Ethnic pigmentation
historical, physiological and clinical aspects

Ethnic pigmentation

historical, physiological and clinical aspects

H. P. WASSERMANN
B.Sc., M.B.Ch.B. (Pret.), M.Med. (Int. Med.), M.D. (Stell.)

M.R.C. Pigment Metabolism Research Unit,
and Department of Internal Medicine,
University of Stellenbosch, Bellville, South Africa

 1974

Excerpta Medica, Amsterdam
American Elsevier Publishing Company, Inc., New York

ISBN Excerpta Medica 90 219 2062 x
ISBN American Elsevier 0 444 15051 x
Library of Congress Catalog Card No. 73–77909

Publisher: Excerpta Medica
                  335 Jan van Galenstraat
                  Amsterdam
                  P.O. Box 1126

Sole Distributors for the USA and Canada:
                  American Elsevier Publishing Company, Inc.
                  52 Vanderbilt Avenue
                  New York, N.Y. 10017

Printed in The Netherlands by Drukkerij Hooiberg, Epe

Preface

Chapter I gives an outline of the general theme of this volume: there is probably more to skin pigmentation than meets the eye.

Chapter XX summarizes the concept that ethnic pigmentation is the result of an adaptation of the reticuloendothelial system to disease stressors in various geographical areas. It has become linked to the cultural heritage of these geographically confined populations, even though they are now widely disseminated over the globe.

The chapters in between will, I hope, stimulate investigation into those areas where the significance of melanin has been inadequately researched in the past.

Acknowledgements

The author would like to thank the following for their kind permission to reproduce certain of the figures:

The Editor of the *South African Medical Journal* for Figures 8, 14, 20, 21, 22 and 24.

The publishers (S. Karger, Basle) of *Dermatologica* for Figures 9 and 10.

The Editor of *Agressologie* for Figure 23.

The Johns Hopkins University Press for Figures 1 and 2.

W. B. Saunders and Co. for Figure 3.

The Wellcome Trustees for Figures 4 and 6.

The Editors of *Surgery, Gynaecology and Obstetrics* for Figure 5.

The author would also like to thank:

Messrs. Blue Crane Books for permission to quote an extensive verse from Mr. V. C. Mutwa's book.

The Africa Institute of South Africa for permission to use their maps in Figure 28.

Mrs. G. van der Walt for help with translations and for typing the manuscript, and the secretarial assistance of Mrs. D. Kögler and S. Theron.

Dr. G. L. Kalsbeek, Amsterdam, for the preparation of the Index.

Contents

Section IV.
Clinical aspects of ethnic pigmentation

Chapter I

The colour problem and the problem of colour

Colour is a visual phenomenon, dependent on a physical stimulus, physiologically processed and psychologically interpreted. Colour can be perceived only by the few in the animal kingdom endowed with colour vision: among the vertebrates a few fishes, most of the birds, and in mammals only the higher primates including man.

Colour vision in man aids the identification of objects, it provides aesthetic pleasure from the decorative use of colour, and it is applied for its symbolic significance, e.g. signal and warning lights on instrument panels, or as a symbol for the identification and use of some commercial products (Wright, 1967).

In human relations the 'colour problem' resides in the use made of colour for object identification, while the problem of colour lies in its symbolic significance (Wassermann, 1972).

THE COLOUR PROBLEM

The extent to which race is, in fact, associated with skin colour is evident from Deighton's (1957) summary: '. . . race relations, or rather bad race relations, are in themselves nothing new. What is perhaps new is the desire to make them the subject of serious academic study, which arises from the anxiety with which the white peoples regard their relationship with the coloured.' No other racial characteristic is as easily defined as the colour of the skin. Sentiments of consciousness of kind or recognition of unlikeness are most unlikely to arise because of a difference in skull form or blood group, but are most likely to do so when there is as visible a difference as skin colour.

The term 'race' has been used for isolated communities such as Reindeer Lapps and Coastal Lapps, for continental groups (African, Asian, European) and even for the whole species ('the human race'). Zoologists use 'race' as a subdivision of species, and for this reason the human species may be subdivided into races. 'However, there is no lower limit and without further specification the term race simply indicates a biologically perpetuating subdivision of species' (Laughlin, 1968). A colour coding system was the first system for race classification and persists to the present day. It has the advantage of simplicity and visibility. There are some disadvantages which are of more theoretical than practical consequence. Between whites and blacks (Bantu, Negro and Australian aborigine) there is no overlap in skin colour, and the discriminatory power of this characteristic is absolute. In the brown races, e.g. Indian, Amerindian, Cape Coloured, some overlap in skin colour between both black and white races does exist, but it is doubtful whether any other visible physical characteristic would aid in classification of an individual into one or other of these racial groups. The position, in fact, is that an easily visible physical characteristic allows both scientist and layman to 'classify' an individual as belonging to a black, brown or white racial group and to be correct in their classification more than 90% of the time.

Racial and ethnic groups

Krogman (1945) pointed out that the thought content of the word 'race' from the very beginning 'had in it the idea of a transmissible biological type.'

In modern medical literature preference is given to 'ethnic' groups instead of 'racial' groups. Deniker's suggestion that the word 'race' should be reserved 'for groups of mankind possessing well-developed and primarily heritable physical differences from other groups', and 'ethnic group' for the grouping 'on linguistic, sociological and especially geographical affinities', seems useful (Count, 1950, p. 207).

The differentiation is especially important because skin colour, a heritable physical difference, does not necessarily fit the ethnic grouping (e.g. Bantu and Negro; American Negro and Cape Coloured) nor does it agree with other heritable characteristics which have often been suggested as a basis for racial classification (e.g. blood groups). Boyd suggested that the basic relationship between some Europeans, Asiatics and Africans in the distribution of their blood groups indicates that the development of differences in pigmentation is of more recent evolutionary origin than that of blood groups (Count, 1950, p. 637).

The interests of a classifier should be stated as well as his purpose for classification. It is obvious that the needs of the physical anthropologist, interested in the history of the human species, differ somewhat from those of the clinician who will also be interested in the effect of cultural pattern on health, e.g. tribal taboos on diet, customs in clothing and child-rearing, as well as the distribution of genes which influence disease patterns and which are now of increasing importance in pharmacogenetics. As this monograph is concerned with ethnic pigmentation in its biological and clinical context, it is useful to use the term 'race' in a different connotation from 'ethnic group', as Deniker originally suggested. The 'well-developed and primarily heritable physical difference' in which we are interested is skin pigmentation, and 'colour coding' is therefore preferred when referring to races.

The term European, Asian, African, Australian and American has become fairly meaningless because Africa is inhabited by whites of European extraction who have never been out of the continent for several centuries, and inhabited parts of the continent long before the migration of black men. 'African' should thus be reserved as a collective noun for Egyptians, Arabians, Hottentots, Bushmen, Cape Coloureds, and English- or Afrikaans-speaking whites as well as for Bantus, Negroes and Nilotes. Similarly, the American Negro is related more closely, both as regards skin colour and language and disease pattern, to the Cape Coloured of South Africa than to the Negro or Bantu people from which he originated. In a recent study Klineberg and Zavalloni (1969) investigated the self-identity of blacks in 6 university populations in various parts of Africa. In all countries except Senegal national identity was mentioned more frequently than African identity. Concerning their self-identity, they found that the proportion mentioning Africa ranged from a low 7% to a high of only 18% in Ghana. Klineberg (1971) states: 'Some of the young blacks in the United States appear to be more African than the Africans in this respect.'

There seems to be little logic in retaining a colour name (Negro) in one instance, and preferring a geographical name (Caucasian) in another, when, for example, American Negroes are more often brown than black, and most whites have never set foot in the Causasus. For the same reason, and because language, culture and social custom bear additional significance to genetic factors in the aetiology of disease, ethnic groups within races should be indicated (Table I).

Table I

Race	Ethnic groups
White	The various nations speaking primarily European languages, e.g. English, German, French or modern derivations therefrom, e.g. Afrikaans, and perhaps 'American' English
Brown	American Negro Cape Coloured Indian (India)*
Black	Bantu Negro Australian aborigine
Yellow	Japanese Chinese
Red	Indian (America)

---

* Within ethnic groups considerable variation in pigmentation may occur: e.g. some Indians are black rather than brown, while northern Indians would pass for Mediterranean whites. The ethnic divisions, as indicated here, roughly group together populations frequently studied in relation to skin colour. Extrapolations, often not valid, are sometimes made from a study on a 'brown' population (e.g. American Negro) to explain findings in a 'black' population (e.g. African Negro).

It is fully appreciated that the tendency to *colour contraction* does not make colour description completely accurate for the race as a whole. Colour contraction signifies the expansion of the colour scale when dealing with a narrow range of colour. A farmer might refer to 'red soil' when a brownish-red would be more appropriate (Wright, 1964). 'White' is a colour contraction for flesh-coloured, defined in *Methuen's Handbook of Colour* (Kornerup and Wanscher, 1963) as the 'colour of the flesh of the Caucasian race'. It is evident that the purist could object to colour coding, for the *hue* of human skin colour is in all cases orange to red, but varies in a *tonal scale* from pale through pale yellow, sunbrown or tan to negro – a colour defined as 'the colour of the skin of a person of the Negroid race'. Apart from evidence presented from reflectance spectrophotometry (Wassermann, 1971), it is of interest to note that both flesh colour (6B3) and negro (6F3) occur on the same colour plate in *Methuen's Handbook of Colour*, as tonal and saturation variants of orange (6A8), but this is one of the 'problems of colour'.

THE PROBLEM OF COLOUR

The *concept* of colour preceded colour naming, and it would be reasonable to assume that a colour was only named when materials for its use were available. Cave artists used 5 colours (red, yellow, orange, brown and black) and these represent the earliest colour names (Kornerup and Wanscher, 1963). As whites are frequently referred to as 'reds' by people of the black or brown races in their own languages, these colours are coincidentally also a colour coding of races, and were used for this purpose by the Ancient Egyptians (Haddon, 1934).

That colour was naïvely regarded as an attribute of objects is evident from the *naming* of colours, e.g. lemon green, copper, bottle green, canary yellow, sky blue, calypso red (Kornerup and Wanscher, 1963). The finesse and number of colour names used by individuals is determined by the civilization in which they live (Ray, 1953).

We can summarize the modern view of colour perception in the words of Kalmus (1970) '. . . it is a computed value (output) derived from the input of a number of retinal receptors, according to their spectral absorption properties, spatial relations, and previous exposure.' We learn to name the computed sensation and to associate it with certain objects in our environment. All men are significantly influenced by their perception of colour. Even in spite of Newton, we subconsciously consider colour an attribute of objects because of our cultural heritage over many millennia. The connotative meaning of colour names are soundly entrenched in the culture of people wherever they are and regardless of their sophistication.

It should be emphasized that, even though colour perception can be scientifically explained and colour can be objectively measured, it is the *connotative meaning* of colour names and the cultural heritage which, as an infant, condition man to consider colour as an attribute of objects (Williams, 1964, 1966).

The problem of colour is that it elicits an emotional response, has deep-rooted symbolic significance, and is always associated with objects.

Racial prejudice

As skin colour is used as a means of object identification and the *problem of colour* is that its connotative meanings symbolize certain emotional responses, it is perhaps inevitable that this phenomenon should become part of a political and sociological problem.

Racial or ethnic prejudice requires: (1) the existence in a community of two or more groups easily distinguishable from one another by a characteristic such as skin colour which is highly visible, (2) the creation of false stereotyped ideas, and (3) the existence of feelings of insecurity and frustration among members of the in-group (Richmond, 1957).

Skin colour is intimately involved in sociopolitical ideologies. Klineberg (1971) states, 'I wonder whether we take skin colour seriously because it has high visibility, or whether it has high visibility because we take it seriously.' The fact remains that the problems of race relations are identified by the colour of the races involved. Klineberg (1971), looking back on more than 40 years of observation of the American racial scene, would say that many of them were working towards the goal of colour-blindness but he admits, 'We soon discovered that we could not be colour-blind, at least not yet.' He refers to black separatism emerging in the U.S.A. after white-instituted integration, a black nationalism which envisages a separate black nation in the U.S.A.

This political problem has influenced scientific studies on race and ethnic physiology in so far as Ingle (1967), with reference to the intellectual abilities of blacks in the U.S.A., states: 'Individuals interested in further studies (in that field) find that many who are concerned with the advancement of the Negro, hold that closed systems of belief are necessary to unite theory and social action,' a situation also referred to by Humphreys (1969). This reverse racism, if it creates an artificial reality by selectively discouraging research on controversial issues not yet settled by satisfactory or convincing data, can in the long run only be damaging to scientific progress. It does, however, indicate another problem of colour as it concerns ethnic pigmentation: Forced (or pretended) 'colour-blindness', where it exists in the field of scientific research, solves no problem but merely shelves it. It may even lead to frustrated behaviour and aggression (Ingle, 1967; Humphreys, 1969).

Racial physiology and pathology

The existence of physiological differences between races constitutes an experiment of nature in the sense that, in the course of evolution, the man most suitable to particular conditions was selected. To study and unravel these relationships is the task and privilege of the scientist. It is evident that racial skin colour is the result of the presence of melanin in an easily visible location. Mason (1967) introduced his paper on the structure of melanin: 'It is a pity that the structure of melanin, the understanding of which is fundamental to so many biological, medical, social and economic problems, remains an enigma after 50 years of study.' These words were used to qualify the often stated dogma of biochemistry 'that biological function is explainable only in terms of chemical structure and reactivity.'

Ethnic pigmentation was the natural phenomenon which stimulated pigment research. Most of what we know about melanin and melanogenesis results from dermatological interest in pigment anomalies. To look at melanin in the skin only is to neglect its significance in the organism as a whole. If Virchow was correct in his view that 'the significance of the constituent parts will at all times be found only in the whole,' a skin-bound view of melanin obscures its biological significance.

In a recent review (Wassermann, 1970) I pointed out that 'the biological significance of melanin may in the past have been overlooked because of its *visibility*; a bio-electronic key to fundamental mechanisms of cancer, extrapyramidal disease and schizophrenia may have been overlooked because it so obviously appeared in the *skin*.'

Colour and society

'The imaginations which people have of one another are the solid facts of society' (C. H. Cooley).

The sociological implication of artificial ethnic colour change was explored by whites who disguised themselves as Negroes and reported the psychological effects of this colour change (Griffin, 1960; Halsell, 1969). Their experiences show that whites will be taken for blacks if they are black.

In many countries, but especially in the U.S.A. and South Africa, 'passing' from one racial or ethnic group to the other occurs. There are different degrees of passing, accompanied by different degrees of estrangement from the Negro group and emotional identification with the white community, but, in contrast to occasional temporary passing or passing for convenience, Drake and Cayton (1962) consider that 'for a Negro to pass socially means sociological death and rebirth.'

Henshel (1971) reviewed some of the problems accompanying ethnic colour change in the U.S.A. and cites some references to the volume of trade and economics involved in the sale of skin creams and hair straighteners. He quotes estimations of 25,000 to 300,000 individuals annually passing from black to white. In the South African Cape Coloured group passing to white occurs, but it does not occur among the Bantu. This is due partly to the physical difficulty: American Negroes, due to white admixture, correspond in skin colour to the Cape Coloured. The African Negro and Bantu are on average much darker and have a higher incidence of kinky hair than the former ethnic groups. Some discussion has recently started in South Africa favouring ethnic integration between Cape Coloureds and whites, and racial segregation between Bantus and whites.

Black pride, the rise of black militancy and the 'black is beautiful' movements, new in the U.S.A., are of course old and natural manifestations of nationalism amongst the Bantus and Negroes in Africa. This is the basis of success for Bantu home lands, although economic factors still complicate its application.

A significant new direction in thought on ethnic pigmentation and sociological issues, which is apparent from Henshel's (1971) review, is the possibility of an 'alteration technology'. Mass acceptance of such a technology would ultimately strive to change ethnic pigmentation. It is envisaged that improvement of the psoralens might *enpigment* whites, and monobenzyl ether of hydroquinone may *depigment* Negroes to an acceptable intermediate colour, thus providing whites with a tan and lightening Negroes to the colour of tanned whites. Melanocyte-stimulating hormone may be a more effective darkener. Henshel (1971) considers the technological possibility from the viewpoints of whether or not it will work, be used, and its mass acceptance. The last (mass acceptance) might have worked before the rise of 'black militancy' in the U.S.A., but now it would appear less certain. The direct and indirect consequences are considered from the social, economic, political and psychological aspects. But this once again raises the biological question: Is melanin merely a skin pigment or does it have a physiological significance beyond the skin? As extrapyramidal disease and schizophrenia bear a relationship to melanin, as discussed in Chapter 19, further urgent research on the functional role of melanin in the organism as a whole is required.

If technological alteration of ethnic pigmentation should be undertaken at the stage which *dermatological* research on pigmentation has reached at present, and before the overall physiology of extracutaneous melanin is satisfactorily known, unexpected results might lead to a worse crisis than was experienced with the thalidomide disaster. Controversy at present existing on moral, religious and other aspects of organ transplantation indicates the necessity of careful and extensive theoretical evaluation of new technological possibilities.

CONCLUSION

This Chapter is to some extent an explanation of the scope of this monograph. It is clear that in the 'colour problem' use is made of colour for object identification, and this identifies the race problem. The 'problem of colour', on the other hand, lies in its symbolism, which adds certain psychological and emotional judgements to man's inability (through all ages) to live harmoniously with his fellow-men who differ in important aspects from his particular group. If, by analogy, the predominance of melanin in the skin is considered as a mere decorative use of colour by nature, we may not only misdirect research and remain ignorant of the functional significance of melanin but may actually misapply recent technological advances.

Ethnic pigmentation is discussed in the sections entitled 'historical', 'physiological' and 'clinical' aspects, because our main interest is melanin pigmentation in man. Biological man has a cultural heritage and a technological ability which continually seeks practical application of his knowledge.

The *history of scientific thought* on ethnic pigmentation is included because apparently no attempt at a systematic study has been made. It explains to some extent the misapplication of scientific and pseudoscientific fact for ideological purposes, but also indicates the selectivity of research endeavours to concentrate on those aspects of pragmatic value.

The *physiology of ethnic pigmentation* is of course basically similar in all men, and the general body of scientific fact has been briefly reviewed with emphasis on *ethnic differences* rather than the larger *biological similarities*. The *clinical aspects* concentrate on the neglected or currently emerging problems in relation to melanin and extrapyramidal disease, schizophrenia and cancer rather than on the purely dermatological aspects.

REFERENCES

COUNT, E. W. (1950): *This is Race*. Henry Schuman, New York, N.Y.

DEIGHTON, H. S. (1957): History and the study of race relations. *Man*, 57, 123.

DRAKE, ST. C. and CAYTON, H. R. (1962): *Black Metropolis*. Harper and Row, New York, N.Y.

GRIFFIN, J. H. (1960): *Black like Me*. Signet, New York, N.Y.

HADDON, A. C. (1934): *History of Anthropology*. Watts and Co., London.

HALSELL, G. (1969): *Soul Sister*. The World Publishing Co., Cleveland, Ohio.

HENSHEL, R. L. (1971): Ability to alter skin color: Some implications for American society. *Amer. J. Sociol.*, 76, 734.

HORTON, C. P. and CRUMP, E. P. (1958): Growth and development. III. Skin color in Negro infants and parents: Its relationship to birth weight, reflex maturity, socio-economic status, length of gestation and parity. *J. Pediat.*, 52, 547.

HUMPHREYS, L. G. (1969): Racial differences: Dilemma of College admissions. *Science*, 166, 167.

INGLE, D. J. (1967): Editorial: The need to study biological differences among racial groups: Moral issues. *Perspect. Biol. Med.*, 10, 497.

KALMUS, H. (1970): Review Article: Reflections on abnormal colour vision and theories of colour. *J. med. Genet.*, 7, 294.

KLINEBERG, O. (1971): Black and white in international perspective. *Amer. Psychol.*, 26, 119.

KLINEBERG, O. and ZAVALLONI, M. (1969): *Nationalism and Tribalism among African Students*. Mouton, Paris.

KORNERUP, A. and WANSCHER, J. H. (1963): *Methuen's Handbook of Colour*. Methuen and Co., London.

KROGMAN, W. M. (1945): The concept of race. In: *The Science of Man in the World Crisis*, pp. 42–49. Editor: R. E. Linton. Columbia University Press, New York, N.Y.

LAUGHLIN, W. S. (1968): Race: A population concept. *Eugen. Quart.*, 13, 326.

MASON, H. S. (1967): The structure of melanin. In: *Advances in Biology of Skin, Vol. VIII: The Pigmentary System*, pp. 293–312. Editors: W. Montagna and F. Hu. Pergamon Press, London.

RAY, V. F. (1953): Human color perception and behavioral response. *Trans. N.Y. Acad. Sci.*, 2, 98.

RICHMOND, A. H. (1957): Theoretical orientations in studies of ethnic group relations in Britain. *Man*, 58, 124.

WASSERMANN, H. P. (1970): Melanokinetics and the biological significance of melanin. *Brit. J. Derm.*, 82, 530.

WASSERMANN, H. P. (1971): Human skin colour. *Dermatologica (Basel)*, *143*, 166.
WASSERMANN, H. P. (1972): The colour problem and the problem of colour. In: *Essays on Tropical Dermatology, Vol. II*, pp. 50–59. Editor: J. Marshall. Excerpta Medica, Amsterdam.
WILLIAMS, J. E. (1964): Connotations of color names among Negroes and Caucasians. *Percept. motor Skills*, *18*, 721.
WILLIAMS, J. E. (1966): Connotations of racial concepts and color names. *J. Personality soc. Psychol.*, *3*, 531.
WRIGHT, W. D. (1964): *The Measurement of Colour*. Hilger and Watts, London.
WRIGHT, W. D. (1967): *The Rays are not Coloured*. Hilger and Watts, London.

Section I

Historical aspects

The development of scientific thought
on ethnic pigmentation

*The scientific ideas of a given age are
much more than a bald portrait of Nature:
they reflect men's untiring desire to
match their forms of thought against the
testimony of things.*

S. Toulmin and J. Goodfield (1965):
The Discovery of Time. Hutchinson, London.

Chapter II

Myths, legends and Scriptures
on ethnic pigmentation

INTRODUCTION

The development of scientific thought can only be reconstructed if the time concept of a particular age is appreciated.

The dawn of history was in a sense the dawn of the discovery of time, and this was discussed by Toulmin and Goodfield (1965). In tracing the history of scientific thought on ethnic pigmentation the background afforded by their work is essential to grasp the significance of the most ancient sources of history: myth, legend and Scriptures.

Before the art of writing, memory could serve as a reliable source for a short period only. Memory was aided by reciting in rhythm and rhyme some earlier histories. 'Beyond the time-barrier imaginations entered a new world in which, for lack of trustworthy testimony, they were driven back onto speculation and myth' (Toulmin and Goodfield, 1965, p. 23). With the growth of factual knowledge, myths as a historical source and analytic tool gradually fell into disrepute.

Giambattista Vico was hailed as the 'Mendel of history' and his *Scienza Nuova* of 1725 was far in advance of his times. He critically examined myths to uncover the *living thought* from which they originated. In his view they were 'not poetic fancies; nor fictions of the priests; nor heroic legends magnified through the lens of the past. They represented rather Man's first crude but honest efforts to understand the world of Nature and live in harmony with it' (Toulmin and Goodfield, 1965, pp. 125–129). Likewise, legend consisted of transmitted memory. Before the invention of writing the bards of primitive nations could recite traditional epic poems. Vico regarded legends as being significant too: 'In their fables the nations have, in a rough way and in the language of the senses, described the beginning of the world of the sciences, which the specialized studies of the scholars have since clarified for us by reasoning and generalization' (Toulmin and Goodfield, 1965).

Egyptian, Mesopotamian, Ionian and classical Athenian scientific thought lacked a time perspective, but Judeo-Christian thought was bound to time. The latter therefore exerted a great and significant influence on scientific thought even to the present time. In the words of Dobzhansky (1962): 'Christianity is a religion that is implicitly evolutionistic in that it believes history to be meaningful: its current flows from the Creation, through progressive revelation of God to man, from man to Christ and from Christ to the Kingdom of God.'

History developed because people everywhere sought information about the origin and beginning of things as they found them. In contrast to myths which are purely speculative explanations, legends are immediate precursors of history, but even the 'earliest written history by the most favourably placed men in the ancient world only possesses authentic records going back to 4000 years, this being the very outside limit' (Toulmin and Goodfield, 1965, p. 29); the appreciation of the antiquity of the earth is of fairly recent date.

MYTHS

Hopf (1909) discussed the various creation myths of nations. He found that close examination of these traditions reveals the fact that in every case a process of generation is presupposed, a fact occupying a still more prominent position in those doctrines of creation held by all polytheistic races, whether civilized or uncivilized. The union of two primitive beings, male and female, is supposed to occur even in those who believe man to have simply arisen from the earth.

According to Egyptian, Babylonian and Phoenician cosmogony, the creation of the world and man results from the union of two primitive beings, the male fair, the female dark. (This is paradoxical as the female is the lighter sex, a fact known to Renaissance painters of Adam and Eve.)

Creation myths in which something is created out of nothing are rare among North American Indians and non-existent among the Eskimoes. There is always doubt whether the original man in such myths represents a native concept or a borrowing from Christianity in post-Columbian times. Interest in origin varies from one tribe to another and evidence of such interest can be seen in the number of features accounted for.

If this holds true in general, it can be assumed that in isolated communities whose only contact is with fairly homogenous people there would be no need to account for various races. Most of the oldest creation myths, therefore, do not mention skin colour.

Mutwa (1964), a Zulu born from a long genealogy of Zulu medicine-men and schooled in the tradition of his tribe, has presented in English (verse) the traditional creation myth of the Bantu, and this has several features in common with Negro creation myths elsewhere in Africa (Beier, 1966):

'The Great Spirit created the Universe for reasons that nobody must endeavour to fathom. The Tree of Life is the most revered deity throughout Bantu-Africa – a being half plant and half animal' (Mutwa, 1964). According to this myth a race of men originated from the union of the Great Mother *Ma* and the Tree of Life:

> *'The Holy Ones of Kariba Gorge tell us*
> *That the first men to walk the earth*
> *Were all of a similar kind.*
> *They looked exactly alike, and were all of a similar height,*
> *And their colour was red like Africa's plains.*
> *In those days there were no black-skinned or dark-brown men;*
> *No Pygmies and Bushmen, nor Hottentots either.'*

This First People (Amarire) died and
> *'. . . were later to be known*
> *As the Race that Died.'*

The Bantu creation myth described the First People as red, which is the most accurate description for 'white people' and quite common in early descriptions of skin colour by dark races. 'Phoenician' means red skin, Russians with their rusty hair were originally 'Rustians', and 'Batuli', the north-Nigerian word for whites, also means 'redskin' (Simons, 1961).

The Bantu myth, then, accounts for Bushmen and Pygmies and finally for the Bantus themselves, the latter, however, having a father (Odu) different from the others (Gorogo):

After her marriage to Gorogo, chief of the Frogmen, Amarava brought forth eggs from which hatched:

> *'A yellow frog-like people*
> *Cunning little rascals these –*
> *The Bushmen and the Pygmies.'*

The Bantus were born from the marriage with Odu and their skin colour is described:

> *'Some were as black as a much-used pot;*
> *Some were brown and even yellow-brown.'*

In contrast to the very uniform First People the Second People had diversity in colour, stature, and intellect:

> *'In short, my children, they exactly resembled*
> *the puzzling muddle of present day humanity!'*
> (Mutwa, 1964).

The origin of certain legends is completely different in style from those referred to above: God created all men black, but then gave them the opportunity of washing themselves clean. The white men washed themselves all over, leaving powerless water for the Negroes who could thus only cleanse the palms of their hands and the soles of their feet which explains the white palms and soles of Negroes. Other similar legends were collected by Simons (1961). These myths and legends have a sophistication not found in the primitive myths and legends and must date from a more modern age. Such tales may have been invented for propaganda purposes, or to explain some socioeconomic situation or other, e.g.

the Fiji island tale which narrates that those who behaved badly turned black, receiving few clothes, that the moderate sinners (Tongans) became brown, getting more clothes, and that the whites, who were well behaved, received most clothes of all. This group of myths must not be considered in the same light as the ancient ones.

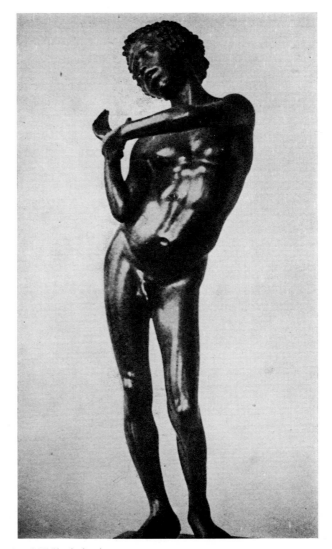

Fig. 1. *Example of Hellenistic Art*
Described as 'the best known and probably finest statuette of an Ethiopian' (Beardsley, 1929). Bronze statuette, 0.20 m high (Paris, Bibliothèque Nationale). Discovered amongst Roman bronzes in 1763 at Châlon-sur-Saône, universally accepted as of Hellenistic origin. (From Beardsley, 1929, *The Negro in Greek and Roman Civilization. A Study of Ethiopian Type*. The Johns Hopkins University Press, Baltimore, Md. Courtesy of the Publishers.)

In Africa this distinction between genuine creation myths and later fabrications may in future become more difficult in view of the changing concepts of the self and the supernatural (Vilakazi, 1962).

LEGENDS AND ART

The evidence of cave paintings, the portrayal of red Egyptians, yellow Semites or Asiatics, black Southerners or Negroes and white Westerners or Libyans by 19th Dynasty (1350–1205 B.C.) Egyptian artists, confirms the fact that differences in skin colour contributed towards the division op people into groups.

The Greeks had, according to Josephus writing in 70 A.D., very little sense of the past and even the Trojan War (1250 B.C.) was a legendary event to them. This perhaps enhanced the originality of their speculations (Toulmin and Goodfield, 1965).

Beardsley (1929) reviewed the contact between Ethiopians and ancient Greek and Roman civilizations as portrayed in art and literature. Poets and writers differentiated between an Eastern and Western Ethiopian. The name derives from αἴθος and ὀψς: a man with a (sun)burned face. They were mythical figures who dwelt in areas of either the rising or setting of the sun, a blameless race of men who held sacrificial feasts attended by the gods. The mythical Ethiopians described by Homer, Hesiod, Aeschylus, Herodotus and others were 'in the first place ... really Greek, a product of Greek imagination and a tradition of Greek literature' (Beardsley, 1929).

The artists, however, portrayed what they saw and one finds not only the humour and caricature that portrayed 'this strangeness which made the Ethiopian an object of entertainment to them, but (also) the pathos of an exile from his own land' (Figs. 1 and 2). 'This sentimentality', Beardsley (1929) continues, 'is nowhere met in the later and more matter-of-fact Roman art.'

Negro slaves were comparatively rare in Greece. They were brought to Greece by the Persian invasion and not through military action. The Romans built up important colonies in Africa through military campaigns and vast numbers of slaves were brought to Rome. The possession of Ethiopian slaves was apparently a status symbol in Rome. In early literature the Greek αἰθίοψ (Aethiops) was transliterated into Latin. The word *niger*, from which so many modern languages derive their designation for black people, was apparently seldom used in antiquity (Beardsley, 1929). 'The Roman attitude toward the Ethiopian ... is far less kindly than the Greek,' but Beardsley warns that: 'How early the Roman attitude crystallized into racial feeling is hard to say, and as those who express it are chiefly satirists one must be careful in drawing conclusions.'

There was some prospect of an alliance between history and natural philosophy in the 6th century B.C., but then historians (Herodotus and others) parted from scientists (Pythagoras, Aristotle). Although he had no evolutionary concept in mind, Aristotle spoke of a ladder or Scale of Nature. To him this was a factual observation regarding the existing world of living things (Toulmin and Goodfield, 1965, p. 38).

Aristotle (384–322 B.C.) extended his concept to climate as well. People from the cold northern parts of Europe were characterized by their fearlessness, but their lack of intelligence hindered the forming of political organisations. The intelligent, resourceful Asian lacked drive. The Greek, geographically in the middle, was destined to rule the world. He considered the Ethiopian a cross between a gorilla and a man. This idea was based on material collected by the

Fig. 2. *Example of Hellenistic Art*
Bronze Negro boy, height 0.183 m (New York, Metropolitan Museum of Art). (From Beardsley, 1929, *The Negro in Greek and Roman Civilization. A Study of Ethiopian Type*. The Johns Hopkins University Press, Baltimore, Md. Courtesy of the Publishers.)

Carthaginian who encountered gorillas in Africa on his journeys, and the description of Ethiopians by Herodotus.

Herodotus (484–425 B.C.) and Hippocrates (460–377 B.C.) explained different races as the result of environmental influences, although Hippocrates thought that acquired characteristics could become hereditary.

Poseidonios (135–51 B.C.) also saw a causal relationship between environment and different races.

These concepts held sway especially in anthropological thinking until fairly recently, and in subsequent Chapters reference will again be made to them.

MONOTHEISTIC SCRIPTURES

The Bible

The Bible contains no specific reference to *ethnic* pigmentation in either the Old or the New Testament. Reference is made to the tanned skin of a bride:

> *'I am very dark, but comely,*
> *O daughters of Jerusalem,*
> *Like the tents of Kedar,*
> *Like the curtains of Solomon.'*
> *(Song of Solomon, 1, 5).*

And to the appearance of her husband:

> *'Who is this that looks forth like the dawn,*
> *Fair as the moon, bright as the sun,*
> *Terrible as an army with banners.'*
> *(Song of Solomon, 6, 10).*

Daniel (5, 6) describes the countenance of King Belshazzar: 'Then the King's colour changed, and his thoughts alarmed him; his limbs gave way, and his knees knocked together.' The complexion of David is described (*I Samuel* 16, 12): 'And he sent, and brought him in. Now he was ruddy, and had beautiful eyes, and was handsome.'

In the New Testament an Ethiopian is described as a eunuch, but his skin colour is not described (*Acts*, 8, 27): 'And behold, an Ethiopian, a eunuch, a minister of Candace the queen of the Ethiopians in charge of all her treasure, had come to Jerusalem to worship.' 'Ethiopian' was in a sense a colour name, as discussed earlier in this Chapter, but it is nevertheless of interest that nowhere in the Bible is skin colour described as an ethnic characteristic.

This total absence of any description of ethnic pigmentation is especially noteworthy as numerous appeals to Biblical authority were made throughout subsequent historical eras.

Neither the nature of the mark of Cain nor the nature of the curse on Ham, son of Noah, is specified in terms of skin colour. Cuvier (1769–1832) apparently revived the suggestion that the curse on the son of Ham was a dark colour. This unfounded claim was used to justify slavery on Biblical grounds.

The conjecture that one of the Magi, or Wise Men of the East, was a Negro was 'a mediaeval innovation to demonstrate the universality of Christianity' (Simons, 1961).

Skin colour does not enter into concepts on the image and likeness of God, and both Jews and Christians are prohibited from worshipping any graven image (*Exodus, 20, 2*).

Sorsby (1958) based his conjecture that Noah was an albino on apocryphal literature and not on canonical Scripture.

Ladell (1964), referring to the fact that Adam and Eve were sent out of the Garden of Eden clothed in 'coats of skin' instead of the few leaves they originally chose implied that if the Garden was situated in a tropical environment, the leaves would be more suitable than the 'coats of skin'. In a similar vein, this may even be construed as evidence that man evolved in an equatorial area (leaf-clothing) and then migrated to a temperate or cold climate (skin-clothing).

The Koran

The early Arabian philosophers, Alkendi, Alfarabi and Ibn Sina, in spite of their acquaintance with Aristotelian philosophy, were orthodox dogmaticians and even among the later sects none would question the teaching of the Koran. Orthodox members of the Hanifilic sect maintain that argument about the articles of faith laid down by the Koran is expressly forbidden by Mohammed (Hopf, 1909).

In the fifteenth Sura it is written: 'God said to the angels: I will make man out of dry earth and black clay, and after that I have made his form perfect and breathed my spirit into him then shall ye fall down and worship him.'

The Koran (*30, 23*) does refer to: 'the diversity of your tongues and complexions. In that surely are signs for those who possess knowledge.' It also (*19, 14*) refers to 'the tribes and sub-tribes' into which men were made 'for greater facility of intercourse'. The division of man into nations and tribes has thus been divinely sanctioned.

Hence, ethnic pigmentation is scarcely mentioned in the Koran.

CONCLUSIONS

The skin colour of original or prehistoric man is not known, and speculations either assume that the first men were of a homogeneous skin colour or that they exhibited the full range of colours from black to white.

In favour of a fairly homogeneous colour is the fact that the earliest written records do not remark on differences in skin colour, and ancient creation myths do not attempt an explanation of differences in skin colour. The Bantu creation myth is the only one I know of which specifically refers to a homogeneously coloured 'First People' who lived before the advent of ethnic pigmentation. Implied in the marriages of Amarava to Odu and Gorogo, and their different offspring, is a concept of genetic transmission of racial characteristics.

'If we go back far enough, we reach a screen of ignorance on to which we can do no more than project *a priori* forms of theory shaped in our minds' (Toulmin and Goodfield, 1965, p. 267).

REFERENCES

BEARDSLEY, G. H. (1929): *The Negro in Greek and Roman Civilization. A Study of Ethiopian Type*. Johns Hopkins Press, Baltimore, Md.

BEIER, U. (1966): *The Origin of Life and Death. African Creation Myths*. William Heinemann, London.

DOBZHANSKY, T. (1962): *Mankind Evolving: The Evolution of the Human Species*. Yale University Press, New Haven, Conn.

HOPF, L. (1909): *The Human Species*. Longmans, Green and Co., New York, N.Y.

LADELL, W. S. S. (1964): Terrestrial animals in humid heat: Man. In: *Handbook of Physiology, Section 4: Adaptation to the Environment*, pp. 625–659. Editors: D. B. Dill, E. F. Adolph and C. G. Wilber. American Physiological Society, Washington, D.C.

MUTWA, V. C. (1964): *Indaba, My Children*. Blue Crane Books, Johannesburg.

SIMONS, R. D. PH. G. (1961): *The Colour of the Skin in Human Relations*. Elsevier Publ. Co., Amsterdam.

SORSBY, A. (1958): Noah – an albino. *Brit. med. J.*, 2, 1587.

TOULMIN, S. and GOODFIELD, J. (1965): *The Discovery of Time*. Hutchinson, London.

VILAKAZI, A. (1962): Changing concepts of the self and the supernatural in Africa. *Ann. N.Y. Acad. Sci.*, 96, 670.

Chapter III

The mediaeval period and the Renaissance

Throughout the mediaeval period not only Aristotle 'with his cool and limpid sanity, with his knowledge, which never becomes cynical, of the common man, with his inspired common sense . . .' (Knowles, 1962, p. 5), but also Plato 'with his unforgettable picture of Socrates, with his deep moral earnestness and lofty idealism . . . with his vision of the godlike soul and its immortal destiny . . .' (Knowles, 1962, p. 4) directed the thoughts of men. The two systems (Platonian and Aristotelian) have more in common than is frequently supposed. 'For both, the universe has a design and a purpose, for both, the good is equated with the real, with the true and with the beautiful, and the good life is the goal of all ordered human endeavour' (Knowles, 1962, p. 6).

From 350 till 500 A.D. the influence of ancient civilization was in decline, and the Christian Church was attaining social maturity. At this stage the profound influence of St. Augustine on the system of Christian thought emerged and held sway until Lutheranism, Calvinism and Jansenism gave rise to new insight and discussion in the 16th and 17th centuries (Knowles, 1962, p. 33).

While the social maturation of Christianity is sometimes regarded as a factor in the decay of science, Singer and Underwood (1962, p. 69) point out that 'science was in headlong decay before Christianity was in a position to have any real effect on pagan thought.' Indeed, Christianity was a 'protest and a revulsion against the prevailing and extremely pessimistic pagan outlook' (Singer and Underwood, 1962, p. 69), which deprived men everywhere of a motive for living. These ages were 'dark' because, while the intellectual heritage of Greece and Rome was held in high esteem in both the Eastern Muslim Empire and the Christian world of the West, people were awaiting the end of the world.

The Renaissance or Age of Enlightenment came gradually and at varying times, between 800 A.D. and 1050–1450 A.D., to the different lines of scientific thinking. Various scholars pointed out the debt Galileo, Vesalius and Copernicus owed to Aristotle. The idea of a gradual development of Life could be read into Aristotle's 'Ladder of Life' even though he did not appreciate the evolutionistic implication, and Titus Lucretius Carus in his *De Rerum Natura* attempted to explain the origin of life and its gradual advance. In man's development from a savage to a civilized being he suggested various adaptive procedures. Galen introduced a teleological view and steered the early beginnings of adaptive biology in the direction of an evolutionistic concept. The Galenic tradition was maintained and consolidated throughout the medieval period. Disease was believed to be a disturbance in the natural harmony of the body, the result of a disequilibrium in the four humours. The idea of humours, partly derived from Egyptian speculations on the presumed principle of putrefaction, ultimately developed to a humoral concept which had a significant influence on the way of thinking of Renaissance writers on ethnic pigmentation. This is evident from lengthy discussions on the role of 'yellow bile' in particular, which may colour the skin and sclerae, and 'black bile', the humour closest to death, which is formed from coldness (from the air) and dryness (from the earth). Weight was given to this concept by Hippocrates' views on ethnic pigmentation.

As pointed out in the previous Chapter, 'Christianity is a religion that is implicitly evolutionistic in that it believes history to be meaningful' (Dobzhansky, 1962), and with the growth of Christianity the evolutionistic concept, which so markedly influenced the concept of race, gained momentum. There were many concepts in biology which involved the assumption of progressive *change* long before Darwin crystallized it into a comprehensible theory. In German 'Entwicklungsgeschichte' and in English the 'Development Hypothesis' embodied such a concept of change. Herbert Spencer (1820–1903) is credited with the introduction of the word 'evolution' in its present sense. Darwin did not use the word 'evolution' anywhere in his *Origin of Species*, except that the last word in this work is the word 'evolved' (Oppenheimer, 1967, p. 206). The word 'race' was an ill-defined term, used to embrace both nations, ethnic groups and specific biological subgroups. Only gradually it emerged as a term denoting a specific breeding group. Subsequent to its rather loose usage, then, the biological concept of race came to include nations and all conceivable subdivisions of Man.

Ethnic pigmentation identifies races. In discussing the history of scientific thought on ethnic pigmentation it is important to realize, at this stage, that the early mediaeval concepts of evolution ultimately gave rise to a concept which later was to enhance the growth of racism and racialistic discrimination. As pointed out by Haller (1971), 'evolutionary dysteleology' designated inferior and superior positions achieved in the struggle for the survival of the fittest to people differing in skin colour. Indeed, in the 19th century U.S.A. many were awaiting the extinction of the black man by natural selection.

MEDIAEVAL THOUGHT ON ETHNIC PIGMENTATION

Legends which sprang up around the healing saints Cosmas and Damian, practitioners of medicine, are perhaps the most typical of Byzantine thought (A.D. 200–1500) on medicine. These practitioners practised faithhealing and were martyred under Diocletian (A.D. 303). A legend tells of a man with gangrene of the left leg who collapsed at the door of the church of Saint Cosmas and Saint Damian in Rome. He dreamed that the Saints transplanted the left leg of a corpse to his stump, after amputation of the gangrenous part. On awakening he had, indeed, two sound legs, but as the donor was a Negro the recipient's right leg was white now, and his left leg black. This legend was illustrated by Fra Angelico and by Fernando Gullegos (Singer and Underwood, 1962, p. 68). The legend and the paintings were reproduced recently in popular magazines reporting on recent advances in organ transplantation.

Lack of thought or discussion on ethnic pigmentation was probably due to lack of contact with, and knowledge of, the existence of men with a skin colour different to that of mediaeval Europeans. Further interest and development in this field did not occur until the Crusades, the travels of Marco Polo, and the journeys of discovery by the seafaring nations, notably the Portuguese and the Spaniards, acquainted Europeans with the great diversity of peoples inhabiting the earth. In studying the revival of scientific thought on ethnic pigmentation, it is remarkable how heavily the Renaissance workers relied on travellers' descriptions of foreign races. How naive people were, is shown by their ready acceptance as fact that the people of Formosa had tails. It must be remembered, however, that superstition about the effects of environment and prenatal influences on teratology was still prevalent. Scientific fact, time-honoured tradition, the authoritarian dogma of the Ancients, and fantastic conjectures from a few facts were gradually still being assembled in proper perspective (Glenister, 1964).

The transition, gradual as it was, from the Dark Ages to the Age of Enlightenment created the intellectual climate which fostered the start of original and experimental enquiry into the phenomenon of ethnic pigmentation.

Prominent in this transition were men like Leonardo da Vinci (1452–1519) who questioned Galen's views. Paracelsus, the 'Luther of Medicine', introduced (1520) the polygenetic theory of the origin of man against the monogenetic theory. Although thereby defying Scriptual authority, he was 'as devoutly religious as Luther and believed that he presence of God was manifest throughout all nature' (Poynter, 1971).

Georges Louis Leclerc, Comte de Buffon (1707–1788), described by Toulmin and Goodfield (1965) as 'less of an individual scientist than a committee', was one of the early 'evolutionists'. He was fully acquainted with the various travel descriptions of his time, and he had a great influence on Lamarck. Like Paracelsus, he attempted to reconcile the conflict between theological and scientific thinking: 'There is no difference between the truths that God has revealed, and those which He has permitted us to discover by observation and enquiry' (Count, 1950, p. 3 : 704). The bold concepts of these men stimulated the subsequent investigation and thought on ethnic pigmentation.

REFERENCES

COUNT, E. W. (1950): *This is Race*. Henry Schumann, New York, N.Y.
DOBZHANSKY, T. (1962): *Mankind Evolving: The Evolution of the Human Species*. Yale University Press, New Haven, Conn.
GLENISTER, T. W. (1964): Fantasies, facts and foetuses: The interplay of fancy and reason in teratology. *Med. Hist.*, *8*, 15.

HALLER, J. S. (1971): *Outcasts from Evolution. Scientific Attitudes of Racial Inferiority, 1859–1900,* p. 210. University of Illinois Press, Urbana–Chicago–London.

KNOWLES, D. (1962): *The Evolution of Mediaeval Thought.* Longmans, Green and Co., London.

OPPENHEIMER, J. M. (1967): *Essays in the History of Embryology and Biology.* Massachusetts Institute of Technology Press, Cambridge, Mass.

POYNTER, N. (1971): *Medicine and Man.* Watts and Co., London.

SINGER, C. and UNDERWOOD, E. A. (1962): *A Short History of Medicine.* Clarendon Press, Oxford.

TOULMIN, S. and GOODFIELD, J. (1965): *The Discovery of Time.* Hutchinson, London.

Chapter IV

Rebirth of scientific thought
on ethnic pigmentation (1600–1800)

The revival of ancient scientific knowledge first stimulated an interest in *anatomy*. The simultaneous renaissance of art (Michelangelo, Raphael, Dürer and Leonardo da Vinci) required some knowledge of the skeleton and muscles to portray the human form. Leonardo da Vinci (1452–1519), a notable artist, also excelled as a scientist. In his notebooks he remarked that 'the seed of the father has power equal to that of the womb because, if a white male produced a child in a black woman the colour of the child was brown' (Linscott, 1957).

Galenic *physiology* was changed by Jean François Fernel (1497–1558) when he became Professor of Medicine at Paris. The humoral theory of ancient medicine greatly influenced his work *Universa Medicina* (1554). His concept of medicine was based on the basic sciences of physiology and pathology. Paracelsus, meanwhile, stressed the necessity of teaching medicine from personal experience, and also introduced chemistry into medicine.

Sir Isaac Newton (1642–1727) established the *universality of natural law*, and thereby destroyed the further influence of mediaeval scientific speculation.

To illustrate this period in scientific thought on ethnic pigmentation, the works of some early anatomists will be discussed. The physiological approach is perhaps best illustrated by the work of Le Cat, who provides a general review of the concepts of that time, and the interdisciplinary nature of pigmentation research is best foreshadowed by Mitchell's (1747) application of Newton's colour theory to pigmentation. His work was apparently the first to originate from the New World.

THE ANATOMISTS

Alexis Littré (1658–1726), a French surgeon, described his observations on the skins of whites and blacks: The skin is composed of three parts: (1) The innermost part is called the *proper skin*. At the internal surface are round or oval glandular grains and the roots of the hair. At the external surface are the excretory ducts of these glands, the hair and an infinite number of small *mammelons* which are the organs of touch. (2) Stretched on the skin proper is a *reticular membrane*, pierced like a net by small holes through which these structures pass. (3) This membrane, in turn, is covered by the *epidermis* of which the external surface is smooth, but the internal surface irregular, forming little alcoves where the ends of the mammelons are situated.

In the black skin (of the Moor), the proper skin and the epidermis are as white as that of the European and it is only the reticular membrane which is black (and which is visible through the transparent epidermis).

Littré, referring to Malpighi's studies in which he claimed that the black colour of the reticular membrane was caused by a thick and gelatinous black juice which it contained, reinvestigated this theory himself by carrying out an autopsy on a Moor. For a period of 7 days he infused a piece of skin in warm water, and another in spirits of wine. Neither of these 'powerful solvents' could extract the colour. He concluded that this colour was thus part of, and adherent to, the reticular membrane.

After boiling a piece of skin, he found small 'bottles' the size of 'grains of seed' developing, which were filled with quite clear fluid. On cooling, this fluid formed a jelly-like substance, very transparent and not resembling a black and glutinous juice at all. And thus Littré thought that the black colour was in part due to the reticular membrane, and in part due to the action of very warm air. For the latter statement he found some evidence in the fact that Moors are born white. Littré also observed that that part of the glans penis which was not covered by the prepuce was black like the rest of the skin. The rest of the glans, which was covered, was perfectly white. He remarks that some male infants of Moors are born with a black spot on the end of the penis and this extends itself over the rest of the body. He thought this could be due to the action of the air. In passing, he noted that 'not only males, but all Moorish infants have at birth black nails on their extremities.'

The reticular layer was named by Malpighi, and this layer, as the anatomical site of ethnic pigmentation, was of interest to all the anatomists.

Bernardo Siegfried Albinus (1697–1770), Professor of Anatomy and Surgery at Leyden, was called 'the greatest anatomist of his time' by Singer and Underwood (1962, p. 150) (Fig. 3). Appointed to the Chair at the age of 24 he collaborated with Boerhaave in a superb edition of the collected works of Vesalius. His greatest work, however, was the *Tabulae Scleri et Musculorum Corporis Humani*. He supervised the illustration (by Ladmiral) and his technique was ahead of his time: He selected the most suitable examples from many dissections. To preserve perspective, two nets of appropriate size were used through which the part to be sketched was viewed. His *Sede et Causa Coloris Aethiopum et Caeterorum Hominum* (1737) reviews earlier work while presenting his own findings.

He found the skin of all people regardless of their ethnic colour to be clear white (candidus), but not completely white. It was slightly stained with the colour of the reticulum; so lightly that he at first thought the skin of the blackest man to be white. In Ethiopians the staining could be observed better. Riolan, quoted by Malpighi, thought that the skin of the Ethiopian was whiter than snow. Ruysch considered it dull-white (albus), as did Malpighi, while Santorini regarded it as clear white (candidus). With these descriptions Albinus had to disagree. He takes great care to point out that he was not deceived by accidental staining due to rupture of the corpus reticulare, an artefact with which he was well acquainted. Ruysch also noted that rupture of the corpus reticulare could stain the skin; such staining was then due to the epidermis. From this it is apparent that both Ruysch and Albinus were aware that pigmentation of the dermis occurred naturally in Negroes.

Fig. 3. *Bernardo Siegfried Albinus (1697–1770)*
  Described as 'the greatest anatomist of his time', he published *Sede et Causa Coloris Aethiopum et Caeterorum Hominum* in 1737. (From Garrison, 1929, *An Introduction to the History of Medicine*, 4th ed., p. 336. W. B. Saunders and Co., Philadelphia, Pa. Courtesy of the Publishers.)

On the other hand, while the corpus reticulare contained most of the pigment, he agreed with Riolan that the cuticula also contained pigment, but confusion of terminology was apparent at this early stage of pigment research: early anatomists distinguished between epidermis and dermis only, calling the former the cuticula at times. When 'cuticula' was used, he points out, both the epidermis and the reticular layer were intended. Ruysch remarked that the epidermis was ash-coloured in the Ethiopian although the reticular layer was always a bright black (niger).

He agreed with Winslow that the epidermis apparently consisted of layers and, as the inner part was more pigmented, he considered that the outer layers of the epidermis were indeed a continuation of the inner (or reticular) layer. He found the epidermis to be black, but transparent and therefore much less black than the reticular layer. He pointed out that Santorini described it as black, and Ruysch as ash-coloured. When Malpighi described it as white, it was merely to denote that it was not pitch black as was the reticular layer with which he contrasted it.

He then discussed the reticular layer: The colour is darker where it joins the dermis and is lighter on the epidermal side. This explains why the Ethiopian is not as black as his reticular layer when seen from outside. The deeper part of the reticulum cannot be seen through its outer part and through the epidermis. He refers to Littré who remarked that a pitch-black reticulum yields a sooty colour viewed through the epidermis.

The reticular layer is also darker where it touches the papillae of the skin and fills the interspaces between the papillae, than where it surrounds the apices. He remarked that the appearance of an 'ox-tongue', as described by Malpighi, was not due to perforations of the reticular layer, but to thinning caused by the papillae. The palms and soles, however, did not exhibit papillae, but rather compressed fibres.

He pointed out that the skin of the Ethiopian was not equally dark in all areas, due to variations in the reticular layer. He compared the reticulum of skin from the cheeks, mammae, abdomen, arms, thighs, knees, legs, feet, hands, soles, palms, fingers and toes of one person and remarked that one could doubt whether all came from the same woman. The white areas in an Ethiopian (soles, heels, fingers and palms) contain a reticulum which is nearly white, but not a homogeneous white, as it contains several specks of darker colour. This also applied to the reticulum beneath the nails.

Perhaps typical of his exactness and methodological approach, Albinus studied these skin areas, not only in an Ethiopian, but also in an exceptionally white woman, a rather dark woman, a very dark (European) woman and a 'semi-Ethiopian'. In all cases the colour of the reticular layer corresponded in intensity to the skin colour, but in whites the reticulum of the palms and soles was yellow. Darker reticular layers were found over the genitalia and pubes. A specimen from the scrotum of a European was similar in its reticular layer to that over the tibia of an Ethiopian (Fig. 4).

He repeated the experiments of Littré, and found that the reticulum retained its colour in spite of washings in water and alcohol. In absolute alcohol the colour was retained for over a year. In the course of such prolonged experiments he found that the reticular layer eventually disintegrated in water, colouring the water but not the resistant epidermis.

In speculating on the cause of differences in ethnic pigmentation, one now sees the lack of contemporary physiological thought. Albinus' entire discussion centres around the views of ancient Greek scholars: Strabo and Herodotus, observing the phenotypes of racial cross-breeding speculated on white and black semen, but Aristotle refuted this explanation. Pliny and Lucretius are quoted in support of the view that proximity to the sun explains blackness and this is put forward as the consensus of ancient opinion. Galen expressed a view which was rather sophisticated: heat is lost through the skin but the excessive heat gain from an external source leads to more heat retention and a scorching of the skin.

He remarked astutely that the white colour of the new-born Ethiopian changes to black in 8 to 10 days, but in new-born whites a similar change occurs from red to that of a normal baby's skin colour. With this observation it should be remembered, however, that Ethiopians do not become white in Europe nor even in the far northern ice fields, and that they reproduce blacks as long as intercourse occurs with other members of their race. Likewise, whites in the tropics do not become black, although they do acquire a tan (as also occurs on exposure to the sun elsewhere in the world), and do not produce darker offspring.

Fig. 4. Illustration from B. S. Albinus' anatomical treatise on ethnic pigmentation, comparing skin from variously pigmented individuals as well as nail colouration. (From Albinus, 1737, *Dissertatio Secunda Sede et Causa Coloris Aethiopum*. T. Haak, Leyden. Courtesy of 'The Wellcome Trustees'.)

The albino Moor remains the same colour even though living in sunny areas. Albinus therefore favours genetic factors above environmental factors in the explanation of ethnic pigmentation. He also pointed out that the white scars in Ethiopians (e.g. after extensive burns with boiling water) are similar to the scars which occur in whites although the contrast is more readily visible.

Concerning the colour of the first man, he considers that Adam must have been red because he was created from the clay of the earth and 'Adam' means red. Various interpretations of the Bible are discussed, and he points out correctly that the Bible itself gives no further clue to the origin of ethnic pigmentation. He was also the first to point out that the blood contained in arteries and veins contributes to the skin colour, as seen in blushing, and for this season obese people tend to be paler than lean people. This paleness is also seen in dropsy patients and in consumptives. Similar changes due to illness contribute to a dullness of the otherwise shiny black appearance of healthy Ethiopians. Loss of weight may be important, because lean people have a duller skin colour than the obese.

Considering the crude and macroscopic observations at his disposal, and the general scientific background of his era, Albinus impresses the modern reader as a critical observer with a scientific approach to a problem masked at that time by superstition, general impressions and legendary explanations.

It is difficult now to assess the importance his approach had on the general scientific climate of his era, but his work illustrates the fact that many of the early anatomists were fully aware of the findings of their contemporaries.

THE PHYSIOLOGICAL APPROACH

'Claude Nicolas Le Cat . . . was one of the early physicians to contribute to this reformation and make eighteenth century French medicine and surgery outstanding' (Lurie, 1960).

Le Cat was born in Bléracourt, Picardy, on September 6, 1700. At the College of Soissons he first studied philosophy and ecclesiastics before changing to architecture and mathematics. Finally, because of his ability in natural science, he became an apprentice to his father, a surgeon. He studied under Winslow, Peyronie, Guérin and Morand. Between 1732 and 1738 he was awarded all the competitive prizes offered by the Academy of Surgeons of Paris. He published many papers on the principles of medicine, surgery, astronomy, electricity, history and archaeology, as well as communications to the Royal Academy of Science of Rouen. He preceded Duchenne (1806–1875) by a century in using electricity in the diagnosis and treatment of nervous diseases. He incidentally described Courvoisier's law (as formulated by Ludwig George Courvoisier a century later), but at the time he was more interested in the effect of obstructive jaundice on skin colour than in the diagnostic significance of his discovery (Fig. 5).

Lurie (1960) concludes his biographical sketch: 'Claude Nicolas Le Cat lived in an age of transformations, changes and revolutions. A learned man, versed in many branches of science, a teacher and a surgeon of reputation, he was a product of his era . . . he is a representative of the more important and enlightened surgeons of his era and helped perpetuate the evolution of the modern surgeon.'

To understand the era of Le Cat, it must be realised that in that era 'the belief in the teratogenic powers of maternal impressions reigned supreme' (Ballantyne, 1904). Little was known of the physiology of reproduction and of intrauterine life, but, as Ballantyne (1904) states: 'Credulity would indeed seem to have reached a maximum when it began to be asserted and believed that conception might occur through the imagination alone.' Riolan believed that while imagination could alter the properties of the uterine contents, it could not change the species. Monster births, up to that time, were held to be the result of bestial or Satanic intercourse. It is interesting to note that the Boyle who conceived Boyle's Law (of the relation between pressure and volume in gases) was content to accept that a mother who had a speckled child conceived such a child, because she used to gaze at some speckled, red pebbles during her pregnancy. It was only towards the middle of the eighteenth century that the work of Blondel became well known and accepted, although his work was published in 1727. He showed, by careful consideration of the facts and arguments, that the theory of maternal impressions was unsupported by experience, by reason, or by anatomy. Blondel's work was supported by Albert von Haller, with whom Le Cat had a fierce argument on the theory of sensibility and irritability. Le Cat's argument was critically

Fig. 5. *Claude Nicolas le Cat (1700–1768)*
He published the first comprehensive physiological treatise on ethnic pigmentation in 1765, with a full review of the literature of his era and many original observations. 'A learned man, versed in many branches of science... a product of his era.' (From A. L. Lurie, 1960, *Surgery, Gynecology and Obstetrics, 111.* 247. Courtesy of the Editors.)

analysed by Von Haller, and shown to be faulty, in a paper read at Göttingen in 1752. Boerhaave, with his authoritative views on many problems in medicine, favoured the old theory. Le Cat seems to have favoured Krause's suggestion of a nervous communication between the mother's uterus, the placenta and the foetus.

Ballantyne, writing in 1904, considered that at the beginning of the present century the theory of maternal impressions was still very much alive and was strengthened by the 'views that group themselves around 'Christian Science' and 'Mind Cures'.'

The work of Le Cat, entitled *Traité de la Couleur de la Peau Humaine en général, de celle des Nègres en particulier, et de la Métamorphose d'une de ces Couleurs en l'autre, soit de Naissance, soit accidentellement*, appeared in 1765.

The Frontispiece is discussed at length as to its symbolic significance, as was the custom at the time (Fig. 6). The publication is indicated as a response to the phenomenon described in a letter in *Feuille Hebdomadaire* of March 2, 1764. In this letter the metamorphosis of a well-known Parisian woman to the colour of an Ethiopian was described, and the problem of the explanation of this phe-

H. Gravelot del.   Bacheley sculp.
non vultus, non color vnus. Virgil L. vi.

TRAITÉ
DE LA COULEUR
DE LA PEAU HUMAINE
EN GÉNÉRAL,
DE CELLE DES NEGRES
EN PARTICULIER,
ET DE LA MÉTAMORPHOSE
D'UNE DE CES COULEURS EN L'AUTRE,
SOIT DE NAISSANCE, SOIT ACCIDENTELLEMENT ;

Ouvrage divisé en trois Parties.

PAR M. LE CAT,

Ecuyer, Docteur en Médecine, Chirurgien en Chef de l'Hôtel-Dieu dé Rouen, Lithotomiste Pensionnaire de la même Ville, Professeur-Démonstrateur Royal en Anatomie & Chirurgie, Correspondant de l'Académie Royale des Sciences de Paris, Doyen des Associés Regnicoles ; de celle de Chirurgie, Membre des Académies Royales de Londres, Madrid, Porto, Berlin, Lyon ; des Académies Impériales des Curieux de la Nature, de S. Pétersbourg, de l'Institut de Bologne, & Secrétaire perpétuel de l'Académie des Sciences de Rouen.

A AMSTERDAM.

M. DCC. LXV.

Fig. 6. Frontispiece of Le Cat's Treatise. The symbolic picture portrays a scene in America, where beneath a simple tent a French lady is attended by her maid mixing a cordial. The American Indian is surprised by his image as seen in a mirror held by a Negro. (From Le Cat, 1765, *Traité de la Couleur de la Peau Humaine.* Reproduced from the original Manuscript in the Wellcome Library. Courtesy of 'The Wellcome Trustees'.)

nomenon was put to Le Cat. His explanation was apparently criticized and he takes exception to the severity of the criticism, especially as this was apparently very personal and acrimonious.

The work itself is a rather lengthy, but very full review, of the eighteenth century views on skin pigmentation, and ethnic pigmentation in particular.

Of interest is the general organisation of the work: In the first section the problem of the colour of the skin is discussed in 4 articles: Colour of races, origin of races, the anatomy of the skin and, finally, the substances providing colour to the skin.

The second part concerns itself with the Ethiopian colour, its origin and, remarkable for this period, comparative studies on the squid (ink-fish) and the similarity of its pigment to that of the skin.

The third part considers metamorphosis of skin colour, and here albinism is differentiated from vitiligo; also pigmentation due to longstanding jaundice is considered (with the description of Courvoisier's law in a case of carcinoma of the pancreas).

Part one starts with a description of the various skin colours in different climates, but exceptions are noted such as a 'race as white as milk' dwelling in the centre of tropical Africa. In other respects these people resembled the other blacks of the regions. He also refers to travel descriptions by Struys which describe people with tails in Formosa. He stressed the occurrence of more than two colours and many features of the people of newly discovered countries.

In Article II he discusses the origin of the several races. As the 'Bible and tradition of all people' (*sic*) proclaims that whites were the original race, it has to be explained how other races developed from them. He discards the mark of Cain and the curse on Ham. He remarks that those who believed that the sons of Noah were white, brown and black established their arithmetic to fit the known races. Had they known of the fourth or copper-coloured race they would have allotted 4 sons to Noah. Even these 4 brothers would be hard put to explain that race with tails living on Formosa. But even if this is accepted, it has still to be explained how Noah and his white wife could produce children all differing in colour.

If a curse solved the problem of the originator of a black race, it still has to be explained where the cursed man found a wife of similar colour.

He then remarks on the stupidity of invoking a curse to explain the origin of a whole race as this would tend to make people consider such a race as inferior. He believes that, although the Negroes 'are not our equals, they are nevertheless just as good, wise and clever as whites.'

He then goes on to review the various explanations put forward by Ancient Greek poets, travellers and scientists. He comes to the conclusion that the effect of sunlight and climate was probably decisive in creating different races. Ingeniously, he compares Joshua of the Bible to Phaeton of Greek mythology. Joshua prayed for the sun to stand still and the legend of Phaeton confirms this event. In the evening in Israel, the sun would be directly above the land of the Negroes. The darker Mediterranean people support this fact.

The alternative theory that people derived their colour from the colour of the earth from which they were created is discussed at length. He modifies this view to suggest that the diet as derived from various soils may influence skin colour. A final hypothesis, which he attributes to Vossius, suggests that a black skin came as a consequence of a skin disease, and that the black races originated from the marriage of two such sufferers.

In Article III he reviews the work of the anatomists on the epidermis, reticular layer and dermis. He explains striae gravidarum as the result of overstretching of the skin with rupture of the reticular membrane.

Considerable attention is given to the nerves of the skin which produce (1) glands to keep the skin supple as well as juices to keep the skin sensitive, (2) hair and (3) sense organs. The vascular system contains blood and lymph, the former rendering the skin red, especially in eczema and inflammation, but also in blushing, while the latter is responsible for the white colour.

The nervous secretions are gelatinous, and the condensation of this nervous secretion forms the reticular layer, and this, eventually, the epidermis.

The concept then, briefly, is that the dermis, containing nerves which secrete a mucus, condensed to form the reticular layer, while other juices, leaking through to condensate with amniotic fluid, formed the epidermis. In the latter, however, several other materials from the immediate environment are captured. The effect of heat and sun dries this layer and makes it impermeable. On this basis is explained the shedding of skin by snakes, and also other skin diseases in man.

Leeuwenhoek's observation of pores in the epidermis, estimated at 125,000 in a piece of skin the size of a grain of sand, strengthened Le Cat's opinion that continuous secretion adds to the epidermis. He also refers to microscopy performed by himself, but considers that he has less experience in this field than Leeuwenhoek and Malpighi, although his observations are in general agreement. He believes that sweat derives from the lymph vessels in the skin.

To explain the formation of the reticular layer from body fluids (including nervous secretions), he absorbed blood, bile and lymph from whites and blacks on pieces of linen, and noted that their colours were the same. These fluids are not, as held by several contemporaries, the cause of ethnic differences in pigmentation. (Santorini ascribed the colour of Negroes to black bile, Morgagni thought the blood of Negroes to be black, but later corrected himself – sec p. 55.)

His physiology is based on the various juices of the body which must derive from the blood, but, because gastric juice differs so markedly from lymph, it must be the nerves which determine their final nature. In the choroid of the eye, nerves are close to a black ink-like substance (similar to the reticular layer). Similar black pigments are to be found in many glands, including the suprarenal glands. Essentially then, nerves influence fluid exuding from blood vessels so that it becomes a black pigment. (At this stage he announces himself as the possessor of the fundamental knowledge of the colour of the Negro, but modestly admits that he only saw a glimmering of the light, as one lost deep in a labyrinth. It is still a long way to complete the journey). He then learnt of Meckel's announcement that the medulla oblongata of the Negro has a bluish colour. He dissected brains and discovered that they consist of a grey cortex and white medulla, the latter having a bluish sheen in blacks. He thus concludes that the brain produces the pigment (which he named ethiops) and that this is conveyed by nerves to the choroid, the skin and the several glands. The brain is undoubtedly a 'spermatic part' and here he refers to Strabo's opinion that the colour of the skin is in the seed of the parents. (The 'spermatic nature' of the brain could thus determine the colour of the skin of the offspring.) He points out that when he refers to the ethiops as a spermatic fluid, he means a nervous secretion and not the white fluid derived from the testes. This still leaves unsolved the reason why whites should have so much ethiops in the choroid of the eye but not elsewhere.

He then digresses to an excursion in comparative anatomy, the most interesting part of which is the identification of the similarity of the ethiops of the ink-fish to that of the choroid of the eye and the reticular layer. (This deduction proved to be completely correct and in recent years many studies on squid melanin have been done.) He identified the granular nature of the pigment when dried, whether it be derived from the ink of the squid, the choroid of the eye or the reticular layer of the skin.

In the third part, clinical conditions are considered. Bile, considered originally by Barrère as the cause of the blackness of Negroes, is discussed at length and also his comparisons of Negro blood and bile. (The comparison of linen strips soaked in blood and bile from whites and Negroes was performed as a double blind study. Several observers were asked to point out differences in the linen stains marked according to their origin but covered and unknown to either Le Cat or his colleagues.)

He gives considerable attention to Negroes born white and remaining so throughout life. The parents were black, the eyes were reddish and the pupil red 'as the red glow of dawn'. The hair was a sandy colour. The eyes 'shivered' and vision was poor in daylight. The eyes are exactly like the eyes of white rabbits. White inhabitants of his town had 2 or 3 children suffering from the same condition because their mother was alarmed by a white rabbit when expecting them. The choroid of the white rabbit is black, but the retina white. In the white Negro absence of pigment in the choroid allows light scattering which explains his poor vision in sunlight. The wavering and shivering iris accounts for the poor ability to focus, and habitual squinting further impairs vision.

This clinical description of albinism is as accurate as any in modern textbooks of dermatology. (Lionel Wafer (1699) also gave an accurate description of albinism.)

Occasionally it occurs that black children are born to white parents, although this phenomenon is more rare than albinism. Here he interposes that he does not warrant the truth of the many stories told. He had no personal experience of such cases, but is willing to accept maternal impressions as the cause, as in the 'case reported recently' where a pregnant woman was frightened by the Negro valet of a prince.

He then discusses acquired metamorphosis and accurately describes several case histories of vitiligo starting in small areas and then progressing in symmetrical distributon over the hands and face, and depigmentation following on burns by boiling water.

Finally, sudden greying of the hair (King Henry III of Navarre's moustache turned grey in a few hours after proclaiming the Edict of Nantes) also confirmed his conclusion that emotions operating through the nerves determine the pigmentation of the body. Subsequently case reports of whites who turned black are discussed. These are puzzling descriptions. In some cases, I suspect, chloasma of pregnancy could be the diagnosis (most cases occurred during pregnancy and all concern females), but in two individuals fever and systemic illness were present which suggests a diagnosis of tuberculosis, Addison's disease and uraemia.

Le Cat considered regional darkening to be the result of a skin disease (a foot turning black but recovering later). In one case emotional disturbances and depression were marked.

Le Cat remarks that bronzing of the forehead is normal in pregnancy, and he attributes the same thing occurring in the case of an unmarried woman with amenorrhoea, but not pregnant, to a similar mechanism. Melancholia as described in some cases turned his thoughts to jaundice and darkening of the skin. Nevertheless, these cases, although puzzling to Le Cat, were considered to be brought about by multifactorial causes.

He then embarked on an investigation of 'black jaundice'. The first personal case was an aged woman with obstructive jaundice due to gallstones in a fibrotic gallbladder, calculi filling what remained of the small gallbladder.

His second case is described in detail. Pierre Paulard, 80 years old, developed jaundice, emaciation and fever, and two weeks before his death his jaundice turned black. 'Where the duodenum receives the hepatic and pancreatic ducts he had a scirrhous, necrotic tumour and therefore his excretory ducts were completely obstructed; from that came the reflux of bile and pancreatic juice. The gallbladder was large and completely distended. The bile in this pouch was the darkest I had ever seen; at the same time it was extremely thick and very viscous.' The brain was not discoloured by jaundice. In a footnote he remarks that in the autumn of 1763 he saw such tumours at the same site with reflux to a distended gallbladder in several cases. 'It would appear as if I had an epidemic disease of these organs.' A century later Ludwig George Courvoisier formulated his law with reference to the gallbladder and pancreatic carcinoma.

On examining the black bile he found that dilution with water rendered it yellow as normal bile. On mixing bile with spirit of nitre it turned a dark green, then purple after an initial white colour on the paper (Fouchet's test). Alkalis did not affect the bile, but all acids turned it green. This differs from the reactions observed on the ethiops. He concludes that black jaundice does not explain either ethnic hyperpigmentation or the metamorphosis of whites to blacks.

What did Le Cat achieve? Judged within the era in which he lived, he critically examined popular notions and speculations and disproved most of them. He conducted chemical tests on ethiops (melanin) and demonstrated the similarity of skin, choroid and squid melanin, and he was able to differentiate chemically bile, black in appearance, from ethiops (melanin). He contrasts obstructive jaundice, due to a shrivelled gallbladder with stones, with his cases of pancreatic carcinoma with obstruction of the common duct and distention of the gallbladder. He provided a full and accurate description of albinism which he differentiated from vitiligo and posttraumatic depigmentation. Considered in the context of the physiology and pathology of his time, he gave the first reasoned explanation of ethnic pigmentation on the basis of the slender physiological principles known or erroneously accepted at the time. His was truly the first attempt at a physiological and biochemical investigation of skin pigmentation. His microscopic instruments were crude and would be surpassed by better instruments in the next century, but in many ways he pioneered pigment research.

THE PHYSICAL APPROACH TO SKIN PIGMENTATION

Johann Mitchel's treatise of 1747 was probably the first on ethnic pigmentation from the New World. Mitchel, a member of the Royal Society, wrote from Urbana, Virginia, to Peter Collinson, also a member of the Royal Society: 'I am afraid that this communication will arrive too late for the prize competition of the Academy of Bordeaux, so I would ask you only to communicate this to the Royal Society if it merits so much honour. Should it be well received, I leave the publishing to you in your learned and witty wordings.'

In the letter he also points out that his observations do not agree with the findings of European workers who report black juices in the reticular layer. He suspects that because these workers used dead bodies they found a paste-like substance which they interpreted as a reticular layer filled with black mucus.

He propounds several theorems which he then proves from his observations, e.g.:

Theorem I: The colour of whites is derived from the colour which is transmitted through the epidermis. It is due more to the colours of parts below the epidermis than due to the epidermis itself.

The colour of various parts (lips, palms) is related to the thickness of the epidermis over these parts. Blushing and erythema in fever is due to blood, because it blanches on pressure. In jaundice the epidermis, which contains no vessels according to Malpighi, cannot be stained and the yellowness comes from below the epidermis. Oedema and anaemia are also cited in evidence.

The epidermis, therefore, is a transparent skin and is analogous to the cornea of the eye through which the colour of the iris may be seen. The cause of this transparency is discussed later. According to Newton, the epidermis would reflect light because the interspaces between its particles are small and it would thus appear white. In vivo, however, the spaces are filled with fluid of about the same density as the particles and would thus be transparent. In oblique light the thick and roughened epidermis of the palms can be seen to be transparent, but when it flakes off due to disease it is dried out and appears white.

Theorem II: The skin of blacks is thicker and of a denser tissue than that of whites, and is not transparent.

Evidence for this theorem is that, at venesection, the skin of blacks feels more solid and thicker than that of whites. He found it more difficult to raise blisters by Spanish fly poultices or local heat in blacks than in whites. They do not sunburn as easily as whites. A black body absorbs more heat and thus the skin must be thicker and more resistant to heat if it does not blister even in spite of this additional heat load.

In blacks with a thinner skin, it feels harder in winter when not covered with fatty sweat. This is also the case in fevers. Furthermore, blacks do not suffer from the skin diseases (scruffiness, prickly heat or eschars) which occur commonly in those with a tender skin, and likewise blushing is not observed. Therefore the skin is not transparent enough to allow observation of changes in blood or other colouring matters.

Newton's theory of light and colour claims that if light and colour are absent, darkness and blackness result. He then investigated this lack of transparency.

He used epispastics (Liq. cantharides) to raise blisters. Especially over the fingers, where the skin of blacks is about twice as thick as that of whites, the roof of the blister consists of an outer part and inner part, the latter appearing black. The blister base is of the same colour as in whites. Scraping the skin shows that the outer skin consists of layers of flakes which, when totally removed, leave a base as white as in Europeans. He identifies the black layer as the reticular layer of Malpighi. A slightly more transparent upper skin explains the copper colour of American Indians and mulattoes. The nerves and vessels of the skin proper terminate in this reticular layer, but nerves pierce the layer, although vessels, except for sweat gland ducts, do not.

As nothing is found in black skin which does not also occur in white skin, the colour of the blacks is not due to black juices or liquid parts.

He discusses fully that he was enthusiastic about the suggestion by Malpighi and other workers that the reticular layer contains an oily black substance, especially as he could conceive that the heat of the sun could concentrate this substance to darken the skin. Such a substance would probably also appear in sweat and this would, thus, lighten the skin. As he could not demonstrate such a substance in living skin he can, however, not accept this attractive theory. He refers to the early work of Littré who could not extract this substance in ordinary solvents. But even the strongest solvents used would be less powerful than fire or Spanish fly which indeed raised blisters. This should surely discolour the blister fluid if any liquid coloured substance was present in the skin, but this is not the case.

Theorem V: The epidermis, especially its outer part, has interspaces and flakes which are 200 times smaller than the parts of the body from which their colour derives and is, therefore, divided into two parts.

Isaac Newton claimed that the parts of a body which cause its colour are 600 times smaller than those visible to the naked eye. Leeuwenhoek showed that a piece of skin that is just visible had 125,000 interspaces and thus 125,000 smaller parts. 125,000 divided by 600 = 208⅓. These parts of the skin must, therefore, be 200 times smaller than those parts which could lend it its colour.

The transparency of the epidermis must be due to its interspaces and the particles of the skin are too small to reflect light, and so colour the skin. People with a very thick skin are more yellowish than those with a thinner skin and, according to Newton's optics, yellow results from an incomplete transmission of white light.

The gradations of ethnic pigmentation are thus, from the whitest European, through the copper-coloured Indians and yellow Asians to the blackest Moor, solely dependent on the amount of light transmitted through the epidermis. The more scattering of light occurs in the epidermis, the less light is reflected to the eye and the darker does the individual appear. In blisters, the yellowish fluid is visible through white skin but not through black skin, again illustrating the lack of transparency.

Undoubtedly black skin scatters and absorbs practically all light. According to Newton's concept of the particles involved, black skin must contain much smaller particles than white skin because as soon as particles reach a certain size they reflect light. At a time when cellular structure was not yet generally accepted as fundamental to all living tissues, Mitchel came remarkably close to realizing that the essential cause of black skin was the subcellular particles, contained within the epidermal cells of black skin, but lacking in white skin.

Newton's colour theory is then elaborated on, and further everyday observations on colour mixing are discussed in terms of the new physics of light and refraction. A very interesting conclusion is reached at the end of Part. I:

'From this we may deduce truly:

1. That between the blacks and the whites, with respect to their colour, there does not exist such a large, unnatural and incomprehensible difference that it would be impossible to derive this from a common origin, as some people, ignorant of the theory of colours, would believe and ascertain, even if it is in conflict with the teaching of the Holy Scripture.

2. That the epidermis, apart from its other utility, also serves to maintain the correspondence of colours throughout the World.'

In the second part, *Theorem VII* states:

The influence of the sun and the living conditions in hot countries is the most important cause of the colour of the blacks, Indians and Moors. The living conditions prevalent amongst most white nations are such as to make their colour whiter than it originally was or naturally should be.

Some remarkable deductions, ahead of his time, in this section are:

1. All people living in the same latitude do not have the same skin colour. This is because the environment operates through (a) the nature and geography of the land and (b) the customs of the people.

Under (a) is discussed sunlight reflection from the arid white sands of the desert which is much greater than from other soils, the plant life, shade, and the availability of water. Under (b) is discussed clothing, housing, hunting and the custom of anointing the body with various oils and plant juices.

The adverse factors in white civilizations are excessive clothing, warm beds, excessive eating and drinking, a tendency to sit by the fireside and to bath frequently, and an easy and promiscuous life. This tends to make them paler than they should be.

He complains about the lack of historical works in Virginia and insufficient contact with the literature of Europe.

2. He considers it possible that all races might have developed from a single

forebear and separate creations need not be postulated. The fact that a black man in northern climes does not turn white, while Spaniards known to him turned nearly as dark as the Indians of America when living in the warmer parts of America, as did an Englishman who lived for three years amongst Indians with full acceptance of their mode of living, is explained simply by the analogy that it is easier to dye a white cloth than to discolour a black one.

These examples of 18th century scientific work on ethnic pigmentation indicate some far-sighted, remarkably accurate deductions reached with crude but dedicated efforts at experimentation. They also show the beginning of anatomical, physiological, chemical and physical approaches to a problem which even today remains a multidisciplinary research problem and yields the most promising information to interdisciplinary efforts.

REFERENCES

ALBINUS, B. S. (1737): *Sede et Causa Coloris Aethiopum et Caeterorum Hominum.* J. Graal and H. de Leth, Amsterdam.

BALLANTYNE, J. W. (1904): *Antenatal Pathology and Hygiene.* W. Green and Sons, Edinburgh.

FAULL, R. L. M., TAYLOR, D. W. and CARMAN, J. B. (1968): Soemmering and the substantia nigra. *Med. Hist.*, *12*, 297.

LE CAT, C. N. (1765): *Traité de la Couleur de la Peau Humaine en général, de celle des Nègres en particulier, et de la Métamorphose d'une de ces Couleurs en l'autre, soit de Naissance, soit accidentellement.* M. M. Rey, Amsterdam.

LINSCOTT, R. N. (1957): *The Notebooks of Leonardo da Vinci*, p. 205 (abridged, from the translation by E. MacCurdy). Modern Library, New York, N.Y.

LITTRÉ, A. (1702): *Histoire de l'Académie Royale des Sciences*, Article XIII. Paris.

LURIE, A. S. (1960): The evolution of the modern surgeon. *Surg., Gynec., and Obstet.*, *111*, 247.

MITCHEL, J. (1747): Versuch von den Ursachen der verschiedenen Farben der Menschen. *Hamburgisches Magazin.* Georg Christian Grund, Hamburg.

SINGER, C. and UNDERWOOD, E. A. (1962): *A Short History of Medicine.* Clarendon Press, Oxford.

WAFER, L. (1699): A new voyage and description of the Isthmus of America, giving an account of the author's abode there. In: *Collection of Voyages, 3rd ed., Vol. III*, pp. 261–463. Reprint, Burrows Bros., Cleveland, Ohio, 1903.

Chapter V

The nineteenth to the mid-twentieth century

Two reviews on the history of pigmentation research open with the following statements: *Research on the melanotic pigment of the skin was initiated by Henlé (1843) and G. Simon (1840)* (Meirowsky, 1940) and: *The significant study of melanin pigmentation dates from relatively modern times* (Becker, 1959). As is shown in the previous Chapter, however, the scientist of the 19th century had a sound anatomical basis, both in the knowledge that pigment was found to be located in the reticular membrane and in the few early chemical observations of Le Cat (1734) and Littré (1702) on the nature of pigment. The 19th century scientist applied the techniques of microscopy and chemistry to this field, and named the pigment under discussion 'melanin'.

When and how the name melanin came into use is as uncertain as the chemical nature of the pigment which it describes. Skinner (1961) attributes the term to Vizio in 'the early nineteenth century', but Becker (1959) gives Robin (1873) credit for being the originator of this term. Laennec (1826) gave the classic description of melanoma which he called 'la mélanose'.

The early microscopical studies were done before staining methods were available and pigment was therefore an ideal subject for Heusinger (1823) and Simon (1840).

Slack (1844) expresses the frustration of the mid-19th century when he remarks on the, by then well-known, reticular membrane between the cuticle and cutis: 'But here, in this mucous membrane, lies all the difference in the colour of man, be it what it may; in an arrangement of the particles of matter too minute to be detected by the most powerful glass of the optician, too subtile for the nicest test of the chemist.' Judd (1838) and Hurt (1865) commented on their observations of Negro skin and referred to the importance of ethnic pigmentation in the diagnosis of disease. Hurt (1865) also attacks the popular belief, current at the time, in the physiological identity of races, pointing out that the temporary changes in pigmentation due to sunburn revert to normal. He expressed his concept of a dynamic steady state of pigment in clear terms: 'every particle of the matter of which an organized animal body is composed is subject to displacement by the process of disintegration and absorption, and that, by a calculation which at least approximates to accuracy, at any particular time, is removed and replaced by new material, at least several times within the period of ordinary life.'

(This was contemporary with Bernard's concept of the *milieu intérieur*, but more than half a century ahead of Cannon's concept of homeostasis.) He speculates that the difference in the physiology of pigmentation may be associated with the known differences in the manifestations of disease in ethnic groups.

The late 19th century saw several significant directional changes in the research on pigmentation:

1. Speculation on ethnic pigmentation ceased, and the new stain technology for microscopy was applied to elucidate the *mechanisms* of pigmentation.

This change in emphasis is probably due to the clinical interest in pigmentary changes which fell within the field and growing specialization of dermatology.

2. Increasingly, comparative studies on animals were being performed by biologists, and attemps at integrating and reviewing research results were made. Rabl (1896) reviewed studies on vertebrate pigmentation and cites 71 references between 1892 and 1896.

3. The cell theory of Schleiden and Schwann in the early 19th century together with the cellular pathology of Virchow and the concept of the *milieu intérieur* of Claude Bernard became of signal interest. The scientist at the close of the 19th century became engrossed in a specialized cell which produced pigment and occurred in a milieu of various cell types, in a situation where it was relatively exposed to the influence of sunlight as well as being within easy reach of the scalpel. Schwann actually illustrated both mature and immature pigment cells from the skin of the tail of a tadpole.

The interest in the general physiology of pigmentation (e.g. pigmentation in pregnancy, brain pigment etc.) yielded to a more specialized interest in the physiology of skin.

4. The transport of pigment from the skin was of central interest towards the close of the century, but then disappeared completely from the literature after 1923.

5. Specialization is evident in the temporary divorce between melanin chemistry and synthesis, and melanocyte function, reunion taking place after the perfection of electron microscopy in the 1950's.

The tremendous acceleration of research and the synthesis of research findings over the last 30 years is evident when comparing the unanswered questions in Meirowsky's review of the century (1940) with Becker's (1959) review and finally comparing both with the contemporary review of the past two decades by Fitzpatrick et al. (1967).

MELANIN RESEARCH (1847–1928)

Three significant analyses of melanin were made. Professor J. W. Mallet (1876) reported studies on behalf of his pupil Dr. F. P. Floyd. He studied pigment granules still enveloped by the cell structure as obtained from scrapings of skin washed with alcohol and ether to remove fat. His studies were criticized by Abel and Davis (1896) (see below).

The pigment of hair was studied by Sorby (1878). This study comments on different pigments obtained, including a red pigment. He quantitatively divided hairs studied for their relative blackness and relative redness. On this scale red hair scored 100.0 for relative redness, followed by 5.0 for reddish brown hair, 3.7 for brown hair, 'the author's own blackest hair' 0.3 and the feathers of the rook 0.02. For relative blackness the feathers of the rook score 50.0, 'the author's black hair' 3.0, Negro's hair 1.0 and red hair 0.0.

His tables do not show the *quantity* but *quality* of the colour. '. . . as far as the quality is concerned, my own browner hair and that of the Negro agree (1.0), but the total quantity in the latter is ten times as great as in the former . . .'

Microscopically the light-brown and sandy hairs contained a small quantity of black pigment granules varying from 1/30,000th to 1/50,000th of an inch. Apart from commenting on the amount of pigment contained, comment is made, too, on the influence the structure of the hair has on its colour. In the Negro, if the production of black pigment should fail, it could become red, as occasionally described (no reference is given).

The study by Abel and Davis (1896) merits further attention. They refer to the physiological importance of various pigments including (1) those with well-understood functions such as haemoglobin and biliary pigments, (2) those with obscure physiological functions such as the pigments of melanotic tumours, and the retinal and choroidal coats of the eye and of the hair, and (3) the colouring matter in serum, urine and fats. This appears to be the first attempt to classify melanin as one of several classes of biological pigments.

The dark pigments occurring in the heart, liver, kidneys, thyroid gland, supra-renal body and testicles, on the pia mater and in nerve cells were known, but received no attention.

About the pigment in the Negro's skin they remark: '. . . should this pigment prove to be identical with that in the skin of the white races, this knowledge might throw great light on many anomalous cases of pigmentation; for example, the bronzed skin of Addison's disease, the brownish patches appearing on the face and other parts of the body during pregnancy . . .' Naevi and freckles are mentioned, as well as the pigmentary changes occurring in psoriasis, lichen ruber planus and xeroderma pigmentosa, and those following on chronic irritation.

They describe the extraction of pigment from the epidermis with water, alcohol and ether, the removal of hair, 'a tedious process requiring many days of labour', followed by treatment with alkalis to disintegrate the epidermis. Acids, with the exception of nitric acid, do not dissolve the pigment. The gradual disintegration of the epidermis was followed microscopically until only brownish particles, clearly distinguished by an immersion lens, remained. These granules tended to aggregate with a contour suggestive of the original cell form, but dispersed on light pressure on the cover slip. Chemical analysis showed epidermal and hair pigment to be very similar in its carbon, hydrogen, nitrogen, sulphur and oxygen content:

	Pigment of epidermis	*Pigment of hair*
Carbon	51.83	52.74
Hydrogen	3.86	3.53
Nitrogen	14.01	10.51
Sulphur	3.60	3.34
Oxygen	26.70	29.88
	100.00	100.00

Iron content was of special interest at the time because of the possible derivation of melanin pigment from haemoglobin. Three methods were used, but the gravimetric method was considered the most accurate. From 0.3863 g, 0.0134 g of ash was obtained and this contained 0.000385 g of iron, an iron content corresponding to 0.099% for the pigment.

They also found that the pigment was bound to a colourless ground substance of protein. They thought (1) that the iron content was too small to relate the pigment to haemoglobin, but (2) that the high sulphur content, while it argued against its derivation from haemoglobin, did suggest that it derived from the protein moiety to which the pigment is bound.

An analysis of the entire skin, except that of the palms and soles, of the cadaver of a tall slender Negro yielded an epidermis weighing 34.08 g; 9.9306 g of this epidermis yielded 0.2182 g of pigment. From this a weight of 0.8789 g was calculated for pigment in the entire epidermis. This epidermis was thinner than usual and the colour browner (not black) than usually found.

Assuming a 65% water content of cells, they calculated the average Negro to contain 3.3 g pigmentary granules or 1 g pigmentary substance per average body surface. (Apparently no similar calculations have been made since and this figure is still occasionally quoted.) They also concluded that the pigment of black skin differs only in amount and not in kind from that deposited in the skin of the white man.

The structure of complex molecules can be elucidated by either analytical or synthetic approaches. In the classical work of H. S. Raper (1928), who suggested that when tyrosine or dopa is oxidized enzymatically, the resulting melanin is a polymer derived from indole-5,6-quinone, the synthetic approach is adopted. The analytical approach yielded most success in the hands of Nicolaus (1962) and co-workers (Piatelli et al., 1962).

MELANOCYTES

Discovery

Using a gold impregnation technique, Langerhans (1868) identified nerves in the skin and dendritic cells in the skin and hair matrix. His interest was in the terminal nerves and not in pigmentation and a melanogenic function was not attributed to these cells (Giacometti and Barss, 1969).

The first description of isolated dendritic or stellate pigment cells filled with light-brown or golden-yellow granular pigment, in the connective tissue of eyelids, should be credited to Waldeyer (1871). In 1884 Riehl found such cells in the papillae of hair, and Retterer (1887) saw them in an 8 cm human foetus.

These cells were thought to originate from the corium, or from epithelial cells, or from wandering cells. The confusion at the end of the 19th century is evident from Piersol's (1890) review in which he, as a contemporary of the early workers referred to by Meirowsky (1940) and Becker (1959), *critically* discussed their contributions: The explanation most generally adopted was that 'the pigment, in a preformed condition, is carried into the epithelium through the agency of the wandering connective tissue cells; in support of this view, the repeatedly observed entrance of the branched pigmented cells of the cutis into the epidermis is offered as convincing evidence.'

'A second doctrine ascribes to the leucocytes the transportation of the pigment granules, previously formed within the blood vessels, to the superficial epithelium, while a third theory entirely reverses the generally accepted order of things, contending that the pigment originated locally within the epithelial cells, which latter undergo the astonishing metamorphosis of becoming directly converted into the large branched pigment cell, capable of wandering from the epithelium into the cutis . . .'

His own studies on lizard, rabbit, rat, sheep and cat embryos as well as advanced foetal and adult human skin, including that of the Negro, is then presented. He found that in the lizard embryo pigment appeared scantily and irregularly at the edges of the cell, but it soon aggregated immediately about the nucleus. The spherical cell gradually changed to a stellate one, the form of which became more pronounced as the amount of pigment increased. These cells 'passed into the epithelium while still immature and unpigmented; influenced by the same conditions which determine the appearance of pigment in certain cells of the cutis . . . resulting in the unfolding of their unmistakable nature as pigment cells.'

At this time pigment was generally held to be preformed elsewhere. All dark-brown or blackish pigments were regarded as products of the breaking down of the colouring matters of the blood, but Maass (1889) concluded that melanins are not derived from the blood: 'thus far, a positive genetic relation with haemoglobin has not been established for any normal pigment'; only the pigment of the liver and testicles gave strong evidence 'of a genetic relation to haemoglobin.'

Piersol (1890) concludes from his observations: (1) the pigment was formed *in loco* in these cells, which migrated *in embryo* into the epidermis. (2) Later . . . 'the pigment cells (of the cutis) send processes into the epithelium, and thereby contribute additional pigment to the epidermis.' (3) There is no conclusive evidence of the origin of pigment within the epithelial cells of the epidermis.

This little-known article by Piersol (1890) is perhaps one of the most advanced and accurate in its interpretation. In fact, it foreshadowed the concept of the 'epidermal melanin unit' by Fitzpatrick and Breathnach (1963) and it also put Aeby's (1885) and Kölliker's (1887) wandering cells and leucocytes in their proper role as scavengers of pigment produced by these cells.

Delépine (1891), as a physiologist, discussed observations in many clinical conditions and was content to attribute melanogenesis to epithelial cells of the epidermis, but could refute the general physiological view of its derivation from haemoglobin. He was especially interested in the transport of melanin and the increased deposition of melanin in internal organs following on a melanosis of the skin from any cause whatsoever.

Apparently the *function* of the melanocyte was first discovered and accurately described by Piersol (1890), although many workers described dendritic cells with pigment.

The origin of melanocytes from the neural crest was demonstrated in amphibians (Du Shane, 1943), birds (Dorris, 1939) and in mammals (Rawles, 1940).

Research on pigment-forming cells was stimulated by Bloch's discovery (1917) that a 1 : 1,000 solution of L-3,4-dihydroxyphenylalanine (dopa) at pH 7.4 blackens dendritic cells at the epidermodermal junction. These cells were called 'melanoblasts'. The dopa reaction is non-specific as oxidative enzymes in leucocytes yield a positive reaction as well, but later the perfection of the tyrosine reaction by Fitzpatrick et al. (1950) would greatly increase specific recognition of melanocytes.

CONTROL OF MELANOGENESIS

Endocrinology developed from the early 20th century with the concept of 'hormones', named by Bayliss and Starling (1902). Although the influence of pregnancy on pigmentation had held the interest and imagination of researchers since the 18th century, it remained for Steinach (1912) to observe the increase in areolar pigmentation after ovarian transplants to castrated male guinea-pigs. Further work in this area was discussed by Becker (1959).

Addison's disease (1855) was well known in 1874 when Darby described a woman with the clinical features of the disease, on whom he had operated some 20 years previously for a 'fibrocystic tumour of the breast'. He demonstrated the kidneys and adrenals in which he could find no autopsy evidence of any disease. This 'tended to create a doubt in his mind of the correctness of the theory which associated bronzed skin with disease of the suprarenal capsules.' Harvey Cushing (1932) remarked that nearly all diseases of the pituitary are associated with visible deviations in skin pigmentation. It remained, however, for Calkins (1950) to suggest the influence of ACTH and MSH on the pigmentation of the skin in Addison's disease.

Environmental factors

The one known factor clearly influencing skin pigmentation, known since the ancient sun worshippers, was sunlight. Modern research in this field started with Finsen who developed a 'very strong arc-lamp' in December 1896, and studied the effect of light on the skin. He reviewed his earlier work on man, including albinos, and differentiated the reactions due to shorter wavelengths and heat rays, discussing photochemical reactions following exposure to light. He, like Widmark, described the ability of light to cause an inflammatory reaction, and he also found ultraviolet light to be bactericidal. He referred to the 'chemical (ultraviolet) rays' and differentiated their effects from those of heat rays (Finsen, 1900).

Hasselbalch studied the transmission of ultraviolet light by the epidermis, and was followed by several other workers using refined techniques and original approaches (reviewed by Everett, 1964; Everett et al., 1961, 1966). Blum (1948), in particular, explored this field with special reference to the carcinogenetic properties of sunlight and the marked difference in reaction between the white and black races. These studies merged with the larger field of photobiology which, in the case of human skin, received an additional stimulus in the discovery of the free radical properties of melanin.

Genetic factors

Although Hippocrates suspected genetic determination of ethnic pigmentation, little is known of the genetic transmission of human pigmentation. This field abounds in many unanswered questions, mostly studied in small mammals, e.g. mice. The 1940's started the era where '. . . new techniques of biochemical and morphological inquire into molecular genetics have permitted the development of an increasingly clear outline of the problem and contributed highly important information towards its solution' (Quevedo, 1969).

NON-MELANOCYTE MELANIN

Lerner (1955) reviewed melanin pigmentation in the light of 'melanin formed from tyrosine when the principal reactions take place in the melanocyte.' One neglected area is indicated as that of *non-melanocyte melanin* including the melanin of ochronosis in alkaptonuria, and melanosis coli.

By establishing the melanocyte as a cell type, *sui generis*, from the neural crest, other cells as possible melanogenic cells were largely ignored till the work of Okun (1965, 1967) and Okun et al. (1970) concentrated on the mast cell and produced convincing evidence that this cell can produce melanin although its relative overall importance is still uncertain.

Extracutaneous melanin pigmentation featured prominently in works up to the middle of the 19th century, but interest appears to be returning to this field only since recent developments established: (1) diffuse melanosis as a rare side-effect of long-term phenothiazine therapy, (2) L-dopa (a melanin precursor) as the 'treatment of choice' in Parkinsonism, a condition associated with selective depigmentation of neuromelanin-containing basal ganglia, and (3) evidence suggesting that lipofuscin is a misnamed lipomelanin.

CONCLUDING COMMENT

'Pigment cell research' once again became 'melanin biology research' in the 1950's: knowledge of protein biosynthesis expanded rapidly, differential centrifugation techniques developed and electron-microscopic techniques were refined. The subcellular localization of melanin biosynthesis could be studied in a way which is still sufficiently recent to excite admiration for the newly developed technology.

The reviews of the history of pigment research by Meirowsky (1940), Becker (1959) and Fitzpatrick et al. (1967) should be read consecutively to appreciate the rapid advances made since 1940. Fitzpatrick's (1967) especially succeeds in capturing the excitement of the 1940–1966 era.

Ethnic pigmentation is genetically determined, but genetic mechanisms operate at the enzyme level and they are regulated by control mechanisms.

Melanin may influence enzyme systems and we again appear to be at the dawn of a new era in pigment research. The valuable emphasis on *pigment cell function* is now shifting to a more promising emphasis on melanin biology, which can hardly any longer be held to reside only in the skin.

REFERENCES

ABEL, J. J. and DAVIS, W. S. (1896): On the pigment of the Negro's skin and hair. *J. exp. Med., 1*, 361.

ADDISON, T. (1855): Diseases of suprarenal capsules. *London med. Gaz., 43*, 517.

AEBY, C. (1885): Die Herkunft des Pigmentes im Epithel. *Zbl. med. Wiss., 23*, 273.

BAYLISS, W. M. and STARLING, E. M. (1902): The mechanism of pancreatic secretion. *J. Physiol. (Lond.), 28*, 325.

BECKER, S. W. (1959): Historical background of research on pigmentary diseases of the skin. *J. invest. Derm., 32*, 185.

BLOCH, B. (1917): Das Problem der Pigmentbildung in der Haut. *Arch. Derm. Syph. (Berl.), 124*, 129.

BLUM, H. F. (1948): Sunlight as a causal factor in cancer of the skin of man. *J. nat. Cancer Inst., 9*, 247.

CALKINS, E. (1950): Personal communication. Cited by Lerner and Fitzpatrick (1950).

CUSHING, H. (1932): Function of the interbrain pigmentary effect. In: *Papers relating to the Pituitary Body, Hypothalamus and Parasympathetic Nervous System*, p. 28. Charles C. Thomas, Springfield, Ill.

DARBY (1874): Exhibition of 'Tumours and Miscellaneous Specimens'. *Proc. path. Soc. Dublin (New Ser.), 5*, 249.

DELÉPINE, S. (1891): On cutaneous pigment (as an antecedent of haemoglobins). *J. Physiol. (Lond.), 12*, 27.

DORRIS, F. (1939): The production of pigment by chick neural crest in grafts to the 3 day limb bud. *J. exp. Zool., 82*, 131.

DU SHANE, G. (1943): The embryology of vertebrate pigment cells. I. Amphibia. *Quart. Rev. Biol., 18*, 108.

EVERETT, M. A. (1964): Biochemical changes induced by ultraviolet light. *Derm. trop.*, *3*, 97.

EVERETT, M. A., ANGLIN, J. H. and BEVER, A. T. (1961): Ultraviolet induced biochemical alterations in skin. I. Urocanic acid. *Arch. Derm.*, *84*, 717.

EVERETT, M. A., YEARGERS, E., SAYNE, R. M. and OLSON, R. L. (1966): Penetration of epidermis by ultraviolet rays. *Photochem. Photobiol.*, *5*, 533.

FINSEN, N. R. (1900): Neue Untersuchungen über die Einwirkung des Lichtes auf die Haut. *Mitt. Finsens med. Lysinst.*, *1*, 8.

FITZPATRICK, T. B., BECKER JR., S. W., LERNER, A. B. and MONTGOMERY, H. (1950): Tyrosinase in human skin: Demonstration of its presence and of its role in human melanin formation. *Science, 112*, 223.

FITZPATRICK, T. B. and BREATHNACH, A. S. (1963): Das epidermale Melanin-Einheit-System. *Derm. Wschr.*, *147*, 481.

FITZPATRICK, T. B., MIYAMOTO, M. and ISHIKAWA, K. (1967): The evolution of concepts of melanin biology. In: *Advances in Biology of Skin, Vol. VIII: The Pigmentary System*, pp. 1–29. Editors: W. Montagna and F. Hu. Pergamon Press, Oxford.

GIACOMETTI, L. and BARSS, M. (1969): Paul Langerhans: a tribute. *Arch. Derm.*, *100*, 770.

HENLÉ, F. G. J. (1843): Allgemeine Anatomie. In: *Lehre von den Mischungs- und Formbestandteilen des menschlichen Körpers*. L. Voss, Leipzig.

HEUSINGER, C. F. (1823): *Untersuchungen über die anomale Kohlen- und Pigment-Bildung in dem menschlichen Körper, mit besonderer Beziehung auf Melanosen, erhöhte Venosität, gelbes Fieber, und die schwarzgalligen Krankheiten der älteren Aerzte.* J. F. Baerecke, Eisenach.

HURT, G. (1865): Color of the skin – physiologically considered – its permanency and evidence of diversity of species. *St. Louis med. surg. J. (New Ser.)*, *2*, 385.

JUDD, W. (1838): Memoir on the structure of the Negro's skin. *Lancet, 2*, 426.

KÖLLIKER, A. (1887): Über die Entstehung des Pigmentes in den Oberhautgebilden. *Z. wiss. Zool.*, *45*, 713.

LAENNEC, R. T. H. (1826): *Traité de l'Auscultation médiate et des Maladies des Poumons et du Coeur.* Editions J.-S. Chaunde, Paris.

LANGERHANS, P. (1868): Über die Nerven der menschlichen Haut. *Virchow's Arch. path. Anat.*, *44*, 325.

LERNER, A. B. (1955): Melanin pigmentation. *Amer. J. Med.*, *19*, 902.

LERNER, A. B. and FITZPATRICK, T. B. (1950): Biochemistry of melanin formation. *Physiol. Rev.*, *30*, 91.

MAASS, F. (1889): Zur Kenntniss des körnigen Pigmentes im menschlichen Körper. *Arch. mikr. Anat.*, *34*, 452.

MALLETT, J. N. (1876): On the chemical character of the pigment of the Negro's skin. *Chem. News*, *34*, 179.

MEIROWSKY, E. (1940): A critical review of pigment research in the last hundred years. *Brit. J. Derm. Syph.*, *52*, 205.

NICOLAUS, R. A. (1962): Biogenesis of melanins. *Rass. Med. sper.*, *9, Suppl. 1*, 1.

OKUN, M. (1965): Histogenesis of melanocytes. *J. invest. Derm.*, *44*, 285.

OKUN, M. (1967): Pigment formation in mast cells in tissue culture. *J. invest. Derm.*, *48*, 424.

OKUN, M., EDELSTEIN, L., OR, N., HAMADA, G. and DONNELLAN, B. (1970): Histochemical studies of conversion of tyrosine and dopa to melanin mediated by mammalian peroxidase. *Life Sci.*, *9*, 491.

OKUN, M. R., EDELSTEIN, L. M., OR, N., HAMADA, G. and DONNELLAN, B. (1970): The role of peroxidase vs. the role of tyrosinase in enzymatic conversion of tyrosine to melanin in melanocytes, mast cells and eosinophils. *J. invest. Derm.*, *5*, 1.

PIATELLI, M., FATTORUSSO, E., MAGNO, S. and NICOLAUS, R. A. (1962): The structure of melanins and melanogenesis. II. Sepiomelanin and synthetic pigments. *Tetrahedron, 18,* 941.

PIERSOL, G. A. (1890): Development of pigment within the epidermis. *Penn. Univ. Sch. Med. med. Bull., 11,* 571.

QUEVEDO, W. C. (1969): Genetics of mammalian pigmentation. In: *The Biologic Effects of Ultraviolet Radiation (with Emphasis on the Skin),* p. 315. Editor: F. Urbach. Pergamon Press, London.

RABL, H. (1896): Pigment und Pigmentzellen in der Haut der Wirbeltiere. *Ergebn. Anat. Entwickl.-Gesch., 6,* 439.

RAPER, H. S. (1928): The aerobic oxidases. *Physiol. Rev., 8,* 245.

RAWLES, M. E. (1940): The development of melanophores from embryonic mouse tissues grown in the coelom of chick embryos. *Proc. nat. Acad. Sci., 26,* 673.

RETTERER, E. (1887): Sur le lieu et le mode de formation du pigment cutané chez les mammifères. *C.R. Soc. Biol. (Paris), 39,* 150.

RIEHL, G. (1884): Zur Kenntniss des Pigments im menschlichen Haut. *Vjschr. Derm. Syph., 11,* 33.

ROBIN, C. P. (1873): *Anatomie et Physiologie Cellulaire.* Baillière, Paris.

SIMON, G. (1840): Über die Struktur der Warzen und über Pigmentbildung in der Haut. *Arch. Anat. Physiol. wiss. Med.,* 169.

SKINNER, H. A. (1961): *The Origin of Medical Terms.* Williams and Wilkins Co., Baltimore, Md.

SLACK, D. B. (1844): An essay on the human color. *Boston med. surg. J., 30,* 475, 495, 518.

SORBY, H. C. (1878): On the colouring matters found in the human hair. *J. roy. anthropol. Inst. G.B. Ireland, 8,* 1.

STEINACH, E. (1912): Willkürliche Umwandlung von Säugetiere-Männchen in Tieren mit ausgeprägt weiblichen Geschlechtcharakteren und weiblicher Psyche. *Pflügers Arch. ges. Physiol., 144,* 71.

WALDEYER, W. (1871): Xanthelasma palpebrarum. *Virchow's Arch. path. Anat., 52,* 318.

Chapter VI

Hypotheses and theories of ethnic pigmentation

Research does not merely aim to add to
the sum of our knowledge, but to provide
us with understanding and insight into
dynamic interrelationships.

Iago Gladston (quoted by Hopps, 1961).

Ramon y Cajal referred to hypothesis as 'our most valuable intellectual tool' and Hopps (1961) presented a diagram of the 'wheel of research' as follows:

Observation ⟶ Analysis ⟶ Synthesis
⟶ Testing ⟵

As a concept, 'hypothesis' has changed through the centuries. Medawar (1967, p. 138) defines the modern meaning thus: '. . . a hypothesis is an imaginative pre-conception of *what might be true* in the form of a declaration with verifiable deductive consequences.' Further on he states that 'the formulation of a hypothesis carries with it an obligation to test it as rigorously as we can command skills to do so' (Medawar, 1967, p. 145). In this frame of reference ideas on ethnic pigmentation, at least early in history, were theory rather than hypothesis if theory is defined as 'any hypothesis or opinion not based upon actual knowledge' (*Dorland's Medical Dictionary*, 1965). On the other hand the knowledge available becomes increasingly more meagre the further we go back in history. As more facts support a theory, it might eventually become a hypothesis which can be tested and so lead to other observations which modify the hypothesis and build on it, creating further hypotheses to be tested.

ENVIRONMENTAL HYPOTHESES

Hippocrates (460–377 B.C.) ascribed the physiognomy of people to the climate in which they were born and lived: 'The Scythian race is tawny from the cold, and not from the intense heat of the sun, for the whiteness of the skin is parched by the cold and becomes tawny. The Scythians have ruddy complexions on account of the cold, for the sun does not burn fiercely there. But the cold causes their fair skins to be burnt and reddened.'

'... but such as dwell in places which are low-lying, abounding in meadow and ill-ventilated, and who have a larger proportion of hot than cold winds and who make use of warm waters, ... are rather of a dark than of a light complexion, and are less likely to be phlegmatic than bilious; courage and laborious enterprise are not natural in them, but may be engendered in them by means of their institutions.'

'Those who live on thin, ill-watered, and bare soils ... are likely to be ... rather hard and well-braced, rather of a blond than a dark complexion, and in disposition and passions haughty and self-willed' (Chadwick and Mann, 1950, pp. 19-41).

Aristotle (384-322 B.C.) generalized this concept to include intellect and behaviour as well. Neither could conceive of the possibility that these types were selected by environmental influences to survive in the respective climes.

During the 18th century the concept was further elaborated on by Littré (1702) and several other observers, commenting on the fact that blacks were frequently born very light but darkened on exposure to the light and air. The effect of sunburn and tanning enhanced this view. Galen, as pointed out by Albinus (1747), believed that the added heat of the sun scorched the skin because the natural heat of the body usually escapes through the skin. If it is no longer required to heat the body, because this is done by an external source, it scorches the skin on escaping. The temporary nature of tanning and its unlikeliness, as an acquired change, to affect the offspring was mentioned in the 19th century (Slack, 1844).

The mechanism by which light and its spectral composition affects tanning received serious attenton since Finsen's (1900) work with ultraviolet radiation.

It was also common knowledge, especially to travellers in areas with bright sunlight, that tanning afforded protection against the deleterious effects of sunlight. It was assumed that pigment provided a protective barrier against sunlight, very much as a sunfilter would. On this basis, blacks have been thought to be better adapted to life in the tropics, and this has been attributed to natural selection. This suggestion was very cautiously made by Charles Darwin. Blum (1961) subjected this hypothesis to critical examination, concluding that 'when one attempts such an examination one cannot but be surprised that such far-reaching conclusions, based on such tenuous evidence, should have received so much credence.' He reviews physiological mechanisms and the effects of sunlight in relation to the spectra involved, and points out that sunlight adds to the heat load of the body and exerts specific effects by photochemical radiations in the ultraviolet which have carcinogenic and antirachitic action.

As far as the adaptive value is concerned, he drew up a tentative balance sheet which indicates the biological assets of the black skin as far as sunburn and cancer of the skin are concerned, but a liability as far as solar heat under a high environmental temperature is concerned. It has little effect as far as rickets are concerned. Blum (1961) warns 'that it seems so easy to read adaptive value into almost any aspect of the organism, particularly if our understanding of both

physiology and environment is incomplete.' He concludes that the relationship
of melanin to sunlight seems one of minor weight in the survival of human races.

Even if the distribution of the dark-skinned races is compared to the distribution of sunlight, it does not appear to give strong support to this theory. The
heat load of the humid tropics may, theoretically, favour a white skin, but Ladell
(1964) finds that indigenous tropical men do not show excessive adaptation to
heat; they sweat less than temperate climate men resident in the tropics. It may
be due to economy of energy expenditure, but cultural adaptations are few.

When Blum (1961) illustrates his conclusions on the adaptive role of pigment
by saying that black skin would be highly adaptive to life on one of the snow-
capped mountains near the equator, it rings like Sir Samuel Manuwa's comment
on the evidence regarding adaptation in humid heat: 'Africa is no place for the
Black Man' (Ladell, 1964).

Coon (1966) criticized the 'no races, only climes' school of thought which
tends to take an isolated characteristic (e.g. skin colour or blood groups) and plot
its distribution on the world map 'like isobars on a weather map'. The same factors leading to depigmentation in northern Europe tend to be associated with the
darkest skin pigmentation in Negro Africa.

One should, however, at this stage be aware of a subtle change in premise in
the environmental hypotheses: Hippocrates and his contemporaries thought
climate was an explanation of the races which lived in a particular region. In the
theory of evolution *survival* value is necessarily attached to an adaptive change.
It is obvious that pigmentation *does* adapt the skin to sunlight by immediate pigment darkening and tanning, and, as is abundantly evident from the marked
difference in incidence of skin cancer in blacks and whites in the same solar
region, it does afford effective protection against solar keratoses and skin cancers.
As this is a late effect, rarely incapacitating before middle-age, it obviously has
no survival value. To be effective as a factor favouring survival adaptive pigmentation must be associated with other more potent mechanisms (Blum, 1961).

This subtle change in premise has, however, another unintentional and often
ignored consequence: In the theory of the survival of the fittest different degrees
of fitness are ascribed to a particular environment. Evolutionary theory may thus
lend a pseudoscientific authority to sociological and political practices, similar
to the way in which Biblical authority was misquoted to justify slavery. A consideration of this problem is beyond the scope of this monograph, but it is fully
discussed under the provocative title *Outcasts from Evolution* by Haller (1971).

The protective function of melanin, its mechanism of action, and the effect
on melanogenesis and the melanocyte are of practical clinical significance, and
even though the environmental hypothesis does not satisfactorily explain ethnic
pigmentation, it has greatly advanced our knowledge of the physiology of skin
pigmentation.

HEREDITARY AND GENETIC HYPOTHESES

Hippocrates believed that the reproductive material came from all parts of the individual's body and that characteristics were directly handed down to the progeny. Moulding of the head could just as well be inherited as baldness and blue eyes. Aristotle questioned this view because voice, nails, hair and way of moving could not contribute to the reproductive material, since they were either intangible characteristics or resided in dead tissues. He remarked that children may resemble a grandparent more closely than their parents. He thought that reproductive material consisted of nutrient material diverted from its route to a particular part, to that of the reproductive pathway. Modifications of these views persisted till Weissmann postulated his theory on the continuity of germ plasma in 1883. Mendel's conclusions of 1866 discarded the classical view of heredity, and this was rediscovered independently in 1900 by De Vries, Correns and Von Tschermak (Whitehouse, 1969, pp. 1–5).

Darwin's view of heredity corresponded to that of Hippocrates except that he supposed minute granules of cells of constituent parts to be cast off and transported to the reproductive cells.

In explaining ethnic differences Aristotle, relying on hearsay evidence from the early travellers, described the Ethiopian as a cross between a gorilla and a man. Hippocrates noted that skin colour is intermediate to that of the parents in White × Dark crosses, and thus considered that hereditary factors were important in pigmentation.

The *concept* of heredity is of early origin, but the *mechanism* of gene transfer could not be guessed. The word 'race' embodied the idea of 'a transmissible biological type' from the very beginning (Krogman, 1945). As far as early hypotheses are concerned, it was apparently never doubted that this was a hereditary characteristic, but confusion about the mechanism of transfer gave rise to some interesting ideas.

Blood transmission

One of the early theories was that racial characteristics were transmitted by the blood. Forms of modern speech, still in common use, indicate that this concept was fairly entrenched in the lay mind, e.g. 'it runs in the blood', 'his Irish blood is up'. Up to the early 1940's, several anthropological works find it necessary to explain the fallacy of this concept (e.g. Ashley Montagu, 1942, p. 186; Dobshanzky, 1943).

Morgagni (1769, Letter 68, Art. 13) describes a black boy who died of tuberculosis: 'And if, as you read, at the same time, the accurate observations of this very ingenious man upon that, and upon another black, as far as relates to their blackness also; you should happen to be surprised, that, in the dissection of that apoplectic black, which I formerly sent to you (Letter V, Art. 17), and which I made 50 years ago at Venice, no remark was made in regard to the blackish, or brown parts, in the brain of these men, and none in regard to their black, rather than red blood; I would have you know that I had it not in my power to dissect that body before night: and you know that the light of the sun is one thing, and the light of candles another.'

There are several discussions in the early manuscripts on the colour of the blood, and Le Cat (1765) discusses his personal observation of the similarity in colour of white and black people's blood at great length. This scientific refutation of a simple error in reasoning is nevertheless important because of the popularity of the concept of blood transmission.

This hypothesis probably also accounts for the persistent speculation on the derivation of melanin from bile (Le Cat, 1765), haemoglobin (Delépine, 1891) or other substances in the blood.

Semen

Black semen in the Negro was mentioned by Herodotus and contradicted by Aristotle (Albinus, 1737), but was mentioned again by Paauw (Gould and Pyle, 1896). Strabo also thought semen an important means of transmitting colour (Albinus, 1737).

Prenatal influence

The hypothesis that maternal impressions of a pregnant woman may influence her offspring was popular even in Biblical times (*Genesis, 30*) and is also found in the works of certain Greek, Roman, and early Christian authors. Galen believed in the power of maternal imagination when influenced by pictures, and Soranus of Ephesus spoke of ape-like children born to women who looked at monkeys at the time of conception. The white daughter of the black king and queen of Ethiopia was explained by Heliodorus as being the result of the queen's contemplation of a statue of Andromeda at the time of impregnation. Avicenna stressed the belief that infants resembled in colour the things seen by the parents at the time of conception.

From the 17th century some agreed that maternal impressions could alter the uterine contents but that they could not change the species. Swammerdam in 1672 told of a woman who saw a Negro during her pregnancy and then washed herself in warm water to prevent her child being born black. At birth the baby was white except for the areas between the fingers and toes and the wrinkles of the face, which the mother had carelessly neglected in her washing (Ballantyne, 1904, p. 112).

Le Cat (1765) observed acutely, but his interpretations were limited by the concepts current in his time. He adhered firmly to the theory of prenatal influences on offspring to explain pigmentary anomalies.

This theory probably explains why travellers, scientists and physicians were greatly interested in cases of vitiligo and albinism during the 18th and 19th centuries. The hereditary nature of albinism was suspected since ancient times. Sorsby (1958) based his idea that Noah was an albino on the pseudepigraph *The Book of Enoch the Prophet*. Such interest in albinism increased the knowledge not only of the heredity of the condition, but also of its clinical significance.

The genetic mechanism of ethnic pigmentation still requires elucidation. As in the 18th century, hereditary anomalies of pigmentation still offer the most fruitful field of study for the elucidation of the genetic mechanisms involved in pigmentation of the skin.

ENDOCRINOLOGICAL HYPOTHESES

Sir Arthur Keith, in his presidential address to the section of anthropology of the Royal Society in 1919, maintained that the overwhelming majority of anthropologists was convinced that all varieties of living human races descended from a common ancestral stock, and that some varieties had departed less from the original pattern than others. Natural and sexual selection had given 'the Negro, Chinaman and European their distinctive features of race, skull and body as well as certain characteristics of mind.'

Clinical endocrinology was at that time developing rapidly. Mongolian features could be explained by thyroid deficiency, negroid features by both thyroid and adrenal deficiencies.

Fantham (1932) discussed endocrine function in relation to personality and concluded that particular personality traits result from a fundamental, inherited endocrine constitution which separates mankind into white, yellow and black races.

Animal colour change (e.g. fishes, chameleons) was known to Aristotle, and was most extensively studied during the past century. Nervous control of melanocytes in fish was demonstrated by Pouchet (1876), but Adler (1914) found that hypophysectomised tadpoles were silvery in appearance. This was confirmed by many workers. Huxley and Hogben (1922) showed that injection of pituitary extracts darkened urodele larvae.

The extensive literature on the research of the operative humoral mechanisms in this regard was reviewed by Waring (1963). While *mammals* served as the source of the extracted pituitary hormones they were assayed on *amphibians*. Geschwind et al. (1956) and Lerner and Lee (1956) isolated homogenous active peptides with melanocyte-stimulating properties. Lerner et al. (1959) have described the isolation and chemistry of the pineal hormone (melatonin) which aggregates pigment granules in amphibians.

PIGMENTATION FOR CONCEALMENT: RUDIMENTARY EVOLUTIONARY RESIDUE

Cowles (1959), considering human and animal pigmentation, emphasized the role of pigmentation for reasons of camouflage amongst animals, and successfully extrapolated this theory to Negro skin colour in the tropics. This role becomes tenuous in races other than Negro, in areas other than the tropics. Cowles thus concluded that 'it seems reasonable to presume that pigmentation, like numerous other morphological traits of man, has persisted long after its utility had been reduced by changes in his way of life.' He refers to pigmentation as a 'vestigial remainder of a very remote past'. This hypothesis was reconsidered by Quevedo (1969).

RETARDATION OF DEVELOPMENT HYPOTHESIS

Bolk (1929) proposed a 'hypothesis of retardation as an aetiological factor in the development of the genus *Homo*. Metaphorically, human life progresses like a retarded film.' This hypothesis draws heavily on the concepts of Keith. Bolk (1929) states that the explanation of racial characteristics through natural and sexual selection, according to Lamarck and Darwin, had yielded to 'a general tendency to trace back the origin of new species to the action of internal factors' (i.e. hormones) which he considered as 'a rational interpretation of racial features'. His hypothesis considers that development is retarded progressively so that evolutionary development preserves a more foetal-like condition.

'The principal physiological phenomenon of the process of anthropogenesis was an increase of the average duration of individual existence, each period of life – the foetal, infantile, juvenile, the adult, and the period of senescence – having participated in this extension' (Bolk, 1929).

'The rate of development, as well as the course of all other vital phenomena, appears therefore to be retarded during the process of anthropogenesis. This is the main content of what I call the hypothesis of retardation as an aetiological factor in the development of the genus Homo' (Bolk, 1929). His remarks on skin colour, as one of the many racial characteristics considered, are of some interest, and are based on some observations discussed in the Chapter on 19th Century thought:

'The color of the skin – the feature on which the historically oldest anthropological system was founded' is introduced as follows: 'Although we cannot supply absolute evidence, no expert doubts but that the ancestral form from which man originated possessed a colored skin; we are, however, fully ignorant about its shade and the intensity of the pigmentation' (Bolk, 1929). White skin is a persisting foetal condition, which started from an ancestor with a black skin, in whose offspring hair and iris colour were suppressed more and more. 'The Nordic races are the farthest retarded, while albinism is the pathological final state of this decolorating process.' Darkening with age is the 'last utterance of the process of pigmentation'. He believes that the darkening of the new-born Negro, a process which is much more accelerated than that which happens in whites, supports his concept of retardation.

This hypothesis had little, if any, influence on further development in the study of ethnic pigmentation.

DISEASES AS SELECTIVE FACTORS

The environmental hypotheses discussed above are subject to the dangers incumbent on teleological reasoning: melanin is formed for pigmentation of the skin, and pigmentation is a means of environmental adaptation. This happens in whites subjected to solar radiation and protects them from further sunburn; therefore the black man is very well protected from the sun. In recent years it became clear that the white man's burden in the tropics is not merely solar radiation. The adaptation of the black man to tropical conditions is, however, remarkably effective because he has survived malaria, multiple parasites and exotic tropical disease, despite hazards of intense solar radiation and, more often than not, poor nutrition, for several ages (Stamp, 1962).

VITAMIN D AND ETHNIC PIGMENTATION

Loomis (1967) relates the distribution of races according to latitude to adaptations to solar ultraviolet radiation and vitamin D synthesis. 'Selection against the twin dangers of rickets on the one hand and toxic doses of vitamin D on the other hand would explain the worldwide correlation between skin pigmentation and nearness to the equator.' Valid criticisms of this paper were made by Blois (1968) and by Blum (1968). The criticism of the 'no races, only climes' school as presented by Coon (1966) also applies to this argument in general. The relation of vitamin D and skin colour has intrigued many in so far as its possible role in survival is concerned. A useful survey was made by Bekemeier (1969).

If the question of adaptation to a tropical environment, as sketched above, involves defence against the multiple challenges of disease and climate, the problem may be rephrased as follows: 'Does adaptive change to tropical conditions enhance skin pigmentation.' A verifiable hypothesis, based on the physiological observations which are discussed more fully below, could be proposed (Wassermann, 1965, 1969).

SURVIVAL BY RES HYPERACTIVITY WITH INCIDENTAL SKIN DARKENING

In the tropics, 'man's principal organ of defence', his reticuloendothelial system (RES), is challenged by bacteriological, parasitological and viral agents. The defensive action of the RES is embodied in (1) its phagocytic functions and (2) its humoral action in the production of specific antibodies. The activity of the RES is inversely related to adrenocortical activity. There is both direct and indirect evidence of lesser adrenocortical activity in hyperpigmented races and evidence of increased RES activity. Decreased adrenocortical activity would enhance pigmentation which, incidentally, would also protect against the minor hazard, as far as survival is concerned, of solar radiation.

While this hypothesis would explain the physiological difference visible as ethnic pigmentation, it certainly also involves the homeostasis of the genetic, humoral, and cytological factors involved in melanokinetics, perhaps best expressed as a differently set homeostat in races of different skin colour. As this involves, however, a pigment which acts as a stable free radical, the biological significance (or function) of melanin may partly account for differences in some disease manifestations and the incidence of disease in various ethnic groups (Wassermann, 1970).

The implications are that: (1) The hypothesis is verifiable by experiment and investigation, and changing conditions in many tropical countries as well as more effective international communication should facilitate such studies which were difficult to undertake until fairly recently. (2) In view of an environment naturally hostile to all inhabitants of the earth, all ethnic groups should potentially be able to benefit from a study of the advantages and disadvantages of those adaptive measures selected by millennia of evolutionary change for particular ethnic groups. (3) A skin-bound view of melanin as a decorative, screening or camouflaging device may retard and limit the application of its biophysical properties to a single organ.

FINAL COMMENT

It is evident that each of the foregoing hypotheses is built on the observations and rests on the general scientific foundations of the particular era in which it was postulated. In refuting or testing such hypotheses further facts ermerge; it is as valuable to discover that certain assumptions are not justifiable as it is to discover a new principle. For the sound foundations on which we can build our concepts of ethnic pigmentation we are greatly indebted to the erroneous hypotheses and conceptual errors of the past.

Each of these hypotheses, as could be expected from the factual base from which extrapolation has started in each case, contains elements of truth. In this sense, the hypotheses are not rival hypotheses; each subsequent one amplifies the preceding one in view of the increasing body of knowledge, often gained in the investigation of existing hypotheses.

REFERENCES

ADLER, L. (1914): Metamorphosestudien an Bactrachierlarven. I. Extirpation endokriner Drüsen. A. Extirpation der Hypophyse. *Wilhelm Roux' Arch. Entwickl. Mech. Org.*, *39*, 21.

ALBINUS, B. S. (1737): *Sede et Causa Aethiopum et Caeterorum Hominum.* J. Graal and H. de Leth, Amsterdam.

BALLANTYNE, J. W. (1904): *Antenatal Pathology and Hygiene.* W. Green and Sons, Edinburgh.

BEKEMEIER, H. (1969): Evolution der Hautfarbe und kutane Vitamin D Photosynthese. *Dtsch. med. Wschr.*, *94*, 185.

BLOIS, M. S. (1968): Vitamin D, sunlight and natural selection. *Science, 159,* 652.

BLUM, H. F. (1961): Does the melanin pigment of human skin have adaptive value? *Quart. Rev. Biol., 36,* 50.

BLUM, H. F. (1968): Vitamin D, sunlight and natural selection. *Science, 159,* 652.

BOLK, L. (1929): Origin of racial characteristics in man. *Amer. J. phys. Anthrop., 31,* 1.

CHADWICK, J. and MANN, W. N. (1950): *The Medical Works of Hippocrates.* Blackwell Scientific Publications, Oxford.

COON, C. S. (1966): *The Living Races of Man,* p. 209. Jonathan Cape, London.

COWLES, R. B. (1959): Some ecological factors bearing on the origin and evolution of pigment in the human skin. *Amer. Natural., 93,* 283.

DELÉPINE, S. (1891): On cutaneous pigment (as an antecedent of haemoglobins). *J. Physiol. (Lond.), 12,* 27.

DOBSHANZKY, TH. (1943): Genetics and human affairs. *The Teaching Biologist, 12,* 102.

DORLAND'S MEDICAL DICTIONARY (1965): *24th ed.,* p. 1568. W. B. Saunders Co., Philadelphia–London.

FANTHAM, H. B. (1932): Glands and personality. *S. A. J. Sci., 29,* 589.

FINSEN, N. R. (1900): Neue Untersuchungen über die Einwirkung des Lichtes auf die Haut. *Mitt. Finsens med. Inst., 1,* 8.

FREEMAN, F. R. (1967): Vit. D and skin pigments. *Science, 158,* 579.

GESCHWIND, I. I., LI, C. H. and BARNAFI, L. (1956): Isolation and structure of the melanocyte stimulating hormone from porcine pituitary glands. *J. Amer. chem. Soc., 78,* 4494.

GOULD, G. M. and PYLE, W. L. (1896): *Anomalies and Curiosities of Medicine.* Julian Press, New York, N.Y.

HALLER, J. S. (1971): *Outcasts from Evolution. Scientific Attitudes of Racial Inferiority, 1859–1900.* University of Illinois Press, Urbana, Ill.

HOPPS, H. C. (1961): On the philosophy of research. In: *Concepts of Medicine,* p. 213. Editor: B. Lush. Pergamon Press, London.

HUXLEY, J. S. and HOGBEN, L. T. (1922): Experiments on amphibian metamorphosis and pigment responses in relation to internal secretions. *Proc. roy. Soc. B, 93,* 36.

KEITH, A. (1919): The differentiation of mankind into racial types. *Nature (Lond.), 104,* 301.

KROGMAN, W. M. (1945): The concept of race. In: *The Science of Man in the World Crisis,* pp. 42–49. Editor: R. E. Linton. Columbia University Press, New York, N.Y.

LADELL, W. S. S. (1964): Terrestrial animals in humid heat. In: *Handbook of Physiology, Section 4: Adaptation to the Environment,* p. 625. Editors: D. B. Dill, E. F. Adolph and C. G. Wilber. American Physiological Society, Washington, D.C.

LE CAT, C. N. (1765): *Traité de la Couleur de la Peau Humaine en général, de celle des Nègres en particulier, et de la Métamorphose d'une de ces Couleurs en l'Autre, soit de Naissance, soit accidentellement.* Amsterdam.

LERNER, A. B. and LEE, T. H. (1958): Isolation of melanocyte-stimulating hormone from hog pituitary gland. *J. biol. Chem., 221,* 943.

LERNER, A. B., CASE, J. D. and HEINZELMAN, R. V. (1959): Structure of melatonin. *J. Amer. chem. Soc., 81,* 6084.

LOOMIS, W. F. (1967): Skin-pigment regulation of vitamin D biosynthesis in man. *Science, 157,* 501.

MEDAWAR, P. B. (1967): *The Art of the Soluble.* Methuen and Co., London.

MONTAGU, M. ASHLEY (1942): *Man's most Dangerous Myth: The Fallacy of Race.* Columbia University Press, New York, N.Y.

MORGAGNI, J. B. (1769): *The Seats and Causes of Diseases investigated by Anatomy, Vol. III,* p. 580 (Book V, Letter 68, Article 13) (Translated from the Latin by Benjamin Alexander, London). Hafner, New York, N.Y.

POUCHET, G. (1876): Des changements de coloration sous l'influence des nerfs. *J. Anat. (Paris), 12,* 1.

QUEVEDO, W. C. (1969): Pigmentary patterning (Panel discussion on the functions of melanin by M. S. Blois, T. B. Fitzpatrick, F. Daniels Jr. and W. C. Quevedo). In: *The Biologic Effects of Ultraviolet Radiation*, p. 325. Editor: F. Urbach. Pergamon Press, Oxford.

SLACK, D. B. (1844): An essay on the human color. *Boston med. surg. J.*, *30*, 475, 495, 518.

SORSBY, A. (1958): Noah – an albino. *Brit. med. J.*, *2*, 1587.

STAMP, L. D. (1962): Climatic limitations to development in the tropics. *Proc. nutr. Soc.*, *21*, 84.

WARING, H. (1963): *Color Change Mechanisms of Cold-Blooded Vertebrates*. Academic Press, New York, N.Y.

WASSERMANN, H. P. (1965): Human pigmentation and environmental adaptation. *Arch. environm. Hlth.*, *11*, 691.

WASSERMANN, H. P. (1969): Melanin pigmentation and the environment. In: *Essays on Tropical Dermatology*, Vol. *I*, pp. 50–59. Editors: R. D. G. Ph. Simons and J. Marshall. Excerpta Medica, Amsterdam.

WASSERMANN, H. P. (1970): Melanokinetics and the biological significance of melanin. *Brit. J. Derm.*, *82*, 530.

WHITEHOUSE, H. L. K. (1969): *Towards an Understanding of the Mechanism of Heredity*. Edward Arnold, London.

Section II

Descriptive statistics of ethnic pigmentation

We see, not what we look at but what we look for.

W. B. Bean (1958):
Vascular Spiders and Related Lesions of the Skin, p. 322. Blackwell Scientific Publications, Oxford.

Chapter VII

Skin colour

Variation in human skin colour is remarkable in that the variation between different populations is often very great by comparison with that within populations.

Harrison and Owen (1964).

Finally it may be said that although indigenous tropical man may be the right shape for his environment, even a teleologist must confess himself baffled when it comes to color.

Ladell (1964).

In describing ethnic pigmentation one is concerned with the average pigmentation of a particular ethnic group. It is usually assumed that ethnic pigmentation refers to skin colour only, but this is not the case. The black man (Negro, Bantu, Australian aborigine) nearly always exhibits dark-brown to black irides, black hair and fundal pigmentation. Certain pigment anomalies (e.g. albinism, moles, mongolian or sacral spots) have a marked predilection for particular ethnic groups.

Quite apart from the population as a whole, individuals have areas that are both lighter and darker than the colour of the larger part of their body. These lighter and darker areas are more obvious in individuals of an intermediate colour than in the very blond or very dark individual. In the face, the lower eyelid, the upper lip and the centre of the cheek are darker while the upper eyelid, the supraorbital ridge, the malar prominence, the tip of the nose and the point of the chin, as well as the undersurface of the chin, are paler than the rest of the skin. The areas immediately in front of and behind the ears are also paler than average (Niedelman, 1945). In all ethnic groups genital skin, nipples, back of the neck and lower belly are darker than average, while the palms and soles, the back of the heel region, the clavicular region and the sternal region are paler than the average pigmentation of the individual. The posterior midline is also lighter than the rest of the body pigmentation.

METHODS OF DESCRIPTION

There are three methods of description and all three have a specific place in the study of ethnic pigmentation. The oldest and fairly accurate method is verbal description. Until the early fifties of this century matching of the skin, hair or eye colour with arbitrary standards was very popular. The most objective and repeatable quantitative method, however, is reflectance spectrophotometry.

Verbal description is required for gross description and, more specifically, for details such as freckles, moles, birthmarks and mongolian spots. It is the only commonly used method for eye colour, and is often employed in the description of hair and oral pigmentation. Pigmentation of skin appendages (e.g. nails) and special skin regions (sole of the foot) are usually described by this method.

Verbal description of ethnic skin colours can be accurate. Indeed, some colour names have been derived from an original pigment name and in such cases the words for corresponding pigments and colours are often identical. A colour name must be so characteristic of the colour's appearance that it is readily understood by others. In *Methuen's Handbook of Colour* the following descriptive names appear: *Flesh,* derived from 'the colour of the flesh of the Caucasian race', is defined as 'an average flesh colour which differs from the special colour names applied to the complexion such as pale, pale, yellow, sunburn, sunbrown or tan.' *Negro,* 'the colour of the skin of a person of the Negroid race, covers a fairly wide range of colours. Related to Somalis and flesh.' Thus also definitions for *Eye Blue, Eye Brown,* and *Eye Grey* are found as 'the colour of the iris'. 'Blonde' has the same colour appearance as 'bamboo' and 'flax', but is specifically used to describe hair colour. Other hair colours are: flaxen, platinum blonde, dark blonde, golden brown and hairbrown. Grey variations of hair are: ash blonde, golden grey, ash grey. Golden or reddish variations are: golden blonde, reddish blonde, red-haired, golden, golden yellow, reddish golden, titian (red), and henna (Kornerup and Wanscher, 1963).

Expansion of the colour scale (Wright, 1964, p. 235) occurs when verbal description of skin colour is used to designate populations and leads to the less accurate terms white, yellow, black, brown and red. The generalized descriptions (e.g. flesh) apply to the 'usual' appearance of Caucasoid people, but for accurate description the smaller intragroup pigmentations must be accounted for, even though, between populations, colour scale expansion does not affect description in such a way that a white, a brown or a black man are confused.

Colour matching is the usual method used for describing hair colour, e.g. Fischer-Saller Hair Colour Scale (Sunderland, 1965), but it is often employed for eye colour as well (Martin's Eye Colour Chart). Von Luschan's skin colour tablets have apparently not been used since abridged reflectance photometry came into general use.

Visual matching with colour standards allows comparison of findings but the results are not consistently reproduced in repeat experiments. Gates (1949) found that those coloured papers for describing skin colour, suitable for African people, were not suitable for use with Australian aborigines (Gates, 1960, 1961). Von Luschan's colour tablets were more widely used, and spinning tops to which colours could be added (the percentage of black usually being the recorded figure) enjoyed a brief popularity. I suspect that the difficulty experienced by Gates (1961) is partly due to the fact that, as in the case of Von Luschan's tablets, different *hues* were used in the tablets (Figs. 7 and 8). We measured the Von Luschan tablet colours with X, Y and Z filters and found the dominant wavelength to vary through the greater part of the visible spectrum (unpublished). The actual situation for skin in vivo, however, is that the dominant wavelength of all colours of human skin is limited to the orange-to-red part of the spectrum, and differences in saturation and tone determine the shading of the hue (Wassermann, 1971).

Fig. 7. *Von Luschan's Skin Colour Tablet*
  The range of colours towards the white end of ethnic pigmentation.

Reflectance spectrophotometry is the method of choice for the objective study of skin pigmentation and colour definition and is widely employed in population studies (Edwards and Duntley, 1939; Weiner, 1951). It is an objective and repeatable method for both colour definition in terms of hue, saturation and tone (Buckley and Grum, 1964; Wassermann, 1971) and for spectral reflectance curves (Garrard et al., 1967).

Portable reflectance spectrophotometers came into use with the study of Weiner (1951). These instruments, of which two types (the Evans Electro-selenium Company (EEL) instrument and the Photovolt Corporation's instrument) are available, give an abridged curve as plotted from readings at a few selected wavelengths. Garrard et al. (1967) studied the comparability of the two instruments and calculated various conversion equations for the two instruments.

Both operate on the same principle: Light, from a standard source (electric bulb) passes through interchangeable filters with known transmission curves, to strike the surface of the skin at a fixed angle. It is partly absorbed, and partly reflected to activate a photoelectric cell in the pickup head. The output of the photoelectric cell is recorded on a galvanometer. The percentage of light reflected from the skin at a given wavelength is compared to the amount which is reflected from a pure white standard. The standard is a magnesium carbonate block in the case of the EEL instrument, and a standardized white tile in the case of the Photovolt instrument. The reflectance from the standard at a given wavelength is adjusted to read 100% on the galvanometer. The more light reflected at a given wavelength from the skin, the closer the skin's reflectance approaches 100%.

Fig. 8. *Von Luschan's Skin Colour Tablet*
Reverse side, with the darker skin colours.

The advantages of reflectance spectrophotometry are: The incident light used and the distance between light source and object are invariable. Subjective factors inherent in the visual methods are excluded, and the continuous nature of readings from skin surfaces are numerical values which may be subjected to statistical evaluation.

The method has found some use in hair pigmentation studies when sufficient hair was available (Reed, 1952; Sunderland, 1956; Barnicot, 1956) and was modified for limited studies on oral pigmentation (Volker and Kenney, 1960; Bolden, 1960).

The EEL type instrument was more widely used in anthropological studies (Weiner, 1951; Harrison and Owen, 1956, 1964; Barnicot, 1958; Tobias, 1963; Das and Mukherjee, 1963; Walsh, 1963; Harmse, 1964; Weiner et al., 1963, 1964; Huizinga, 1965; Ojikutu, 1965; Harrison and Salzano, 1966; Harrison

et al., 1967; Sunderland, 1967; Wassermann and Heyl, 1968) while the Photovolt instrument was used especially by American workers (Lasker, 1954; Garn
et al., 1956*a,b;* Lee and Lasker, 1959; Ungria, 1965; Collins et al., 1966; Mazess,
1967).

A useful review of the methods of measurement of skin colour in vivo was
made by Gibson (1971).

THE USE OF THE REFLECTANCE SPECTROPHOTOMETER

Authors frequently use 'skin colour measurement' indiscriminately and synono-
mously with 'skin reflectance measurement'. Both these separate measurements
can be performed with the help of these instruments (Buckley and Grum, 1964;
Wassermann, 1971).

The sites of measurement may be varied according to the type of research to
be done. Garn et al. (1956) suggested that measurement of the least exposed,
most exposed and areolar skin gives information on basic pigmentation, ability
to tan and endocrine status respectively. Tobias (1963) estimated the effect of
environmental influence by expressing the percentage relationship of upper
arm and forehead skin reflectance as an index of the individual's *tanning ability.*
A *mean exposure index* could be derived from the summed reflectance at all 9
wavelengths from the forehead.

For comparative studies in different population groups the preferable site for
recording is the medial aspect of the upper arm, because it is least affected by
environmental factors, has a poor tanning ability and the medial epicondyle
serves as a bony landmark for an exact placing of the rim of the spectrophotometer head. Ojikutu (1965) found that of the eight body areas studied, this area
showed the least variation.

THE DATA OBTAINED BY REFLECTANCE SPECTROPHOTOMETRY

Studies by Harrison and Owen (1956) showed that the reciprocal of the reflectance value at any one wavelength had a linear relationship with the melanin
concentration. This relationship of melanin to the reflectance value is least
affected by the blood supply to the skin in the red part of the spectrum (Harmse,
1964). Reflectance readings at 685 nm would thus give a fairly accurate estimation of the melanin content of the skin.

From his reflectance studies Findlay (1966) concludes that 'epidermal reflection is a function of the amount of melanin present' and that 'epidermal
transmission depends both on the amount and state of oxidation of melanin.
None of these factors can at present be assessed from reflection curves of intact
skin however complete, and there seems to be no purpose in refining the methods
without additional information which would be needed to make them meaningful.'

Anthropological studies, concerned with gene effects on pigmentation, tended
to read more into the reflection curve than melanin concentration only. Harrison

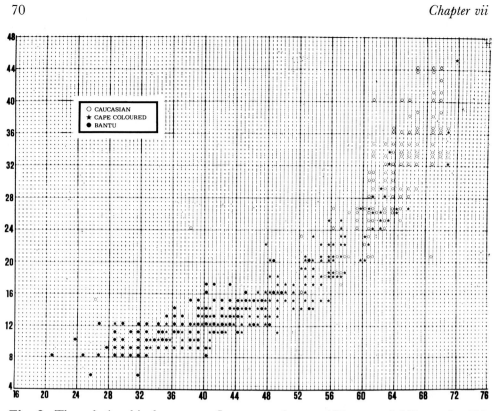

Fig. 9. The relationship between reflectance values at 425 nm and 685 nm for 681
individuals from 3 racial groups (white, brown and black). (From Wassermann, 1971, *Dermatologica (Basel)*, *143*, 166. Courtesy of the Editors.)

and Owen (1964) suggested that environmental interaction with genes is least
at 545 nm, and that better scaling for genetic effects could be obtained by a
log-transformation of values at 425 nm and an antilog-transformation of values
at 685 nm.

Regardless of the wavelengths employed, epidermal melanin concentration is
measured by reflectance spectrophotometry in different ethnic groups. The
mathematical relationship, however, varies at different wavelengths. If the
reflectances obtained from 425 nm and 685 nm are plotted for each individual
from three populations (white, brown and black), a smooth continuous curve
indicates the increasing amount of melanin in the skin (Fig. 9), and this curve
indicates that melanin absorbs more heavily at the blue end of the spectrum
than at the red.

PIGMENTATION OF THE SKIN

Edwards and Duntley (1939) used a Hardy recording reflectance spectrophotometer to study the reflectance, in the visible spectrum, from the skin. From the

reflectance curves they concluded that arterial and venous blood, carotenoids, melanin and 'melanoid' pigments contribute to the colour of the skin. The major variable is melanin.

The colour of the skin

Colour perception is a psychophysiological process. Physical measurements concern the energy at a particular wavelength. To make measurement of spectral reflectances meaningful an attempt should be made to bring spectral reflection in relation to the psychophysiological mechanisms of colour perception.

Psychophysiological considerations in relation to colour perception

HUE

The sensation of whiteness is associated with a reflection of light, in which energy from all regions of the visible spectrum are equally represented, no single region being in excess over any other region. With loss of this equality of distribution of energy from the various spectral regions, due to absorption of a part of the total spectrum, the reflected light appears coloured. Should the fraction absorbed be large, the object appears black. A pigment selectively reduces the energy in certain parts of the spectrum relative to the rest. Red surfaces would reflect highly at the red end of the spectrum. The boundaries between the colour sensation produced and the different wavelengths are ill-defined and gradually merge with the next. From an examination of all reported reflectance curves it is obvious that the hue of the human skin is red, as the highest reflection in all cases occurs at the red end of the spectrum.

SATURATION

In a red object the dominant reflection is from the red end of the spectrum. Should the energy from all other parts of the spectrum increase, the red colour will become diluted with white, i.e. desaturated. Conversely, from a nearly black hue, saturation would increase as total absorbance decreased. The highest saturation of any hue would thus be obtained about midway between total reflectance and total absorbance. Saturation therefore refers to the extent to which one wavelength predominates over all others (Wright, 1964).

LUMINOSITY

If the surface of a diffusely reflecting body is kept white but illumination is progressively reduced the surface would still remain white. If, however, the surface is blackened so as to become a less effective reflector, the surface will appear dark grey. The lightness or darkness of a given surface is closely correlated with the fraction of the incident light reflected by the surface, but not with the absolute amount of light in the reflected beam (Wright, 1964).

Buckley and Grum (1964) showed that the only pigment the epidermis contained was melanin. Measurements in vitiliginous areas and normal areas in the same patient (Cape Coloured, Fig. 10) suggest that there is no *a priori* reason to assume that other factors apart from melanin concentration affect racial skin colour. Harrison and Owen (1964) found that the reciprocal of the reflectance value at 655 nm and 685 nm showed a nearly linear relationship to melanin concentration over a wide range, and this was supported by the findings of Harmse (1964) on bloodless living human skin. This would be expected because melanin, not having a particularly strong absorption in red, would by its concentration diminish the high energy of reflected light.

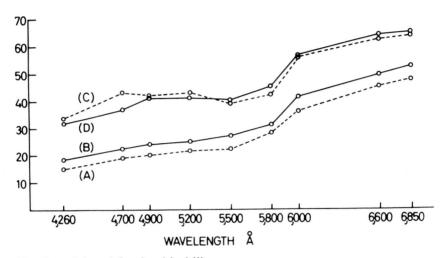

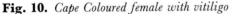

WAVELENGTH Å

Fig. 10. *Cape Coloured female with vitiligo*
Reflectance values from vitiligo and normal skin on the same patient (Cape Coloured) as compared to the curve of mean values for 100 normal white and 100 normal Cape Coloured individuals. Normal skin (A) compared with mean curve of 107 normal CC females (B). Vitiliginous skin area (C) compared with mean curve of 109 white females (D). (From Wassermann, 1971, *Dermatologica (Basel)*, *143*, 166. Courtesy of the Editors.)

With an increase in the melanin content of the skin a depression of the curve occurs but it is more marked in the blue end of the spectrum, than in the red. The absorption band of haemoglobin, marked in the region of 545 nm in light coloured skin, disappears with increasing melanin concentration.

It is thus obvious that what is seen is the red hue of haemoglobin as viewed through a filter containing melanin, whose spectral absorption is strong in the blue region and weak in the red region.

From the above considerations, suggesting a red hue due to haemoglobin for all races, one would expect the colour differences among races to be caused solely by melanin. The explanation of differences in saturation and lightness should then be due to the interposition of a melanized filter between the eye and the red skin colour. This filter theory would agree with the concept of an 'epidermal melanin unit' as the functional unit of pigmentation (Fitzpatrick and Breathnach, 1963), for the *amount* of melanin dispersed in epidermal cells, and not the density of melanocytes, determines skin colour (Wassermann, 1971).

In terms of colour specification the *hue* of white, black and brown skin was orange to red, no difference being found between races (Wassermann, 1971), although in vitro white skin had a slightly more orange tint than brown skin (American Negro) (Buckley and Grum, 1964). The colour *saturation* was higher in American Negro skin (Buckley and Grum, 1964) and in Cape Coloured skin (Wassermann, 1971). Both are conventionally described as brown rather than black. In the case of the Bantu, saturation again decreased (Wassermann, 1971). *Luminance* decreased from 'white' through 'brown' to 'black' skin.

It may thus be said that the colour of human skin in all races is orange to red, but differs in saturation and tone from 'flesh colour' (6B3) through various tones of pale yellow (2A3), sunbrown (6D5) and tan (6D6) to Negro (6F3). The designations in brackets refer to the colour plates in *Methuen's Handbook of Colour* (Kornerup and Wanscher, 1963) (Plate 6 is of an orange hue, the letter and figures following indicating various tonal shadings and saturation of the orange hue).

FACTORS INFLUENCING INDIVIDUAL SKIN COLOUR IN ALL ETHNIC GROUPS

Regional differences

The description of darker and paler areas on an individual was studied more objectively with reflectance measurements. In black people the abdomen was darkest and the lumbar region lightest, as in white people, though in the latter case the means showed smaller differences. The darkest area in whites was over the upper thigh, and the lightest over the lumbar region. In Syrian/Iranian people the sternum and upper thigh were darkest (Ojikutu, 1965) (Fig. 11). A similar study of Pacific and Asian groups, measuring other areas, found the forehead to be the darkest and the axilla the lightest area, except in the Australian aborigine where the axillae were as dark as the forehead (Walsh, 1963) (Fig. 12). In both sexes the areola was the most pigmented, and in males this was similar to the pigmentation of the scrotum (Garn et al., 1956a).

Age

Throughout life there is a gradual increase in reflectance of the unexposed skin (it becomes lighter) while the exposed skin gradually darkens through life. The areola becomes gradually lighter, and Garn et al. (1956a, 1963) consider that this is due to a decrease in hormonal activity with age. This holds true for all races but is more easily seen in whites.

At birth new-born Bantu babies are but slightly darker than new-born white babies.

There are a few objective studies on the normal darkening of the skin with increasing age. Thus the new-born New Guinean infant has relatively little melanin except in the sacral and scrotal skin. The forehead has more melanin than the forearm and chest wall and this difference is maintained throughout life. After birth the skin rapidly acquires pigment, so that at the age of 6 months the forehead, forearm and axilla are already as dark as in the young adult (Walsh, 1964).

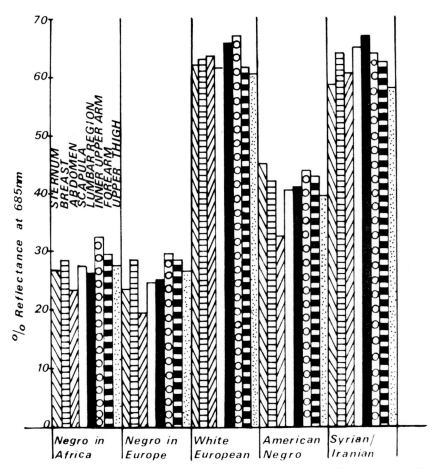

Fig. 11. % Reflectance values at 685 nm from 8 body areas of the same individual in 5 ethnic groups. (From data by Ojikutu, 1965, *Homo, 16,* 77.)

In Tibetans forehead pigmentation is darker in males than in females throughout life, although the difference becomes statistically significant only during middle and late adolescence. The unexposed medial upper arm reflectance showed that girls were darker than boys during early adolescence (boys 13–14

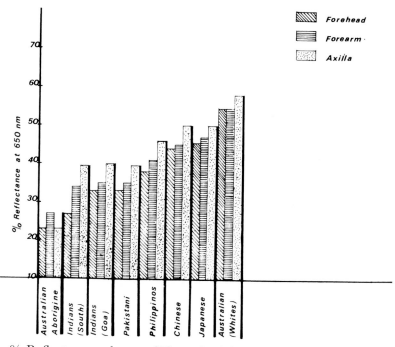

Fig. 12. % Reflectance values at 650 nm in Asian and Pacific people from 3 body
areas in 8 ethnic groups. (From data by Walsh, 1963, *Journal of the Royal
Anthropological Institute*, *93*, 126.)

years, girls 10–12 years), but during middle adolescence (boys 14–16 years, girls
12–14 years) pigmentation was similar, and in late adolescence females (14–16
years) emerged significantly lighter than males (16–18 years) (Kalla and Tiwari,
1970).

Sex and exposure to the sun

The adult female is the lighter sex. This was confirmed for South African whites,
Cape Coloureds and Bantu (Wassermann and Heyl, 1968), for Mexican Para-
choans (Lasker, 1954*a*), Negroes of the Yoruba tribe (Barnicot, 1958) and Indians
of Brazil (Harrison and Salzano, 1966; Garn et al., 1956*a*; Walsh, 1963). Some
lightening occurs with maturity probably due to lesser exposure to the sun. The
increase in difference with aging between forearm and upper arm reflections,
especially in males, indicates that exposure to sunlight is an important factor
in this difference.

In the Bantu, school children were lighter than pre-school children who spent
a greater deal of time outdoors and wore less clothing (Weiner et al., 1964).
Similar findings were also reported for Australian aborigines (Abie, 1961). In
the Tibetan study it appeared that hormonal changes throughout adolescence
clearly also contributed to the sex difference (Kalla and Tiwari, 1970) becoming
established with attainment of adulthood.

Seasonal variation in skin colour is very obvious in whites, but less easily noticed in brown or black people. With the exception of Lasker's (1954*b*) study on young American white adults, seasonal variation in pigmentation was apparently not objectively studied.

Hormonal factors

It is known that several hormones influence pigmentation (p. 173) under clinical conditions, but in healthy people the observable effect is most obvious during pregnancy (Garn et al., 1956*b*). The greatest change in skin colour occurs in the areola which shows the earliest and most marked decrease in reflectance from a mean of 15% in both sexes, to individuals with values of less than 3.5% during pregnancy.

The areola of the breast in men darkens in puberty, as in the case of females, but in females the effect of pregnancy is added to this. There appears to be a cumulative effect of repeated pregnancies on areolar pigmentation. The increased pigmentation of the areola observed after the age of 60 years is darker the greater the number of pregnancies experienced (Garn and French, 1963).

The chloasma of pregnancy is well known and is more readily observed in people with a lighter complexion, although the *change* in pigmentation is more pronounced in those with a darker complexion.

Apart from its physiological occurrence during pregnancy, chloasma is at present frequently seen in women taking oral contraceptive drugs. The incidence increases from 4% during the first year of use to 37% after 5 years of use. The cosmetic effect is the only reason in most instances for consulting the physician (Carruthers, 1966) (see further on p. 176).

Skin pigmentation in relation to the menstrual cycle is a common occurrence. From a questionnaire which I circulated amongst student nurses, some change in pigmentation was reported by about 75% of those replying to the questionnaire, mostly a periocular darkening. Especially those with premenstrual discomfort in the breasts were aware of darkening of the areola (unpublished study). Snell and Turner (1966) reported similar findings from a questionnaire, but little change was recorded by reflectance spectrophotometry. This is perhaps a result of the regional preference of pigment change. The premenstrual darkening is more marked in darker individuals.

POPULATION STUDIES

The form of the reflection curve differs very little between population groups. Maximum reflectance occurs at 685 nm, the absorption band for haemoglobin between 500 and 600 nm causes a trough in the curve but is less marked where melanin concentration is high, and the minimal reflectance occurs at 425 nm (Fig. 13). The differences in white, brown and black skinned groups were only in the levels of percentage reflectance attained, with the qualification that increasing melanin content depressed reflection more towards the blue part of the spectrum than at the red part.

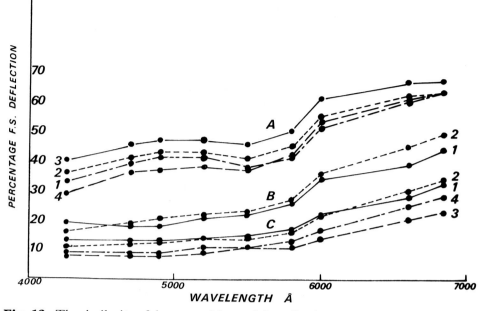

Fig. 13. The similarity of the general form of the reflection curve in white (A), brown (B) and black (C) races.

A₁,₂ = 50 English individuals (each curve).
A₃ = 74 German students and American soldiers in Germany.
A₄ = 108 white South Africans.
B₁ = 12 American Negro soldiers.
B₂ = 103 Cape Coloureds, South Africa.
C₁,₃,₄ = Negroes: 108 at Lagos, 100 Yoruba and 52 Ibo, respectively.
C₂ = Bantu: 104 Xhosas, South Africa.

References: A₁, C₃, C₄ = Barnicot (1958).
A₂ = Harrison and Owen (1964).
A₃, B₁, C₁ = Ojikutu (1965).
A₄, B₂, C₂ = Wassermann and Heyl (1968).

The American Negro corresponds in colour and reflectance values to the Cape Coloured ethnic group of South Africa and is intermediate between whites and African Negro and/or Bantu. Both Bantu and Negro have similar reflectance curves. Plotting the reflectance values at 685 nm gives a general idea of the melanin content of the skin in the different races. In the study by Wassermann and Heyl (1968) the melanin content, estimated in this way, was plotted for whites, Cape Coloureds and Bantu. A fairly narrow distribution curve was obtained in whites. The Cape Coloured curve showed two peaks and was very broad, extending from that of the lightest coloured white to well below the average Bantu colour (Fig. 14).

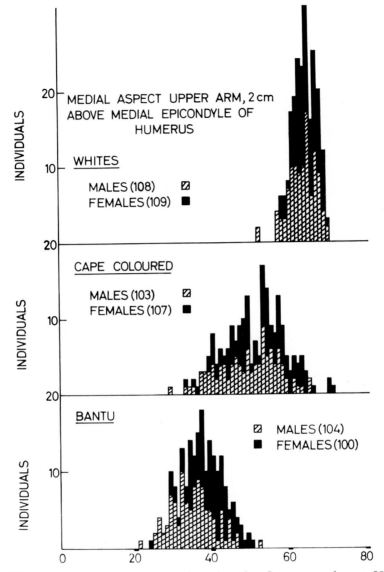

Fig. 14. Skin melanin content expressed as the % reflectance value at 685 nm for 3 racial groups (Bellville, South Africa). Note the double peak in the histogram for Cape Coloureds. A similar double peaked curve would be expected in the American Negro. (From Wassermann and Heyl, 1968, *South African Medical Journal*, *42*, 98. Courtesy of the Editors.)

INHERITANCE OF SKIN COLOUR IN MAN

Very little is known about skin colour inheritance in man although several studies have been undertaken.

Stern (1953) estimated the Caucasian alleles in the American Negro at 30%, but Reed (1969) more recently estimated them at 20%. Revising his earlier studies, Stern (1970) found that the best agreement with observations is obtained from 3 and 4 gene pair models. He emphasizes the uncertainties of the treatment of data and refers to the studies of Harrison and Owen (1964) on first and backcross generations in hybrid families which also indicate that the number of effective factors, i.e. recombining units involved in pigmentation, is 3 or 4.

Mating in humans is not completely at random but is strongly guided by social factors. Anthropological evidence is against the hypothesis that attractiveness of biological characteristics influences mate selection, but Hulse (1967) refers to studies indicating that this might, in fact, be true (see also Section IV, p. 198). Among Japanese he found that in both sexes and in all areas the mean reflectance values of upper social class groups were higher (lighter skin colour) than those of middle and lower class groups, the difference being most pronounced in males. He concluded that social selection for light skin colour has had some genetic effect.

Reflectance spectrophotometry was used to determine the differences in pigment in monozygous and dizygous twin groups, and a close correlation between similarity of skin colour and degree of genetic identity was found (Collins, et al., 1966).

SUMMARY

Normal skin colour in man is dependent on haemoglobin in both oxygenated and reduced state, carotenoids and melanin. Racial and ethnic variations in skin colour depend solely on differences in epidermal melanin content, the only pigment present in the epidermis. The colour is an orange to red hue, maximally saturated in brown races, while the lightness or darkness of an individual depends on the fraction of incident light reflected, i.e. the tone of the orange-red hue.

The distribution of melanin varies in different regions of the body and although often verbally described, it can be measured objectively. It is influenced by hormones, especially after puberty and in pregnancy, and by exposure to the sun. This applies to all races and ethnic groups.

Little is known about the inheritance of skin colour in man. Racial variation in skin colour is one facet of the complex of genetic variation. Social factors and the attractiveness of biological characteristics do seem to influence mate selection and further complicated studies on genetic influences.

REFERENCES

ABIE, A. A. (1961): Recent fieldwork on the physical anthropology of Australian aborigines. *Aust. J. Sci.*, *23*, 210.

BARNICOT, N. A. (1956): The relation of the pigment trichosiderin to hair colour. *Ann. hum. Genet.*, *21*, 31.

BARNICOT, N. A. (1958): Reflectometry of the skin in Southern Nigerians and in some Mulattoes. *Hum. Biol.*, *30*, 150.

BOLDEN, T. E. (1960): Histology of oral pigmentation. *J. Periodont.*, *31*, 361.

Buckley, W. R. and Grum, F. (1964): Reflection spectrophotometry. *Arch. Derm.*, *89*, 110.

Carruthers, R. (1966): Chloasma and oral contraceptives. *Med. J. Aust.*, 2, 17.

Collins, R. N., Lerner, A. B. and McGuire, J. S. (1966): The relationship of skin colour to zygosity in twins. *J. invest. Derm.*, *47*, 78.

Das, S. R. and Mukherjee, D. P. (1963): A spectrophotometric skin colour survey among four Indian castes and tribes. *Z. Morph. Anthrop.*, *54*, 190.

Edwards, E. A. and Duntley, S. Q. (1939): Pigments and colour of living human skin. *Amer. J. Anat.*, *65*, 1.

Findlay, G. H. (1966): The measurement of epidermal melanin by reflectance. *Brit. J. Derm.*, *78*, 528.

Fitzpatrick, T. B. and Breathnach, A. S. (1963): Das epidermale Melanin-Einheit-System. *Derm. Wschr.*, *147*, 481.

Garn, S. M. and French, N. Y. (1963): Postpartum and age changes in areolar pigmentation. *Amer. J. Obstet. Gynec.*, *85*, 873.

Garn, S. M., Selby, S. and Crawford, M. R. (1956a): Skin reflectance studies in children and adults. *Amer. J. phys. Anthrop. New Ser.*, *14*, 101.

Garn, S. M., Selby, S. and Crawford, M. R. (1956b): Skin reflectance during pregnancy. *Amer. J. Obstet. Gynec.*, *72*, 974.

Garrard, G., Harrison, G. A. and Owen, J. J. T. (1967): Comparative spectrophotometry of skin colour with E.E.L. and Photovolt instruments. *Amer. J. phys. Anthrop.*, *27*, 389.

Gates, R. R. (1949): *Pedigrees of Negro Families*. The Blakiston Co., Toronto.

Gates, R. R. (1960): The genetics of Australian aborigines. *Acta genet. med. (Roma)*, *9*, 7.

Gates, R. R. (1961): The histology of skin pigmentation. *J. roy. micr. Soc.*, *80*, 121.

Gibson, I. M. (1971): Measurement of skin colour in vivo. *J. Soc. cosmet. Chem.*, *22*, 725.

Harmse, N. S. (1964): Reflectometry of the bloodless living human skin. *Proc. Kon. ned. Akad. Wet.*, Ser. C, *67*, 138.

Harrison, G. A. and Owen, J. J. T. (1956): The application of spectrophotometry to the study of skin colour inheritance. *Acta genet. (Basel)*, *6*, 481.

Harrison, G. A. and Owen, J. J. T. (1964): Studies on the inheritance of human skin colour. *Ann. hum. Genet.*, *28*, 27.

Harrison, G. A., Owen, J. J. T., da Rocha, F. J. and Salzano, F. M. (1967): Skin colour in Southern Brazilian populations. *Hum. Biol.*, *39*, 21.

Harrison, G. A. and Salzano, F. M. (1966): The skin colour of the Caingang and Guarani Indians of Brazil. *Hum. Biol.*, *38*, 104.

Huizinga, J. (1965): Reflectometry of the skin in Dogons. *Proc. kon. ned. Akad. Wet.*, Ser. C, *68*, 289.

Hulse, F. S. (1967): Selection for skin colour among the Japanese. *Amer. J. phys. Anthrop.*, *27*, 143.

Kalla, A. K. and Tiwari, S. C. (1970): Sex differences in skin colour in man. *Acta Genet. med. (Roma)*, *19*, 472.

Kornerup, A. and Wanscher, J. H. (1963): *Methuen's Handbook of Colour*. Methuen, London.

Ladell, W. S. S. (1964): Terrestrial animals in humid heat. Man. In: *Adaptation to the Environment. Handbook of Physiology*, pp. 625–659. Editors: D. B. Dill, E. F. Adolph and C. G. Wilber. American Physiological Society, Washington, D. C.

Lasker, G. W. (1954a): Photoelectric measurement of skin colour in a Mexican Mestizo population. *Amer. J. phys. Anthrop. New Ser.*, *12*, 115.

Lasker, G. W. (1954b): Seasonal changes in skin colour. *Amer. J. phys. Anthrop.*, *12*, 553.

Lee, M. M. C. and Lasker, G. W. (1959): The sun-tanning potential of human skin. *Hum. Biol.*, *31*, 252.

Mazess, R. B. (1967): Skin colour in Bahamian Negroes. *Hum. Biol.*, *39*, 145.

Niedelman, M. L. (1945): Abnormalities of pigmentation in the Negro. *Arch. Derm. Syph. (Chic.)*, *51*, 1.

Ojikutu, R. O. (1965): Die Rolle von Hautpigment und Schweissdrüsen in der Klima Anpassung des Menschen. *Homo*, *16*, 77.

Reed, T. E. (1952): Red hair colour as a genetical character. *Ann. Eugen. (Lond.)*, *17*, 115.

Reed, T. E. (1969): Caucasian genes in American Negroes. *Science*, *165*, 762.

Snell, R. S. and Turner, R. (1966): Skin pigmentation in relation to the menstrual cycle. *J. invest. Derm.*, *47*, 147.

Stern, C. (1953): Model estimates of the frequency of white and nearwhite segregants in the American Negro. *Acta genet. (Basel)*, *4*, 281.

Stern, C. (1970): Model estimates of the number of gene pairs involved in pigmentation variability of the Negro-American. *Hum. Hered.*, *20*, 165.

Sunderland, E. (1956): Hair-colour variation in the United Kingdom. *Ann. hum. Genet.*, *20*, 312.

Sunderland, E. (1965): Hair colour of the population of Tristan da Cunha. *Nature (Lond.)*, *208*, 412.

Sunderland, E. (1967): The skin colour of the people of Azrac, eastern Jordan. *Hum. Biol.*, *39*, 64.

Tobias, P. V. (1963): Studies on skin reflectance in Bushmen-European hybrids. In: *Proceedings, II International Congress on Human Genetics, Rome, 1961*, p. 461. Istituto G. Mendel, Rome.

Ungria de Diaz, A. G. (1965): La pigmentación de la piel en los indigenas Guahibos. In: *Homenaje a Juan Comas en su 65 Aniversario, Vol. II*, p. 63. Libros de Mexico.

Volker, J. F. and Kenney, J. A. (1960): The physiology and biochemistry of pigmentation. *J. Periodont.*, *31*, 346.

Walsh, R. J. (1963): Variations of melanin pigmentation of the skin in some Asian and Pacific people. *J. roy. anthrop. Inst.*, *93*, 126.

Walsh, R. J. (1964): Variation in the melanin content of the skin of New-Guinea natives at different ages. *J. invest. Derm.*, *42*, 261.

Wassermann, H. P. (1971): The colour of human skin. Spectral reflectance versus skin colour. *Dermatologica (Basel)*, *143*, 166.

Wassermann, H. P. and Heyl, T. (1968): Quantitative data on skin pigmentation in South African races. *S. Afr. med. J.*, *42*, 98.

Weiner, J. S. (1951): A spectrophotometer for the measurement of skin colour. *Man*, *253*, 152.

Weiner, J. S., Harrison, G. A., Singer, R., Harris, R. and Jopp, W. (1964): Skin colour in Southern Africa. *Hum. Biol.*, *36*, 294.

Weiner, J. S., Seberg-Montefiore, N. C. and Peterson, J. N. (1963): A note on the skin colour of Aguarana Indians of Peru. *Hum. Biol.*, *35*, 470.

Wright, W. D. (1964): *The Measurement of Colour*. Hilger and Watts, London.

Chapter VIII

Albinism, xanthism and red skin in ethnic groups

Albinism occurs in all animals, and in all races of man. The condition in man was reviewed by Fitzpatrick and Quevedo (1966) and Witkop (1970). It is due to a heritable defect in the melanocytes of various parts of the body but it is usually not a complete inability to produce any melanin. An anatomical classification was recommended to prevent the confusion arising from terms such as complete, perfect, incomplete, imperfect, generalized and partial (Fitzpatrick and Quevedo, 1966; Witkop, 1970).

Oculocutaneous albinism (complete, perfect, incomplete, imperfect, generalized) consists of hypopigmentation of the fundus oculi and translucent irides, with congenital nystagmus and diffuse absence of normal skin and hair pigmentation. It is inherited as an autosomal recessive. Tyrosinase-positive and tyrosinase-negative types occur (Witkop et al., 1963, 1970). These studies provide an explanation for differing phenotypic descriptions of albinism as well as evidence for genetic and biochemical heterogeneity of oculocutaneous albinism.

Ocular albinism consists of ocular changes but normal skin and hair pigmentation. It is inherited as a sex-linked recessive.

Cutaneous albinism (partial, white forelock, piebaldism) consists of a congenital patterned loss of melanin on the extremities and ventral thorax, usually with a white forelock. Although heterochromia iridis may be present, ocular albinism does not occur. The condition is inherited as an autosomal dominant trait.

INCIDENCE OF ALBINISM IN ETHNIC GROUPS

The difference in the incidence of albinism in ethnic groups was recently noted by several observers from Britain on their first contact with communities in Borneo (Abrahams, 1972), Nigeria (Watkins, 1972) and South America (Mansell, 1972). Increasing travel by European scientists can be expected to increase awareness of the great variation in incidence among different ethnic groups.

The first authenticated case in an Australian aborigine was only recently described by Walker (1969), who believes that a lower birth rate and higher infant mortality with the resulting small population of full-blood aborigines (80,207 in 1966) is responsible for the apparent rarity of albinism among Australian aborigines, rather than an excessive rarity of the responsible gene.

Barnicot (1952) gives the frequency of albinism in Italy as 1/29,000, in Norway 1/9,650, and in Glasgow as 1/12,500 and thus concludes that the incidence of 5/14,292 in Southwestern Nigerian Negroes is higher than in most parts of Europe. This higher frequency cannot be explained on the basis of consanguineous marriages as these are rare in Nigeria.

There is some suggestion from observers that albinism has a high incidence among Mozambique Bantu people, but its incidence is certainly not very obviously different from the ethnic groups of South Africa.

An incidence of albinism of 1 : 3500 was recently reported among Bantus in the Transkei (Rose, 1972).

The highest incidence occurs in American Indians. Woolf (1965) made a census of 23 Southwest Indian populations varying in size between 150 persons in the Picuris tribe of New Mexico to about 90,000 in the Navajo. The prevalence ranges from 1/140 persons among the Jemez to 1/3,750 among the Navajo. On the other hand, 17 of the 23 populations had no albinos at all. The Hopi of Arizona and the Zuni of New Mexico have a frequency of about 1/200, which is similar to that of the extensively studied Cuna Moon-Children (Keeler, 1953, 1964a, b).

Reed (1965) presented a hypothesis that the frequency of an original mutant of the gene for albinism may increase initially as a result of genetic drift in some tribes, and after that 'the frequency of the mutant gene may rise to an equilibrium value dependent upon the extent of inbreeding and chromosomal identity in the isolate.' Woolf and Dukepoo (1969) explain the high incidence by the acquisition of the gene by migration and then by cultural selection and isolation. They believe that albinism will decrease rapidly among the Hopi Indians with the decline of their culture.

ETHNIC INCIDENCE OF THE TYROSINASE-POSITIVE AND -NEGATIVE TYPES

In Negro families, albino parents had normally pigmented offspring. Witkop et al. (1970) found such a father to be tyrosinase-negative, i.e. his hair bulbs failed to produce pigment when incubated with tyrosine, but the mother was tyrosinase-positive. Tyrosinase-positive individuals experience a gradual accumulation of pigment in eye, skin and hair with age, so that they have golden yellow hair, pigment accumulation at the pupillary borders, a cream-coloured skin and moderate nystagmus and photophobia. Tyrosinase-negative albinos have dead-white hair, a pink skin, translucent grey blue irides, a severe nystagmus and photophobia.

In North Carolina the two types occur with equal frequency but both are more common in Negroes, the tyrosinase-positive type being about twice as frequent as the tyrosinase-negative type. These relative frequencies are reversed in Caucasians (Witkop et al., 1970).

EFFECT OF ALBINISM ON THE INDIVIDUAL

Albinism is detrimental to the patient. Albinos are sensitive to sunlight, suffer from myopia and nystagmus and are prone to skin cancer.

The skin cancer in albinos is squamous-cell carcinoma, and metastases are a frequent cause of death. Basal-cell carcinoma occurs in normal Indians and rarely, if ever, metastasizes, but this condition is rarely found in any albino. The malignant lesions appear in the teens and early twenties and metastases are probably the chief cause of death. Of 74 albinos only 5.4% survived to 40 years (Keeler, 1962, 1964a). Pigmented and non-pigmented naevi occur in albinos and may give rise to malignant melanoma (Oettlé, 1963). Large pigmented freckles often develop in the light exposed skin areas of albino Negroes (Barnicot, 1952).

Apart from these lethal conditions, albinos were found to be physically less muscular, about 10% less in body weight, and liable to several anthropomorphic differences in comparison with normal American Indians. There was a high incidence of seborrhoeic keratosis and solar elastosis. The protein-bound iodine was high, and a distinct body odour was noted in Cuna Indians (Keeler, 1968).

In the Cuna Moon-Children, Keeler (1964b) found that the children, though not mentally retarded, did suffer psychologically nevertheless. This suffering was caused by restricted physical ability and social isolation within their group resulting in 'overcompensation, repression and massive denial as major defense mechanisms'. Keeler (1964b) could find no difference between the albino group and control group in the number with personality problems.

There was no difference in the scores in formal intelligence tests, except for a significant difference in IQ in one test (Arthur Adaptation of the International Performance Scale). This test depends heavily on vision and the poor vision of albinos may account for this result (Keeler, 1964b).

POSSIBLE EXPLANATIONS FOR HIGH ETHNIC INCIDENCE

It is unlikely that a deleterious gene would reach a high frequency in several American Indian populations by chance alone. Some selective mechanism may thus be suspected. This has been studied especially in the American Indian populations and was discussed fully for the Hopi Indians by Woolf and Dukepoo (1969).

GENETIC DRIFT

If one or more of a few early settlers carried the gene for albinism in a small isolated community, a relatively high incidence might be attained by chance alone. If one or more of the founders were heterozygous for the gene the incidence would further increase.

On the other hand the relative reproductive (Darwinian) fitness of albinos is low (Keeler, 1964a; Woolf and Grant, 1962). In present-day European and Japanese populations it is about 0.7 to 0.8 for albinos, but in the past it was probably 0.4 to 0.5 (Neel et al., 1949). (A relative reproductive fitness of 0.4 implies that albinos have a functional offspring of 40 for every 100 left by the normally pigmented of their group.) When the heterozygote has a reproductive advantage a relatively high frequency of a deleterious recessive gene may be maintained (Woolf and Dukepoo, 1969).

CULTURAL SELECTION

Keeler (1964a) suggested that infanticide reduced the incidence of Cuna albinos before the reign of Supreme Chief Nele Kantule, and again since his death. He selected several towns as civilized, less civilized and uncivilized and found the corresponding prevalence as 144, 54 and 32 per 10,000 population respectively. This depends on their respective attitudes towards infanticide. On the other hand, Woolf and Dukepoo (1969) reported that among Hopi Indians inbreeding was high in comparison to various European, white American and Japanese populations, but not more so than amongst other Southwestern American Indians. They found that albinos were protected in Hopi society and that a positive attitude existed towards them. They point out that for the Hopi albino incidence, acquisition of the gene by migration (or mutation) and maintenance by cultural selection seems likely, but that this does not necessarily explain the high incidence in the Cuna, Jemez or Zuni Indians.

OCULAR ALBINISM

A type of ocular albinism occurs in which melanin is absent from the eye, and another type in which retinal and iris pigment is markedly reduced but not absent. The skin and hair are normally pigmented.

This condition is inherited as an X-linked recessive. Several loci on the X-chromosome are fairly well known, and on this chromosome genes for the Xg blood group, X-linked ichthyosis, angiokeratoma corporis diffusum (Fabry's syndrome), glucose-6-phosphate dehydrogenase, colour-blindness and haemophilia A occur. Fialkow et al. (1967) constructed a tentative map for the X-chromosome and considered the Xg locus to be within measurable distance of that for ocular albinism (Pearce et al., 1968; Vogel, 1969; Went et al., 1969).

CUTANEOUS ALBINISM

The Waardenburg syndrome is apparently rare in the darker races but was reported in the Bantu (Scott and Van Beukering, 1962; Bwibo and Mkono, 1970), the American Negro (Di George et al., 1960), the Indian (Ghosh, 1962) and in the Cape Coloured (De la Harpe, 1962) and probably accounts for some of the occasional blue-eyed Bantu described in the literature (Soussi, 1965). Considering Deol's hypothesis (1970), one wonders whether this defect should be classified as a form of albinism, and whether it is really related to piebaldism (Section IV, see p. 236).

XANTHISM

Xanthism, a condition previously considered as partial albinism (Loewenthal, 1944; Pearson et al., 1913) but now known to be distinct from albinism, occurs in African Negroes with a frequency of about 1/500 to 1/1000 in Southern Nigeria. There is a conspicuous reddening of the hair and skin pigment and sometimes dilution of iris colour. 'In a population with dark skin pigment and uniformly dark hair and iris pigmentation the segregation of such a condition can be very striking' (Barnicot, 1953). Although the mothers had black hair, children with xanthism had copper-red to reddish-brown hair. The skin was light, often copper coloured, but skin and hair did not always correlate closely. Barnicot described one with yellowish-red hair and approximately normal skin colour and another with brownish-red hair and a very pronounced copper colour. In 6 of the 23 individuals the eye colour was medium brown, but in the rest it was as dark as in the general population. The colour darkens with age. Clarke (1959) presented a colour plate of xanthism in a Negro.

RED SKIN IN NEW GUINEA INDIGENES

What appears from description to be a very similar condition was investigated by Walsh (1971) in New Guinea. The subjects were conspicuous among their relatives and clansmen because of their reddish-brown colour in contrast to the black skin pigmentation. Young children appeared almost red. The hair colour does not show close association with the intensity of the reddish-brown skin colour, varying from the usual black to very fair, almost white. An incidence of about 2% was estimated in 6 villages. Skin reflectances were higher than in black skins but much less than in albinos. Skin biopsy did not reveal any other pigment than melanin, but a soluble pigment could not be excluded. Walsh (1971) thinks that the colour may be due to a precursor metabolite of melanin production, e.g. red dopachrome or a derivative. The metabolic error is thought to result from an autosomal recessive gene. Pedigrees and a colour plate are presented by Walsh (1971).

The relation of xanthism to red skin in New Guinea indigenes is at present unknown (Walsh, personal communication). Rose (1972) has seen a similar condition in Bantu (Xhosa tribe of the Transkei).

Distinctive melanocytes, with thicker dendrites were reported in red-skinned New Guineans. The morphological difference suggests a variation of function of melanocytes in red-skinned New Guineans (Nixon, 1972).

SUMMARY

Several variants of albinism occur and its ethnic incidence varies considerably. The X-chromosome is the most completely mapped chromosome, and the gene for ocular albinism occurs within measurable distance from genes for other X-linked clinical conditions. At least 2 biochemical variants of oculocutaneous albinism are known and further epidemiological surveys and intensive studies on high frequency groups could be very rewarding in providing insights into population genetics, clinical associations and fundamental mechanisms of skin pigmentation. Xanthism and red-skinned New Guineans should be compared, and further research on the underlying mechanisms should be worthwhile.

REFERENCES

ABRAHAMS, P. H. (1972): Albinos in Borneo. *Lancet, 1,* 101.
BARNICOT, N. A. (1952): Albinism in Southwestern Nigeria. *Ann. Eugen. (Lond.), 17,* 38.
BARNICOT, N. A. (1953): Red hair in African Negroes. A preliminary study. *Ann. Eugen. (Lond.), 17,* 211.
BWIBO, N. O. and MKONO, M. D. (1970): Waardenburg's syndrome in an African child. *Hum. Hered., 20,* 19.
CLARKE, G. H. V. (1959): *Skin Disease in the African.* H. K. Lewis, London.
DE LA HARPE, P. L. (1962): Waardenburg's syndrome. A case report in a South African family. *S. Afr. med. J., 36,* 920.
DEOL, M. S. (1970): The relationship between abnormalities of pigmentation and of the inner ear. *Proc. roy. Soc. A, 175,* 201.
DI GEORGE, A. M., OLMSTEDT, R. W. and HARLEY, R. D. (1960): Waardenburg's syndrome. *J. Pediat., 57,* 649.
FIALKOW, P. J., GIBLETT, E. R. and MOTULSKY, A. G. (1967): Measurable linkage between ocular albinism and Xg. *Amer. J. hum. Genet., 19,* 63.
FITZPATRICK, T. B. and QUEVEDO JR, W. C. (1966): Albinism. In: *The Metabolic Basis of Inherited Disease,* 2nd ed., Chapter 14, p. 324. Editors: J. B. Stanbury, J. B. Wyngaarden and D. S. Frederickson. McGraw-Hill Book Co., New York, N.Y.
GHOSH, S. (1962): Waardenburg's syndrome. *Ind. J. Child. Hlth, 11,* 448.
JONES, J. A. (1964): Rio Grande albinism. *Amer. J. phys. Anthrop., 22,* 265.
KEELER, C. E. (1953): The Caribe Cuna Moon-Child and its heredity. *J. Hered., 44,* 163.
KEELER, C. E. (1962): Albinism, xeroderma pigmentosum, and skin cancer. *Nat. Cancer Inst. Monogr., 10,* 349.
KEELER, C. E. (1964a): The incidence of Cuna Moon-Child albinos. *J. Hered., 55,* 115.
KEELER, C. E. (1964b): The Cuna Moon-Child syndrome. *Derm. trop., 3,* 1.
KEELER, C. E. (1968): *Behaviour Synthesis through Pigment Gene Pleiotropy. Reprints and Essays,* pp. 349, 356.

LOEWENTHAL, L. J. A. (1944): Partial albinism and nystagmus in Negroes. *Arch. Derm. Syph. (Chic.)*, *50*, 300.

MANSELL, M. A. (1972): Albinos in South America. *Lancet*, *1*, 265.

NEEL, J. V., KODANI, M., BREWER, R. and ANDERSON, C. (1949): Incidence of consanguineous matings in Japan, with remarks on estimation of comparative gene frequencies and expected rate of appearance of induced recessive mutations. *Amer. J. hum. Genet.*, *1*, 156.

NIXON, P. F. (1972): Paper read at the 8th International Pigment Cell Conference, Sydney.

OETTLÉ, A. G. (1963): Skin cancer in Africa. *Nat. Cancer Inst. Monogr.*, *10*, 197.

PEARCE, W. G., SANGER, R. and RACE, R. R. (1968): Ocular albinism and Xg. *Lancet*, *1*, 1282.

PEARSON, K., NETTLESHIP, E. and USHER, C. H. (1911): *A Monograph on Albinism in Man. Draper's Company Research Memoirs, Biometric Series VI*. Department of Applied Mathematics, University College, London. Dulan, London.

REED, S. C. (1965): Speculations about human albinism. *J. Hered.*, *56*, 64.

ROSE, E. F. (1972): Personal communication from paper read at the 8th International Pigment Cell Conference, Sydney.

SCOTT, F. P. and VAN BEUKERING, J. A. (1962): The Waardenburg syndrome: Report of an abortive case. *S. Afr. med. J.*, *36*, 299.

SOUSSI, J. (1965): Incidence of blue eyes in South African Negroes. *S. Afr. J. med. Sci.*, *61*, 243.

VOGEL, F. (1969): Does the human X-chromosome show evidence for clustering of genes with related functions? *Amer. J. hum. Genet.*, *17*, 475.

WALKER, A. C. (1969): Albinism in a full-blood aboriginal child. *Med. J. Aust.*, *2*, 1105.

WALSH, R. J. (1971): A distinctive pigment of the skin in New Guinea indigenes. *Ann. hum. Genet.*, *34*, 379.

WATKINS, S. M. (1972): Albinos in Nigeria. *Lancet*, *1*, 203.

WENT, L. N., DE GROOT, W. P., SANGER, R., TIPPETT, P. and GAVIN, J. (1969): X-linked ichthyosis: linkage relationship with the Xg blood groups and other studies in a large Dutch kindred. *Ann. hum. Genet.*, *32*, 333.

WITKOP JR., C. J. (1970): Albinism. In: *Advances in Human Genetics, Vol. II*, p. 61. Editors: H. Harris and K. Hirschhorn. Plenum Press, New York, N.Y.

WITKOP JR., C. J., NANCE, W. E., RAWLS, R. F. and WHITE, J. G. (1970): Autosomal recessive oculocutaneous albinism in man: evidence for genetic heterogeneity. *Amer. J. hum. Genet.*, *22*, 55.

WITKOP JR., C. J., VAN SCOTT, E. J. and JACOBY, G. A. (1963): Evidence for two forms of autosomal recessive albinism in man. In: *Proceedings, II International Congress on Human Genetics Rome, 1961*, p. 1064. Istituto Gregorio Mendel, Rome.

WOOLF, C. M. (1965): Albinism among Indians in Arizona and New Mexico. *Amer. J. hum. Genet.*, *17*, 23.

WOOLF, C. M. and DUKEPOO, F. C. (1969): Hopi Indians, inbreeding and albinism. *Science*, *164*, 30.

WOOLF, C. M. and GRANT, R. B. (1962): Albinism among the Hopi Indians in Arizona. *Amer. J. hum. Genet.*, *14*, 392.

Chapter IX

Racial differences in
normal pigmented markings of the skin

Although the skin is usually free from pigmentary lesions at birth, pigmented lesions occurred in 15.6% of American Negro infants and only 2.7% of white American infants (Pratt, 1953). The occurrence of mongolian or sacral spots largely accounts for this difference.

Naevi

At the age of 2 junction naevi appear as pinpoint-sized, flat, pigmented spots usually on the upper parts of the body. They frequently follow on stress situations (e.g. infection). In light complexioned children and albinos they are flesh-coloured, but much darker in children of the darker races.

Naevi enlarge and darken during puberty and pregnancy, and new ones continue to appear up to the age of 40, when they gradually start fading (Lerner, 1955). Senile lentigines appear from the age of 45 onward.

RACIAL INCIDENCE OF MOLES

The average incidence of moles, as recorded in 1000 white patients, was 14.6 per person (Pack et al., 1952). Pack et al. (1963) report on the incidence of pigmented naevi and their pattern of distribution in Negroes, Chinese, Philippinos, Indians, Bantus, Japanese, Mestizos, Maoris and American Indians from the Chaco in Paraguay. There was a paucity of moles in dark-skinned people but a great frequency in the Mestizos of mixed white and Indian parentage. Statistics on the American Negro differ but Pack et al. (1963) found an average of 2 naevi per person in contrast to 15 to 18 per white American male. From Table II it is evident that lighter skinned races have a higher incidence of moles. With notable exceptions, most moles occur on the trunk, and least on the leg.

Comedones

The pigmentation of the central plug of comedones (blackheads) is darker in

Table II

Ethnic incidence of naevi, and its regional distribution

	Ethnic group	Naevi per person (averages)	Head and neck	Trunk	Arms	Legs
	American Negroes	2		43.4	7.4	
Low	Bantus	3	10.4	47.7		
incidence	Indians	9		39.1	17.2	
group	Maya-Guarani Indians	3	64.7			3.1
	Maoris	3	67.1			3.4
	Philippinos	26		34.6		15.7
High	Japanese	16	40.4			13.5
incidence	Chinese	30		31.5		16.6
group	Mestizo Indians	26		37.9		15.9
	American whites	14.6		No data available		

(From data by Pack, Davis and Oppenheim, 1963, *Annals of the New York Academy of Sciences*, *100*, 719.)

dark skin than in light skin as would be expected since the colour is due to melanin (Blair and Lewis, 1970; Goodhead, 1970).

Freckles

Freckles (ephelides) are round or irregular flat spots of light-brown colour and appear from the age of 5 onward. They bear a definite relation to sunburn and suntan. They become less apparent after the age of 20 due to the gradual darkening of the skin.

Nicholls (1968) found a parallel increase of freckles and moles in the age range from 7 to 17 years, and a much greater frequency and area of pigmented birthmarks in those who were heavily freckled. In those with pigmented spots of the iris the frequency of moles was increased.

The development of birthmarks antenatally, and of freckles and moles postnatally, is probably the response to exposure to ultraviolet radiation. Nicholls (1968) also suggested that red hair and heavy freckling represents a homozygous state for a single gene which in the heterozygous state is responsible for brown hair and freckling. According to Lerner (1955) freckling is due to a single dominant gene linked with red hair, and both genes are associated with the same chromosome.

In the lighter Cape Coloured people, especially in children, freckles may be seen, but they are rarely visible in the Bantu.

Racial incidence of café-au-lait spots

The significance of these brown macules of variable size and shape in the diagnosis of neurofibromatosis is not as widely appreciated as it should be (Whitehouse, 1966). The racial incidence is thus of clinical importance. They usually appear after birth. Approximately 10% of normal persons and 90% of patients with neurofibromatosis have café-au-lait spots. However, only 0.2% of normal persons have 3 or more of such lesions, but about 75% of those with neurofibromatosis have this number (Crowe and Schull, 1953).

Whitehouse (1966) studied 365 children under 5 years of age: A significantly greater number (22%) of black children had 1 café-au-lait spot than white children did (11%). Two café-au-lait spots were recorded in 5% of black children as against 2% of white children. Only 1 white child was seen with more than 2 café-au-lait spots (i.e. 3 spots), while 3 black children had more than 2 spots (i.e. 4, 5 and 8 respectively). The mother of the child with 4 spots, and also his maternal grandmother, had multiple spots. Neither had diagnosable evidence of neurofibromatosis or related disease. The one with 5 spots was normal, but the one with 8 spots was mentally retarded, and below the third percentile in size for age. His mother had neurofibromatosis.

Histological examination may assist in deciding the clinical significance of café-au-lait spots, as those associated with neurofibromatosis have a higher melanocyte count and giant melanin granules, in contrast to those occurring in patients without neurofibromatosis (Johnson and Charneco, 1970).

Racial incidence of mongolian or sacral spots

The typical mongolian spot refers to the blue-grey spot, 1 to 10 cm or more in diameter, in the lumbosacral region of new-born babies and small children. They appear in the 4th month of foetal life but sometimes only after birth, and usually disappear in childhood. The author has, however, occasionally seen mongolian spots persisting into early adult life in the Cape Coloured, especially in women. In Central European ethnic groups its incidence varies between 1 and 5% and in Brazilian whites it was reported to occur in 5%. In Asian ethnic groups an incidence of 95 to 100% was claimed. An incidence of 80% and 87% was reported in Peruvian Indians and Brazilian Negroes respectively, while the incidence was 41% in people of mixed parentage and their offspring (Thomas, 1965). Lerner (1955) reported an incidence of 60% in American Negro infants but only 0.5% in white American infants. These spots are thus found in all racial and ethnic groups. Lerner and Lerner (1958) suggest that this difference in incidence represents only a variation in the pigment-producing capacity in infants of dark colour. The dermal melanocytes, which are responsible, may later be masked due to the increase in pigmentation and density of the epidermis in later childhood.

The mechanism of inheritance of sacral spots has not been precisely determined because this would require histological studies to assess the presence of melanocytes with low melanogenetic abilities.

Tanning in races

Immediate pigmentation (pigment darkening) occurs in the Bantu (Kooij and Scott, 1954), American Negro (Monash, 1963) and other dark-skinned races as in the lighter-skinned races. Newly formed melanin is of a lighter brown colour than older pigment. Under the influence of sunlight melanin darkens by photo-chemical oxidation. Tanning of the skin follows on the photochemical inflammation produced by ultraviolet radiation (see p. 226).

This explains to some extent the darker skin colour in the exposed parts of all races (Ojikutu, 1965; Weiner et al., 1964; Tobias, 1963) and also the lighter colour of Negroes studied after prolonged residence in Europe as compared to those in their country of origin. Environmental effect on skin pigmentation was, however, found to be greatest in Europeans as compared to other races (Ojikutu, 1965).

Linear pigmentation demarcation in ethnic groups

The arms and chest of some individuals show sharply divided areas of pigmentation. Along the anterior aspect of the arm a sharp border may separate the lateral dark portion from the medial lighter area. The line fades towards the shoulder and the elbow. It was initially thought that this demarcation line was peculiar to the Japanese (Miura, 1951, 1952) but it was found to be fairly common in American Negroes (Futcher, 1940; Johnson and Pillsbury, 1940) and was observed in a white European immigrant to South Africa and in Bantu and Cape Coloured people as well (Wassermann, 1969). It was observed in only one individual among 431 Cape Coloureds and Bantu of both sexes, and thus appears to be less common there than in the American Negro.

Racial pigmentation of the sole of the foot

Pigmentation of the sole of the foot is extremely rare in whites, but pigmentation of the sole of the foot in the Bantu (Lewis, 1967; Gordon and Henry, 1971) is possibly related to the high incidence of melanoma in the foot of the Bantu (Lewis, 1967). Similar pigmentation in the palm of the hand occurs as well (Lewis, 1967).

The most extensive and dependable statistics available for melanoma in races in Africa are those of Oettlé (1966). He found the greatest incidence in whites and it was about half as high in Cape Coloureds and Bantu. It is rare in Indians. While sunlight does not appear to be a major precipitating factor of melanomas in whites in South Africa, minor traumata may explain the frequency of melanomas on the weight-bearing areas of the sole in Bantu people.

Recently Bentley-Phillips and Bayles (1972) examined the feet of 150 rickshaw boys of Durban whose bare feet are habitually exposed to gross trauma. No evidence of traumatic melanoma was found.

Lewis (1967) graded sole pigmentation in normal Bantu as: no pigmentation,

I; areas of light-brown to dark-brown pigment of various sizes and often with an irregular outline, II; discrete small black areas of pigmentation with clearcut margins, III. The incidence in two available studies using this gradation is shown in Table III. The highest incidence of Grade III pigmentation was found in tribes with the highest incidence of melanoma of the foot (Lewis, 1967).

Table III

Pigmentation of the sole of the foot in the Bantu

Degree of pigmentation		
I	II	III
10–42[1]	45–70	8–28 % (11 Bantu tribes)
39.3[2]	54.5	6.1%

1. Lewis, 1967, *British Journal of Cancer, 21*, 483.
2. Gordon and Henry, 1971, *South African Medical Journal, 45*, 88.

Sex and age distribution in three grades (% of age groups of each sex)

	I		II		III	
	M	F	M	F	M	F
0–9 years	86	78	14	20	0	2
10–19 years	29	36	61	64	10	0
20 years +	7	19	79	76	14	5

Note the increase with age in males with Grade III pigmentation.
(From data by Gordon and Henry, 1971, *South African Medical Journal, 45*, 88.)

Skin colour and eccrine sweat gland distribution

Negroes have a larger number of active sweat glands in all the body areas studied and also sweat more profusely than whites. The number of sweat glands, however, separates the black and white races less well than skin pigmentation. A negative but not significant correlation was found between density of sweat glands and average reflection values of the skin for all body areas and in all racial and ethnic groups studied. Other pertinent earlier studies are also reviewed by Ojikutu (1965). Apparently this does not hold for the Australian aborigines, where equal numbers of eccrine sweat glands occur as in whites, but the glands are larger in size than in the former (Green, 1971).

SUMMARY

The occurrence of pigmented marks (naevi, freckles, café-au-lait spots, mongolian spots and linear pigment demarcation) is not limited to any particular race, but the incidence varies considerably between races. Some of these anomalies have known clinical associations, e.g. café-au-lait spots with neurofibromatosis and sole pigmentation with melanoma of the foot. Further information should be collected for different ethnic groups.

REFERENCES

BENTLEY-PHILLIPS, B. and BAYLES, M. A. H. (1972): Melanoma and trauma. A clinical study of Zulu feet under conditions of persistent and gross trauma. *S. Afr. med. J.*, *46*, 535.

BLAIR, C. and LEWIS, C. A. (1970): The pigment of comedones. *Brit. J. Derm.*, *82*, 572.

CROWE, F. W. and SCHULL, W. J. (1953): Diagnostic importance of café-au-lait spots in neurofibromatosis. *Arch. intern. Med.*, *91*, 758.

FUTCHER, P. H. (1940): The distribution of pigmentation on the arm and thorax of man. *Bull. Johns Hopk. Hosp.*, *67*, 372.

GOODHEAD, D. T. (1970): Electron spin resonance identification of melanin in comedones. *Brit. J. Derm.*, *83*, 182.

GORDON, J. A. and HENRY, S. A. (1971): Pigmentation of the sole of the foot in Rhodesian Africans. *S. Afr. med. J.*, *45*, 88.

GREEN, L. M. A. (1971): The distribution of eccrine sweat glands of Australian Aborigines. *Aust. J. Derm.*, *12*, 143.

JOHNSON, B. L. and CHARNECO, D. R. (1970): Café-au-lait spots in neurofibromatosis and in normal individuals. *Arch. Derm.*, *102*, 442.

JOHNSON, H. M. and PILLSBURY, D. M. (1940): Congenital linear pigmentation of Negroes. *Arch. Derm.*, *42*, 739.

KOOIJ, R. and SCOTT, F. P. (1954): Primêre of direkte pigmentasie van die huid as gevolg van sonlig in Suid-Afrika. *S. Afr. med. J.*, *28*, 433.

LERNER, A. B. (1955): Melanin pigmentation. *Amer. J. Med.*, *19*, 902.

LERNER, A. B. and LERNER, M. R. (1958): Congenital and hereditary disturbances of pigmentation. *Bibl. paediat. (Basel)*, *66*, 308.

LEWIS, M. G. (1967): Malignant melanoma in Uganda (Relationship between pigmentation and malignant melanoma on the soles of the feet). *Brit. J. Cancer*, *21*, 483.

MIURA, O. (1951): On the demarcation lines of pigmentation observed among Japanese on inner sides of their extremities and on anterior and posterior sides of their medial regions. *Tohoku J. exp. Med.*, *54*, 135.

MIURA, O. (1952): A supplement to the demarcation lines of pigmentation observed among Japanese on inner sides of their extremities and on anterior and posterior sides of their medial regions. *Tohoku J. exp. Med.*, *56*, 1.

MONASH, S. (1963): Immediate pigmentation in sunlight and artificial light. *Arch. Derm. (Chic.)*, *87*, 686.

NICHOLLS, E. M. (1968): Genetic susceptibility and somatic mutation in the production of freckles, birthmarks and moles. *Lancet*, *1*, 71.

OETTLÉ, A. G. (1966): Epidemiology of melanomas in South Africa. In: *Structure and Control of the Melanocyte*, p. 292. Editors: G. Della Porta and O. Mühlbock. Springer-Verlag, Berlin.

OJIKUTU, R. O. (1965): Die Rolle von Hautpigment und Schweissdrüsen in der Klima-Anpassung des Menschen. *Homo, 16,* 77.

PACK, G. T., DAVIS, J. and OPPENHEIM, A. (1963): The relation of race and complexion to the incidence of moles and melanoma. *Ann. N.Y. Acad. Sci., 100,* 719.

PACK, J. T., LENSON, N. and GERBER, D. M. (1952): Regional distribution of moles and melanomas. *Arch. Surg., 65,* 862.

PRATT, A. G. (1953): Birthmarks in infants. *Arch. Derm. Syph. (Chic.), 67,* 302.

THOMAS, E. (1965): Über den Mongolenfleck. *Arch. Kinderheilk., 172,* 263.

TOBIAS, P. V. (1963): Studies on skin reflectance in Bushman-European hybrids. In: *Proceedings, II International Congress of Human Genetics, Rome, 1961,* p. 461. Edizioni Istituto G. Mendel, Roma.

WASSERMANN, H. P. (1969): Peculiar pigment-division along Voigt's line in a European and in a Xhosa woman. *Dermatologica (Basel), 135,* 461.

WEINER, J. S., HARRISON, G. A., SINGER, R., HARRIS, R. and JOPP, W. (1964): Skin colour in Southern Africa. *Hum. Biol., 36,* 294.

WHITEHOUSE, D. (1966): Diagnostic value of the café-au-lait spot in children. *Arch. Dis. Childh., 41,* 316.

Chapter X

Ethnic pigmentation of
skin appendages and adjacent regions

Mass movement and easier intercontinental air transport caused the rediscovery of some well-known pigmentation patterns in ethnic groups foreign to their new region. This of course leads to critical studies and frequently unmasks unfamiliarity with available literature.

A. APPENDAGES OF THE SKIN

Pigmentation of the nails

Although the occurrence of nail pigmentation was noted early in this century (Montgomery, 1917; Templeton, 1926; Monash, 1932), it was regarded as a new sign of malnutrition (Bisht and Lucknow, 1962). It was found as a familial congenital condition due to naevi (Caron, 1962), in Addison's disease (Kawamura, 1958; Allenby and Snell, 1966; Bissell et al., 1971) and it was observed subsequent to roentgen or γ-irradiation of the nail and the nailbed (Sutton, 1952; Shelley et al., 1964). The clinical significance of these findings would depend on the ethnic group of the patient.

Pigmentation of the nails of the fingers and toes is unusual in normal whites (Popkin, 1970), not uncommon in the Cape Coloured or American Negro, but common in the Bantu and African Negro.

Samman (1965) divides brown or black pigmentation of the nail into (*a*) the whole or a large part of the nail, (*b*) the edge of the nail and (*c*) longitudinal streaks.

The anatomy of the nail was described by Pardo-Costello and Pardo (1960) and by Samman (1965), and its embryological development by Zaias (1963), but although they discuss nail pigmentation in their monographs, no mention is made of melanocytes in the nailbed or nail matrix. Lerner and McGuire (1964) deduced the presence of melanocytes capable of responding to melanocyte-stimulating hormone (MSH) in the nail matrix, from the appearance of a broad horizontal band of pigmentation on the nails following MSH administration.

The first anatomical and histological study of nail pigmentation was made by

Higashi (1968) and Higashi and Saito (1969) who reviewed the literature on nail pigmentation up to that date. In specimens from Japanese subjects, melanin granules could be demonstrated in the nail matrix. Dopa-positive melanocytes were present in the lower 2 to 4 layers of the normal nail matrix, but few or none were found in the lowest layer. The number of dopa-positive melanocytes was approximately 300 per mm^2 in the distal areas of the intermediate nail matrix (Higashi and Saito, 1969). Histological findings in the nail matrix, corresponding to pigmented bands, revealed an increase in the activity and number of dopa-positive melanocytes.

Nails grow continously at a rate of 0.5 to 1.2 mm per week (Hillman, 1955), and extensive long-term observations of nail growth during periods of health and illness were made by Bean (1953, 1968). Finger- and toenails thus provide a long-sustained record of profound temporary abnormality of control of skin pigment which might otherwise pass unnoted (Thomas, 1964).

WHITES

The healthy nail is pinkish in colour with a smooth shiny surface except for the lunule which appears white due to the looseness of the nailplate. Melanin pigmentation is unusual in normal white individuals.

Longitudinal pigmentation

Bondy and Harwick (1969) described 2 white females with Cushing's syndrome who developed longitudinal nail pigmentation after bilateral adrenalectomy in the one case, and unilateral adrenalectomy for a functioning adrenal cortical adenoma in the other, in whom, after recurrence of hyperadrenocorticism, the other adrenal was also removed. Both patients became hyperpigmented in exposed areas and developed longitudinal nail pigmentation. Plasma levels of ACTH in the first case were normal, but plasma MSH (normal up to 0.09 ng per ml) was 6.1 ng per ml.

Longitudinal nail pigmentation in whites is usually ascribed to a junctional naevus in the matrix (Noble and Ferrin, 1952). Popkin (1970) pointed out that longitudinal nail pigmentation in whites is so unusual that it should not be ignored, but should be investigated by a biopsy of the nailfold to exclude a junctional naevus because such naevi may undergo malignant change, and should be surgically removed. According to Higashi (1968), however, such an assumption is not based on histological evidence. Apart from Noble and Ferrin's case where a benign junction naevus could be demonstrated, those described by Dougherty (1960), Harvey (1960), and Walker and Stewart (1955) were histologically naevoid and Kukita's (1961) case had a lentigo.

Whole nail

The author has seen a white woman, suffering from systemic lupus erythematosus, who developed diffusely pigmented nails. A period of cortisone therapy, which was discontinued before consultation, caused a light band of normal nail colour behind the dark band. A rough idea of the time periods involved could be obtained if rate of nail growth was taken as 0.5 mm per week.

CAPE COLOURED AND AMERICAN NEGRO

In healthy Cape Coloured males the author estimates nail pigmentation to be somewhat higher than the incidence of 11.4% found in Japanese by Kawamura (1958). Pigmentation is apparently less frequently seen in Cape Coloured women, but accurate statistics are not available. The nail of the Cape Coloured and American Negro is similar in other respects to that of whites. In contrast to Negroes and Bantu the lunule is usually well marked, as it is in Indians (Pardo-Costello and Pardo, 1960).

Longitudinal pigmentation

Longitudinal pigmentation, not uncommon in the darker races, was described in an American Negro with primary adrenal insufficiency (Addison's disease), but the pigmentation of the nails disappeared progressively on cortisone therapy (Bissell et al., 1971).

Whole nail

Thomas (1933) described transverse bands of pigmentation in all the finger nails of an American Negro woman with hyperthyroidism and congenital heart disease who developed a thyroid crisis on induction of anaesthesia. The thyroid was irradiated with radium and the transverse bands corresponded to the time of radium exposure.

NEGRO AND BANTU

The lunule is visible in the thumbs only, being absent or very small in the fingers (Pardo-Costello and Pardo, 1960).

The nail in many Bantu is also diffusely brownish black, especially in the darker individuals. Nail pigmentation probably occurs in nearly 50% of Bantu, but no definitive studies could be found. Apart from the fairly common diffuse pigmentation of the whole nail, longitudinal pigmentation is common, appearing as pigment streaks on the nail.

SUMMARY

The nail matrix contains melanocytes, but should be considered one of the most poorly pigmented areas of the body. With increasing pigmentation, as seen in different racial groups, visible nail pigmentation becomes increasingly more common, and is a further manifestation of general melanin pigmentary activity in the individual.

Any stimulus which may increase skin pigmentation may also increase pigmentation of the nails, often as longitudinal streaks, occasionally as pigmentation of the whole nail. There is insufficient evidence to postulate that streaks in whites should always be biopsied. It is a fairly frequent finding in brown people, and common in black people.

Hair pigmentation

Rook (1969) discussed the functions of hair and its clinical significance. In mammals, hair serves the functions of protection, display and sensation. Moulting in man is no longer seasonal, but, as in other species, moulting cycles of the hair are influenced by hormones. Cyclical hair loss is occasionally found in women and may be enough to cause them concern (J. Marshall, personal communication). Hormones controlling somatic growth and sexual maturation also control the pattern of hair growth in man. Its function as a sensory organ is rudimentary in man.

Human hair colour depends on the number of pigment granules present, their size and shape, arrangement and distribution in the hair shaft, and their colour. Electron microscopy shows that the large oval granules in black hair have an internal structure very different from that of the small granules of blond hair. With the exception of red hair, the pigment is melanin.

Dark hair predominates in the world, and it is mainly in the northwestern part of Europe that the incidence of blonde and red shades is high. In dark-haired populations there may be considerable variation in the amount of pigment but differentiation of shades becomes increasingly difficult as hair approaches a black colour. In particular countries variations in hair colour (frequently associated with a change in distribution of eye colours) occur, e.g. in Italy and in the United Kingdom the distribution of red hair resembles that of blood group O to some extent, although there is a discrepancy in East Anglia (Harrison et al., 1964, pp. 224-225).

VARIATION IN THE INDIVIDUAL

Like skin colour, hair colour varies according to body site in the same individual. Genital hair is usually lighter than scalp hair and often has a reddish tint even in those with brown pubic hair. The hair on the lower and lateral aspects of the scrotum is lighter than that on the pubes (Grobbelaar, 1952). A reddish tint to brown hair is also more common in axillary hair than on the scalp in brown-haired individuals. While Grobbelaar (1952) found red axillary hair in 33% of his series of whites, it was only occasionally observed by workers among Rehoboth Coloureds in South Africa, Bavarian and Swiss children. The hair covering of some races is scanty, e.g. the beard of the American Indian, and the body hair of the Cape Coloured. Van Wyk (1939) recorded the distribution of body hair in 133 Cape Coloured males as profuse in 3, medium in 11, weak in 22, very weak in 48, and absent in 49. The Bantu and Negro have very little hair on the arms and legs or on the chest and back, but beard, axillary and pubic hair may be of an average normal density. Green (1971) reported the Australian aborigine as having less body hair and fewer sebaceous glands than white Australians. Black- and brown-haired individuals often have red or auburn sideburns.

AGE AND HAIR COLOUR

Hair colour darkens with age (Sunderland, 1956). Miszkiewicz (1965) found that the predominantly blond hair colour of males and females between 13 and 24 months of age in a Polish population changed to a predominantly dark colouring at about the age of 15. This was ascribed to hormonal influences in puberty.

Greying of the hair is the most obvious sign of aging in man. The normal age for the onset of greying in white races is 34.2 $\pm$ 8.6 years (Rook, 1969). The first appearance of greying may be misleading, as visual impression of degrees of greying is strongly influenced by the contrast between the original colour and white. The first signs of greying are thus more readily seen in dark hair, but fair hair appears to turn completely grey sooner than dark hair. At the age of 50, 50% of people are at least 50% grey irrespective of sex or hair colour (Keogh and Walsh, 1965). The impression among many medical observers is that the Bantu starts to grey at a fairly high age, and the author agrees. The older Bantu, however, do not know their exact age, but in Bantu whose age was known I found grey hair uncommon between 40 and 50 years of age. A peculiar phenomenon, occasionally seen in even young Bantu, is single white hairs occurring between the black, and more often on the occipital region of the head. It may be a familial condition.

There is an impression amongst practitioners in Bantu areas of South Africa that greying occurs in earlier age groups now than a generation ago. It was suggested that this phenomenon might be related to increased emotional stress (Scott, 1970). The Cape Coloured apparently does not differ from whites. Premature greying of the hair may be associated with arteriosclerosis (Lebon et al., 1957) and it is also increased in hyperthyroidism and in pernicious anaemia. The latter 2 conditions are rare in the Bantu. Metchnikoff (1901) suggested that phagocytosis of melanin may be the cause of natural greying of hair due to old age.

Greying of hair in old age was found to be due not to corpuscular colour but to the impression arising from the actual colour of the hair keratin and from the reflection of light on the boundary surfaces and islets of interfibrillary matrix (Orfanos et al., 1970). Herzberg and Gusek (1970) found the melanocyte population greatly reduced in number or totally absent in grey hair, but pigment transfer from melanocytes was normal. Another view holds that greying is due to the progressive loss of tyrosinase activity by the melanocytes of hair follicles. In Addison's disease it may be reversed at this stage by increased melanocyte-stimulating hormone (MSH) output, and clipping of the hair also stimulated melanogenesis in guinea-pigs (Clive and Snell, 1967).

SEX DISTRIBUTION

Keogh and Read (1963) found that fair hair was relatively less common in white Australian women than in men. The difference was statistically significant. Although red hair was seen more frequently in women than in men, the difference was not statistically significant.

HAIR FORM

A tangled fluffy mass of short spirally coiled hairs, often described as 'woolly', is the universal type of hair form in the Bantu and Negro. A modification of this type is the peppercorn which occurs in grouped islands on the scalp of Hottentots and Bushmen (the Koisan people of Africa). Straight or slightly wavy hair occurs in Caucasians and in many hybrid groups. Indian hair is also straight. According to Howells (1937), 'The Australian aborigines are a major race which represents an earlier stage in the development of *Homo sapiens* than does any other existing race ... its characteristic wavy hair is probably older than the woolly hair of the Negro.'

A comparison of form, colour and other indices in Caucasoid (St. Louis whites, 1928), Mongoloid (Chinese students, Wisconsin University, 1922), Negroid (Northern Zululand, South Africa, 1913) and Australian aborigine hair was made by Trotter et al. (1956). Their findings are presented in Table IV.

Table IV

The hair in various ethnic groups

	Aborigine	Negroid	Mongoloid	Caucasoid
Form	Wavy	Kinky	Straight	Wavy
Colour	Brown-black	Brown-black	Brown-black	Brown
Cross-sectional area	0.0036–0.1041	0.0031	0.0060	0.0033
Percentage with medulla	35–66	26	73	36

(From data by Trotter et al., 1956, *American Journal of Physical Anthropology*, **14**, 649.)

Population studies

Reflectance studies were made by Gardener and MacAdams (1934), Reed (1952), Sunderland (1956) and Barnicot (1956) and a colorimetric estimation of extracted pigment was done by Hanna (1956), but the usual method employed in population studies was a comparison with Fischer's (1907) hair colour chart, or as modified by Fischer and Saller (1928).

In general, the highly pigmented races have black or black-brown hair. The yield of melanoprotein extracted from pooled hair of many individuals was 951 mg, 701 mg, 600 mg and 225 mg per 100 g of hair for Bantu, Indian, Cape Coloured and Caucasian groups respectively (Wassermann, 1970).

In the population of Tristan da Cunha, a predominantly darkly pigmented people, Sunderland (1965) found that black-brown hair colour predominated (90.08%); brown (6.87%), dark-blond (2.29%) and red hair (0.76%) were much less frequent. The female group had a greater incidence of brown hair (8.96%), but fewer had black-brown hair (88.06%) than in the male group (4.69 and 92.19% respectively). In those with dark-blond hair males predominated (3.12% against 1.49%).

The correlation of hair colour with skin colour and eye colour is seen from data by Keogh and Read (1963) for Australian whites. Dark hair occurred in 62% of those with sallow skin, but in only 27% of those with a fair skin, where fair hair was the commonest. In the sallow complexion group 4.2% had fair hair. Hazel-grey eyes were commonest in all 3 skin colour groups, but blue eyes predominated in the fair-skinned group.

In white South Africans there was a correlation between hair colour and eye colour which was statistically significant at the 1% level, but correlation with skin colour was not statistically significant (Grobbelaar, 1952).

INHERITANCE OF HAIR COLOUR

Little is known about the inheritance of hair colour. In the dark races there is intense selection for dark hair, but in Caucasians there is no strong selection in favour of any particular colour. It is possible that a large number of genes for hair colour exist, many producing almost identical phenotypes.

The inheritance of red hair was more extensively studied than the other varieties of hair colour. Red hair is said to occur in about 3% of English whites but in more than 11% of the population of Scotland. The inheritance of red hair appears to be dominant to its absence and hypostatic to brown and black (Rife, 1967) in contrast to the earlier held view that it is recessive to non-red (Singleton and Ellis, 1964). Red-haired children often change to brown-haired, sandy-haired or auburn-haired adults. Further studies on genetic linkages of red hair could provide information of fundamental importance because red-haired people suffer from poor protection against sunburn.

The significance of hair colour in mate selection is discussed on p. 197 et seq.

SUMMARY

Dark hair predominates in the world, and it is mostly in white races that red and blond shades occur. Variations occur in the same individual, and hair colour tends to darken with age. Fair hair appears to be less common in women than in men (of the white race).

Hair form differs among ethnic groups, the woolly type being universal among Bantu and Negroes.

Greying of hair was the subject of several recent studies. Although the Bantu start to grey at a later age than whites, recent impressions are that the present generation starts to go grey at an earlier age.

Population studies confirm the predominance of black and dark-brown hair among dark ethnic groups.

Little is known about the inheritance of hair colour, most studies concerning themselves with the inheritance of red hair.

B. PIGMENTATION OF ADJACENT REGIONS

Eye pigmentation

Visible pigmentation of the eye concerns 3 parts of the eye: the iris, cornea and sclera. Functionally more important is retinal pigmentation which, however, is not directly visible.

IRIS PIGMENTATION

Eye colour, in general, ranges from blue to very dark brown in Caucasians and is nearly always dark brown to black in the Negro or Bantu. Blue eyes occur less often in Cape Coloureds than in Caucasians.

The colour of the eye depends on the relationship of melanin in the anterior structures of the iris and the deep purple pigment in the posterior aspect of the iris.

Anatomy of the iris

The iris is a thin, circular contractile disc perforated slightly towards the nasal side by the pupil. It consists of 4 layers: The outermost layer consists of flattened endothelial cells and is heavily pigmented in Negroes, but in Caucasians with dark-coloured irides some, but usually much less, pigment granules may be seen too. The second layer, or stroma, consists of fibrous connective tissue and cells containing pigment in dark-eyed individuals. The pigment consists of yellow or yellow and brown granules. The third layer consists of the circular and radial muscle fibres of the ciliary muscle. The innermost layer consists of two layers of pigmented epithelial cells, the pigment being retinal melanin.

The histological differences between the irides of the African Negro and those of the white race were compared by Emiru (1971). In the Negro it is mainly the thicker and more pigmented anterior border that is very markedly different from the iris of the white person, but more abundant branching pigment cells can also be seen in the stroma of the Negro iris. There is an impression that the Negro iris may be thicker.

The sphincter pupillae, dilator pupillae and the posterior pigment epithelium did not appear to differ in the 2 races.

A sex difference in the colour of the eye exists in all ethnic groups but is more noticeable in the Caucasian where the spectrum of eye colours ranges from blue to very dark brown. This sex difference in the colour and structure of the iris is more marked in the adult than in the child (Ziegelmayer, 1954).

Eye colour is anatomically determined as follows (Skinner, 1955):

a. Blue eyes are due to the Tyndall effect or Rayleigh scattering when viewing the dark pigment of the posterior layer through the overlying layers. Different shades of blue are due chiefly to the structure, texture and colour of the overlying fibrous layers.

b. Grey eyes are due to the effect of a thin, very superficial layer of melanin, usually appearing yellow rather than brown, on the blue iris as described above.

c. Green and brown eyes with their various shades are due to the presence, localization and amount of melanin in the middle and anterior layers of the iris, depending to some extent on whether or not the pigment is more yellow or more brown.

d. Brown, dark-brown and yellowish-brown eyes are due to heavily pigmented superficial layers which completely obscure the posterior pigment.

e. Black eyes are actually so intensely dark brown with such heavily pigmented superficial layers that the dark pupil cannot readily be distinguished from the iris.

f. Pink irides occur in albinos due to the total lack of pigment in superficial layers so that arterial blood in the vessels of the iris can be seen through the superficial layers. The retinal melanin is also absent.

The description of eye colour

Iris colour can be matched to the eye colour tablet of Martin but it is rarely used. Most studies on eye colour usually reduce their findings to blue, intermediate and brown-black colours.

The description of eye colour in a group of white students by Skinner (1955) also gives an indication of the difficulties involved in designing a satisfactory objective method for eye colour:

Around the periphery of the iris (limbal area) a dark ring may often be seen in light-coloured irides. This is due to the absence of anterior pigment in this circle, allowing the dark posterior pigment to be seen. In dark eyes the line is not discernible.

Summarizing the description further: The anterior pigment tends to be evenly distributed over the whole front of the iris (40.6%) rather than concentrated around the pupil (34.8%) in those eyes with a dark ring at the periphery. In those eyes without a dark ring at the periphery the pigment tends to be concentrated around the pupil (43.9%) rather than being evenly distributed (31%). In all eyes considered together the pigment was concentrated around the pupil (43.9%) more often than being evenly distributed (33.6%). It is more often concentrated in isolated patches or in a radiating pattern (18.1% than haphazardly distributed over the entire iris (7.6%).

This pattern of distribution probably holds true for all ethnic groups, but is difficult to observe in the very dark, nearly black iris.

Eye colour in different ethnic groups

Most studies classify eye colour in a few broad divisions. Grobbelaar (1952) describes numbers on the *Augenfarbentafel* of Martin, and groups them together as follows:

No.	2, 3	Very dark brown			7, 8	Greenish	
	4	Brown	Brown		9, 10	Dark grey	Intermediate
	5, 6	Light brown			11, 12	Light grey	

	13, 14	Dark blue	Blue
	16	Light blue	

10%, equally distributed among whites, blacks and browns. The incidence in Guatemala (8.9%) and in Mexico (8.6%) was less than in tropical Africa (12.1%). In 665 individuals with this pigmentation it occurred on the nasal side in 312, on the temporal side in 268, and it was bilateral in 114.

PIGMENTATION OF THE FUNDUS OF THE EYE

Although not directly visible, ophthalmoscopic investigation of the fundus of the eye is a routine procedure in general medicine, and a description of its melanin pigmentation fits logically into this Chapter.

The colour of the normal fundus of the eye ranges from orange to vermilion. In brunettes the fundus is more darkly tinted to an Indian-red colour. In the darker ethnic groups, e.g. Cape Coloured, Bantu and Negro, the colour may vary from that of brunettes to a chocolate brown, or at times, purplish hue. Ophthalmologists find it useful to describe the fundus as of average, blonde, brunette or negroid variety (Ballantyne and Michaelson, 1962).

The red hue, as in the skin, is due to oxyhaemoglobin, but the wide variety of colouration is due to the varying quantities of melanin in the retinal hexagonal cells and in the choroid.

The pigment epithelium of the human *retina* shows pigment granules at the 4th week (5–6 mm stage) and is completely pigmented by the 5th week (10 mm stage) and is well filled with pigment granules at birth, but the *choroid* is unpigmented. As the retinal pigment fades with age, choroid pigmentation increases throughout life and progressively tints the average fundus to a greyish brown in old age. Miyamoto and Fitzpatrick (1957) found that retinal fading is *apparent* only as area increases, but pigmentation remains essentially the same through life. In the macular area pigment stippling occurs normally and is due to the retinal layer of pigmented hexagonal epithelium. In these cells the pigment is distributed unequally.

The negroid fundus is found in dark-skinned races, and its colour is due to the heavily pigment-loaded stroma of the choroid. The retinal layer, on the other hand, may be even less densely pigmented than in many European eyes (Ballantyne and Michaelson, 1962).

Albinotic fundi, at the other extreme, have maximum visibility of choroidal vessels due to scanty pigmentation of all layers of the retina and choroid, but 'no albino eye has yet been found to be completely lacking in pigment' (Ballantyne and Michaelson, 1962). Pigment-bearing cells, both retinal and choroidal, are present as in the normal eye. The granules may be recognized microscopically although deficient or lacking in colour.

The differentiation of the macula in albinotic eyes is incomplete and is accompanied by nystagmus and poor visual acuity.

Optic discs. The pale-red to yellowish optic disc is sometimes partly encircled by a narrow pale border, the scleral ring. When the retinal pigment layer is thickened before it impinges on the optic nerve it gives the appearance of a pigmented ring outside the scleral ring. In the black races a pigment crescent or ring at or just outside the edge of the optic disc is of common occurrence but it may also occur normally in white races.

Sharp lines of distinction cannot be drawn between moderate degrees of departure from the 'average' fundus and extreme forms which may be considered as anomalous or pathological. Brunettes may have a 'melanosis' which would be normal in the fundus of a Negro.

The pigment in the retina has been assumed to be melanin, because of the failure of pigment synthesis in the retinal pigment epithelium of the complete albino. Miescher (1923) demonstrated dopa-oxidase by histochemical methods in retinal pigment epithelium. Retinal pigment epithelium is derived from the neural ectoderm. Miyamoto and Fitzpatrick (1957) demonstrated in chick embryos the enzymatic oxidation of L-dopa and L-tyrosine to melanin, and its inhibition against L-dopa, but not against L-tyrosine, by copper. In this respect the enzyme is similar to mammalian tyrosinase. Tyrosinase was first detectable on the 6th day and increased to maximal activity on the 10th day. There was an abrupt decline after the 12th day and no tyrosinase activity was present on or after the 14th day of development. They could also show tyrosinase activity in the retinal pigment epithelium of a 15-day mouse embryo and a 6-month human foetus.

The function of retinal melanin in the optical system of the eye is clearly to limit the scattering of light, and albinos, therefore, have poor vision in sunlight. Their vision in moonlight or subdued light is known to be normal, and this contributed to the dubbing of San Blas Indian albinos as Moon-Children (Keeler, 1953).

LENS PIGMENTATION

The lens of the eye of most diurnally active animals including man shows various shades of yellow, amber and brown, while it is colourless in nocturnal animals.

Zigman (1971) presented evidence that this colour may result from the photo-oxidation of the aromatic rings of amino acids (e.g. phenylalanine, tryptophan and tyrosine) to quinones. Reduced glutathione or ascorbic acid (at 0.001 M excess) markedly inhibited the formation of photoproducts of tryptophan or *p*-aminobenzoic acid.

These coloured products bind firmly to lens and other proteins at their amino and sulphydryl groups.

In natural sunlight the 365 nm light on a cloudless, sunny day was approximately 300 μw/cm^2 which corresponds to 75% of the energy of the laboratory lamp used in his studies. There is evidence that ultraviolet light may be damaging to the retina, and the pigments so formed would thus protect the retina. By blocking shorter waves it would also sharpen the retinal image. The disadvantage would be the lowered water solubility which may contribute to the brunescent type of human cataract. This melanin pigment differs from other eye pigments in as far as it is of non-melanocyte origin.

There are no comparative studies available, but according to these findings populations exposed to areas with high-intensity ultraviolet radiation in sunlight would be expected to show more lens pigmentation and in such populations this pigmentation may be a significant adaptive change.

SUMMARY

Eye colour differs markedly among the races, any eye colour other than black being highly exceptional in Negroes and Bantu. Brown races (e.g. Cape Coloured) occasionally have intermediate and blue eyes. The pigmentation of the iris shows varying patterns which make the value of objective measurement doubtful, even if a satisfactory method should be found.

Scleral pigmentation occurs in all races, but is only marked in the darker races. The pigment spots are found surrounding the limbus around the perforating branches of ciliary arteries and veins, or along intrascleral nerve loops.

Corneal pigmentation may result from local adrenalin instillation, but in tropical countries (especially those inhabited by yellow and black races) triangular corneal pigmentation occurs. In Venezuela white, black and brown ethnic groups had an equal incidence.

Fundal pigmentation is well known and ranges from average to the darker brunette or negroid varieties and the lighter blonde variety. Tyrosinase activity in embryos reaches a maximum and then disappears. Fading of pigment in the retina with age is due to increase in size of the pigment layer without corresponding melanogenesis.

Lens pigmentation results from photo-oxidation of aromatic amino acids to melanin. The melanin is non-melanocytic in origin, and it occurs only in diurnally active animals, including man. It may have adaptive significance.

Oral pigmentation

GINGIVAE AND BUCCAL MUCOUS MEMBRANE

Normal pigmentation of intraoral tissues is a relatively frequent finding, but received little attention after its first systematic study by Adachi (1903) and its description in the French literature (Bonnet, 1912) until the first symposium on oral pigmentation was held in 1959. Many studies, reviewed chronologically by Dummett and Barens (1967), have appeared since that time. Early studies on Australian aborigines were discussed by Brown (1964). Steigmann (1965) refers to studies on Rumanians, Gypsies, Negroes, Latin Americans and Hindus in discussing his observations on Yemenite Jews. Extensive studies on American Negroes were made by Dummett (1945, 1946). Yoshiaki et al. (1956) studied oral pigmentation in Japanese, and Raut et al. (1954) studied Indians in Bombay. In Africa, oral pigmentation in blacks is known to be very common, but most studies have been concerned with its relationship to oral melanoma rather than its systematic description. Van Wyk (1970) reported on the normal oral pigmentation of Bantu in South Africa.

Although Volker and Kenney (1960) and Bolden (1960) used a modified reflectance spectrophotometric evaluation, the Dummett oral pigmentation index (DOPI) assessment technique is easier. Bolden (1966) modified Dummett and Gupta's original method, and assigns zero to no clinical pigmentation, 0.03–1.0 to mild light-brown colouration of gingival tissues, 1.03–2.0 to moderate (medium-brown or mixed pink and brown colour), and 2.03 to 3.0 to heavy clinical pigmentation (deep brown or blue black). The mouth is divided into arches corresponding with the teeth and the DOPI assessment, then, is the sum of assigned estimates of components divided by 28 or 32 unit spaces.

In Bolden's study all whites had a DOPI assessment of zero (25 individuals) while only 9.4% of 156 American Negroes were zero. The remaining 90.6% American Negroes had an assessment of between 0.3 and 3.0.

Healthy gingivae range from a pale pink to deep bluish purple, with many intermediate colours. The colour depends on activity of melanogenesis, epithelial cornification, depth of epithelization and gingival vascularity. Non-pigmented gums are found more often in fair-skinned individuals, and pigmented gums are usually seen in dark-skinned persons. Oral pigmentation was observed in newborn infants as early as 3 hours after birth and in some cases it was the only sign of pigmentation on the body (Dummett and Barens, 1967).

Apart from physiological melanin pigmentation, several pharmacological agents (Dummett, 1964), and also metallic foreign bodies (Orban, 1956) as well as physical trauma (Penev, 1970) may cause oral pigmentation. Dummett (1962) classified oral pigmentation into primary and secondary melanin pigmentations, non-melanic pigmentation and the oral melanoclasis.

It is very obvious that the statement (Dunlop, 1963) 'pigmentation of the buccal mucous membrane if not pathognomonic of Addison's disease is nearly so' does not apply to highly pigmented races, and even in whites there are many exceptions.

In whites buccal pigmentation does occur; in Britain the incidence of buccal pigmentation was found to be as high as 5% in whites against 38% in the coloured races (Fry and Almeyda, 1968). In all these cases adrenal function tests were done and shown to be normal.

Dark-skinned races

The incidence of oral pigmentation in blacks is high. It was found in all but 2 of 122 Bantu individuals in Van Wyk's (1970) study. The gums were most consistently pigmented, less often (60%) in American Negroes (Dummett and Barens, 1967) than in Bantu (99%) (Van Wyk, 1970).

Oral pigmentation is usually symmetrical, the upper gums quantitatively more pigmented than the lower, and the buccal surfaces more than the lingual surfaces. Both upper and lower gums were usually pigmented (105/122) but, in a few, only the upper (5/122) or the lower (2/122) gums were pigmented (Van Wyk, 1970). The hard palate showed pigment in 61% of Dummett's and 83% of Van Wyk's series.

In approximately half of the people in Van Wyk's (1970) survey, the lips showed diffuse pigmentation, and the cheeks were patchily pigmented, while about one-third had diffusely pigmented cheeks.

The tongue was pigmented in 15% of Dummett's cases, while in Van Wyk's study the ventral surface was pigmented in just under 50%, mostly confined to the fimbriae. No general pattern was found, the pigmentation varying from pinpoint spots to large blotches.

Van Wyk (1970) found pigmentation of the floor of the mouth in about 12% of Bantus.

The American Negro corresponds in skin colour to the Cape Coloured, and the Bantu to the West African Negro. It would thus appear that in these 2 ethnic groups, oral pigmentation is more marked in the darker racial group.

In Indians, Pakistanis and West Indian Negroes a higher incidence of lip pigmentation (43–65%) and lower incidence of gingival pigmentation (16–17%) were found than in the 2 studies discussed above (Fry and Almeyda, 1968).

Dummett (1970) recently reported the emotional reaction to oral pigmentation. False teeth, until recently manufactured in a bright pink, contrast strongly with the normal gingival colour of American Negroes, and several such patients insisted on a more suitable colour.

PIGMENTATION OF THE TONGUE

Fry and Almeyda (1968) found no tongue pigmentation in 49 Indians and Pakistanis, and tongue pigmentation was indeed described as a familial pigment anomaly in an Indian family (Rao, 1970). Kaplan and Hurley (1967) described it as an uncommon normal variation. Such pigmentation was seen in children at 4 years of age, unassociated with other oral pigmentation. It was found in 9% of over 1,700 Negroes (Kaplan, 1961) which is less than Dummett's findings in American Negroes and Van Wyk's findings in Bantu. Kaplan and Hurley (1967) found an incidence of 0.4% in American Negroes but none in whites. It is not clear whether or not the same pigmentation was discussed in each case. Kaplan and Hurley (1967) report histological findings as well as Van Wyk (1970). Rao (1970) describes the pigmentation as ash-coloured, Kaplan and Hurley (1967) as brown. Cases of tongue pigmentation which I have seen in Cape Coloureds and Bantu, as well as occasionally in whites, were mostly bluish black or brown in colour.

Pigmentation of the nasal cavity

Friedman (1958) stated: 'The occurrence of benign melanoma in the nasal cavity has not yet been confirmed; indeed, pigment is lacking in the nasal mucosa except in the olfactory area.' Few melanomas, however, occurred in the olfactory area; most were found in the septum, inferior turbinate and middle turbinate, in that order of frequency.

Lewis and Martin (1967) examined 66 medical students, nurses and clerical staff of Nilotic, Nilo-Hamitic and Bantu ethnic groups, and also 30 biopsies from autopsy material. Pigmentation in the nasal vestibule varied from no pigmentation to dark, brownish-black spots usually most noticeable just anterior to the mucocutaneous junction on the nasal septum. The term 'ectopic pigmentation' was only employed for those cases which had a distinct band of normal mucosa between the pigment-containing area and the mucocutaneous junction. Most common was a collection of minute specks of melanin 'akin to a dusting of black pepper, over an area which varied from approximately 0.25 cm² to 1.0 cm².' Ectopic pigmentation, as defined, occurred in 13.5% of the series, the most common site being the anterior part of the septum. No correlation was found between the degree of pigmentation of the skin of the nasal vestibule and the occurrence of ectopic melanin. Histologically melanocytes occurred in both the stratified squamous mucosa and in the junctional areas between the respiratory columnar epithelium

SUMMARY

Oral and nasal cavity pigmentation follows the same pattern found in ethnic pigmentation in general: Its incidence increases with increasing darkness of skin colour. There is no evidence to support the suggestion that oral pigmentation is nearly pathognomonic of Addison's disease. Indeed, it is only in the white races that its occurrence is infrequent, but decidedly not unknown.

REFERENCES

ADACHI, B. (1903): Das Hautpigment beim Menschen und bei den Affen. *Z. Morph. Anthrop.*, *6*, 1.

ALLENBY, C. F. and SNELL, P. H. (1966): Longitudinal pigmentation of the nails in Addison's disease. *Brit. med. J.*, *1*, 1582.

BALLANTYNE, A. J. and MICHAELSON, I. C. (1962): *Textbook of the Fundus of the Eye*, p. 31 *et seq.* E. and S. Livingstone, Ltd., London.

BARNICOT, N. A. (1956): The relation of the pigment trichosiderin to hair colour. *Ann. hum. Genet.*, *21*, 31.

BEAN, W. B. (1953): A note on fingernail growth. *J. invest. Derm.*, *20*, 27.

BEAN, W. B. (1968): Nail growth, twenty-five years' observation. *Arch. intern. Med.*, *122*, 359.

BISHT, D. B. and LUCKNOW, M. D. (1962): Pigmented band on nails: A new sign in malnutrition. *Lancet*, *1*, 507.

BISSELL, G. W., SURAKOMOL, K. and GREENSLIT, F. (1971): Longitudinal banded pigmentation of nails in primary adrenal insufficiency. *J. Amer. med. Ass.*, *215*, 1667.

BOLDEN, T. E. (1960): Histology of oral pigmentation. *J. Periodont.*, *31*, 361.

BOLDEN, T. E. (1966): The oral pigmentation index (DOPI) – Adaptation to populations with permanent and deciduous dentitions. *N.Y. St. dent. J.*, *32*, 203.

BONDY, P. K. and HARWICK, H. J. (1969): Longitudinal banded pigmentation of nails following adrenalectomy for Cushing's syndrome. *New Engl. J. Med.*, *281*, 1056.

BONNET, L. M. (1912): La pigmentation des muqueuses. *Lyon méd.*, *119*, 107.

BROWN, T. (1964): Oral pigmentation in the Aborigines of Kalumburu, Northwest Australia. *Arch. oral Biol.*, *9*, 555.

CARON, G. A. (1962): Familial congenital pigmented naevi of the nails. *Lancet*, *1*, 508.

CLIVE, D. and SNELL, R. (1967): Effect of alpha-MSH on mammalian hair color. *J. invest. Derm.*, *49*, 314.

DOUGHERTY, J. W. (1960): Linear pigmentation of the fingernail. *Arch. Derm.*, *82*, 126.

DUMMETT, C. O. (1945): Clinical observations on pigment variations in healthy oral tissues of the Negro. *J. dent. Res.*, *24*, 7.

DUMMETT, C. O. (1946): Physiologic pigmentation of the oral and cutaneous tissues in the Negro. *J. dent. Res.*, *25*, 451.

DUMMETT, C. O. (1962): A classification of oral pigmentations. *Milit. Med.*, *127*, 837.

DUMMETT, C. O. (1964): Oral mucosal discolorations related to pharmacothera-peutics. *J. oral Ther. Pharmacol.*, *1*, 106.

DUMMETT, C. O. (1970): Mental attitudes toward oral pigmentations. *Milit. Med.*, *134*, 19.

DUMMETT, C. O. and BARENS, G. (1967): Pigmentation of the oral tissues: A review of the literature. *J. Periodont.*, *38*, 369.

DUNLOP, D. (1963): Eighty-six cases of Addison's disease. *Brit. med. J.*, *2*, 887.

EMIRU, V. P. (1971): Response to mydriatics in the African. *Brit. J. Ophthal.*, *55*, 538.

FISCHER, E. (1907): Die Bestimmung der menschlichen Haarfarben. *Bl. dtsch. Ges. Anthrop.*, *38*, 141.

FISCHER, E. and SALLER, K. (1928): Eine neue Haarfarbentafel. *Anthrop. Anzeit*, *5*, 238.

FRIEDMAN, I. (1958): *Cancer*. Editor: R. W. Raven. Butterworth, London.

FRY, L. and ALMEYDA, J. R. (1968): The incidence of buccal pigmentation in Cau-casoids and Negroids in Britain. *Brit. J. Derm.*, *80*, 244.

GARDENER, B. B. and MACADAMS, D. L. (1934): Colorimetric analysis of hair colour. *Amer. J. phys. Anthrop.*, *19*, 187.

GREEN, M. A. (1971): The distribution of eccrine sweat glands of Australian aborig-ines. *Aust. J. Derm.*, *12*, 143.

GROBBELAAR, C. S. (1952): The distribution of and correlation between eye, hair and skin colour in male students at the University of Stellenbosch. *Ann. Univ. Stellen-bosch*, *28*, Sect. *A/1*.

HANNA, B. L. (1956): Colorimetric estimation of the pigment concentration in hair of various colour grades. *Amer. J. phys. Anthrop.*, *14*, 153.

HARRISON, G. A., WEINER, J. S., TANNER, J. M. and BARNICOT, N. A. (1964): *Human Biology, An Introduction to Human Evolution, Variation and Growth*. Oxford University Press, London.

HARVEY, K. M. (1960): Pigmented nevus of nail. *Lancet*, *2*, 848.

HERZBERG, J. and GUSEK, W. (1970): Das Ergrauen des Kopfhaares. Eine histo- und fermentchemische sowie elektronen-mikroskopische Studie. *Arch. klin. exp. Derm.*, *236*, 368.

HIGASHI, N. (1968): Melanocytes of nail matrix and nail pigmentation. *Arch. Derm.*, *97*, 570.

HIGASHI, N. and SAITO, T. (1969): Horizontal distribution of the dopa-positive melanocytes in nail matrix. *J. invest. Derm.*, *53*, 163.

HILLMAN, R. W. (1955): Finger nail growth in the human subject. Rates and varia-tions in 300 individuals. *Hum. Biol.*, *27*, 274.

HOWELLS, W. W. (1937): Anthropometry of the natives of Arnhem Land and the Australian race problem. *Papers Peabody Mus. Amer. Archeol. Ethnol.*, *16/1*, 1. Harvard University.

HUXLEY, H. J. and SHELLY, W. B. (1959): Melanocytic striae in scars and nails. *Arch. Derm.*, *80*, 268.

JAY, B. (1967): Pigmented lesions of the conjunctiva. I. *Brit. J. Ophthal.*, *51*, 862.

JAY, B. (1968): Pigmented lesions of the conjunctiva. II. *Brit. J. Ophthal.*, *52*, 70.

KAPLAN, B. J. (1961): The clinical tongue. *Lancet*, *1*, 1094.

KAPLAN, B. J. and HURLEY, H. J. (1967): Prominent pigmented papillae of the tongue. *Arch. Derm.*, *95*, 394.

KAWAMURA, T. (1958): Pigmentatio longitudinalis striata unguium and pigmentation of nail plate in Addison's disease. *Jap. J. Derm.*, *68*, 10.

Keeler, C. (1953): The Caribe Cuna Moon Child and its heredity. *J. Hered.*, *44*, 163.

Keeley, K. J. (1962): Pigmented bands on nails. *Lancet*, *1*, 866.

Keogh, E. V. and Read, G. (1963): The distribution of skin, hair and eye colours in an Australian population. *Aust. J. exp. Biol. med. Sci.*, *41*, 405.

Keogh, E. V. and Walsh, R. J. (1965): Rate of greying of human hair. *Nature (Lond.)*, *207*, 877.

Krejci, L. and Harrison, R. (1970): Epinephrine effects on corneal cells in tissue culture. *Arch. Ophthal.*, *83*, 451.

Kukita, A. (1961): A case of pigmented stripe of the nail (lentigo unguium). *Jap. J. Derm.*, *71*, 1010.

Lagraulet, J., Borrey, F. and Bard, J. (1967): La pigmentation triangulaire de la cornée des pays tropicaux. *Bull. Soc. Path. exot.*, *60*, 312.

Lebon, J., Duboucher, G., Claude, R. and Hadida, A. (1957): Affections cardio-artérielles et cavité précose. *Algérie méd.*, *61*, 871.

Lerner, A. B. and McGuire, J. S. (1964): Melanocyte-stimulating hormone and adrenocorticotrophic hormone: their relation to pigmentation. *New Engl. J. Med.*, *270*, 539.

Lewin, K. (1965): The normal fingernail. *Brit. J. Derm.*, *77*, 421.

Lewis, L. (1954): Microscopic studies of fetal and mature nail and surrounding soft tissue. *Arch. Derm. Syph. (Chic.)*, *70*, 732.

Lewis, M. G. and Martin, J. A. (1967): Malignant melanoma of the nasal cavity in Ugandian Africans. Relationship of ectopic pigmentation. *Cancer*, *20*, 1699.

Metchnikoff, E. (1901): On the process of hair turning white. *Proc. roy. Soc. B*, *69*, 156.

Miescher, G. (1923) Die Pigmentgenese im Auge. *Arch. mikr. Anat.*, *97*, 326.

Miszkiewicz, B. (1965): Alters- und Geschlechts-Unterschiede der Haarfarbe in Polen. *Homo*, *16*, 49.

Miyamoto, M. and Fitzpatrick, T. B. (1957): On the nature of the pigment in retinal pigment epithelium. *Science*, *126*, 449.

Monash, S. (1932): Normal pigmentation in the nails of the Negro. *Arch. Derm. Syph. (Chic.)*, *25*, 876.

Montgomery, D. W. (1917): A pigmented stripe in the nail. *J. cutan. Dis.*, *35*, 99.

Noble, J. F. and Ferrin, A. (1952): A pigmented naevus of the fingernail matrix. *Arch. Derm. Syph. (Chic.)*, *65*, 49.

Orban, B. (1956): Discolorations of the oral mucous membrane by metallic foreign bodies. *J. Periodont.*, *17*, 55.

Orfanos, C., Ruska, H. and Mahrle, G. (1970): Das weisse Haar alternder Menschen: Über die Feinstruktur der Haare. *Arch. klin. exp. Derm.*, *236*, 395.

Pardo-Costello, V. and Pardo, O. A. (1960): *Diseases of the Nails, 3rd ed.* Charles C. Thomas, Springfield, Ill.

Penev, S. G. (1970: Peribuccal pigmentation as an artifact. *Brit. J. Derm.*, *82*, 40.

Popkin, G. L. (1970): More on nail bands (Letter to the Editor). *New Engl. J. Med.*, *282*, 1216.

Rao, D. C. (1970): Tongue pigmentation in man. *Hum. Hered.*, *20*, 8.

Raut, R. B., Baretto, M. A., Mehta, F. S., Sanjana, M. K. and Shourie, K. L. (1954): Gingival pigmentation: Its incidence amongst the Indian adults. *J. All-India dent. Ass.*, *26*, 1.

Reed, T. E. (1952): Red hair colour as a genetic character. *Ann. Eugen.*, *17*, 115.

Rife, D. C. (1967): The inheritance of red hair. *Acta Genet. med. Roma*, *16*, 342.

Rook, A. (1969): Hair colour in clinical diagnosis. *Irish J. med. Sci.*, *2*, 415.

Samman, P. D. (1965): *The Nails in Disease*, pp. 13–14. William Heinemann Medical Books, Ltd., London.

Scott, E. H. M. (1970): White hair in Bantu. *S. Afr. med. J.*, *44*, 368.

Shelley, W. B., Rawnsley, H. M. and Pillsbury, D. M. (1964): Postirradiation melanonychia. *Arch. Derm.*, *90*, 174.

Singleton, W. R. and Ellis, B. (1964): Inheritance of red hair for six generations. *J. Hered.*, *55*, 261.

Skinner, J. H. (1955): The percentage distribution of Deniker's six European races in male students at the University of Stellenbosch. *Ann. Univ. Stellenbosch*, *31*, Sect. A/2.

Soussi, J. (1964): Blue eyed Africans. *S. Afr. med. J.*, *38*, 20.

Soussi, J. (1965): Incidence of blue eyes in South African Negroes. *S. Afr. J. med. Sci.*, *61*, 243.

Steigmann, S. (1965): The relationship between physiologic pigmentation of the skin and oral mucosa in Yemenite Jews. *Oral Surg.*, *19*, 32.

Sunderland, E. (1956): Hair colour variation in the United Kingdom. *Ann. hum. Genet.*, *20*, 312.

Sunderland, E. (1965): Hair color of the population of Tristan da Cunha. *Nature (Lond.)*, *208*, 412.

Sutton, R. L. (1952): Transverse band pigmentation of fingernails after X-ray therapy. *J. Amer. med. Ass.*, *150*, 210.

Templeton, H. J. (1926): Pigmented stripe in the nail. *Arch. Derm. Syph. (Chic.)*, *14*, 533.

Thomas Jr., H. M. (1933): Pigment in nails during hyperthyroidism. *Bull. Johns Hopk. Hosp.*, *52*, 315.

Thomas Jr., H. M. (1964): Transverse bands in fingernails. *Bull. Johns Hopk. Hosp.*, *115*, 238.

Trotter, M., Duggins, O. H. and Setzler, F. M. (1956): Hair of Australian aborigines (Arnhem Land). *Amer. J. phys. Anthrop.*, *14*, 649.

Van Wyk, C. W. (1970): Mouth pigmentation in a group of healthy South African Bantu. *S. Afr. med. J.*, *44*, 177.

Van Wyk, G. F. (1939): A preliminary account of the physical anthropology of the Cape Coloured people (males). *Ann. Univ. Stellenbosch*, *17*, Sect. A/2.

Volker, J. F. and Kenney Jr., J. A. (1960): The physiology and biochemistry of pigmentation. *J. Periodont.*, *31*, 346.

Walker, A. E. and Stewart, J. J. (1955): Subungual pigmented naevus. *Arch. Derm.*, *71*, 421.

Wassermann, H. P. (1970): Ethnic differences in natural melanoproteins. *Dermatologica (Basel)*, *141*, 44.

Wassermann, H. P. and Heyl, T. (1968): Quantitative data on skin pigmentation in South African races. *S. Afr. med. J.*, *42*, 98.

Yanoff, M. (1969): Pigment spots of the sclera. *Arch. Ophthal.*, *81*, 151.

Yoshiaki, A., Suetaka, T. and Sakuma, I. (1956): A statistical investigation of gingival pigmentation. *Shika Gakuho*, *56*, 93.

Zaias, N. (1963): Embryology of the human nail. *Arch. Derm.*, *87*, 37.

Ziegelmayer, G. (1954): Geschlechtsunterschiede in der Irisbeschaffenheit. *Acta anat. (Basel)*, *21*, 116.

Zigman, S. (1971): Eye lens colour: Formation and function. *Science*, *171*, 807.

Section III

Physiology of ethnic pigmentation

*If we once realize that the colour of an
organism is not an isolated characteristic
forced upon it, as it were, from without,
but may be merely the outward expression
of its constitution, we may surely hope
not only to be delivered from many
laborious hypotheses as to the use of
colour in particular cases, but also may
perhaps learn something of the
physiology of colour.*

M. I. Newbigin (1898): *Colour in Nature.*
John Murray Ltd., London.

Chapter XI

General physiology and biochemistry of pigmentation: Classical concepts

*The racial differences in pigmentation
are physiological and not anatomical.*

Szabo (1959).

From our description of ethnic pigmentation in the preceding Chapters, it follows that ethnic pigmentation is a *quantitative* difference in pigmentation between different races. Apart from the much greater deposition of melanin in the skin of a black man than in the skin of a white man, melanin pigmentation occurring in the nailbed, the oral cavity and the eye, as well as the tendency for the iris and hair of the darker races to be predominantly black, expresses a functionally higher activity of melanogenesis. This is seen especially in whites where Addison's disease tends to pigment those skin appendages and adjacent regions which are normally pigmented in darker races, but not so frequently pigmented in whites. The 2 problems – *why* are some people hyperpigmented (or conversely, hypopigmented), and *how* is this brought about? – suggest an analysis of the normal physiology of pigmentation and its mechanisms of control. The following Chapters aim at such a review. The emphasis, however, will be on the *differences*, rather than the basic similarities, between ethnic groups.

MICROSCOPIC ANATOMY OF ETHNIC PIGMENTATION

Histological aspects

Differences in ethnic pigmentation are due to differences in melanin content. On vertical sections in white skin melanin is found mainly in the basal layer of the epidermis, but in dark-skinned races melanin can be seen in the upper layers of the epidermis and also in phagocytes in the upper dermis. Although epidermal cells up to the stratum corneum contain melanin in all races, this is very marked in dark races. Stratum corneum melanin actually rubs off onto a swab or white paper in very dark individuals.

MELANOCYTES

The melanocyte is a specialized cell containing many yellow to golden-brown pigment granules, which are formed in the cell. This is achieved by tyrosinase synthesized in the cell. This enzyme initiates melanin synthesis and results in melanin formation in melanosomes.

Melanocytes develop from melanoblasts which originate from the neural crest (Dushane, 1943; Rawles, 1940, 1948) and then invade the epidermis, where they can be distinguished from Malpighian or keratinizing cells by their dopa-positivity. In the epidermis they exhibit dendrites; although they are cuboidal epithelial cells in the retina, they become semispherical with blunt pseudopodia on dissociation, and in tissue culture they assume an elongate dendritic form and ultimately present the appearance of fibroblasts or typical skin melanocytes (Trinkaus, 1963). Masson (1948) revived the concept that melanocytes transfer their products into the neighbouring Malpighian cells by cytocrine action, i.e. they 'injected' their melanin into neighbouring cells. Melanocytes form a loosely connected network at the dermo-epidermal interface and because of the dermal papillae orthodox transverse sections give a false impression of the distribution and relationship of melanocytes to keratinocytes.

Melanocytes also occur in the hair follicles associated with the hair matrix and melanin is transferred to these cells as in the case of epidermal cells. Tyrosinase activity in hair melanocytes varies according to the growth cycle of hair (Kukita, 1957).

The epidermis may be separated from the dermis by trypsin or sodium bromide (Medawar, 1941; Szabo, 1955; Starrico and Pinkus, 1957) and the network of melanocytes can be inspected in situ after applying the dopa-technique. This technique was used by Szabo (1954, 1955, 1959) and Starrico and Pinkus (1957), who found that there was no significant racial difference in the distribution of melanocytes. Becker and Zimmermann (1955) and Zimmermann and Becker (1959) determined the number of melanocytes in the Negro foetus.

Distribution and functional activity

Melanocytes were always present in all skin regions investigated, regardless of whether they were exposed to sunlight or covered by clothing (Szabo, 1959).

After exposure to *natural sunlight* the density of melanocytes increased as the amount of melanin in the epidermis increased. Szabo (1967) found no increase in melanocyte density although tyrosinase activity increased 72 hours after irradiation. He concluded that mammalian epidermis is able to increase its melanin content without recourse to an increased density of melanocytes. Under natural conditions, however, the pigmentary process may be combined with mitotic activity of melanocytes.

Several workers suggested that the pigmentation following on ultraviolet radiation is due to an increase in number of functioning melanocytes *and* increased tyrosinase activity (Becker, 1948; Becker et al., 1952; Bischitz and Snell, 1959; Fitzpatrick et al., 1950; Peck, 1930; Quevedo and Grahn, 1958; Quevedo and Smith, 1963; Quevedo et al., 1965; Snell, 1963). Pathak et al. (1965) found no significant increase in the density of melanocyte population in response to a single dose of 300 nm monochromatic irradiation although there were morphological changes indicating increased *functional* activity. Tyrosinase activity was enhanced after 72 hours. *Their conclusion was that melanogenesis is more dependent on the functional activity of melanocytes than on numerical increase of these cells.*

Distribution in body areas

Great differences in the density of melanocytes in various body regions exist (Szabo, 1959). The average of 1560 melanocytes per mm^2 for all body regions shows great variation due to both regional and individual variations. The highest relative density was in the epidermis of the head, the lowest in the trunk. The density of melanocytes in nasal and oral epithelia and in the epidermis of the sole of the foot is intermediate between the density in the epidermis of the head and skin of the body in general. Melanocytes are symmetrically distributed throughout the body and no significant sexual difference could be demonstrated (Szabo, 1959).

'It is also true of the human race that the colour of the skin is not the expression of melanocyte density, but that of the specific color produced by physiologically different melanocytes' (Szabo, 1959).

A notable exception to studies finding no numerical difference in melanocytes of different ethnic groups is that of Mitchell (1968), who found more melanocytes in the epidermis of aborigines than in white Australians.

The relative proportion of melanocytes to Malpighian cells is 4 to 5 Malpighian cells to each melanocyte in the cheek, and about 10 to 12 in the epidermis of the thigh and arm (Szabo, 1959). This information, being of little value to the histopathologist who has to judge the incidence of melanocytes from vertical skin biopsies, was assessed by Cochran (1970) who found that 1 cell in 10 in the basal layer is a melanocyte. The incidence in adults was higher than in children and foetuses, probably decreasing with age. High density areas were again found to be the face, neck and upper limbs, and Cochran (1970) advanced the hypothesis that the high density in these areas may be due to their proximity to the neural crest.

There is a decrease in melanocyte numbers in the aged skin (Fitzpatrick et al., 1965) but this coincides with epidermal atrophy, so that the ratio of melanocytes to keratinocytes remains constant (Frenk and Schellhorn, 1968).

While the melanocyte system, with the exception of the Australian aborigine (Mitchell, 1968), is numerically not different in different races, the difference in its functional activity can be seen and thus constitutes an anatomical difference in epidermal cells.

EPIDERMAL CELLS IN ETHNIC GROUPS

By stripping the skin with adhesive tape single layers of epidermal cells can be obtained (Pinkus, 1951), which can be removed and stained for investigation (Keddie and Sakai, 1965). Epidermal cells contain visible melanin granules sparsely distributed through the cell in whites, and with many intermediate variations in individuals at the darker end of the spectrum of white skin colour. There is a relative increase in the number of granules in the cells from the brown races (e.g. Cape Coloured) to the black races (e.g. Bantu), where the density of

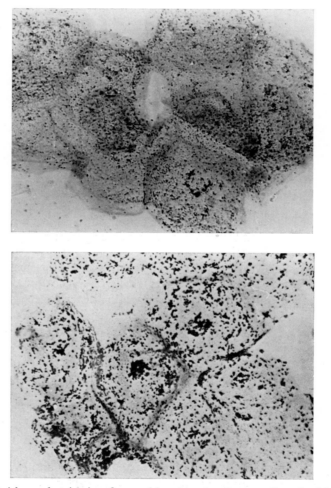

a

b

Fig. 15. *a.* Epidermal stripping from white skin showing small and widely dispersed melanin granules.
    b. Epidermal stripping from Cape Coloured skin. Note larger granules, more densely packed.
    c. Epidermal stripping from Bantu skin. Note size of granules and the tendency to clump together.

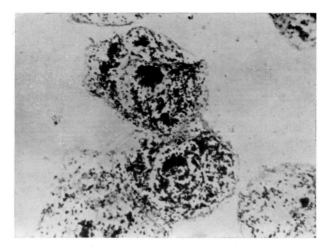

c

granules in the cells is very markedly more than even in the darkest white (Figs. 15*a*, *b* and *c*).

In the epidermis of whites the granules are smaller and usually distributed at random through the cell, but in those cells which contain a larger amount of melanin, a tendency to form clumps in the cell can be seen. In the Bantu the granules are larger than in whites, and darken with ammoniated silver nitrate in about half the time required in white preparations, and often reveal centrally situated clumps of melanin granules, resembling in appearance the nucleus of the cell. When counterstained with Giemsa's stain, and in the deeper layers of the epidermis, such clumps of melanin were frequently associated with nuclei or nuclear remnants. While nuclei or nuclear remnants were of frequent occurrence in the deeper layers (10th–15th strippings) of Bantu skin, they were only rarely seen in whites. Their appearance suggests that:

(1) The melanin granules in the cell are distributed according to metabolically active regions around the nucleus and/or (2) the nucleus is preserved longer when surrounded by melanin accumulations (Wassermann, 1968).

Cytological aspects

Melanocytes are best known in the skin and hair, the leptomeninges (Becker et al., 1952), the choroid and retina of the eye. They probably occur elsewhere in the body as well (see p. 140 et seq.), but little is known of their distribution.

Melanocytes may either retain their melanin ('continent melanocytes'), or may donate granules to neighbouring cells ('secretory melanocytes'). This pigment donation was called 'cytocrine activity' by Masson (1948).

The greater functional cytocrine activity in darker races is evident from the greater amount of melanin secreted into epidermal cells and in the general consequences of such pigment transfer to associated cells as described in the previous section.

Recent evidence suggests that the epidermal cell may be the active component in this transfer instead of the melanocyte, as implied by the cytocrine theory:

Epithelial cells are capable of actively ingesting portions of melanocytes whether or not dendrites are present (Mottaz and Zelickson, 1967; Drochmans, 1961; Prose et al., 1965; Prunieras, 1969; Potter and Medenica, 1968; Klaus, 1969). Following transfer, melanosome packages are digested and the melanin granules dispersed throughout the cytoplasm of keratinocytes (Klaus, 1969).

Studies on cell culture of the epidermis allowed interesting observations on the process of pigment donation in vivo (Cohen and Szabo, 1968) and electron-microscopic studies of melanin phagocytosis by cutaneous vessels in a cellular blue naevus suggest that these cells participate in melanosome degradation (Sato and Kukita, 1969). The differentiation of melanophagocytosis and melanin synthesis is aided by the demonstration of acid phosphatases, an enzyme present in active melanophages but not in melanocytes. At a subcellular level the presence of melanin in lysosomes or in the form of melanosomes, together with the demonstration of lytic or synthetic enzymes, allows the recognition and differentiation of phagocytes and melanocytes (Mishima, 1966).

In in vitro cell cultures of primarily epidermal cells, the phagocytosis of melanin granules and Indian ink particles could be observed (Blois, 1968).

Ultrastructural aspects

Melanin is formed and deposited on cytoplasmic particles in melanocytes. Tyrosinase is bound to these organelles. Briefly, the work of Seiji et al. (1961, 1963) and the related aspects (reviewed by Seiji, 1967; Fitzpatrick et al., 1967; Toda et al., 1968) which led to the morphological and functional concept of the *melanosome*, may be summarized as follows:

Tyrosinase, the melanin-forming enzyme, is synthesized, like other proteins, on the ribosomes and transferred via the endoplasmic reticulum to the Golgi area, where it is incorporated into vesicles (as in the case of other enzymes synthesized in cells: Golgi endoplasmic-reticulum lysosome (GERL) hypothesis). The further development may be divided into Stages I–IV: Stage I melanosomes consist of tyrosinase and a protein matrix; Stage II melanosomes (or premelanosomes) have a fully developed membranous structure but there is no melanization. During Stage III melanin deposition accumulates on the inner membranes until in Stage IV the characteristic periodicity (100Å) of their internal structure (Schroeder, 1969) is completely obscured by the melanin deposition, so as to form a uniformly dense particle. (This terminology is in accordance with that of Toda et al. (1968), but also in current use are the definitions of Fitzpatrick et al. (1966).)

At the ultramicroscopic level, as would be expected from the merging of morphology and function evident in other fields of physiology, the functional differences in ethnic pigmentation find a morphological basis: Epidermal melanocytes in very light whites with blue eyes and red hair have practically no melanosomes in the perikarya. The dendrites contain few or no Stage III and IV melanosomes, and the epidermal cells few melanosomes. Darker whites lack Stage IV melanocytes in the dendrites, although they occur in the epidermal cells. Brown-skinned races (Mongoloids) have many Stage II, III and IV melanosomes in the perikarya of their melanocytes, and blacks (Negroes) have mainly Stage IV melanosomes in this area of their melanocytes (Szabo et al., 1968).

A racial difference also exists in the 'packaging' or arrangement of melanosomes in epidermal cells. In whites and browns (Chinese) Szabo et al. (1969) found that melanosome groups of 2 or more were enclosed by a membrane. In the Negro and also in the Australian aborigine (Mitchell, 1968) the melanosomes are found as single bodies. (The reader is referred to the excellent electron micrograms in the references cited in this section.) Similar racial differences could be seen when functional activity was increased by ultraviolet radiation in the different races studied.

The size of the melanosomes is probably critical in this phenomenon (Wolff and Konrad, 1971).

Epidermal cells may play an active role in the phagocytosis of portions of melanin-laden dendrites of melanocytes (Fitzpatrick and Breathnach, 1963; Mottaz and Zelickson, 1967), and its removal from melanocytes may regulate melanin synthesis in the melanocyte (Hadley and Quevedo, 1967). The free radical acceptor properties of melanin (p. 137) may be involved, if it is assumed that melanosomes are transported to areas where free radicals are generated by metabolic activity (Wassermann, 1967, 1968).

A functional unit may be defined as the morphological complex of structures which perform all the functions of that organ (e.g. the nephron in renal physiology). When the skin is considered as the organ of pigmentation, the concept of the epidermal melanin unit, as conceived by Fitzpatrick and Breathnach (1963), is a most important concept. At the outset, the author must state his personal reservations: (1) He accepts the epidermal melanin unit as the morphological functional unit of skin pigmentation, and suspects a similar relationship to exist between melanocytes and their adjacent cells elsewhere in the body. (2) He believes that this is a model to study the control of pigmentation, but (3) that the functional significance of *melanin* is not necessarily related to this functional unit. It may be likened to the relationship of the nephron to the control of the H^+ ion concentration of the body; it may be part of the homeostatic mechanism but does not constitute the whole of the mechanism.

THE EPIDERMAL MELANIN UNIT

Melanocytes, through their functional activity, fill epidermal cells to varying degrees with their cytocrine activity (although the phagocytic ability or potential of the epidermal cell may be of equal or prime importance) (Fitzpatrick and Breathnach, 1963; Mottaz and Zelickson, 1967; Hadley and Quevedo, 1966, 1967). It is not, however, the admittedly important detail of the *mechanism* of transfer, but the fact that the pigmentation of the skin, visible to the observer, depends on the integrated functional activity of the melanocyte and its constellation of epidermal cells, that allows a systematic physiological approach to pigmentary phenomena. It is in this context that the concept of Fitzpatrick and Breathnach (1963) of an integrated multicellular system of the melanocyte and its related epidermal cells as an 'epidermal melanin unit', is a significant conceptual advance.

The 'physiological' and 'morphological' colour changes of amphibians and reptiles (Waring, 1963) depend on neurogenic, hormonal and physical influences, and this can be studied in the vertebrate epidermal melanin unit (Hadley and Quevedo, 1966, 1967), but little is known about the regulation of the 'epidermal melanin unit' in mammals. The technique for studying mammalian melanocytes in vivo (McGuire, 1966) may, however, be a suitable method for such experimental investigation.

It is known that ethnic pigmentation depends on *genetic factors*. Such genetic factors, however, operate as gene control of specific enzymes (1 gene : 1 enzyme theory).

Hormones influence skin pigmentation profoundly and endocrine influences can thus be expected to influence the epidermal melanin unit. *Chalones* may be defined as inhibitory hormones produced by particular organs which exert homeostatic control on organ function.

Genetic factors in ethnic pigmentation

At the level of the 'epidermal melanin unit' (EMU), genetic factors involved in ethnic pigmentation can at present only be indirectly extrapolated from studies on animals (mice, guinea-pigs). Some 70 genes at 40 loci are known to influence colouration of mice and may be grouped together as:

(*a*) *genes acting through the cellular environment,* which would control the origin, migration and differentiation of melanoblasts, and the type of melanin synthesized in the melanocyte (yellow, brown or black melanosomes);

(*b*) *genes acting within the melanocyte* controlling its morphology, the matrix structure of melanosomes, the tyrosinase activity in melanosomes and the type of melanin synthesized and

(*c*) *genes acting within the epidermal cells,* which may determine not only transfer of melanosomes (if epidermal cells are the active component in transfer) but also the pattern of melanosome distribution in these cells. (Reviews by Billingham and Silvers, 1960; Foster, 1965; Quevedo, 1969).

Tyrosinase in mushrooms occurs in multiple forms (Jolley, 1967; Robb, 1967). In hamster melanoma 2 tyrosinases were found by Pomerantz (1963). It is not known whether such isoenzymes occur and are involved in human ethnic pigmentation. Chen and Chavin (1967) were able to demonstrate a higher tyrosinase activity in the dorsal integument than in the ventral integument of several vertebrates studied, and the highest tyrosinase activity could be found in rats at the age of rapid melanin formation.

Enzyme activities of the glycolytic pathway in melanocytes were assayed by Adachi (1967). Melanoma melanocytes had higher activity than normal melanocytes and this indicates enzyme adaptation in the mammalian melanocyte system.

Adachi (1967) speculated that such adaptation may be controlled by co-factors such as nicotinamide adenine nucleotides and adenine nucleotides. These adaptive changes may result from continuous integration of minor change in activity. In mouse melanomas the amelanotic melanoma possessed almost twice as much enzyme activity as the melanotic melanoma.

Thus far, the only enzyme definitely involved in ethnic pigmentation appears to be *glutathione reductase* (Halprin and Ohkawara, 1966). Circumstantial evidence indicated reduced glutathione as the inhibitor of melanin formation from tyrosine and dopa (Rothman et al., 1946). Halprin and Ohkawara (1966, 1967) found that reduced glutathione was present in vivo in concentrations shown to be inhibitory to in vivo melanin formation. Glutathione reductase activity and reduced glutathione were lower in Negro skin than in white skin. Some evidence indicated that this difference may be due to genetic changes in deoxyribonucleic acid (DNA), resulting in three different glutathione reductase molecules in Negro skin, all of which are different from the Caucasian enzyme (Fig. 16).

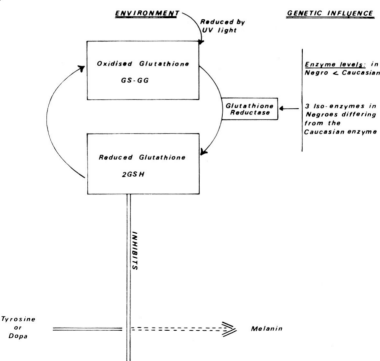

Fig. 16. Diagrammatic summary of the role of glutathione reductase in ethnic pigmentation as proposed by Halprin and Ohkawara (see text). (From data by Halprin and Ohkawara, 1966, *Archives of Dermatology*, *94*, 355.)

Hormonal factors

α-MSH administration leads to gross hyperpigmentation in man with increased melanosomes in epidermal cells, and increased dendricity of melanocytes with increased melanocyte-epidermal cell transfer (Snell, 1967), but the pituitary-adrenal axis, gonads and thyroid influence pigmentation in addition to MSH.

There is, at present, convincing evidence that in Bantu and Negroes, as compared to whites, endocrine differences exist (p. 173 et seq.).

As a homeostatic factor in the control of pigmentation the epidermal and melanocytic chalones (Bullough and Laurence, 1964; Bullough et al., 1967; Bullough, 1970) may maintain the apportioning of epidermal and melanocytic components of the EMU by control of mitotic rates in these cell lines. It cannot, at present, be considered as a major factor in ethnic pigmentation.

Theoretically, because of the negative feedback control of melanogenesis in the melanocyte by epidermal removal of melanosomes, controlling factors may operate on either of the components or on both. If, as suggested (Wassermann, 1967), melanin transfer between cells is determined by a redox potential gradient (melanin as electron acceptor migrating to areas with a high rate of free radical formation) metabolic changes or differences in epidermal cells alone may increase both melanocytic activity and melanosome transfer. Glutathione reductase may operate in this way (Fig. 17).

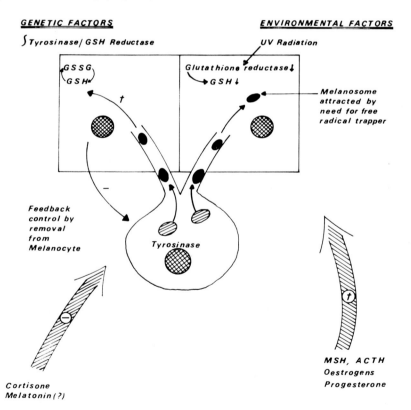

Fig. 17. Control of the epidermal melanin unit by genetic factors (left) which determine rate of free radical formation and melanin migration and (right) environmental influences on this system (theoretical possibilities).

Thus far, the best known local mechanisms of pigmentation were discussed. A further point merits consideration: If melanosome removal controls the melanocytic production of melanosomes by a negative feedback mechanism, a continuous high rate of removal will be required for an increased melanogenesis. Again, theoretically, it must be assumed that a steady state would only be achieved if melanosomes could satisfy a specific demand in the receptor cell (negative feedback). If unimpeded transfer, regardless of demand, existed, an unstable homeostatic system would result (positive feedback or vicious circle).

These considerations would imply:

1. A specific function for melanin in cellular metabolism, which, if satisfied, would inhibit further transfer to epidermal cells.

2. Removal of melanosomes by any other mechanism would increase melanogenesis. This removal could be by (*a*) degradation of melanin to a functionally inactive state or (*b*) by removal of intact melanosomes from melanocytes by other cells in addition to epidermal cells. These mechanisms may exert additional control over EMU.

Melanin can now be considered especially with regard to its functional significance, and its circulation.

REFERENCES

ADACHI, K. (1967): Enzyme activities in mammalian pigment cells. In: *Advances in Biology of Skin, Vol. VIII: The Pigmentary System*, p. 223. Editors: W. Montagna and F. Hu. Pergamon Press, New York, N.Y.

BECKER JR., S. W. (1948): Dermatological investigations of melanin pigmentation. In: *Biology of Melanomas, Vol. IV*, p. 82 (special publications of the New York Academy of Sciences). Editors: R. W. Miner and M. Gordon. New York Academy of Sciences, New York, N.Y.

BECKER JR., S. W., FITZPATRICK, T. B. and MONTGOMERY, H. (1952): Human melanogenesis: cytology and histology of pigment cells (melanodendrocytes) *Arch. Derm. Syph. (Chic.)*, *65*, 511.

BECKER JR., S. W. and ZIMMERMANN, A. A. (1955): Further studies on melanocytes and melanogenesis in the human foetus and newborn. *J. invest. Derm.*, *25*, 103.

BILLINGHAM, R. E. and MEDAWAR, P. B. (1953): A study of the branched cells of the mammalian epidermis with special reference to the fate of their division products. *Phil. Trans. B*, *237*, 151.

BILLINGHAM, R. E. and SILVERS, W. K. (1960): The melanocytes of mammals. *Quart. Rev. Biol.*, *35*, 1.

BISCHITZ, P. G. and SNELL, R. S. (1959): A study of the melanocytes and melanin in the skin of the male guinea-pig. *J. Anat. (Lond.)*, *93*, 233.

BLOIS, M. S. (1968): Phagocytosis of melanin particles by human epidermal cells in vitro. *J. invest. Derm.*, *50*, 336.

BULLOUGH, W. S. (1970): The rejuvenation of the skin. *J. Soc. cosmet. Chem.*, *21*, 503.

BULLOUGH, W. S. and LAURENCE, E. B. (1964): The production of epidermal cells. *Symp. zool. Soc. Lond.*, *12*, 1.

BULLOUGH, W. S., LAURENCE, E. B., IVERSEN, O. H. and ELGJO, K. (1967): The vertebrate epidermal chalone. *Nature (Lond.)*, *214*, 578.

CHEN, Y. M. and CHAVIN, W. (1967): Comparative biochemical aspects of integumental and tumor tyrosinase activity in vertebrate melanogenesis. In: *Advances in Biology of Skin, Vol. VIII: The Pigmentary System*, p. 253. Editors: W. Montagna and F. Hu. Pergamon Press, New York, N.Y.

COCHRAN, A. J. (1970): The incidence of melanocytes in normal human skin. *J. invest. Derm.*, *55*, 65.

COHEN, J. and SZABO, G. (1968): Study of pigment donation in vitro. *Exp. Cell Res.*, *50*, 418.

DEOL, M. S. (1970): The relationship between abnormalities of pigmentation and of the inner ear. *Proc. roy. Soc. Lond. Ser. A*, *175*, 201.

DROCHMANS, P. (1961): Étude au microscope électronique du mécanisme de la pigmentation mélanique: la distribution des grains de mélanine aux cellules malpighiennes. *Path. et Biol.*, *9*, 947.

DUSHANE, G. (1943): The embryology of vertebrate pigment cells. I. Amphibia. *Quart. Rev. Biol.*, *18*, 108.

FITZPATRICK, T. B., BECKER JR., S. W., LERNER, A. B. and MONTGOMERY, H. (1950): Tyrosinase in human skin: demonstration of its presence and its role in human melanin formation. *Science*, *112*, 223.

FITZPATRICK, T. B. and BREATHNACH, A. S. (1963): Das epidermale Melanin-Einheit-System. *Derm. Wschr.*, *147*, 481.

FITZPATRICK, T. B., MIYAMOTO, M. and ISHIKAWA, K. (1967): The evolution of concepts of melanin biology. In: *Advances in Biology of Skin, Vol. VIII: The Pigmentary System*, p. 1. Editors: W. Montagna and F. Hu. Pergamon Press, Oxford.

FITZPATRICK, T. B., QUEVEDO, W. C., LEVENE, A., McGOVERN, V. J., MISHIMA, Y. and OETTLÉ, A. G. (1966): Terminology of vertebrate melanin-containing cells: a report of the Nomenclature Committee of the 6th International Pigment Cell Conference. In: *Structure and Control of the Melanocyte*, p. 1. Editors: G. Della Porta and O. Mühlbock. Springer-Verlag, Berlin.

FITZPATRICK, T. B., SZABO, G. and MITCHELL, R. (1965): Age changes in the human melanocyte system. In: *Advances in Biology of Skin, Vol. VI: Aging*, p. 35. Editor: W. Montagna. Pergamon Press, Oxford.

FOSTER, M. (1965): Mammalian pigment genetics. *Advanc. Genet.*, *13*, 311.

FRENK, E. and SCHELLHORN, J. P. (1968): Zur Morphologie der epidermalen Melanin Einheit. *Dermatologica (Basel)*, *139*, 271.

HADLEY, MacE. and QUEVEDO JR., W. C. (1966): Vertebrate epidermal melanin unit. *Nature (Lond.)*, *209*, 1334.

HADLEY, MacE. and QUEVEDO JR., W. C. (1967): The role of epidermal melanocytes in adaptive color changes in amphibians. In: *Advances in Biology of Skin, Vol. VIII: The Pigmentary System*, p. 337. Editors: W. Montagna and F. Hu. Pergamon Press, New York, N.Y.

HALPRIN, K. M., and OHKAWARA, A. (1966): Glutathione and human pigmentation. *Arch. Derm.*, *94*, 355.

HALPRIN, K. M. and OHKAWARA, A. (1967): The measurement of glutathione in human epidermis using glutathione reductase. *J. Invest. Derm.*, *48*, 149.

HALPRIN, K. M. and OHKAWARA, A. (1967): Human pigmentation: The role of glutathione. In: *Advances in Biology of Skin, Vol. VIII: The Pigmentary System*, p. 241. Editors: W. Montagna and F. Hu. Pergamon Press, New York, N.Y.

JOLLEY, R. L. (1967): The tyrosinase isozymes. In *Advances in Biology of Skin, Vol. VIII: The Pigmentary System*, p. 269. Editors: W. Montagna and F. Hu. Pergamon Press, New York, N.Y.

KEDDIE, F. and SAKAI, D. (1965): Morphology of the horny cells of the superficial stratum corneum: Cell membranes and melanin granules. *J. invest. Derm.*, *44*, 135.

KLAUS, S. N. (1969): Post-transfer digestion of melanosome complexes and saltatory movement of melanin granules within mammalian epidermal cells. *J invest.Derm.*, *53*, 440.

KUKITA, A. (1957): Changes in tyrosinase activity during melanocyte proliferation. *J. invest. Derm.*, *28*, 273.

MASSON, P. (1948): Pigment cells in man. In: *Biology of Melanomas, Vol. IV*, p. 15 (special publications of the New York Academy of Sciences). Editors: R. W. Miner and M. Gordon. New York Academy of Sciences, New York, N.Y.

McGUIRE, J. S. (1966): Examination of mammalian melanocytes in vivo: A new approach. *J. invest. Derm.*, *46*, 311.

MEDAWAR, P. B. (1941): Sheets of pure epidermal epithelium from human skin. *Nature (Lond.)*, *148*, 783.

MISHIMA, Y. (1966): Cellular and subcellular differentiation of melanin phagocytosis and synthesis by lysosomal and melanosomal activity. *J. invest. Derm.*, *46*, 70.

MITCHELL, R. E. (1968): The skin of the Australian aborigine; a light and electron-microscopical study. *Aust. J. Derm.*, *9*, 314.

MIYAMOTO, M. and FITZPATRICK, T. B. (1957): On the nature of the pigment in retinal pigment epithelium. *Science*, *126*, 449.

MOTTAZ, J. H. and ZELICKSON, A. S. (1967): Melanin transfer; a possible phagocytic process. *J. invest. Derm.*, *49*, 605.

PATHAK, M. A., SINESI, S. J. and SZABO, G. (1965): The effect of a single dose of ultraviolet radiation on epidermal melanocytes. *J. invest. Derm.*, *45*, 520.

PECK, S. M. (1930): Pigment (melanin) studies of the human skin after application of thorium X. With special reference to the origin and function of dendritic cells. *Arch. Derm. Syph. (Chic.)*, *21*, 916.

PINKUS, H. (1951): Examination of the epidermis by the strip method of removing horny layers. *J. invest. Derm.*, *16*, 383.

POMERANTZ, S. H. (1963): Separation, purification and properties of two tyrosinases from hamster melanoma. *J. biol. Chem.*, *238*, 2351.

POTTER, B. and MEDENICA, M. (1968): Ultramicroscopic phagocytosis of synthetic melanin by epidermal cells in vivo. *J. invest. Derm.*, *51*, 300.

PROSE, P. H., SEDLIS, E. and BIGELOW, M. (1965): The demonstration of lysosomes in the diseased skin of infants with infantile eczema. *J. invest. Derm.*, *45*, 448.

PRUNIERAS, M. (1969): Interactions between keratinocytes and dendritic cells. *J. invest. Derm.*, *52*, 1.

QUEVEDO, W. C. (1969): Genetics of mammalian pigmentation. In: *The Biologic Effects of Ultraviolet Radiation (with Emphasis on the Skin)*, p. 315. Editor: F. Urbach. Pergamon Press, London.

QUEVEDO, W. C. and GRAHN, D. (1958): Effect of daily gamma-irradiation on the pigmentation of mice. *Radiat. Res.*, *8*, 254.

QUEVEDO, W. C. and SMITH, J. A. (1963): Studies on radiation induced tanning of the skin. *Ann. N.Y. Acad. Sci.*, *100*, 364.

QUEVEDO, W. C., SZABO, G., VIRKS, J. and SINESI, S. J. (1965): Melanocyte populations in UV-irradiated human skin. *J. invest. Derm.*, *45*, 295.

RAWLES, M. E. (1940): The development of melanophores from embryonic mouse tissues grown in the coelom of chick embryos. *Proc. nat. Acad. Sci. (Wash.)*, *26*, 673.

RAWLES, M. E. (1948): Origin of melanophores and their role in development of color patterns in vertebrates. *Physiol. Rev.*, *28*, 383.

ROBB, D. A. (1967): Concerning the heterogeneity of tyrosinase. In: *Advances in Biology of Skin, Vol. III: The Pigmentary System*, p. 283. Editors: W. Montagna and F. Hu. Pergamon Press, New York, N.Y.

ROTHMAN, S., KRYSA, H. F. and SMILJANIC, A. M. (1946): Inhibitory action of human epidermis on melanin formation. *Proc. Soc. exp. Biol. Med. (N.Y.)*, *62*, 208.

SATO, S. and KUKITA, A. (1969): Electron-microscopic study of melanin phagocytosis by cutaneous vessels in cellular blue nevus. *J. invest. Derm.*, *52*, 528.

SCHROEDER, H. E. (1969): Melanin containing organelles in cells of the human gingiva. I. Epithelial melanocytes. *J. Periodont. Res.*, *4*, 1.

SEIJI, M. (1967): Subcellular particles and melanin formation in melanocytes. In: *Advances in Biology of Skin, Vol. VIII: The Pigmentary System*, p. 189. Editors: W. Montagna and F. Hu. Pergamon Press, New York, N.Y.

SEIJI, M., FITZPATRICK, T. B. and BIRBECK, M. S. C. (1961): The melanosome: a distinctive subcellular particle of mammalian melanocytes and the site of melanogenesis. *J. invest. Derm.*, *36*, 243.

SEIJI, M., SHIMAO, K., BIRBECK, M. S. C. and FITZPATRICK, T. B. (1963): Subcellular localization of melanin biosynthesis. *Ann. N.Y. Acad. Sci.*, *100*, 497.

SNELL, R. S. (1963): The effect of ultraviolet irradiation melanogenesis. *J. invest. Derm.*, *40*, 127.

SNELL, R. S. (1967): Hormonal control of pigmentation in man and other animals. In: *Advances in Biology of Skin, Vol. VIII: The Pigmentary System*, p. 447. Editors: W. Montagna and F. Hu. Pergamon Press, New York, N.Y.

STARRICO, R. J. and PINKUS, H. (1957): Quantitative and qualitative data on the pigment cells of adult human epidermis. *J. invest. Derm.*, *28*, 33.

SZABO, G. (1954): The number of melanocytes in human epidermis. *Brit. med. J.*, *1*, 1016.

SZABO, G. (1955): A modification of the technique of 'skin splitting' with trypsin. *J. Path. Bact.*, *70*, 545.

SZABO, G. (1959): Quantitative histological investigations on the melanocyte system of the human epidermis. In: *Pigment Cell Biology*, p. 99. Editor: M. Gordon. Academic Press, New York, N.Y.

SZABO, G. (1967): Photobiology of melanogenesis: Cytological aspects with special reference to differences in racial coloration. In: *Advances in Biology of Skin, Vol. VIII: The Pigmentary System*, p. 370, Editors: W. Montagna and F. Hu. Pergamon Press, Oxford.

SZABO, G., GERALD, A. B., PATHAK, M. A. and FITZPATRICK, T. B. (1968): Racial differences in human pigmentation on the ultrastructural level. *J. cell. Biol.*, *39/2*, Part 2, 132.

SZABO, G., GERALD, A. B., PATHAK, M. A. and FITZPATRICK, T. B. (1969): Racial differences in the fate of melanosomes in human epidermis. *Nature (Lond.)*, *222*, 1081.

TODA, K., HORI, Y. and FITZPATRICK, T. B. (1968): Isolation of the intermediate 'vesicles' during ontogeny of melanosomes in embryonic chick retinal pigment epithelium. *Fed. Proc.*, *27*, 722.

TRINKAUS, J. P. (1963): Behavior of dissociated retinal pigment cells in heterotypic cell aggregates. *Ann. N.Y. Acad. Sci.*, *100*, 413.

WARING, H. (1963): *Color Change Mechanisms of Cold-Blooded Vertebrates*. Academic Press, New York, N.Y.

WASSERMANN, H. P. (1967): Extension of the concept 'vertebrate epidermal melanin unit' to embrace visceral pigmentation and leucocytic melanin transport. *Nature (Lond.)*, *213*, 282.

WASSERMANN, H. P. (1968): Phenothiazines and leucocytic melanin transport. *Aggressologie*, *9*, 241.

WOLFF, K. and KONRAD, K. (1971): Melanin pigmentation: an in vivo model for studies of melanosome kinetics within keratinocytes. *Science*, *174*, 1034.

ZIMMERMANN, A. A. and BECKER JR., S. W. (1959): Precursors of epidermal melanocytes in the Negro foetus. In: *Pigment Cell Biology*, p. 159. Editor: M. Gordon. Academic Press, New York, N.Y.

Chapter XII

Melanins: cutaneous and extracutaneous

Melanins are an ill-defined class of pigments. They are widely distributed throughout the animal and plant kingdom but their biological function is obscure.

Detailed reviews on the structure of melanin may be found in papers by Mason (1967), Robson and Swan (1966), Nicolaus (1962), Hempel and Männl (1966), Blois (1967), Duchon et al. (1968) and Swan (1973).

Melanocytes are specialized cells containing tyrosinase, and they produce melanin. Raper (1928) and colleagues studied plant tyrosinases and established a metabolic pathway from tyrosine to melanin, which was subsequently modified by Mason (1948). This is known as the Raper-Mason scheme (Fig. 18). Swan (1963) has shown, with labelled precursors, that this may be an oversimplified scheme. Mason (1967) coined the terms *homopolymer* and *poikilopolymer*. According to his concept (and the classical Raper-Mason scheme) melanin is a regular polymer involving a single type of subunit (indole 5,6-quinone) joined by a single type of linkage. The 'poikilopolymer' concept is supported by analytical (Nicolaus and Piatelli, 1965) and physical (Blois et al., 1964) data which suggest that melanins are random polymeric products, i.e. the subunits may consist of dopaquinone, indole 5,6-quinone and indole 5,6-quinone 2-carboxylic acid as monomers (Hempel, 1966). The 'homopolymer' and 'poikilopolymer' views are summarized in Figure 18.

In humans there is conclusive evidence, discussed by Fitzpatrick et al. (1967), that tyrosine is the precursor, and tyrosinase the enzyme, responsible for melanin formation in *melanocytes*. There is, however, no conclusive evidence that the melanocyte is the sole site of melanin formation, nor for the assertion that melanin is formed *only* by melanocytes. This will be discussed subsequently.

Types of melanin

1. EUMELANIN

The Raper-Mason scheme, or its modification for the 'poikilopolymer', probably applies to the melanin formed in melanosomes by melanocytes in man and called eumelanin, to differentiate it from other melanins also formed in man. These melanins are black melanins (*synonym*: allomelanin).

2. PHAEOMELANIN

Both eumelanin and phaeomelanin are products of melanocyte activity, but while they share a common pathway up to the dopaquinone stage, the phaeomelanin pathway then deviates to form 2 isomers of cysteinyldopa (5-S and 2-S) which is oxidized by way of intermediates to phaeomelanin (see Fig. 18). This product differs from eumelanin in the following aspects:

    a. It is soluble in dilute alkali.

    b. Its melanosomes are spherical instead of ellipsoidal as in the case of eumelanin (Parakkal, 1967).

    c. In mice, the genetic loci for its production are different from that of eumelanin.

    d. The colour is yellow to red.

(Prota and Nicolaus, 1967; Prota et al., 1968).

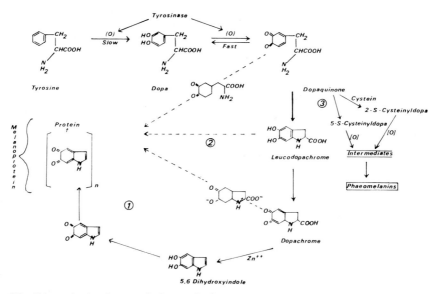

Fig. 18. *Biosynthesis of eu- and phaeomelanin*
    Summary of synthesis of melanins:
    1. Classical Raper-Mason scheme (solid arrows) leading to a homopolymer.
    2. Modified scheme (dotted arrows) leading to a poikilopolymer.
    3. Possible pathway (Prota et al., 1968) of biosynthesis of phaeomelanin.

    This view differs from that of Flesch (1968) who maintained that the iron-containing pigment trichosiderin was the cause of red hair and feathers, and that 2 coexisting but independent pathways could be assumed for red and black pigments.

3. RHEOMELANIN

The transformation of epinephrine, adrenochrome and adrenolutin into plasma-soluble melanins during incubation with human blood plasma at 37°C for 24 hours, was demonstrated by Hegedus and Altschule (1967, 1968). The name was decided on because these melanins were plasma-soluble and brown in colour. They suggested that rheomelanin may be a soluble transport form of melanin which differs from the more familiar deposit forms. This finding indicates that the indole pathway of epinephrine metabolism is available in the plasma of man, since the plasma lacks catecholamine *o*-methyltransferase. All the plasma rheomelanin solutions show the presence of free radicals (Hegedus and Altschule, 1970).

4. NEUROMELANIN

While melanin is known to be formed by melanocytes, and the subcellular morphology of melanogenesis is virtually known, the absence of melanocytes in the central nervous system (except in the meninges) would suggest that neuromelanin is not produced by melanocytes (Duchon et al., 1968). Electron-microscopic studies (Duffy and Tennyson, 1965; Moses et al., 1966) indicate that the neuromelanin granule has a structure more like the lipofuscin granule than the cutaneous melanosome. Moreover, Moses et al. (1966) demonstrated that diamine silver reduction by neuromelanin was limited to a dark, focal and presumably intragranular melanin component. Pakkenberg (1966) was not able to differentiate between melanin, neuromelanin and lipofuscin by microspectrophotometry.

Human and monkey neurons bearing neuromelanin are topographically homologous to rat neurons with high concentrations of the catechol derivatives dopamine and norepinephrine (Barden, 1969). Melanized lipofuscin exhibited the properties of unbleached neuromelanin.

Neuromelanin invested with ferrous sulphide could only be pseudoperoxidatively melanized with dopa or dopamine, if invested with cupric sulphide. Neuromelanin could be further melanized with dopamine after pretreatment with hydrogen sulphide (Barden, 1969). A negative dopa reaction for tyrosinase and positive reactions for the lysosomal hydrolases, acid phosphatases and non-specific esterases were found. Barden (1969) concludes that neuromelanin may be a melanized lipofuscin and discusses the lysosomal genesis of neuromelanin.

Van Woert et al. (1967) demonstrated that lipofuscin, which is synthesized in lysosomes, contains a melanin component, and more recently (1971) they showed that compounds which labilize biological membranes, increase tyrosinase activity in melanoma and new-born mouse skin. They could confirm alteration of the outer melanosomal membrane by digitonin and chlorpromazine, both of which activate tyrosinase activity in melanosomes. Seiji and Iwashita (1965) discovered that melanosomes contained acid phosphatase, the enzyme thought to be localized specifically in lysosomes.

Melanin may also be formed from adrenalin, serotonin, tryptamine and dopamine, and all these melanins have in common free radical signals in their electron spin resonance (esr) spectra (Van Woert et al., 1967).

Thus, neuromelanin is apparently a true melanin according to existing evidence, but the cellular mechanisms for its production are unknown. It is probably formed from dopamine (Van der Wende and Spoerlein, 1963; Van der Wende, 1964), or is the end-product of a tyrosine pathway which produces catecholamines, at least where the hydroxylation of tyrosine is mediated by the enzyme *tyrosine hydroxylase* (Nagatsu et al., 1964; Victor and Bazelon, 1966) and not by the aerobic oxidase, *tyrosinase*. There is a decrease in melanin granules in the cells of the substantia nigra in parkinsonism (see further on p. 254). In patients with parkinsonism, who failed to respond to L-dopa therapy, Birkmayer (1970) found no melanin in the substantia nigra, probably because of the severity of the defect involved in their parkinsonism.

5. LIPOFUSCIN

Apart from Van Woert's statement (1967) that lipofuscin may be a misnomer for a lipomelanin, the position of lipofuscins in pigment chemistry is at present sufficiently uncertain to have to refer at least to the extensive review of Strehler (1964) for a detailed discussion of the histochemistry and ultrastructure of this so-called 'age pigment'. Lipofuscin exhibits enzymatic activities and in isolated particles direct confirmation of the presence of proteins could be found. Chromatography of isolated pigment gave evidence of a number of different classes of lipid components and explains the multiple lipid stainability of lipofuscin in tissue sections.

Strehler (1964) considers the 4 currently popular hypotheses which attempt to explain the origin of lipofuscins, namely:

  a. their possible derivation from the breakdown of mitochondria,
  b. that they may represent secretory bodies formed in the vicinity of the Golgi apparatus,
  c. that they represent the active and inactive remains of lysosomes, and
  d. that they may represent a product of the endoplasmic reticulum.

The pigment moiety appears to be melanin (Siebert et al., 1962; Van Woert et al., 1967), but the isolated granules also contain haems (Björkerud, 1964). Further work is necessary to ascertain what happens to melanosomes entrapped in lysosomes. Are they degraded perhaps and the pigment attached to a lipid-protein substructure? There is increasing evidence that lipofuscin accumulation is not necessarily dependent on aging (Graham, 1970) and it has been demonstrated in liver cells of new-born human infants (Goldfischer and Bernstein, 1969).

6. OCHRONOTIC PIGMENT

In alkaptonuria the inherited deficiency of homogentisic acid oxidase leads to accumulation of homogentisic acid, which leads to dark urine and diffuse pigmentation of connective tissue. Ochronotic pigment cannot be differentiated from melanin by staining methods. Presumably it is a polymer of homogentisic acid of unknown chemical structure, but it is similar to melanin in the following properties: (*a*) Both are bleached by hydrogen peroxide, (*b*) both are soluble in alkali and (*c*) relatively insoluble in hydrochloric acid (O'Brien et al., 1963). Fuchs (1968) was unable to differentiate between dopa polymers and homogentisic-acid polymers. In a case of ochronosis rod-like clear complexes as well as striped pigment granules were found on electron microscopy.

7. MELANOID

The term 'melanoid' should be discarded as obsolete in view of present knowledge. What Edwards and Duntley (1939) described as melanoid is, in retrospect, melanin. What they described as melanin was in fact premelanosomes. For a fuller discussion, see Blair and Lewis (1970).

Identification and properties of melanin

There are no tests which are specific for this somewhat ill-defined class of pigments. Melanins are characterized by extreme stability to chemical reagents and identification rests on a number of different types of observations. The pigments were named for their colour, but all dark pigments are not necessarily melanin. Frequently, however, dark insoluble pigments are referred to as melanin, regardless of their chemistry. The histochemistry of pigments yields little information as far as definitive identification is concerned. It is useful to differentiate between iron-containing (e.g. haemosiderin) and non-iron-containing pigments, but the differentiation from lipofuscin is more uncertain. Pearse (1960) deleted the Chapter on pigments from the last edition (1970) of his textbook of histochemistry. At its best, in our experience, histochemistry allows the conclusion that a pigment is a 'melanin-like pigment'. Optical spectroscopy shows no specific absorption bands in the near ultraviolet or visible spectrum. In the far infrared there are distinctive absorption bands (Blois, 1966) and the infrared spectra of melanins from different sources and of different types are similar in appearance, although there may be some differences in detail (Hackman and Goldberg, 1971).

On alkali fusion eumelanins yield hydroxyindoles and allomelanins give catechol derivatives. Microchemical methods were recently described for the detection of melanin in milligram amounts (Hackman and Goldberg, 1971) and this should be a useful adjunct to a more definitive identification of melanin in unusual sites. Since Commoner et al. (1954) first showed that melanins could be studied by electron spin-resonance (esr) spectroscopy, it was discovered that all melanins are paramagnetic because they contain unpaired electrons within their molecules. This is true for natural and synthetic melanins. The esr spectra, while defining a common property, cannot distinguish between chemically different polymers, e.g. polymers deriving from catechol or dopa (Blois, 1966).

Commoner et al. (1954) presented evidence that the esr signals in tissues were meaningful in the sense that they appeared to be related to metabolism. All tissues that contain melanin yield an esr signal, due, in fact, to the melanin content. The unpaired electron system in melanin is very stable. Daniels (1959) suggested that melanins may protect against radiation damage by acting as a trap for free electrons. 'It is possible that melanin, in a variety of tissues, may act as a similar protective device by serving as a trap for otherwise harmful free radicals of different origins' (Isenberg, 1964).

To develop an identification method employing immunofluorescent techniques, we attempted to produce antibodies against melanin in rabbits. Melanin extracted from human hair and from baboon eyes was used (the latter obtained without chemical manipulation, i.e. the pigment granules were freed after lysis in distilled water only). Subcutaneous melanin was injected with and without Freund's adjuvant and challenged subsequently by intravenous melanin. No antibodies could be demonstrated after 3 months with either precipitation tests or agar gel (Ouchterlony) plates, and no significant change in serum proteins could be demonstrated (Wassermann and Van der Walt, 1973). Similar negative findings were reported by Blois (1965) who suggests that, as no 2 melanin molecules look exactly alike, melanin cannot be identified by the reticuloendothelial system for the formation of antibodies.

Ethnic differences in natural melanoproteins

Extraction of melanoproteins from the pooled hair of a large number of individuals from 4 ethnic groups yielded decreasing amounts of melanoprotein for Bantu, Indian, Cape Coloured and white individuals. In view of the unknown chemical structure of melanin the differences found in organic and inorganic constituents (Table V) cannot be explained at present (Wassermann, 1970a). It may, however, be genetically determined, as in the case of the morphological differences in melanosomes of varous ethnic groups, and their mode of transfer to epidermal cells (Mitchell, 1968; Szabo et al., 1969).

Metal ions and melanin interact by ion exchange and the role of protein in the metal binding is small (Bruenger et al., 1967). It is possible that differences in metal content in the melanoproteins of the various ethnic groups may be related to this interaction.

Table V

Elemental composition of melanoprotein in various ethnic groups

	Carbon (%)	Hydrogen (%)	Nitrogen (%)	Sulphur (%)	Manganese (ppm)	Copper (ppm)	Iron (ppm)
1. Bantu	43.71	4.41	9.74	1.93	6.9	29.8	992
2. Indian	50.14	5.09	11.20	2.93	7.0	50.7	332
3. Cape Coloured	45.43	3.69	9.37	3.02	10.5	334.0	1721
4. Caucasian	47.13	4.19	10.74	3.20	14.0	203.0	941
5. Japanese	51.6	6.5	11.1	1.6	>6.0	139.0	

1–4: From Wassermann, 1970a, *Dermatologica (Basel)*, 141, 44.
   5: From Bolt, 1967, *Life Sciences*, 6, 1277.

Functional activity of melanin(s)

If physiological interest centres around visible (or dermatological) pigment it might be useful to differentiate melanins as eumelanin and phaeomelanin, and to consider neuromelanin and rheomelanin as separate substances.

Melanocytes may not be the only cells that produce melanin. The mast cell has at least a very convincing claim (see p. 144). Wherever it is formed, and by whatever cell type involved, whether it is formed from tyrosine and dopa by tyrosinase, or from primary amines by tyrosine hydroxylase, the final product is a pigment with stable free radical properties.

The skin, in areas with high ultraviolet radiation which generates harmful free radicals in the skin (Pathak, 1967), is protected by this free radical acceptor. The free radical donor which benefits schizophrenic patients, chlorpromazine (CPZ), increases melanogenesis (as a rare side-effect) and may cause extra-pyramidal symptoms as a side-effect. Furthermore, depigmentation of the substantia nigra is the most constant finding in Parkinson's disease and this con-dition benefits by L-dopa therapy (see p. 244). Central to these clinical con-siderations stands melanin, with only 1 known property which may influence biochemical reactions: its paramagnetic property. Szent-Györgyi (1967, 1968) points out 2 stagnant areas of biochemistry: the molecular mechanisms of energy transformation and of hormonal activity. In medicine, according to him, cancer and schizophrenia are similar stagnant fields. 'This suggests that some important factor has been overlooked. Electronic mobility may be this factor, and charge transfer could mediate the electron transfer between molecules' (Szent-Györgyi, 1967).

As previously discussed (Wassermann, 1970*b*), melanin should not be so narrowly defined in chemical-morphological terms that its clinical physiology is obscured.

Except in the case of neuromelanin, accounts of the physiology of melanin pigmentation, thus far, make no mention of melanin occurring elsewhere than in the skin and hair. We may briefly consider what evidence for extra-cutaneous melanin exists, and then try to embrace this wider distribution of melanin within our conceptual knowledge of its circulation and control mecha-nisms. Such knowledge as may be obtained would, in man, naturally be found in autopsy studies in diseased conditions. The tendency to label any internal pigment, which does not appear to be haemosiderin, as lipofuscin, is well known among pathologists. This section will have served a desirable function if it induces more critical analyses of any internal pigment discovered in autopsy studies than is generally performed on routine material at present.

EXTRACUTANEOUS MELANIN

The skin and its appendages are well known for the occurrence of melanocytes and melanin pigment. Melanin pigment occurs in many internal organs, and in contrast to the commonly held view that 'melanocytes are the dermatologist's cells' it is a fact that most vertebrates do have melanocytes widely distributed throughout their various tissues, and specifically in mammals, melanocytes have also been described in tissues other than the skin (Billingham and Silvers, 1960; Nichols and Reams, 1960; Reams, 1963).

Authors reporting on extracutaneous melanin frequently quote Willis (1967): 'Melanoblasts are not cells of a specific type, but are of as many and diverse kinds as there are different tissues capable of producing melanin.'

This statement can be discussed from 3 factual bases:

1. It is possible that melanocytes, in their migration from the neural crest, may occasionally be 'trapped' or become ectopically stranded in tissues other than the skin. It is known that they occasionally develop into primary melanomas in such organs.

2. Consideration should, however, also be given to the second possibility in Willis's statement: 'different tissues capable of producing melanin'. This was recently demonstrated for mast cells.

3. A further possibility, the subject of the most popular debate at the turn of the century, is that melanocytic melanin may be transported elsewhere. This was never disproved, but was simply displaced by the convincing evidence for the derivation of melanocytes from the neural crest.

Extracutaneous melanocytic melanin

OVARIAN TERATOMAS IN THE NEGRO AND BANTU

Lewis (1968) states that melanin pigment must have been observed in the basal layer of the epidermis in the 'skin of dermoid cysts of the ovary by numerous pathologists working amongst Negro peoples, but little reference is made to this in standard textbooks of pathology and gynaecology.'

In his study of the melanin-pigmented components in ovarian teratomas of 80 operative specimens from Ugandan Bantu women, Lewis (1968) found that most of the sites in which melanin-containing cells were present were those sites where adults normally exhibit pigment, i.e. ocular epithelium, meninges and skin. Nevertheless, dendritic pigment cells could be demonstrated in ciliated columnar epithelium resembling respiratory epithelium. The presence of pigment in these cysts is a reflection of the genetically determined pigmentation of Negro races, although pigmented 'skin' in non-Negro teratomas was reported (Lubarsh, 1932). References are given to reports on malignant melanomas originating in ovarian teratomas (Lewis, 1968).

MELANOCYTES IN INTERNAL ORGANS

Oesophagus

Typical dendritic cells with melanin granules were reported in melanosis of the oesophagus (De la Pava et al., 1963).

Prostate

Infrequent reports on melanin in the prostate (Goldman, 1968; Nigogosyan et al., 1963; Simard et al., 1964) were followed up by a study of 330 prostate glands obtained at autopsy (Guillan and Zelman, 1970). In 2 prostates pigmented melanocytes with small elongated dendritic processes were found in the parenchyma. In 1 gland they were in close association with melanin-containing epithelium. Epithelial cells with melanin were found in 13 prostates (4%), and the distribution of the granules was mostly in the basal portions of the cells, but Goldman (1968) found a perinuclear distribution and also a diffuse scattering of pigment in some cells.

Leptomeninges

In the Ugandan Bantu, there was a direct relationship between the depth of pigmentation of the leptomeninges and that of the skin. This would suggest that similar factors operate in the control of melanocytic function in the two sites (Lewis, 1969).

PRIMARY MELANOMAS IN INTERNAL ORGANS

The following section is not presented as an exhaustive review of all reported cases of primary extracutaneous melanomata but rather to indicate some of the various organ systems in which such melanomas were reported.

Nasal cavity and oral tissues

The occurrence of melanocytes in the nasal cavity and oral tissues has been described. Malignant melanomas in the nasal cavity of whites (Harrison, 1968) and Bantu (Lewis and Martin, 1967) are not, therefore, unexpected findings. Primary melanomas were found as primary tumours of the parotid gland (Greene and Bernier, 1961). Oral, nasal and pharyngeal primary melanomas are said to be responsible for 2% of all malignant melanomas. Most of them occurred in the oral cavity, but Mesara and Burton (1968) consider that the approximately 1% which occur in the nasal cavity and sinuses are clinically important because they present as local growths with recurrences for an average of 3 years before they disseminate more widely.

Respiratory system

Upper respiratory tract. Among the non-epidermoid cancers of the *larynx* described by Cady et al. (1968) 4 of the 31 were primary malignant melanomas. In 1964 Pantazapoulos reported a primary laryngeal melanoma and stated that only 7 cases were described at that time.

Lower respiratory tract. Setting rigorous criteria of no past history of excision or of fulguration of a lesion of the skin or mucous membrane, no demonstrable tumour elsewhere, and histological evidence of junctional change with dropping off or nesting of malignant cells with melanin below the bronchial epithelium, and invasion of bronchial epithelium by melanoma cells where the epithelium is not ulcerated, Allen and Drash (1968) meet such criteria when reporting a *primary malignant melanoma of the lung*. Reid and Mehta (1966) and Salm (1963) also described primary melanoma of the lower respiratory tract.

Gastrointestinal tract

A malignant melanoma of the *oesophagus* in a 7-year-old boy, with no autopsy evidence of a primary elsewhere in the body (excepting the eyes), was described by Basque et al. (1970).

Jones (1961) reported a malignant primary melanoma of the gallbladder, while a histologically proven case with cervical metastasis and 14½ year survival was reported by Walsh (1956).

A review of gastrointestinal melanoma was made by Willbanks and Fogelman (1970). Usually metastatic to small intestine (58%), colon (22%), and stomach (26%) as reported by Das Gupta and Brasfield (1964), they also refer to 3 reports on probable primary melanomas. In these instances no primary could be demonstrated and the diagnosis was thus made by exclusion rather than direct evidence.

Genitourinary tract

In the male, blue naevi of the prostate were reported (Nigogosyan et al., 1963; Simard et al., 1964), but apparently only 1 probably malignant melanoma (Berry and Reese, 1953).

Gillenwater and Burrows (1968) reported on urethral melanoma in a white female, and from the literature they found 25 cases reported up to 1967. Ariel (1961) reported on a malignant melanoma of the vagina.

Central nervous system

Malignant melanomata as primary meningeal tumours have been described (Forbes and Maloney, 1950; Gibson et al., 1957; Willis, 1960). Lewis (1969) described a primary melanoma of the leptomeninges in a 7-year-old Bantu girl. A primary malignant melanoma of the spinal cord was described by Hirano and Carton (1960).

It cannot be estimated how often melanocytes in internal organs undergo malignant change, but it did occur in such melanocytes in the systems referred to above.

CLINICAL SIGNIFICANCE OF INTERNAL MELANOCYTES

Special interest attaches to melanocytes in such internal organs with regard to the possible role of a 'solar circulating factor' in inducing malignancy in melanocytes *not* exposed to the sun (Lee and Merrill, 1970). It should be an interesting effort to collect as many of these reports as possible, and the areas in which they occurred, to see whether or not solar exposure may have an influence. Apart from studies from Africa on upper respiratory tract melanomas (Lewis and Martin, 1967), one gets the *impression* that most of the case reports originated in the U.S.A. and very few in Europe. The correlation between depth of skin pigmentation and depth of leptomeningeal pigmentation observed by Lewis (1969) suggests that internal melanocytes are controlled and influenced by similar factors as those in a cutaneous location. If a distribution corresponding to regions with high solar radiation could be demonstrated, it would tend to support Lee and Merrill's hypothesis of a 'solar circulating factor'.

Melanin production in tissues

MELANOSIS COLI

The classical problem in this regard is probably melanosis coli. The term was used by Virchow in 1847 and by Pick, apparently unaware of Virchow's choice of name, in 1911 (Won and Ramchand, 1970). The aetiological factors suggested (heavy metal action in the intestine, the possible decomposition of aromatic proteins, skatole and indole, under the action of peroxidase and its subsequent phagocytosis, the colouring matter of anthracene drugs and chronic constipation) are fully discussed by Won and Ramchand (1970). The phagocytic nature of the phenomenon and pigment transport is stressed by the finding of pigment in the mesocolic lymph nodes.

Ghadially and Parry (1966) studied melanosis coli by electron microscopy of epithelial cells and macrophages. The morphological similarity suggests that macrophages obtained the pigment from epithelial cells, but they could not demonstrate or explain its transfer from epithelial cells to macrophages. They concluded that the pigment contained lipofuscin derived by oxidation of lipids originating from the lipoprotein membrane of sequestrated mitochondria and endoplasmic reticulum.

Hardmeier (1965) distinguished 2 groups of pigment in the intestine: iron-containing haematogenous pigment (haemosiderin) and iron-free pigments (ceroid and melanin). Histochemically the pigment resembled melanin, and spectrophotometric curves of the pigment were similar to those found in metastatic melanoma, in dermoid cysts of the ovary and in oesophageal melanosis. He concluded that the term '*pseudo*melanosis' coli was not justified.

In describing melanosis of the *ileum*, Won and Ramchand (1970) found that histochemical procedures were positive for both melanin and lipofuscin, as in the case of melanosis coli. All the pigment was intracellular, the pigment-bearing cells being crowded in the lamina propria of the mucosa but not in the deeper layers. The large mononuclear cells, on electron microscopy, showed well-preserved mitochondria, smaller in size than the pigment granules. The granules had a complex morphology with considerable variation in size, shape and density. Some granules were surrounded by a distinct membrane, while others showed smooth, rounded or convoluted margins. Smaller granules appeared to clump together to form large irregular pigment aggregates.

The nature of the pigment is still uncertain, but it would appear that, whatever its origin, it is phagocytosed by mononuclears and degraded. Unfortunately, only histochemical differentiation was attempted, suggesting a lipofuscin (or lipo-melanin) or melanin.

NEUROMELANIN

This pigment, a true melanin, was discussed earlier (p. 135).

MELANIN PRODUCTION BY MAST CELLS

The relationship of mast cells to melanogenesis was reviewed by Michels (1938). Since that time few intensive studies have been performed, especially after the neural crest derivation of melanocytes was established. Okun (1965) suggested that mast cells and melanocytes are of similar lineage, and under some circum-stances mast cells represent a transitional phase in the differentiation of melano-cytes. He demonstrated the presence of cells containing mast cell granules and melanin granules in many pathological sections, and found ultrastructural simi-larity between mast cell granules and naevus cell granules. The mast cells could produce dopa melanin, and peroxidase activity could be demonstrated in mast cells, naevus cells and melanocytes. Peroxidase activity was demonstrated in normal and neoplastic melanocytes and casts doubt on the assumption that the histochemical dopa-oxidase reaction reflects melanogenic potential only in per-oxidase-negative cells (Okun, 1967a). The intensive investigations of Okun and Chorzelski (1965) and Okun (1967b) and co-workers (1969, 1970) provided con-vincing evidence that mast cells are capable of melanogenesis. The presence of preformed melanin in mast cells, dopa activity and tyrosinase activity in mast cells stimulated by ultraviolet light, and the pigment formation in mast cells in tissue culture, leaves little doubt as to the melanogenetic potential of this cell line.

In many species a reciprocal relation exists between the numbers of circulating basophils and tissue mast cells. This raises the question of the relationship of the tissue mast cell to the blood basophil. In Cape Coloureds, Bantu and whites of both sexes, a sex difference was demonstrated in direct basophil counts in whites and Cape Coloureds, but this was not found in Bantu. This finding was statistic-ally significant. There was a tendency to a lower basophil count in the Bantu, but it was still within the normal range, and the difference, significant at the 10% level, was not significant at the 5% level (Wassermann et al., 1972).

The circulation of melanin

The skin contains an extensive lymphatic drainage system, most readily ap-preciated by viewing a dermal lymphangiogram in patients with obstruction to lymphatic drainage of the limbs. Lymphatico-venous anastomoses can become patent in such cases (Fig. 19).

Interracial studies showed a very high incidence of melanin deposits in skin-draining lymph nodes in Bantu (85% inguinal, 90% axillary and 44.5%

cervical lymph nodes) while in whites corresponding skin-draining lymph nodes contained melanin deposits in a much lower percentage of cases but in the same numerical order of magnitude (26% inguinal, 20% axillary and 10% cervical). This would strongly suggest melanin transport by lymphatic drainage (Baker, 1964; Gail, 1957).

In the placentae of both white and American Negro women melanin deposits could be demonstrated in 33% and 43% of cases respectively, but in those patients with chronic skin lesions during pregnancy the incidence was 88% and 86% respectively (Ishizaki and Belter, 1960).

Melanin-containing mononuclears could be demonstrated in leucocyte concentrates of the peripheral blood of normal Bantu and Cape Coloured individuals but not in whites (Wassermann, 1965). This finding was confirmed in phenothiazine melanosis in white patients (Satanove, 1966).

There is evidence, however, that leucocyte activity and kinetics are different in the dark races and this may be related to endocrine factors which apparently

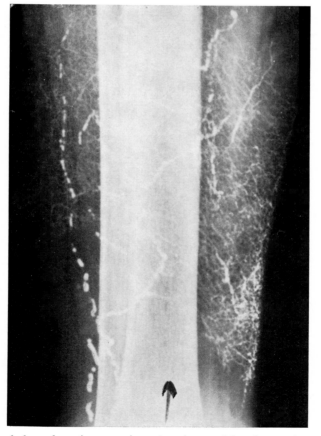

Fig. 19. Dermal lymphangiogram in a patient with obstruction of lymphatic drainage of the leg. Note the extensive lymphatic system of the skin. (Courtesy of Dr. H. O. Prinsloo.)

influence both melanokinetics and leucocytic melanin transport. The role of leucocytes in melanin pigmentation merits more detailed consideration, and will be considered in the following Chapter.

REFERENCES

ALLEN, M. S. and DRASCH, E. C. (1968): Primary melanoma of the lung. *Cancer (Philad.)*, *21*, 154.

ARIEL, I. M. (1961): Malignant melanoma of the vagina. Report of a successfully treated case. *Obstet. Gynec.*, *17*, 222.

BAKER, W. DE C. (1964): Melanin deposits in the lymph glands of Africans in Kenya. *E. Afr. med. J.*, *41*, 15.

BARDEN, H. (1969): The histochemical relationship of neuromelanin and lipofuscin. *J. Neuropath. exp. Neurol.*, *28*, 419.

BASQUE, G. J., BOLINE, J. E. and HOLYOKE, J. B. (1970): Malignant melanoma of esophagus. *Amer. J. clin. Path.*, *53*, 609.

BERRY, N. E. and REESE, L. (1953): Malignant melanoma which had its first clinical manifestations in the prostate gland. *J. Urol. (Baltimore)*, *69*, 286.

BILLINGHAM, R. E. and SILVERS, W. K. (1960): The melanocytes of mammals. *Quart. Rev. Biol.*, *35*, 1.

BIRKMAYER, W. (1970): Failures in L-dopa therapy. In: L-*Dopa and Parkinsonism*, p. 12. Editors: A. Barbeau and F. H. McDowell. F. A. Davis Co., Philadelphia, Pa.

BJÖRKERUD, S. (1964): Isolated lipofuscin granules. A survey of a new field. In: *Advances in Gerontological Research*, *Vol. I*, p. 257. Editor: B. Strehler. Academic Press, New York, N.Y.

BLAIR, C. and LEWIS, C. A. (1970): The pigment of comedones. *Brit. J. Derm.*, *82*, 572.

BLOIS, M. S. (1965): Random polymers as a matrix for chemical evolution. In: *The Origins of Prebiological Systems*, p. 19. Editor: S. W. Fox. Academic Press, New York, N.Y.

BLOIS, M. S. (1966): On the spectroscopic properties of some natural melanins. *J. invest. Derm.*, *47*, 162.

BLOIS, M. S. (1967): A note on the problem of melanin structure. In: *Advances in Biology of Skin, Vol. VIII: The Pigmentary System*, p. 319. Editors: W. Montagna and F. Hu. Pergamon Press, Oxford.

BLOIS, M. S., ZAHLAN, A. B. and MALING, J. E. (1964): Electron spin resonance studies on melanin. *J. Biophys.*, *4*, 471.

BOLT, A. G. (1967): Interactions between human melanoprotein and chlorpromazine derivatives. I. Isolation and purification of human melanoprotein from hair and melanoma tissue. *Life Sci.*, *6*, 1277.

BRUENGER, F. W., STOVER, B. J. and ATHERTON, D. R. (1967): The incorporation of various metal ions into in vivo- and in vitro-produced melanin. *Radiat. Res.*, *32*, 1.

BUCKLE, E. A. (1969): Primary malignant melanoma of the female urethra. *Brit. J. Surg.*, *56*, 548.

CADY, B., RIPPEY, J. H. and FRAZELL, E. L. (1968): Non-epidermoid cancer of the larynx. *Ann. Surg.*, *167*, 116.

COMMONER, B., TOWNSEND, J. and PAKE, G. E. (1954): Free radicals in biological materials. *Nature (Lond.)*, *174*, 689.

DANIELS JR., F. (1959): The physiological effects of sunlight. *J. invest. Derm.*, *32*, 147.

DAS GUPTA, T. K. and BRASFIELD, R. D. (1964): Metatastic melanoma of the gastro-intestinal tract. *Arch. Surg., 88,* 969.

DE LA PAVA, S., NIGOGOSYAN, G., PICKREN, J. W. and CABRERA, A. (1963): Melanosis of the esophagus. *Cancer (Philad.), 16,* 48.

DUCHON, J., FITZPATRICK, T. B. and SEIJI, M. (1968): Melanin 1968: Some definitions and problems. In: *1967–68 Yearbook of Dermatology,* p. 1. Year Book Medical Publishers Inc., Chicago, Ill.

DUFFY, P. E. and TENNYSON, V. M. (1965): Phase and electron-microscopic observation of Lewy bodies and melanin granules in the substantia nigra and locus caeruleus in Parkinson's disease. *J. Neuropath. exp. Neurol., 24,* 398.

EDWARDS, E. A. and DUNTLEY, S. Q. (1939): Pigments and colour of living human skin. *Amer. J. Anat., 65,* 1.

FITZPATRICK, T. B., MIYAMOTO, M. and ISHIKAWA, K. (1967): The evolution of concepts of melanin biology. In: *Advances in Biology of Skin, Vol. VIII: The Pigmentary System,* p. 1. Editors: W. Montagna and F. Hu. Pergamon Press, Oxford.

FLESCH, P. (1968): The epidermal iron pigments of red species. *J. invest. Derm., 51,* 337.

FORBES, W. and MALONEY, A. F. J. (1950): Primary melanomatosis of the leptomeninx. *J. Path. Bact., 62,* 403.

FUCHS, U. (1968): Elektronenmikroskopische Untersuchung des Homogentisinsäure-Melanins bei Ochronose. *Virchows Arch. path. Anat., 344,* 243.

GAIL, D. (1957): Über das Vorkommen von Melanin und Hämosiderin in peripheren Lymphknoten. *Frankfurt. Z. Path., 68,* 64.

GHADIALLY, F. N. and PARRY, E. W. (1966): An electronmicroscope and histochemical study of melanosis coli. *J. Path. Bact., 92,* 213.

GIBSON, J. B., BURROW, D. and WEIR, W. P. (1957): Primary melanoma of the meninges. *J. Path. Bact., 74,* 419.

GILLENWATER, J. Y. and BURROWS, H. M. (1968): Unusual tumors of the female urethra. *Obstet. Gynec., 31,* 617.

GOLDFISCHER, S. and BERNSTEIN, J. (1969): Lipofuscin (aging) pigment granules of the newborn human liver. *J. Cell Biol., 42,* 253.

GOLDMAN, R. L. (1968): Melanogenic epithelium in the prostate gland. *Amer. J. clin. Path., 49,* 75.

GRAHAM, C. E. (1970): Distribution of lipofuscin in the squirrel monkey *Saimiri sciurea. Histochem. J., 2,* 521.

GREENE JR., G. W. and BERNIER, J. L. (1961): Primary malignant melanomas of the parotid gland. *Oral Surg., 14,* 108.

GUILLAN, R. A. and ZELMAN, S. (1970): The incidence and probable origin of melanin in the prostate. *J. Urol. (Baltimore), 104,* 151.

HACKMAN, R. H. and GOLDBERG, M. (1971): Microchemical detection of melanins. *Analyt. Biochem., 41,* 279.

HARDMEIER, TH. (1965): Zur Differenzialdiagnose der Pigmentierungen des Verdauungstraktes. *Path. et Microbiol. (Basel), 28,* 437.

HARRISON, D. F. (1968): Malignant melanomata of the nasal cavity. *Proc. roy. Soc. Med., 61,* 13.

HEGEDUS, Z. L. and ALTSCHULE, M. D. (1967): Studies on aminochromes. II. Behavior of added adrenolutin in blood of normal and psychotic persons. *Arch. int. Physiol. Biochim., 75,* 697.

HEGEDUS, Z. L. and ALTSCHULE, M. D. (1968): Studies on aminochromes. III. Transformation of epinephrine, adrenochrome and adrenolutin into plasma-soluble melanins during incubation in human blood plasma. *Arch. Biochem., 126,* 388.

HEGEDUS, Z. L. and ALTSCHULE, M. D. (1970): Studies on rheomelanins. I. The formation of rheomelanins in human blood plasma from catecholamines, from L-dopa and from some of their derivatives. *Arch. int. Physiol. Biochim.*, *78*, 443.

HEMPEL, K. (1966): Investigation on the structure of melanin in malignant melanoma with H³ and C¹⁴-DOPA labelled at different positions. In: *Structure and Control of the Melanocyte*, p. 162. Editors: G. Della Porta and O. Mühlbock. Springer-Verlag, Berlin.

HEMPEL, K. and MÄNNL, H. F. K. (1966): The conversion of H-3-tyrosine to H-3-dopa in mouse melanoma in vivo. *Biochim. biophys. Acta (Amst.)*, *124*, 192.

HIRANO, A. and CARTON, C. A. (1960): Primary malignant melanoma of the spinal cord. *J. Neurosurg.*, *17*, 935.

ISENBERG, I. (1964): Free radicals in tissue. *Physiol. Rev.*, *44*, 487.

ISHIZAKI, Y. and BELTER, L. F. (1960): Melanin deposition in the placenta as a result of skin lesions (dermatopathic melanosis of placenta). *Amer. J. Obstet. Gynec.*, *79*, 1074.

JONES, C. H. (1961): Malignant melanoma of the gallbladder. *J. Path. Bact.*, *81*, 423.

LEE, J. A. A. and MERRILL, J. M. (1970): Sunlight and the aetiology of malignant melanoma: A synthesis. *Med. J. Aust.*, *2*, 846.

LEWIS, M. G. (1968): Melanin-pigmented components in ovarian teratomas in Ugandan Africans. *J. Path. Bact.*, *95*, 405.

LEWIS, M. G. (1969): Melanoma and pigmentation of the leptomeninges in Ugandan Africans. *J. clin. Path.*, *22*, 183.

LEWIS, M. G. and MARTIN, J. A. (1967): Malignant melanoma of the nasal cavity in Ugandan Africans. Relationship of ectopic pigmentation. *Cancer (Philad.)*, *20*, 1699.

LUBARSCH, O. (1932): Über gefärbte, warzige Muttermäler in der Haut von Eierstocksembryonen. *Virchows Arch. path. Anat.*, *285*, 197.

MAEDA, T. and WEGMANN, R. (1969): Infrared spectrometry of locus caeruleus and substantia nigra pigments in human brain. *Brain Res.*, *14*, 673.

MASON, H. S. (1948): The chemistry of melanin. III. Mechanism of the oxidation of dehydroxyphenylalanine by tyrosinase. *J. biol. Chem.*, *172*, 83.

MASON, H. S. (1967): The structure of melanin. In: *Advances in Biology of Skin, Vol. VIII: The Pigmentary System*, p. 293. Editors: W. Montagna and F. Hu. Pergamon Press, Oxford.

MESARA, B. W. and BURTON, W. D. (1968): Primary malignant melanoma of the upper respiratory tract. *Cancer*, *21*, 217.

MICHELS, N. A. (1938): The mast cells. In: *Handbook of Haematology, Vol. I*, p. 318. Editor: H. Downey. Paul B. Hoeber, Inc., New York, N.Y.

MITCHELL, R. E. (1968): The skin of the Australian aborigine: A light and electron-microscopic study. *Aust. J. Derm.*, *9*, 314.

MOSES, H. L., GANOTE, C. E., BEAVER, D. L. and SCHUFFMAN, S. S. (1966): Light and electron microscopic studies of pigment in human and rhesus monkey substantia nigra and locus caeruleus. *Anat. Rec.*, *155*, 167.

NAGATSU, T., LEVITT, M. and UDENFRIEND, S. (1964): Tyrosine hydroxylase. The initial step in norepinephrine biosynthesis. *J. biol. Chem.*, *239*, 2910.

NICHOLS, S. E. and REAMS, W. M. (1960): The occurrence and morphogenesis of melanocytes in the connective tissues of the PET/MCV mouse strain. *J. Embryol. exp. Morph.*, *8*, 24.

NICOLAUS, R. A. (1962): Biogenesis of melanins. *Rass. Med. sper.*, *9*, *Suppl. 1*.

NICOLAUS, R. A. and PIATELLI, M. (1965): Progress in the chemistry of natural black pigments. *Rend. Accad. Sci., Fis. Matemat. Soc. naz. Sci. Lett. Arte Napoli, Ser. 4*, *32*, 1.

NIGOGOSYAN, G., DE LA PAVA, S., PICKREN, J. W. and WOODRUFF, M. W. (1963): Blue nevus of the prostate gland. *Cancer (Philad.)*, *16*, 1097.

O'BRIEN, W. M., LA DU, B. N. and BUNIM, J. J. (1963): Biochemical pathologic and clinical aspects of alcaptonuria, ochronosis and ochronotic arthropathy. Review of world literature (1584–1962). *Amer. J. Med.*, *34*, 813.

OKUN, M. R. (1965): Histogenesis of melanocytes. *J. invest. Derm.*, *44*, 285.

OKUN, M. R. (1967a): Peroxidase activity in normal and neoplastic melanocytes. *J. invest. Derm.*, *48*, 461.

OKUN, M. R. (1967b): Pigment formation in mast cells in tissue culture. *J. invest. Derm.*, *48*, 424.

OKUN, M. R. and CHORZELSKI, T. (1965): Metachromatic granules in dendritic cells within epithelial structures in alopecia mucinosa. *J. invest. Derm.*, *45*, 129.

OKUN, M. R., EDELSTEIN, L., NIEBAUER, G. and HAMADA, G. (1969): The histochemical tyrosine-dopa reaction for tyrosinase and its use in localizing tyrosinase activity in mast cells. *J. invest. Derm.*, *53*, 39.

OKUN, M. R., EDELSTEIN, L. M., OR, N., HAMADA, G., DONNELLAN, B. and LEVER, W. F. (1970): Histochemical differentiation of peroxidase-mediated from tyrosinase-mediated melanin formation in mammalian tissue. *Histochemistry*, *23*, 295.

OKUN, M. R. and ZOOK, B. C. (1967): Histologic parallels between mastocytoma and melanoma. Demonstration of melanin in tumor cells of mastocytoma and metachromasia in tumor cells of melanoma. *Arch. Derm.*, *95*, 275.

PAKKENBERG, H. (1966): The pigment in the substantia nigra in Parkinsonism. Microspectrophotometric comparison with other sources of human pigments. *Brain Res.*, *2*, 173.

PANTAZAPOULOS, P. E. (1964): Primary malignant melanoma of the larynx. *Laryngoscope (St Louis)*, *74*, 95.

PARAKKAL, P. F. (1967): The transfer of premelanosomes into the keratinizing cells of albino hair follicles. *J. cell. Biol.*, *35*, 473.

PATHAK, M. A. (1967): Photobiology of melanogenesis: Biophysical aspects. In: *Advances in Biology of Skin, Vol. VIII: The Pigmentary System*, p. 397. Editors: W. Montagna and F. Hu. Pergamon Press, Oxford.

PEARSE, A. (1960): *Histochemistry*. Little, Brown and Co., Boston, Mass.

PEARSE, A. (1970): *Histochemistry*. Little, Brown and Co., Boston, Mass.

PROTA, G. and NICOLAUS, R. A. (1967): On the biogenesis of phaeomelanins. In: *Advances in Biology of Skin, Vol. VIII: The Pigmentary System*, p. 323. Editors: W. Montagna and F. Hu. Pergamon Press, Oxford.

PROTA, G., SCHERRILO, G. and NICOLAUS, R. A. (1968): Struttura e biogenesi della feomelanine. IV. Sintesi e proprietà della 5-S-cisteinildopa. *Gazz. chim. ital.*, *98*, 495.

RAPER, H. S. (1928): The aerobic oxidases. *Physiol. Rev.*, *8*, 245.

REAMS, W. M. (1963): Morphogenesis of pigment cells in the connective tissue of the *PET* mouse. *Ann. N.Y. Acad. Sci.*, *100*, 486.

REID, J. D. and MEHTA, V. T. (1966): Melanoma of the lower respiratory tract. *Cancer (Philad.)*, *19*, 627.

ROBSON, N. C. and SWAN, G. A. (1966): Studies on the structure of some synthetic melanins. In: *Structure and Control of the Melanocyte*, p. 155. Editors: G. Della Porta and O. Mühlbock. Springer-Verlag, Berlin.

SALM, R. (1963): A primary malignant melanoma of the bronchus. *J. Path. Bact.*, *85*, 121.

SATANOVE, A. (1965): Pigmentation due to phenothiazines in high and prolonged dosage. *J. Amer. med. Ass.*, *191*, 263.

SEIJI, M. and IWASHITA, S. (1965): Intracellular localization of tyrosinase and site of melanin formation in melanocyte. *J. invest. Derm.*, *45*, 305.

SIEBERT, G., DIEZEL, P. B., JAHR, K., KRUG, E., SCHMITT, A., GRÜNBERGER, E. and BOTTKE, I. (1962): Isolierung und Eigenschaften von Lipofuscin aus Herzgewebe des Menschen. *Histochemie, 3,* 17.

SIMARD, C., ROGNON, L. M. and PILORCE, G. (1964): Le problème du naevus bleu prostatique. *Ann. Anat. path., 9,* 469.

STREHLER, B. L. (1964): On the histochemistry and ultrastructure of age pigment. In: *Advances in Gerontological Research, Vol. I,* p. 343. Editor: B. Strehler. Academic Press, New York, N.Y.

SWAN, G. A. (1963): Chemical structure of melanins. *Ann. N.Y. Acad. Sci., 100,* 1005.

SWAN, G. A. (1973): Current knowledge of melanin structure. In: *Pigment Cell, Vol. I,* p. 151. S. Karger, Basle.

SZABO, G., GERALD, A. B., PATHAK, M. A. and FITZPATRICK, T. B. (1969): Racial differences in the fate of melanosomes in human epidermis. *Nature (Lond.), 222,* 1081.

SZENT-GYÖRGYI, A. (1967): Charge transfer and electronic mobility. *Proc. nat. Acad. Sci. (Wash.), 58,* 2012.

SZENT-GYÖRGYI, A. (1968): Bio-electronics. *Science, 161,* 988.

VAN DER WENDE, C. (1964): Studies on the oxidation of dopamine to melanin by rat brain. *Arch. int. Pharmacodyn., 152,* 433.

VAN DER WENDE, C. and SPOERLEIN, M. T. (1963): Oxidation of dopamine to melanin by an enzyme of rat brain. *Life Sci., 2,* 386.

VAN WOERT, M. H. (1969): Spectral studies of the pigment of the human substantia nigra. In: *Progress in Neuro-Genetics, Vol. I,* pp. 306–310. Editors: A. Barbeau and J. R. Brunette. ICS 175, Excerpta Medica, Amsterdam.

VAN WOERT, M. H., KORB, F. and PRASAD, K. N. (1971): Regulation of tyrosinase activity in mouse melanoma and skin by changes in melanosomal membrane permeability. *J. invest. Derm., 56,* 343.

VAN WOERT, M. H., PRASAD, K. N. and BORG, D. C. (1967): Spectroscopic studies of substantia nigra pigment in human subjects. *J. Neurochem., 14,* 707.

VICTOR, D. J. and BAZELON, M. (1966): Neuromelanin and the olfactory bulb. *Lancet, 2,* 1467.

WALSH JR., T. S. (1956): Primary melanoma of the gallbladder with cervical metastases and $14\frac{1}{2}$ year survival; first histologically proved case. *Cancer (Philad.), 9,* 518.

WASSERMANN, H. P. (1965): Leucocytes and melanin pigmentation. I. Demonstration of pigmented leucocytes in peripheral blood of amphibians, reptiles and normal man. *J. invest. Derm., 45,* 104.

WASSERMANN, H. P. (1967): Phenothiazines and leucocytic melanin transport. *Agressologie, 9,* 241.

WASSERMANN, H. P. (1970a): Ethnic differences in natural melanoproteins. *Dermatologica (Basel), 141,* 44.

WASSERMANN, H. P. (1970b): Melanokinetics and the biological significance of melanin. *Brit. J. Derm., 82,* 530.

WASSERMANN, H. P., MULLER, M. A. and LAUBSCHER, N. F. (1972): Ethnic and sex difference in an interracial study of direct basophil counts. *S. Afr. med. J., 46,* 143.

WASSERMANN, H. P. and VAN DER WALT, J. J. (1973): Antibodies against melanin: The significance of negative results. *S. Afr. med. J., 47,* 7.

WILLBANKS, O. L. and FOGELMAN, M. J. (1970): Gastro-intestinal melanosarcoma. *Amer. J. Surg., 120,* 602.

WILLIS, R. A. (1967): *Pathology of Tumours,* 4th ed., p. 915. Butterworth, London.

WON, K. H. and RAMCHAND, S. (1970): Melanosis of the ileum. *Amer. J. dig. Dis., 15,* 57.

Chapter XIII

Leucocytes and melanin pigmentation

Leucocytic melanin transport received much attention up to the end of the 19th century, but the observations could not be interpreted before identification of melanocytes as the cellular site of melanogenesis, and while some held that leucocytes produced melanin, others thought that melanin was transported from the blood to the epidermis (p. 46).

Leucocytes are transported by the blood but perform their functions extra-vascularly. Homeostatic mechanisms, however, regulate the leucocyte count and the differential distribution of the various types of leucocytes, and this homeostasis is influenced, and often transiently disturbed, by many factors both internal and external.

The relationship of leucocytes to pigmentation is evident in (*a*) the handling of melanin in the inflammatory response, (*b*) the transport of melanin through the body, (*c*) the difference in leucocyte counts and their differential distribution in dark races as compared to whites and (*d*) the association of leucocytic and pigmentary anomalies in several clinical syndromes.

THE INFLAMMATORY RESPONSE

The skin window technique is perhaps the most physiological method for the study of cellular events in aseptic inflammatory reactions. Tissue culture methods do not reproduce either the physiological milieu of inflammation or the temporal sequence of cellular migration (Rebuck, 1940; Riis, 1959; Wassermann, 1961, 1963*a,b*, 1964*b*). The method consists of scraping away epidermis until fine bleeding points and a serosanguineous ooze indicate that the corium has been reached. Although the irritation of a foreign body (e.g. a glass coverslip, chemically clean and sterilized) is sufficient to cause cellular migration (Perillie and Finch, 1960), an antigen to which the patient has not been immunized (e.g. egg-white) leads to a greater cellular reaction and stronger participation of lymphocytes. With an immune antigen (tuberculin in a tuberculin-positive patient) the reaction is further accelerated and intensified (Rebuck, 1947; Rebuck et al., 1951, 1955, 1958, 1960; Wassermann, 1964*b*) (Fig. 20).

The antigen is applied *on* the lesion and covered by a coverslip which may be changed hourly or at greater intervals, thus allowing sequential sampling of inflammatory cells, which migrate to the response and adhere to the coverslip as a single layer of cells.

Most of our studies used egg-white as a non-immune antigen. In whites the reaction proceeds as described by several workers (Rebuck and Crowley, 1955; Braunsteiner et al., 1958; Riis, 1959; Hu et al., 1961) and melanin rarely becomes a striking feature in the reaction.

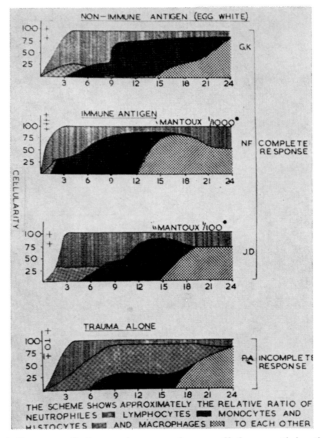

Fig. 20. The influence of the antigen used on cellular participation in the inflammatory response. (From Wassermann, 1964, *South African Journal of Laboratory and Clinical Medicine*, 10, 76. Courtesy of the Editors.)

In the Cape Coloured and Bantu the appearance of melanin in the response is a constant and striking feature observed in several hundreds of people studied over the past decade. Although neutrophils appear within 30 minutes it is usually after a few hours that small dark particles, approximately the size of specific granules, appear in the neutrophils. (If Bantu scrapings are applied to a lesion in a white person, a strong neutrophilic (foreign body) reaction appears, but the neutrophils of the white recipient then also acquire such granules.) As the neutrophils shrink and nuclei start to stain darker, these smaller specks are clumped together to form granules with a distinct green-black appearance on Romanowsky's stain (May-Gruenwald-Giemsa or Wright's stain). Unstained, the granules are yellow-brown to golden-brown.

Neutrophils are essential for the subsequent transformation of lymphocytes to macrophages (Page and Good, 1957), and neutrophil-lymphocyte interactions are seen in which melanin granules are transferred to the lymphocytes. The lymphocytes at first are identical to blood lymphocytes and, in contrast to neutrophils, are mostly dopa-negative. Progressively more lymphocytes obtain dopa positivity during and after the neutrophil-lymphocyte interaction.

Melanin is transferred to lymphocytes at a stage where they are still motile; many handmirror-shaped lymphocytes arrested in active movement and loaded with melanin could be seen and also observed in a warm-stage enclosure in vivo in a moist preparation (Wassermann, 1963*b*; Hu, 1965).

The Bantu response proceeds as in whites, except that as the lymphocytes hypertrophy to macrophages they acquire more granules, and the granules are often either arranged around the edges of vacuoles appearing in their cytoplasm, or at times included in vacuoles as a fairly large clump. In some of the macrophages granules, which exhibited a positive reaction for sulphydryl groups early in the response, appear with a negative reaction. Some evidence suggesting degradation of melanin is seen in the lighter staining of the granules and the loss of sulphydryl reactivity (Wassermann, 1963*a,b*). Most probably, however, it is not the melanin but the protein moiety which is degraded. Some macrophages fuse and show differential labelling with melanin in multinucleate giant cells (Wassermann, 1963*a*).

The melanin labelling allows some differentiation between cells: Monocytes and tissue macrophages show large clumps of melanin early in the response. Lymphocytes acquire smaller and more discrete granules, which only later clump to larger accumulations similar to that of monocytes.

Without antigen, the Bantu generally exhibit a stronger neutrophilic participation and more lymphocytes than whites, but the dominant mononuclear cell type is monocytes. With both egg-white and tuberculin in tuberculin-positive individuals the Bantu shows a richer initial and more persistent neutrophilic participation, and also a stronger lymphocyte invasion at about the 9th hour of inflammation. Macrophages in the Cape Coloured and Bantu response show more frequent and more pronounced dendritic processes which connect with other macrophages or with neutrophils. As the macrophages become filled with melanin granules they round off and dendritic processes become less frequent (Wassermann, 1964, 1967*a*).

The influence of the antigen on cellular participation has been shown (Fig. 20), and the summarized sequence of the response and the corresponding melanin labelling is shown in Figure 21.

For the study of phagocytosis melanin labelling appeared to be a more physiological marker than Indian ink, which invariably leads to a granulocyte influx when applied to the lesion. Melanin labelling in a Cape Coloured with systemic lupus erythematosus (LE) showed that the neutrophils ingesting the polymerized nuclear material to form LE cells were usually the lesser lobed neutrophils, and they were phagocytically more active. The LE cell lobe index is usually to the left of that of the general population of LE cells, and the number of LE cells, as a percentage of neutrophils examined in LE preparations, had a significant negative correlation with the neutrophil lobe index of the preparation (Wassermann, 1963c, 1967b).

In *Xenopus laevis* larvae phagocytosis of melanin by histiocytes is known and could also be demonstrated in the cerebrospinal fluid of young larvae. The phagocytosis by histiocytes and macrophages of melanin was studied by Glombek (1968).

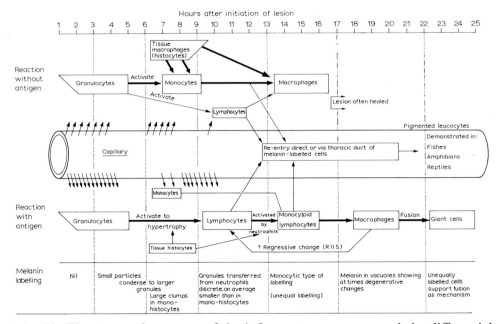

Fig. 21. The temporal sequence of the inflammatory response and the differential melanin labelling. (From Wassermann, 1964, *South African Journal of Laboratory and Clinical Medicine*, **10**, 76. Courtesy of the Editors.)

Phagocytosis of melanin by macrophages in the skin window is also referred to as a 'frequent finding' by Shelley et al. (1969).

The inflammatory response is suppressed by cortisol (Mlczoch and Kohout, 1965), the effective level of which is controlled by a negative feedback with the anterior pituitary ACTH secretion. The number of circulating lymphocytes is also influenced by this mechanism. Thus, the inflammatory response can either retain melanin in macrophages in the dermis (postinflammatory hyperpigmentation) or may enhance its transport to other areas by lymphocytes, as in the case of Addison's disease (Fig. 22).

Melanophagocytosis could recently be studied in the skin window by electron microscopy (Wassermann et al., 1973).

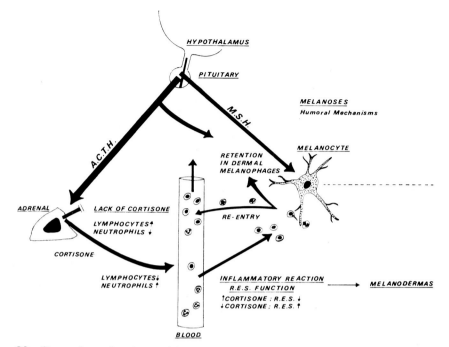

Fig. 22. Control mechanisms of leucocyte and melanocyte function. (From Wassermann, 1965, *South African Medical Journal, 39,* 711. Courtesy of the Editors.)

PHENOTHIAZINE MELANOSIS

At approximately the time of publication of these studies Hays et al. (1964),
Feldman and Frierson (1964), Barnes and Cameron (1966) and Mathelone (1967)
reported on a generalized melanosis found in schizophrenics on prolonged, high-
dosage phenothiazine therapy. The skin showed a blue or slate-grey pigmentation and ocular changes occurred as well. Pigmentation was found especially
in exposed areas, but was unlike suntan; the sclera and cornea showed a hazy-
brown pigmentation. In internal organs the *liver* showed fine granular, yellow-
brown pigment in cells around the central veins, and in macrophages. Similar
deposits were found in the myocardium, kidneys, lungs, large intestines and
thyroid gland. In the brain and meninges occasional macrophages loaded with
pigment were seen in close proximity to capillaries. The pituitary gland showed
granules in subcapsular lymphatic channels (Greiner, 1968).

The pigment was dopa-positive in skin but dopa-negative in internal organs.
It was negative for iron, bile and lipid. It did not polarize light and did not
fluoresce in the wavelength for chlorpromazine. Masson-Fontana staining was
positive, and it could be bleached by hydrogen peroxide. The extracted pigment
yielded esr signals identical with synthetic and frog skin melanin (Greiner, 1968).

There is some doubt, however, about the nature of the pigment. Zelickson (1965) found an increase in the number of melanosomes in the skin of a patient on chlorpromazine. Perry et al. (1964) extracted phenothiazine metabolites from a portion of liver from a patient with melanosis, but after extraction pigmentation was the same. Hashimoto et al. (1966) found an increase in the number of melanosomes in the epidermal cells and in lysosomes of dermal phagocytes in a patient with this melanosis. In the study by Zelickson (1965), electron-dense bodies without recognizable internal structure were noted in endothelial cells and alongside melanosomes within phagocytic lysosomes. Huang (1967) believes that phenothiazine metabolites are loosely associated with melanin.

The observation by Greiner and Nicholson (1965) that increased melanin deposits could be found in autopsy material of schizophrenics from the period 1947–1949, i.e. before phenothiazines were used, would suggest that an internal circulation of melanin is present in schizophrenia, but only markedly accentuated by phenothiazines. This would suggest that there is increased melanogenesis and circulation of melanin in schizophrenia which may be aetiologically related to the condition (see p. 251). Phenothiazines, while improving schizophrenic symptoms, also activate increased melanin transport.

When chlorpromazine was applied to the skin window of normal whites, neutrophils in the early phases showed large vacuoles containing a clear blue-staining material. They increased until about one-third of the cells exhibited this blue-staining material. This material is then transferred to lymphocytes at about the 9th hour, and at this stage granules resembling melanin are found in greater quantity than in the control lesion (on the same arm, and in the same patient). Later, very prominent cytoplasmic vacuolization is found in most of the cells in the experimental lesion giving a foamy appearance to the cells. At this stage a larger number of green-black melanin granules was seen than in the control lesion.

The Bantu response differed markedly from the white response. The experimental lesion was markedly more cellular than the control lesions (as in whites). Vacuolization was not prominent, the blue material could not be seen in the cells, but the experimental lesion showed cells well filled with large and very dense melanin granules more black than the green-black staining seen in the control lesion. The dense, larger and often confluent granules persisted when decreased staining became evident in the control lesion (Wassermann, 1968).

Apparently the chlorpromazine or its metabolites, which appear as a blue-staining material in the white response, lead to increased melanophagocytosis in whites, and are harmful to the cells in so far as they lead to very marked vacuolization. In the Bantu, melanin apparently protects against this change, possibly by forming charge transfer complexes with chlorpromazine.

LEUCOCYTIC TRANSPORT

Pigmented leucocytes can normally be found quite often in amphibians and reptiles, and the liver, spleen and lung, in approximately that order, contain melanin deposits. I studied amphibians with red leg disease (Wassermann, 1964*a*) and found a large histiocytic type of melanin-containing cell in the peripheral blood. Such cells were demonstrated in the blood of both chameleons and tortoises, and confirmed that the pigment was melanin by Lillie's ferrous iron uptake, Schmorl's reaction, bleaching in 10% hydrogen peroxide and dopa reaction (Wassermann, 1965; Fukui and Mitsui, 1965).

In normal Bantu and Cape Coloureds leucocyte concentrates from peripheral blood were studied by similar staining techniques and melanin could be identified in occasional mononuclear cells (Wassermann, 1965). While the above-mentioned article was in press, Satanove (1965) reported findings in the skin window of whites with phenothiazine melanosis similar to our observations in Bantu and Cape Coloureds, and also reported pigmented leucocytes in the buffy coat of their peripheral blood.

We could not find any pigmented leucocytes in leucocyte concentrates from peripheral blood in white patients.

Melanin-containing leucocytes were reported in the bone-marrow cells of patients with metastatic melanoma (Sundberg, 1956; Franklin et al., 1952; Jonsson and Rundles, 1959) and 2 reports on melanin-containing leucocytes in the peripheral blood of patients with melanoma could be found (Goodall et al., 1961; Liebmann, 1929).

LEUCOCYTES AND THE EPIDERMAL MELANIN UNIT (EMU)

The function of leucocytes appears to be integrated with the EMU as follows: Disruption of epidermal melanin units allows leucocytes to transport melanin. When epidermal melanin units are filled to capacity as in hyperpigmentation, whether racial or acquired, the leucocytic system apparently acts as an additional transporting system. As the melanocytic melanogenesis is probably controlled by a negative feedback mechanism from epidermal cells, the leucocytic melanin transport would help to maintain a high rate of melanogenesis. Hyperpigmentation induced by hormones (Addison's disease, hyperthyroidism and anorexia nervosa) and racial pigmentation (see below) are accompanied by an increase in the number of lymphocytes in the peripheral blood. This would indicate that with increased melanogenesis the additional transport system is simultaneously activated. The activation of the additional transport system is associated with increased visceral melanin deposition.

Phenothiazine melanosis shows evidence of increased melanogenesis, leucocytic pigment transport, and visceral pigment deposition. Melanin as electron acceptor binds with the electron donor chlorpromazine, probably by forming charge transfer complexes. These findings would suggest that if the melanin-accepting ability of cells depended on their concentration of electron donors, the transfer of granules would stop on cancellation of the charge by the formation of charge transfer complexes. Chlorpromazine as electron donor, when present in cells, would enhance transfer to epidermal units and leucocytes, and result in visceral pigmentation (Wassermann, 1967*a*, 1968) (Fig. 23).

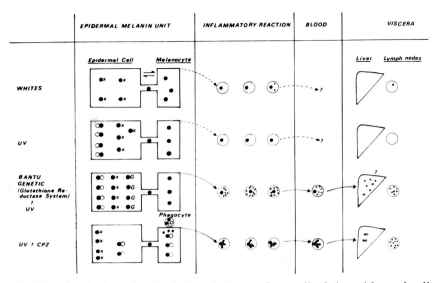

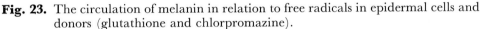

Fig. 23. The circulation of melanin in relation to free radicals in epidermal cells and donors (glutathione and chlorpromazine).

Key: ● Melanin
      × Free radical
      G Glutathione   } Electron donors.
      O Chlorpromazine }

(From Wassermann, 1968, *Agressologie*, *9*, 241. Courtesy of the Editors.)

PERIPHERAL LEUCOCYTE COUNTS IN ETHNIC GROUPS

'Clinicians and pathologists dealing with African patients are familiar with the fact that the distribution of the white cells in the blood of Africans differs from that commonly accepted as normal in persons of European stock' (Moore, 1958a). This is not always so obvious when dealing with ill people, because the Bantu count reverts to that found in whites during illness (Johnstone, 1951) and pregnancy (Moore, 1958b).

The pattern of neutropenia and lymphocytosis has been constantly reported in Negroes and Bantu from various parts of the African continent since 1917, and also in American Negroes, Australian aborigines and Indians in India. It was reported in Bantu and Negroes studied in Europe. The pertinent literature (up to 1965) was reviewed by Wassermann (1966). Since that time similar findings were again reported in American Negroes (Broun et al., 1966) and rediscovered in Britain in West Indians and African Negroes (Barnard, 1967; Davis, 1967; Rippey, 1967) as well as in South African children (Neser, 1968).

The studies up to 1966 were not acceptable because of the paucity of white controls from the same area, the uncertainty as to the presence of malnutrition in the populations studied, the possible effects of altitude, ultraviolet radiation and tropical climate in many areas, and the presence of tropical diseases, especially malaria, but also trypanosomiasis, yellow fever, leprosy, amoebiasis, bilharziasis and intestinal parasitism.

For these reasons a study was done at Bellville, South Africa, at sea level, in an area free of malaria and most tropical diseases, with a Mediterranean temperate climate. Only males were studied to exclude the possible effects of pregnancy or the menstrual cycle. Only economically privileged members of the 3 racial groups (whites, Cape Coloureds and Bantu) were studied and it was required that all individuals should have normal haemoglobin levels. Because of the high incidence of raised erythrocyte sedimentation rates (ESR) in Africa in otherwise healthy Bantu, due to occult malnutrition (Walker et al., 1956; Brönte-Stewart et al., 1961), further selection was applied to obtain individuals with normal ESR's and eosinophil counts. The area is most favourably situated as far as medical personnel is concerned, and the ratio of inhabitants to hospital beds is more than 400 : 1 in this particular area. All individuals had free access to medical facilities, and the conditions of employment required periodic routine medical examination.

The data were not normally distributed in the case of leucocytes and differential counts, but had large 'tails'. Selection procedures decreased the sample size of Bantu disproportionately, and thus the Wilcoxon-Mann-Whitney 2 sample test was employed. Differences were considered significant and highly significant at the 5% and 1% level respectively.

In the Bantu group the total leucocyte count was significantly lower than in Cape Coloured and white groups, a finding best appreciated when the percentage of individuals below the warning level and rejection level for leucocyte counts,

Table VI

	% below warning level (A.E.R.E., Harwell)	% below rejection level (A.E.R.E., Harwell)
Total leucocyte counts		
Turner's English males (1956)	2.4	Nil
Wassermann (1966):		
whites	3.0	Nil
Cape Coloureds	2.9	Nil
Bantu	6.4	1.0
Neutrophil counts		
Turner's English males (1956)	15.8	1.6
Wassermann (1966):		
whites	15.0	2.0
Cape Coloureds	16.5	4.9
Bantu	42.6	13.8

Reversal of neutrophil/lymphocyte ratio occurred in:
9% of whites
16% of Cape Coloureds
48% of Bantu   (Wassermann, 1966)

as suggested by the Atomic Energy Research Establishment at Harwell (Turner, 1953), is compared to English studies (Table VI).

Compared to whites, the Bantu had a neutropenia and lymphocytosis (in both 'relative' and 'absolute' differential counts) which was highly significant (in the group studied as a whole, as well as in the groups selected for an ESR below 10 mm and below 5 mm, and also in the group with an ESR below 5 mm and absolute eosinophil counts below 400 cells per mm³).

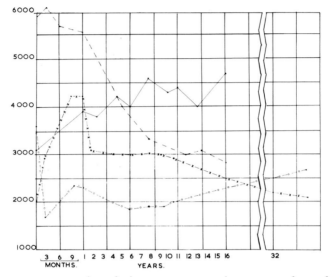

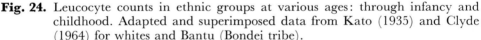

Fig. 24. Leucocyte counts in ethnic groups at various ages: through infancy and childhood. Adapted and superimposed data from Kato (1935) and Clyde (1964) for whites and Bantu (Bondei tribe).
———————— Granulocytes whites
- - - - - - - Lymphocytes whites
o-o-o-o-o-o Granulocytes Bantu
-x-x-x-x- Lymphocytes Bantu
(From Wassermann, 1966, *South African Medical Journal, 46, Supplement 3.* Courtesy of the Editors.)

A reversal of neutrophil lymphocyte ratios occurred in about 9% of whites, 13% of Cape Coloureds, but in 54.8% of Bantu.

Effects of external factors (altitude, climate, seasonal fluctuation and diurnal fluctuation) were critically reviewed and appeared to be of minor importance in acclimatized individuals (Wassermann, 1966).

Considering the intrinsic factors, the Bantu leucocyte picture indicates that lymphocytes predominate up to the age of about 17, while in whites neutrophils exceed the lymphocyte count from the age of about 4. Leucopenia is evident from birth and persists throughout life (Fig. 24) (Kato, 1935; Clyde, 1964).

There is no sex difference apart from a change towards the white pattern in

Bantu females during pregnancy, again reverting to the Bantu pattern 2 weeks post partum.

The conclusion reached was that the factor most likely to be involved in this difference was less adrenocortical activity in the Bantu. The anatomical and the direct and indirect evidence for this conclusion will be considered in the next Chapter (Wassermann, 1966).

The bone marrow in the Negro was studied by Linhard (1956): The erythrocytic precursors did not differ from those in normal whites. Myelocytes in the bone marrow were decreased, and some slight increase in plasma cells was found (also by Blitstein, 1950). The increase in plasma cells correlates with the higher γ-globulins found in Bantu and Negro individuals (Blitstein, 1950; Linhard, 1956).

BASOPHILS IN ETHNIC GROUPS

A reciprocal relationship between tissue mast cells and circulating basophils exists in many species (p. 144). Evidence available at present does not suggest a higher mast cell count in the tissues of different ethnic groups (Pepler and Meyer, 1961). On the other hand, in the study discussed above (Wassermann, 1966), the basophil count derived by indirect methods was 26 and 24 cells per mm³ for whites and Cape Coloureds, and 14 cells per mm³ for Bantu, which represents a significant (p = 0.05) difference.

It is known, however, that this method is inaccurate and therefore this difference was re-examined by a direct counting method for basophils which has been previously evaluated (Wassermann et al., 1971). By this method it could be established that a significant sex difference exists in Cape Coloureds and in whites, but not in Bantu. There is a tendency to a lower count in Bantu males than in whites and Cape Coloureds; this is not significant at the 5% level, but is of significance at the 10% level (Wassermann et al., 1972).

LEUCOCYTIC ANOMALIES AND PIGMENTATION

The studies discussed above would indicate that leucocytic function may be important in the overall physiology of pigmentation. It is therefore of interest that changes in leucocytes accompany certain disorders which show hyperpigmentation as an integral part of the syndrome, e.g. Addison's disease, hyperthyroidism and anorexia nervosa. In all 3 a leucocytic picture closely resembling that often found in dark races occurs, namely lymphocytosis and neutropenia. This picture does not occur in phenothiazine melanosis (A. Satanove and A. C. Greiner, personal communication). The endocrine changes are clearly related to both the pigmentation and the leucocyte count in these syndromes.

In the following disorders which involve leucocytic anomalies as well as pigmentary changes, the mechanism is apparently not an endocrine one:

Chediak-Higashi syndrome

An extensive review of this rare syndrome was made by Sung et al. (1969). Only 35 cases in 23 families had been reported prior to 1969. The characteristic findings in man are: anomalous giant granules in leucocytes, defective pigmentation, photophobia and increased susceptibility to infections. Widespread lymphohistiocytic infiltrations in various organs, interpreted by some as a malignant change in lymphoid tissue, eventually develop and survival beyond adolescence is rare. The association with partial albinism is interesting because a homologous condition was described in Aleutian mink (Leader et al., 1963), in partial albino Hereford cattle (Padgett et al., 1963, 1964; Padgett, 1967) and in the Beige mouse (Lutzner et al., 1967). The genetic leucocytic pigmentation link-up is of interest, and further studies should be rewarding to the pigmentologist.

The cytoplasmic inclusions are present in a variety of cells of neuroectodermal origin (e.g. neurons, astrocytes, choroid plexus epithelium, satellite cells of the dorsal spinal ganglia and Schwann cells) as wel as in cells of other tissues. Neuropathological changes are described and illustrated *in extenso* by Sung et al. (1969) who found that these inclusions resembled lipofuscin in many microscopic and ultramicroscopic characteristics. Especially in relation to neuromelanin, whose cellular derivation is uncertain, although it is regarded as a true melanin (p. 135), it is interesting to note that they found that the pigment was similar in staining characteristics and natural colour to that of normal people, but differed in its larger size, irregular form and tendency to clump or fuse into compact masses. They refer to the studies of Duffy and Tennyson (1965) which suggest that neuromelanin may have a lipofuscin substructure upon which melanin pigment is deposited.

The leucocytic inclusions of giant size might be due to fusion of the smaller ones (Bessis et al., 1961). These granules are the lysosomes of normal leucocytes (Cohn and Hirsch, 1960) and thus it is believed that the large anomalous granules are altered lysosomes (White, 1966). In minks no difference could be found in the amounts of lysosomal acid phosphatase, β-glucuronidase and cathepsin in leucocytes of affected and unaffected animals (Padgett, 1967). Altered premelanosomes, and melanosomes characterized by gigantism of melanin granules, of skin, hair and eyes was described in Chediak-Higashi disease (Pierini and Abulafia, 1958; Stegmaier and Schneider, 1965; Windhorst and Zelickson, 1966; Zelickson et al., 1966). Lipofuscin granules are considered as secondary lysosomes or residual bodies (Novikoff, 1967). Melanin granules have much in common with lysosomes, as indicated by the observation of Van Woert et al. (1971) that substances which increase pigmentation are substances which influence the stability of lysosomal membranes.

The abnormally enlarged granules in neutrophils from animals with the Chediak-Higashi anomaly do not undergo lysis following phagocytosis of bacteria (Padgett, 1967; Padgett et al., 1967), and it is thought by Sung and Okada (1971) that the enlarged granules probably represent the product of insufficient lysosomal digestion. Thus, they remain undigested as the result of a partial enzymatic defect yet to be elucidated.

Acid phosphatase is present in melanosomes and in the Golgi area of melano-cytes. It is not clear how it acquires the enzyme (Seiji and Kikuchi, 1969).

Fanconi's anaemia

An aplastic anaemia which occurs at a very early age and which is associated with a variety of congenital defects (bone abnormalities, especially forearm and thumbs, microcephaly, hypogenitalism and genitourinary tract abnormalities), is most constantly accompanied by hyperpigmentation which may be generalized olive brown or patchy. In the family studied by the author pigmentation was marked in the affected sibs, and was very marked circumorbitally, in a broad band across the abdomen and in other friction areas, but also in many café-au-lait patches.

Aplastic anaemia was universally fatal before anabolic steroid and cortico-steroid therapy was introduced in such cases, but it now has a better prognosis. (Our patient is now 23 years old, married and has been asymptomatic for 6 years as far as the anaemia is concerned.) However, a higher incidence of leukaemia in patients with Fanconi's anaemia has been reported, and may be related to the chromosome anomalies frequently found in these patients (Wassermann et al., 1968). Longer survival may increase the incidence of subsequent leukaemia in these patients.

As far as pigmentology is concerned, the genetic control of both haemato-poiesis and leucopoiesis, and pigmentary, skeletal and other anomalies, is of central interest.

Sea-blue histiocyte syndrome

Up to 1971, 24 cases of the 'sea-blue histiocyte syndrome' have been reported. The syndrome is characterized by hepatosplenomegaly, usually detected in early life, mild thrombocytopenia with or without purpura, and the presence, in the bone marrow and spleen, of the characteristic histiocyte containing granules which stain bright blue or blue-green with Romanowsky stains.

In 3 of the 24 cases brownish pigmentation of the skin was present, and lymphadenopathy in 2 cases. Karayalcin et al. (1971) think it likely that 'acquir-ed' and 'hereditary' varieties exist. They consider that the relationship to histiocytes in the hereditary and acquired lipidoses should be elucidated. This relationship between lipidoses and the lipofuscin depositions in the nervous system was considered for Chediak-Higashi disease by Sung and Okada (1971).

LYSOSOMES AND MELANIN

Leucocytic handling of melanin focuses interest on the role of lysosomes, the intracellular organelles concerned with enzymatic degradation of ingested material. Our studies (Wassermann, 1963, 1964, 1965, 1968) indicate that a change occurs in the staining of ingested melanin in macrophages. Whether or not this is due to a degradation of melanin or the protein moiety, always attached to natural melanins, cannot be ascertained by ordinary microscopy.

Although extremely resistant to clinical and physical methods aimed at its degradation, it was suggested that melanin might be disintegrated intracellularly in old melanoma melanocytes (Mishima and Ito, 1969; Novikoff et al., 1968; Seiji and Ohtaki, 1971), in macrophages (Olson et al., 1970), as well as in epidermal cells (Olson et al., 1970; Hori et al., 1968; Szabo et al., 1969).

Using liver lysosomes, Ohtaki and Seiji (1971) showed that melanosomal protein components were degraded at a steady rate, but melanin labelled with ^{14}C-dopa in mice with melanoma showed that the melanin moiety of melanosomes was not significantly degraded, as judged by the release of radioactivity to the centrifuged supernatant. The random polymeric nature of melanin may protect against enzymatic degradation of the pigment (Blois, 1965).

SUMMARY

The relationship of leucocytes to melanin pigmentation needs further investigation, but at present it appears that (1) leucocytes transport melanin in darker races (2) in whom the peripheral blood leucocyte picture assumes a pattern found in endocrine diseases with hyperpigmentation. (3) Available evidence suggests that this is, in fact, due to lesser adrenocortical function in the darker races. (4) Anomalies associated with pigmentation defects and leucocytic anomalies indicate that genetic control of the lysosomal enzymes may be common to both in the Chediak-Higashi syndrome. Chromosome abnormalities and associated skeletal and genitourinary anomalies with defective haematopoiesis and pigmentation defects might indicate alternative but associated genetic control mechanisms for these organ systems.

The role of lysosomes in melanin physiology is a field of current interest and could yield more specific data in the near future as to what happens to the pigment moiety left intact after degradation of its substructure. It may provide the link between lipofuscin and melanin.

Apart from the fact that a stable free radical which may influence several metabolic pathways is transported in this way by leucocytes, nothing is known of the degradation products of melanosomes and their influence on the metabolism of other organs.

REFERENCES

BARNARD, H. F. (1967): Leucopenia in West Indians and Africans. *Lancet*, 2, 213.
BARNES, G. J. and CAMERON, M. E. (1966): Skin and eye changes associated with chlorpromazine therapy. *Med. J. Aust.*, 1, 478.
BESSIS, M., BERNARD, J. and SELIGMANN, M. (1961): Etude cytologique d'un cas de maladie de Chediak. *Nouv. Rev. franç. Hémat.*, 1, 422.
BLITSTEIN, I. (1950): Hématologie normale des Noirs du Congo Belge. Sang et moëlle osseuse des adultes. *Ann. Soc. belge Méd. trop.*, 30, 1401.
BLOIS, M. S. (1965): Random polymers as a matrix for chemical evolution. In:

The Origins of Prebiological Systems, p. 19. Editor: S. W. Fox. Academic Press, New York, N.Y.

BRAUNSTEINER, H., PAERTAN, J. and THUMB, N. (1958): Studies on lymphocytic function. *Blood, 13*, 417.

BRÖNTE-STEWART, B., ANTONIS, A., ROSE-INNES, T. and MOODIE, A. D. (1961): An interracial study on the serum protein pattern of adult men in Southern Africa. *Amer. J. clin. Nutr., 9*, 596.

BROUN, G. O., HERBIG, F. K. and HAMILTON, J. R. (1966): Leukopenia in Negroes. *New Engl. J. Med., 275*, 1410.

CLYDE, D. F. (1964): A study of mononuclear leucocyte and neutrophil patterns among East Africans partially immune to malaria. *J. trop. Med. Hyg., 67*, 25.

COHN, Z. A. and HIRSCH, J. G. (1960): The isolation and properties of the specific cytoplasmic granules of rabbit polymorphonuclear leucocytes. *J. exp. Med., 112*, 983.

DAVIS, L. R. (1967): Leucopenia in West Indians and Africans. *Lancet, 2*, 213.

DUFFY, P. E. and TENNYSON, V. M. (1965): Phase and electron-microscopic observations of Lewy bodies and melanin granules in the substantia nigra and locus caeruleus in Parkinson's disease. *J. Neuropath. exp. Neurol., 24*, 398.

FELDMAN, P. E. and FRIERSON, B. D. (1964): Dermatological and ophthalmological changes associated with prolonged chlorpromazine therapy. *Amer. J. Psychiat., 121*, 187.

FRANKLIN, J. W., ZAVALU, D. C. and RADCLIFFE, C. E. (1952): Detection of malignant melanoma by bone-marrow aspiration. A report of 2 cases. *Blood, 7*, 934.

FUKUI, A. and MITSUI, T. (1965): A contribution to the study of the pigmented leucocytes in Urodeles. *Okajimas Folia anat. japon., 41*, 285.

GLOMBEK, G. (1968): Die Phagozytose von Melaningranula durch Bindegewebszellen während des Gewebeabbaus der Metamorphose bei *Xenopus*. *Experientia (Basel), 24*, 265.

GOODALL, P., SPRIGGS, A. I. and WELLS, F. R. (1961): Malignant melanoma with melanosis and melanuria and with pigmented monocytes and tumour cells in the blood. *Brit. J. Surg., 48*, 549.

GREINER, A. C. (1968): Phenothiazines and diffuse melanosis. *Agressologie, 9*, 219.

GREINER, A. C. and NICHOLSON, G. A. (1964): Pigment deposition in viscera associated with prolonged chlorpromazine therapy. *Canad. med. Ass. J., 91*, 627.

GREINER, A. C. and NICHOLSON, G. A. (1965): Schizophrenia melanosis. *Lancet, 2*, 1165.

HASHIMOTO, K., WIENER, W., ALBERT, J. and NELSON, R. G. (1966): An electron-microscopic study of chlorpromazine pigmentation. *J. invest. Derm., 47*, 296.

HAYS, G. B., LYLE, C. G. and WHEELER, C. E. (1964): Slate grey colour in patients receiving chlorpromazine. *Arch. Derm., 90*, 471.

HORI, Y., TODA, K., PATHAK, M. A., CLARK, W. H. and FITZPATRICK, T. B. (1968): A fine structure study of the human epidermal melanosome complex and its acid phosphatase activity. *J. ultrastruct. Res., 25*, 109.

HU, F. (1965): The developmental cycle of B26 melanoma cell in culture. *Tex. Rep. Biol. Med., 23*, 308.

HU, F., FOSNAUGH, R. P., BRYAN, H. G. and JACKS, D. (1961): Human skin window. A cytologic method for the study of allergic inflammation. *J. invest. Derm., 37*, 409.

HUANG, C. L. (1967): Isolation and identification of urinary chlorpromazine metabolites in man. *Int. J. Neuropharmacol., 6*, 1.

JOHNSTONE, R. M. (1951): Some observations on the total and differential leucocyte counts in adult male East African natives. *J. roy. Army med. Cps, 97*, 251.

Jonsson, U. and Rundles, R. W. (1959): Tumor metastasis in bone marrow. *Blood, 6,* 965.

Karayalcin, G., Rosner, F. and Sawitsky, A. (1971): Sea-blue histiocyte syndrome in an octogenarian. *Lancet, 2,* 318.

Kato, K. (1935): Leucocytes in infancy and childhood. *J. Pediat., 7,* 7.

Leader, R. W., Padgett, G. A. and Gorham, J. R. (1963): Studies of abnormal leukocyte bodies in the mink. *Blood, 22,* 477.

Liebmann, E. (1929): Über das Auftreten von melaninhaltigen Monozyten bei generalisierter Melanomatosis. *Schweiz. med. Wschr., 59,* 597.

Linhard, J. (1956): Quelques normes hématologiques chez des Africains de la Région de Dakar. *Sang, 27,* 142.

Lutzner, M. A., Lowrie, C. T. and Jordan, H. W. (1967): Giant granules in leukocytes of the Beige mouse. *J. Hered., 58,* 299.

Mathelone, M. B. R. (1967): Eye and skin changes in psychiatric patients treated with chlorpromazine. *Brit. J. Ophthal., 51,* 86.

Mishima, Y. and Ito, R. (1969): Electron microscopy of microfocal necrosis in malignant melanomas. *Cancer (Philad.), 24,* 185.

Mlczoch, F. and Kohout, J. (1965): Das 'Gewebsbild' bei malignen Erkrankungen. Untersuchungen mit der Hautfenstermethode an 214 Fällen. *Klin. Wschr., 43,* 627.

Moore, R. (1958a): The whole blood cell count in the indigenous people of East Africa. *J. trop. Med. Hyg., 61,* 70.

Moore, R. (1958b): The white cell count in the indigenous people of East Africa. *J. trop. Med. Hyg., 61,* 144.

Neser, M. L. (1968): The leucocyte picture in white, Bantu, coloured and Indian school children of 6–15 years as observed during the Pretoria Nutrition Status Surveys of 1962–1965. *S. Afr. med. J., 42,* 444.

Novikoff, A. B. (1967): Lysosomes in nerve cells. In: *The Neuron,* p. 319. Editor: Holger Hyden. Elsevier Publ. Co., Amsterdam.

Novikoff, A. B., Albala, A. and Biempica, L. (1968): Ultrastructural and cytochemical observations on B-16 and Harding-Passey mouse melanoma. *J. Histochem. Cytochem., 16,* 299.

Ohtaki, N. and Seiji, M. (1971): Degradation of melanosomes by lysosomes. *J. invest. Derm., 57,* 1.

Olson, R. L., Nordquist, J. and Everett, M. A. (1970): The role of epidermal lysosomes in melanin physiology. *Brit. J. Derm., 83,* 189.

Padgett, G. A. (1967): Neutrophilic function in animals with Chediak-Higashi syndrome. *Blood, 29,* 906.

Padgett, G. A., Leader, G. W. and Gorham, J. R. (1963): Hereditary abnormal leukocyte granules in mink. *Fed. Proc., 22,* 428.

Padgett, G. A., Leader, G. W., Gorham, J. R. and O'Mary, C. C. (1964): The familial occurrence of the Chediak-Higashi syndrome in mink and cattle. *Genetica, 49,* 505.

Padgett, G. A., Reiquam, C. W., Gorham, J. R., Henson, J. B. and O'Mary, C. C. (1967): Comparative studies of the Chediak-Higashi syndrome. *Amer. J. Path., 51,* 553.

Page, A. R. and Good, R. A. (1957): Studies on cyclic neutropenia. *J. Dis. Child., 94,* 623.

Pepler, W. J. and Meyer, B. J. (1961): Mast cells in the coronary arteries. *Arch. Path., 71,* 209.

Perillie, P. E. and Finch, S. C. (1960): The local exudative cellular response in leukaemia. *J. clin. Invest., 39,* 1353.

PERRY, T. L., CULLING, C. F. A., BARRY, K. and HANSEN, S. (1964): 7-Hydroxy-chlorpromazine: potential toxic drug metabolite in psychiatric patients. *Science*, *146*, 81.

PIERINI, D. O. and ABULAFIA, J. (1958): Manifestaciones cutaneas del sindrome de Chediak-Higashi. *Arch. argent. Derm.*, *8*, 23.

REBUCK, J. W. (1940): On the role of the monocyte in inflammation as demonstrated by a new technique. *Anat. Rec. 76, Suppl. 2*, 46, 93.

REBUCK, J. W. (1947): *Cytology of Acute Inflammation in Man as demonstrated by Two Original Technical Procedures with Especial Reference to the Role of Lymphocytes*. Thesis, University of Minnesota.

REBUCK, J. W., BOYD, C. B. and RIDDLE, J. M. (1960): Skin windows and the action of the reticulo-endothelial system in man. *Ann. N.Y. Acad. Sci.*, *88*, 30.

REBUCK, J. W. and CROWLEY, J. H. (1955): A method for studying leukocytic functions in vivo. *Ann. N.Y. Acad. Sci.*, *59*, 757.

REBUCK, J. W., MONTO, R. W., MONOHAN, S. A. and RIDDLE, J. M. (1958): Potentialities of the lymphocyte, with an additional reference to its dysfunction in Hodgkin's disease. *Ann. N.Y. Acad. Sci.*, *73*, 8.

REBUCK, J. W., SMITH, R. W. and MARGULIS, R. R. (1951): The modification of leucocytic function in human skin windows by ACTH. *Gastroenterology*, *19*, 644.

RIIS, P. (1959): *The Cytology of the Inflammatory Exudate*. Munksgaard, Copenhagen.

RIPPEY, J. J. (1967): Leukopenia in West Indians and Africans. *Lancet*, *2*, 44.

SATANOVE, A. (1965): Pigmentation due to phenothiazines in high and prolonged dosage. *J. Amer. med. Ass.*, *191*, 263.

SEIJI, M. and KIKUCHI, A. (1969): Acid phosphatase activity in melanosomes. *J. invest. Derm.*, *52*, 219.

SEIJI, M. and OHTAKI, N. (1971): Lysosomes in mouse melanoma. *J. invest. Derm.*, *56*, 436.

SHELLEY, W. B., GRIFFITH, R. F. and RAWNSLEY, H. M. (1969): Unique pigment in skin window macrophages. Associated with recurrent painful ankle ulcers: Atrophie noir. *Arch. Derm.*, *99*, 398.

STEGMAIER, O. C. and SCHNEIDER, L. A. (1965): Chediak-Higashi syndrome. Dermatologic manifestations. *Arch. Derm.*, *91*, 1.

SUNDBERG, R. D. (1956): Metastatic malignant melanoma of the bone marrow. *Anat. Rec.*, *124*, 368.

SUNG, J. H., MEYERS, J. P., STADLON, E. M., COWEN, D. and WOLF, A. (1969): Neuropathological changes in Chediak-Higashi disease. *J. Neuropath. exp. Neurol.*, *28*, 86.

SUNG, J. H. and OKADA, K. (1971): Neuropathological changes in mink with Chediak-Higashi disease. *J. Neuropath. exp. Neurol.*, *30*, 33.

SZABO, G., GERALD, A. B., PATHAK, M. A. and FITZPATRICK, T. B. (1969): Racial differences in the human epidermis. *Nature (Lond.)*, *222*, 1081.

TURNER, F. M. (1953): An investigation into the relationship between physiologically low leucocyte counts and sickness absence. *Brit. J. Radiol.*, *26*, 417.

TURNER, F. M. (1956): The white cell count and exposure to radiation hazards: The significance of leucocyte warning and rejection levels in the younger age groups. *Brit. J. indust. Med.*, *13*, 277.

VAN WOERT, M. H., KORB, F. and PRASAD, K. N. (1971): Regulation of tyrosinase activity in mouse melanoma and skin by changes in melanosomal membrane permeability. *J. invest. Derm.*, *56*, 343.

WALKER, A. R. P., FLETCHER, D. C., REYNOLDS, P. A., BERSOHN, I. and SONNENFELD, E. D. (1956): Reduction to normal levels of the high erythrocyte sedimentation rates in apparently healthy South African Bantu men. *Nature (Lond.)*, *177*, 480.

WASSERMANN, H. P. (1961): *Die Effek van 5-Hidroksitriptamien op die Ontwikkeling van die Limfosiet soos waargeneem in die Inflammatoriese Respons.* Thesis, University of Stellenbosch.

WASSERMANN, H. P. (1963a): Fusion of melanin-labelled macrophages to form giant cells observed in vivo. *J. invest. Derm., 40,* 73.

WASSERMANN, H. P. (1963b): Lymphocytes and the transport of melanin. Observations in the inflammatory response. *J. invest. Derm., 41,* 473.

WASSERMANN, H. P. (1963c): An assessment of the phagocytic ability of melanin-labelled L.E. cells and neutrophils in the human skin window. *S. Afr. J. Lab. clin. Med., 9,* 142.

WASSERMANN, H. P. (1964a): Döhle bodies in *Bufo temporaria* afflicted with red leg disease. *Nature (Lond.), 202,* 816.

WASSERMANN, H. P. (1964b): Studies on melanin-labelled cells in the human skin window. *S. Afr. J. Lab. clin. Med., 10,* 76.

WASSERMANN, H. P. (1965): Leucocytes and melanin pigmentation. I. Demonstration of pigmented leucocytes in blood of amphibians, reptiles and normal man. *J. invest. Derm., 45,* 104.

WASSERMANN, H. P. (1966): Leucocytes and melanin pigmentation. II. The leukocyte count and erythrocyte sedimentation rate in Africa. An interracial study and review of the literature. *S. Afr. med. J., 40, Suppl.,* 3.

WASSERMANN, H. P. (1967a): Extension of the concept 'vertebrate epidermal melanin unit' to embrace visceral pigmentation and leukocytic melanin transport. *Nature (Lond.), 213,* 282.

WASSERMANN, H. P. (1967b): Phagocytosis in the L.E. cell phenomenon. *Lancet, 1,* 1112.

WASSERMANN, H. P. (1968): Phenothiazines and leucocytic melanin transport. *Agressologie, 9,* 241.

WASSERMANN, H. P., FRY, R. and COHN, J. (1968): Fanconi's anaemia: Cytogenic studies in a family. *S. Afr. med. J., 42,* 1162.

WASSERMANN, H. P., LAUBSCHER, N. F. and BOTHA, M. V. (1971): Evaluation of an improved method for direct basophil counts. *S. Afr. med. J., 45,* 491.

WASSERMANN, H. P., MULLER, M. A. and LAUBSCHER, N. F. (1972): An ethnic and sex difference in interracial studies of direct basophil counts. *S. Afr. med. J., 46,* 143.

WASSERMANN, H. P., VAN DER WALT, J. J., LUTZ, U. and TIEDT, F. (1973): Electron microscopy of melanophagocytosis in the human skin window. *S. Afr. med. J.,* in press.

WHITE, J. G. (1966): The Chediak-Higashi syndrome. A possible lysosomal disease. *Blood, 28,* 143.

WINDHORST, D. B. and ZELICKSON, A. S. (1966): The pigmentary anomaly of the Chediak-Higashi syndrome. *Clin. Res., 14,* 276.

ZELICKSON, A. S. (1965): Skin pigmentation and chlorpromazine. *J. Amer. med. Ass., 194,* 670.

ZELICKSON, A. S., WINDHORST, D. B., WHITE, J. G. and GOOD, R. A. (1966): Chediak-Higashi syndrome: Hereditary gigantism of cytoplasmic organelles. *Science, 151,* 81.

ZELICKSON, A. S. and ZELLER, H. C. (1964): A new and unusual reaction to chlorpromazine. *J. Amer. med. Ass., 188,* 394.

Chapter XIV

Control mechanisms of pigmentation

As with all systems in the body, there are local homeostatic control mechanisms for pigmentation which have already been discussed (p. 125). The overriding control system for the body as a whole is, however, a function of the endocrine and central nervous system; both are closely integrated at present in our concept of neuroendocrine mechanisms. Hormones may exert their influence on the melanocyte, or primarily, according to the present-day concept of the epidermal melanin unit, on cells removing melanin from the melanocytes, i.e. keratinocytes (Hall, 1969) or phagocytes (Wassermann, 1968). Nervous influences on the effector cells are mediated by the release of chemical substances acting locally on the cell membrane.

If the main interest centres around the *ability* of the melanocyte to respond to chemical influences, it becomes of secondary interest whether or not the substance under discussion reaches the cell through the circulation (hormone from a particular endocrine gland) or by direct contact (neurohumour secreted by a nerve-ending on the cell membrane). Much can also be learned from cell responses to pharmacologically active substances which may compete for that particular receptor.

The author believes that the melanocyte and its secretion product occupy a special place in the evolution of neuroendocrine control mechanisms, and that melanin is indeed a hormone. This is discussed at the end of the Chapter, but for the sake of convenience the nervous system and the endocrine system will be considered separately.

Common to both the endocrine and neurological control, as a 'final common pathway', is the 'first messenger – second messenger' concept of cellular control mechanisms. Interesting work on amphibians has recently been reported, but much remains to be elucidated before valid extrapolations to mammalian systems can be made.

CELLULAR CONTROL BY NEUROHUMOURS AND HORMONES

Sutherland et al. (1965, 1966) formulated the 'first messenger – second mes-

senger' hypothesis: Hormones, as *first messengers*, mediate their actions by controlling the intracellular level of the *second messenger*, cyclic 3′,5′-AMP. Strong
evidence for this hypothesis is the fact that cyclic 3′,5′-AMP can mimic the action
of the first messenger (Sutherland et al., 1968) (Fig. 25).

As far as *amphibian* melanocytes are concerned it was shown (Novales and
Davis, 1967) that cyclic 3′,5′-AMP can mimic the action of melanocyte-stimulating hormone (MSH) on the skin of *Rana pipiens*, and Abe et al. (1969) showed
that darkening of frog skin by MSH is correlated with an increased level of
cyclic 3′,5′-AMP.

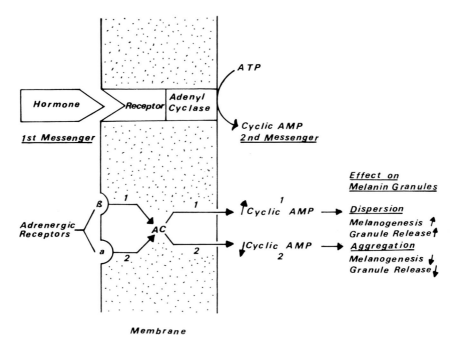

Fig. 25. Function of cyclic AMP in the control of pigmentation. Upper part of
Figure summarizes the concept of Sutherland et al. (1965, 1966), and the
lower part the results of studies by Goldman and Hadley (1969).

Goldman and Hadley (1969) demonstrated melanin *aggregation* in *Anolis*
melanophores in response to α-adrenoceptors and *dispersion* in response to β-
adrenoceptors. Stimulation of β-adrenoceptors, in some other tissues, increases
the intracellular levels of cyclic 3′,5′-AMP (Robinson et al., 1967).

In the epidermal melanin unit of amphibians, Hadley and Quevedo (1966)
postulated that the rate of melanin granule synthesis and transfer of melanin to
epidermal cells is directly related to the *effective* secretory surface of the melanocytes. Granule dispersion is associated with a high rate of melanogenesis and
granule release to epidermal cells, while aggregation of granules within the
melanocyte lowers the rate of melanogenesis and granule release.

In his study on the physiology and pharmacology of colour change in the sand flounder, Scott (1965) found that all drugs causing pigment aggregation when injected subcutaneously were substituted aromatic ethylamines or hydrazines. Epinephrine, norepinephrine, dopamine and methamphetamine were the most potent. Pyrogallol, an inhibitor of catechol-*o*-methyl transferase, drastically potentiated epinephrine and norepinephrine. His studies strongly suggested that a catecholamine (epinephrine, norepinephrine or dopamine) is the transmitter at the chromato-neural junction and that catechol-*o*-methyl transferase is involved in chromatophore physiology.

Thought-provoking to the worker interested in ethnic pigmentation, but of fundamental significance to pigment physiology, is Hadley and Goldman's (1970) finding that within the 'species' *Rana pipiens*, the response of integumental chromatophores to hormonal stimulation in vitro varies markedly between frogs of northern (United States) origin as compared to those of southern (Mexican) origin. Southern frogs fail to lighten in response to catecholamine stimulation because the chromatophores lack α-adrenergic receptors. Darkening is due to β-adrenergic receptors present in frogs from both geographical areas.

The finding that α-adrenergic receptors mediate melanin granule aggregation, and β-adrenergic receptors regulate melanin granule dispersion is of considerable importance (see also Gupta and Bhide, 1967; Goldman and Hadley, 1969, 1970). The 'ethnic difference' in the experiments of Hadley and Goldman (1970) indicates, as they point out, the importance of a knowledge of the genetic background and characteristics of amphibians used in physiological research.

Abe et al. (1969) described the antagonism between MSH-induced increase in cyclic 3',5'-AMP in frog skins and the decrease in this enzyme following norepinephrine. Both MSH and the α- and β-receptor mechanisms locate the control of melanocyte responses to cyclic 3',5'-AMP levels within the cell, in the case of amphibians and reptiles. The lack of effect on pigmentation of various α- and β-stimulators and blockers used clinically in humans, supports other evidence for a lack of significant direct neurological control of human pigmentation.

The title of the following section was advisedly chosen to avoid the confusion of a title such as 'nervous control of pigmentation'. *Direct* nervous control of pigmentation does not exist in man, although it does in teleosts and some reptiles. This does not mean that some *anatomical* association of cholinesterase-positive nerve-endings and dendritic cells could not be shown (Serri and Cerimele, 1967) but simply that convincing evidence for *control* of function does not exist, although there is some evidence for an *influence* on melanocytes of man.

THE NERVOUS SYSTEM AND PIGMENTATION

1. Neuroendocrine mechanisms hold considerable evolutionary interest, and as a general statement it may be said that neurological control of melanocytes was superseded by a predominantly endocrine control in higher vertebrates.
2. The embryology and development of the melanocyte as well as its morphology and functional relationships support the view that the melanocyte is a 'masked primitive neuron' (Burgers, 1966).

The nervous origin of melanocytes

The neural crest appears as a group of epithelial cells, in the early presomite stage, at the side of the neural plate. As the plate folds over to become a tube, the cells come to lie dorsolaterally and then migrate to form a sheet which extends from the brain stem to the lower spinal cord. Apart from melanocytes, the cells also differentiate into spinal ganglia, sympathetic ganglia, chromaffin cells and probably, but this is disputed, Schwann cells. They also contribute to the formation of dental enamel.

The primitive melano*blasts* first appear in the 10-week-old Negro foetus, and the first few melano*cytes* infiltrate the epidermis in the 11th week. They increase rapidly as melanocytes from the dermis populate the epidermis between the 12th and 14th weeks. The dermis becomes depopulated and dermal melanocytes are restricted to a few localized areas such as the sacral or mongolian spot (Zimmerman and Becker, 1959).

The neural crest origin and subsequent migration of melanoblasts probably explains the association of various pigmentary changes with congenital anomalies (e.g. Waardenburg syndrome, neurofibromatosis). For further discussion see p. 235.

Pigmentation in human cutaneous nerves

Pigment zones occur around nerve fibres in the ocular fundus, olfactory epithelium and around the brain and spinal cord. The presence of pigmented cells closely associated with cutaneous sensory and autonomic nerves has been demonstrated (Kawamura et al., 1964). Whether or not intracutaneous naevus cells are directly derived from Schwann cells or nerves in adult skin is still undecided. Mishima (1967) pointed out that without electron-microscopic investigation the pigment around nerve fibres could be explained in several ways: (*a*) by the presence of melanized melanocytes around the nerve fibre which may or may not be derived from inactive melanocytes; (*b*) by the transformation of Schwann cells into melanocytes; (*c*) by the presence of melanophages along the nerve fibre; (*d*) or by the phagocytosis of melanosomes by Schwann cells or other neural structures. In his study of a blue naevus from the cheek of a 16-year-old white youth and a compound naevus on the sole of a 20-year-old American Negro man he demonstrated aggregated melanosomes within a Schwann cell and within the perineural cells of an unmyelinated nerve fibre in the upper corium. Occasionally the aggregates were enclosed with endo- or epineural material by a conspicuous double-layered membrane, but no developmental stages of melanosomes or premelanosomes were seen. He concluded that pigmentation of the peripheral nerves is due to the phagocytosis of melanosomes of extrinsic origin by Schwann cells and other neural structures.

Studies on vitiligo in man

In view of the observations suggesting that vitiligo may be associated with some neural or neurohumoural defect, several studies were made. Breathnach et al. (1966) studied centrally placed biopsies from areas of vitiligo and from normally pigmented skin, as well as marginal skin. They found degenerative and regenerative changes in terminal regions of a small proportion of nerves supplying the central and marginal areas of vitiliginous lesions.

Lerner (1959) suggested that in normal skin 'there is a balance between MSH from the pituitary gland which darkens melanocytes and of a substance from peripheral nerves which lightens them.' He reported on a woman with transverse myelitis whose vitiligo was limited to the area above the cord lesion, in contrast to the usual generalized distribution on vitiligo. Neither did depigmentation develop in or near the surgical scar of a subsequent hysterectomy.

The neurohumoural agent, acetylcholine, at low concentrations caused aggregation of melanin granules within frog epidermal melanocytes, previously dispersed by MSH (Goldman and Hadley, 1968). There is differential responsiveness of dermal and epidermal melanocytes in amphibians (McGuire and Möller, 1966) but it would appear valid, as Goldman and Hadley (1969) point out, in the absence of a satisfactory technique for in vivo study of human melanocytes, to extrapolate from the cytophysiological findings on the *epidermal* melanocyte system of amphibians to the melanocytes of mammals. They conclude that such extrapolation suggests that localized depigmentation (e.g. vitiligo) in mammals may result from increased cholinergic activity in such areas. This supports the view originally taken by Lerner (1959).

More recently, Lerner (1971) proposed a melanocyte-selfdestruction hypothesis to explain the aetiology of vitiligo. According to this hypothesis lethal damage to the melanocyte results from a toxic melanin precursor, which may involve the enzyme tyrosinase (Riley, 1970).

ENDOCRINE CONTROL OF PIGMENTATION

Several recent reviews (e.g. Hall, 1969a; Lande and Lerner, 1967) discussed the influence of hormones on pigmentation, and as far as *ethnic* pigmentation is concerned the reviews on endocrine patterns in the African (Adadevoh, 1967, 1968, 1970; Trowell, 1960; Wassermann, 1966) should provide a perspective of the relative importance of these factors in ethnic pigmentation.

The main uncertainties in our present knowledge concerning endocrine influence on pigmentation are:
1. Most of the studies concern amphibians, in whom the initial studies of Allen (1916) and Smith (1916) indicated the importance of the pituitary. In most instances human hormone assays for melanocyte stimulating hormone MSH and melatonin used *amphibians* to assay the influence of *mammalian* hormones. Only recently have immunoassays become available (Abe et al., 1969).
2. Endocrine studies in the darker races must differentiate an endocrine pattern which has been adapted to a completely different environment from that in which the baseline normals of endocrinology have been established. By this not only the geographical and climatic factors (which are probably of minor

importance in acclimatized individuals) are meant, but also those environmental factors which challenge (as a form of stress) the host's endocrine adaptation from early childhood (malnutrition, malaria and other tropical diseases).
3. Many darker races have increased γ-globulin fractions and a lower albumin fraction in their serum proteins as compared to whites. Hormones are transported, bound to proteins, and the active fraction is the free hormone. It is reasonable to suppose, as unpublished studies at present in progress (Van Heerden and Wassermann) intend to point out, that protein binding of hormones in different ethnic groups may cause differences in free hormone levels with normal function of the target organs.
4. As far as African endocrinology is concerned, communicable and infectious diseases present the most problems for a relatively small number of medical workers, so that most of the studies available at present were made in the Republic of South Africa, the most advanced country on the continent and largely free from the more exotic tropical diseases; but recently significant work has also been done in Nigeria.
5. The American Negro is often presented in American literature as equivalent to the African (Bantu or Negro), but in actual fact he resembles the Cape Coloured of Africa much more closely, not only as far as disease incidence pattern is concerned (Phillips and Burch, 1960), but also in skin colour (Ojikutu, 1965; Wassermann and Heyl, 1968) and in leucocyte counts (Wassermann, 1966).

Pituitary gland

The detailed biosynthesis of MSH in the pituitary is unknown, but the biosynthesis of ACTH in hypophyseal tissue has been studied (Adija et al., 1965). α-MSH, adrenocorticotrophic hormone (ACTH) and β-MSH have structural similarities. The first 2 contain identical amino terminal tridecapeptide sequences, while all 3 share the heptapeptide sequence -Met-Glu-His-Phe-Arg-Try-Gly-. This portion of the molecule is probably directly responsible for eliciting the melanocytic response, and accounts for the MSH activity of even highly purified ACTH.

Releasing polypeptide factors from the hypothalamus control pituitary secretion of the hormone. Taleisnik and Orias (1965) presented evidence for a MSH-releasing factor, while Schally et al. (1965) presented evidence for an inhibitor of MSH release in hypothalamic tissue. The liver is an important MSH-inactivating site, and 4 to 6% of the activity introduced by intramuscular injection in man can be recovered from urine (Lerner et al., 1954).

Lande and Lerner (1967) state that it is 'not possible or wise to extrapolate results from one species to another' and find that the functional significance of the MSH hormones in mammalian species is not clear. Both α- and β-MSH and ACTH darken human skin over a period of days and may be involved in hyperpigmentation associated with pituitary hyperfunction (Lerner, 1960), and in these cases increased levels of β-MSH have been found in man. In the guinea-pig MSH increases melanocyte size and complexity and also intra- and extracellular pigment, but the sexual skin of female guinea-pigs shows greater sensitivity to oestrogens than to MSH (Snell and Bischitz, 1960; Snell, 1962, 1964).

Extra-melanocytic activities, including thyrotrophin-like activity (Cehovic, 1962), influence on neural transmission (Krivoy and Guillemin, 1961) and release of free fatty acids into the serum (Rudman, 1963), have been reported. The possibility that a-MSH may not only be an intermediate in the biosynthesis of ACTH, but also a corticotrophin-releasing factor is of particular interest (Schally et al., 1962). Effects of MSH on cell cultures of melanocytes have been studied (Novales, 1963).

Cortisol or corticosteroids prevent or reverse the hyperpigmentation of bilateral adrenalectomy (Lerner and McGuire, 1964) as they do in the substitution therapy of Addison's disease.

The role of MSH in human pigmentation, and especially ethnic pigmentation, is not clear. Dahlberg (1963) found that daily MSH levels in 5 women reached a peak at the time of increased pigmentation at the beginning and end of the menstrual cycle. McGuinness (1963) found that patients with paler skins had lower levels of urinary MSH output than those with a darker skin colour. On the other hand, no differences were discovered between individuals from light and dark ethnic groups. Synthetic a-MSH and an acetylated 23 amino acid ACTH caused striking hyperpigmentation after 3 days' administration to an American Negro (McGuire and Lerner, 1963).

Ethnic differences in end-organ responsiveness to pituitary hormones is suggested by the finding of subresponsiveness to pituitary growth hormone in Central African Pygmies (Rimoin et al., 1969).

Thyroid hormones

Species variation is evident in the influence of thyroxine on melanin pigmentation. In man, hyperthyroidism may be accompanied by increased epidermal melanin (Robert, 1941; Jeghers, 1944), but little is known of its action on pigmentation at cellular and biochemical levels.

Normal thyroid function in Negroes and Bantu has received little attention. Protein-bound iodine levels are generally lower than in whites (Politzer and Munoz, 1962). Thyrotoxicosis, uncommon in the Bantu and African, seems to have become more prevalent in recent years (Gelfand, 1957; Dancaster, 1970). Long-acting thyroid stimulator (LATS) is present in nearly all cases of Graves' disease, and the inability of the Bantu to form autoantibodies (Zoutendyk, 1970) is suggested as a possible explanation for the rarity of thyrotoxicosis in the Bantu (Dancaster, 1970). Hypothyroidism is extremely rare in the Bantu (Meiring, 1967).

Androgens

These hormones have a complex and ill-understood influence on pigmentation. Stimulation (Flaks, 1948), inhibition (Bischitz and Snell, 1959) and no effect (Snell, 1967) have been reported. Increased pigmentation of several skin areas in states of androgen excess, and decreased pigmentation in these areas in androgen deficiency, indicate the physiological action of these hormones. In the congenital adrenogenital syndrome hyperpigmentation results from the defective hydroxylation of C_{21} hormones with a resultant escape of ACTH from the negative feedback control by cortisol.

Lesser excretion of androgen metabolites has been reported in African males over 30 years of age than in white males (Bersohn and Oelofse, 1957; Clifford and Buldrook, 1966).

Oestrogens and progesterone

The influence of the ovary on skin pigmentation has been known since 1930 (Lipschutz, 1930). Skin colour varies with menstruation (Snell and Turner, 1966) and depends on the synergistic action of oestrogen and progesterone. In birds oestrogens increase tyrosinase activity and this action is inhibited by puromycin, an antibiotic which inhibits protein synthesis (Hall, 1969*b*). The action of oestradiol on the uterus in increasing its protein synthesis points to a possibly similar action in melanocytes (Notides and Gorski, 1966).

The best clinical example of the effect of oestrogens and progesterones on melanin pigmentation is seen in the chloasma resulting from oral contraceptives (Carruthers, 1966, 1967; Gregg, 1966; Quamina, 1967). This is a common side-effect and occurs in all races. It is due to the hormone effects but the precise relationship of oestrogen and progesterones is not known. Oestrogen alone can cause chloasma even in the male, but Carruthers (1966, 1967) suggested that progestogens act on the oestrogen-primed melanocytes (similar to their action on the other reproductive organs in the female), and from his review of the literature he thinks it most likely that chloasma is precipitated by sunlight. He found that the incidence increased from 4% during the 1st year of use to 37% after 5 years of use. In most instances the cosmetic effect is the only reason for consulting the physician.

Most African males over 30 years of age apparently excrete large amounts of oestrogens and few androgen metabolites (Trowell, 1960; Bersohn and Oelofse, 1957; Clifford and Buldrook, 1966).

During pregnancy oestrogen excretion in Africans is greater than in whites and Indians living in Africa, although the normal pattern of increase throughout pregnancy is present (Boulle, 1968).

In the absence of liver disease and leprosy both unilateral and bilateral gynaecomastia is fairly common in African males. Apart from the higher urinary oestrogen levels, target organ sensitivity may also be involved. The effect of malnutrition is, however, probably as important as endocrine factors.

Adrenocortical function in Bantu and Negro

The adrenal cortex is involved indirectly in pigmentation through its negative feedback control of ACTH and possibly MSH secretion.

Lesser adrenocortical function has been generally assumed to be standard in Africans, but some evidence of this has also been found in American Negroes, Indians and Malaysians.

ANATOMICAL EVIDENCE

This does not imply functional differences, but a lesser cortex to medulla ratio has been reported in Africans (Allbrook, 1956), American Negroes (Swinyard, 1940) and West Indians (Stirling and Keating, 1958).

PHYSIOLOGICAL EVIDENCE

Direct evidence for decreased adrenocortical function

Lesser 17-hydroxycorticoid excretion in Africans (Politzer and Tucker, 1958; Barnicot and Wolffson, 1952), Malaysians (Lugg and Bowness, 1954), and Indians (Friedman, 1954) was reported. Postoperatively, there is a lesser increase in Africans undergoing operations of similar traumatic nature than in a control group of whites. This increase was about 35% lower than in the whites (Parkinson et al., 1960).

The pattern in fractionation studies was similar, but the total amounts were less in Negroes than in whites (Higgin and Wolffson, 1958). Similar findings were reported in Egyptians (Awad, 1958).

Recently studies of plasma cortisol levels and hydrocortisone production rates in individuals from East and West Africa revealed levels comparable to those in whites (Adadevoh, 1968). The maximal response of plasma cortisol to insulin-induced hypoglycaemia is retarded in Nigerians compared to whites, occurring after 90 minutes instead of 60 minutes. Cortisol binding by plasma proteins appears to correlate with the hyperglobulinaemia common in Africans, but Adadevoh (1968) thinks this requires confirmation. If differences in plasma protein binding are present and comparable cortisol levels, but lesser urinary excretion of cortisol metabolites, are found it would suggest that the available, functionally active, free cortisol is decreased. Evidence that this may be the case is present in the indirect physiological findings which may depend on adrenocortical activity.

Indirect evidence for decreased adrenocortical activity

This may be seen in the difference in leucocyte differential counts (Wassermann, 1966) discussed in the previous Chapter (p. 158). Leschi (1947, 1948) found that an injection of 20 mg/kg body weight potassium citrate caused a 20% rise in plasma potassium in Negroes but not in whites. Henrotte et al. (1960) confirmed this finding in Indians and whites living in Madras, India. In the case of whites there was a significant correlation between potassium concentration rise and length of stay in Madras. Plasma sodium levels had a mean of 143 mEq/l in whites but a slightly lower mean was found in South African Bantu (Politzer et al., 1954; Politzer and Wayburne, 1957). The same was discovered in interracial studies in Dakar, Senegal and Paris (France) (Leschi, 1948).

The 24-hour urine volume was significantly higher in Bantu than in white South Africans (Modlin et al., 1963) although the authors thought this might be due to differences in diet.

Ladell (1964) speculatively interprets the adrenocortical function in tropical races as follows: 'The evidence does not suggest an 'exhaustion' of the endocrine system, but rather that indigenous tropical man does not need the 'permissive action' of the adrenocortical hormones.'

Studies in most parts of Africa are complicated by the effect of nutrition on adrenocortical function. Cooke et al. (1964) review the literature and confirm a decrease of 17-ketosteroid but not of 17-hydroxycorticoid excretion in malnutrition. They demonstrated a delayed cortisol clearance from the plasma, and concluded that the effects of malnutrition may fall principally upon the enzyme systems involved in steroid metabolism and a quantitative reduction in the response of the adrenal cortex to ACTH.

The position is still unclear but if normal cortisol levels are confirmed in the darker races: (*a*) it still requires an investigation of protein binding of cortisol in the plasma, to explain the discrepancy in plasma levels and urinary metabolite excretion; (*b*) such normal levels may be maintained by increased ACTH secretion if, as Cooke et al. (1964) suggest, reduced enzyme systems lead to a quantitative reduction in adrenocortical response to ACTH; (*c*) the indirect or functional evidence of lesser adrenocortical function may also suggest end-organ subresponsiveness (Rimoin et al., 1969), a point also considered by Adadevoh (1970).

I have suggested (Wassermann, 1965, 1969) that such lesser adrenocortical activity may be due to genetically determined decrease in enzyme levels in the adrenal cortex. This suggestion, in view of the normal cortisol levels reported, need not necessarily be incorrect in so far as it could explain subresponsiveness of the adrenal cortex to ACTH. Much further study is required to elucidate adrenocortical function in dark races.

The hypothesis of decreased adrenocortical activity in dark races is based on observed facts which could best be explained by this mechanism. Its survival value is suggested by evidence that the Bantu has increased reticuloendothelial activity as compared to whites:

i. Increased phagocytic activity of leucocytes for malarial pigment (Roberts, 1948).

ii. Lymphadenopathy, especially supratrochlear lymph nodes, common in blacks in the absence of any clinical or laboratory evidence of disease.

iii. Haemosiderosis in the Bantu is a standard finding, usually attributed to increased dietary iron intake. Yam et al. (1968) could demonstrate iron transport by leucocytes in the buffy coat of venous blood in patients with haemochromatosis and other iron-storage conditions such as transfusion siderosis. The haemosiderosis in the Bantu is probably due to increased iron intake, but increased reticuloendothelial activity may aid the deposition which differs so markedly from Cape Coloureds and whites who, in some cases, also have a high iron intake in assimilable form.

iv. The Bantu and other dark races have higher γ-globulin levels than whites (Arens and Brock, 1954; Bearwood et al., 1962; Brönte-Stewart et al., 1961;

Charmot et al., 1960). Recently it could also be shown that the higher γ-globulin fraction is due to increased levels of immunoglobulin (Ig) G and A in Bantu children (Rosen et al., 1971). In adult Bantu this also includes IgM, and the levels are about one-third higher than in whites (Milner and Calitz, 1971). This finding, occurring in other dark races too (Kalff, 1970; McFarlane et al., 1970) was also found in a white population in those with a darker skin as compared to those of lighter complexion (Suckling, 1968).

INTERRELATION OF NERVOUS AND ENDOCRINE FACTORS IN REGULATION OF MELANOCYTES AND MELANOGENESIS

Since the 1930's speculations on the 'reflex' induction of ovulation in rabbits attempted to incriminate the neurohypophysis in the control of the adenohypophysis. Green and Harris (1947) proposed that the adenohypophysis is controlled by different transmitter substances released into the primary plexus of the hypophyseal portal system. Since then 2 corticotrophin-releasing factors (CRF) have been isolated. α-CRF is apparently identical to α-MSH and β-CRF to vasopressin.

Voitkevich (1966) stated that there are sufficient grounds to consider that MSH is the initial 'pivot' of biosynthesis of somatotrophic hormone and ACTH. Without MSH as precursor the production of the 2 latter hormones might not be possible. He also considered it possible that vasopressin molecules might be 'organizers' of the biochemical complication of MSH to CRF and ACTH, and points to the fact that tyrosine oxidation is the initial step in the biosynthesis of melanin, catecholamine and thyroid hormones. His hypothesis is that as MSH activates melanogenesis, the utilisation of tyrosine for production of noradrenalin and thyroid hormones would be decreased.

It is interesting to note that the whole body of knowledge on hormonal and neurological control of melanocytes is conventionally interpreted to explain a visible pigmentary phenomenon. Assuming no *a priori* function for melanin, the data may be considered in another order:

The melanocyte develops from the neural crest and may rightly be considered as a masked primitive neuron. Specialized neurons in the hypothalamus region secrete polypeptides MSH, CRF, and STH which control secretion by the adenohypophysis of trophic hormones to peripheral endocrine glands. The 'masked primitive neuron' on reaching the epidermis secretes a pigmented substance through its dendrites into other cells (epidermal melanin unit). Other neurons (substantia nigra, locus caeruleus) produce a pigmented substance with near-identical physicochemical properties although its exact biosynthesis is unknown. Melanocytes in the inner ear (of *Rana esculenta* and *Cavia cobaya*) respond to pineal and hypophyseal hormones (Cherubino et al., 1966) and it would seem valid, therefore, to assume that melanocytes elsewhere in the body may respond similarly. If we now consider the pigmentary substance (melanin) as a modified neurosecretion we may consider its possible function. The only area where extensive studies have been performed is in the skin, and convincing evidence for its function as a trap for free radicals formed during ultraviolet radiation has been obtained. If one now postulates a protective function for melanin because it shows an ethnic predilection, corresponding roughly to solar radiation intensity under which various ethnic groups live, we have satisfactorily proved a hypothesis which we have set out to prove: Why does melanin protect against solar radiation? If, on the other hand, we view melanin as a free-radical-accepting hormone (Wassermann, 1968) we may see other biologically significant aspects: The evolution of feedback systems as shown in Figure 26 and the hormonal function of melanin.

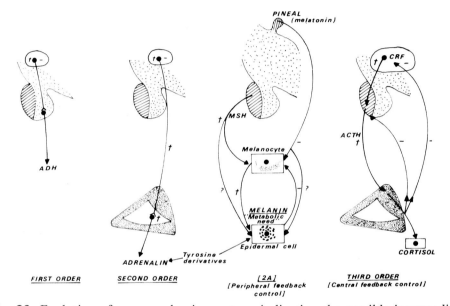

Fig. 26. Evolution of neuro-endocrine systems indicating the possible intermediate position of the peripheral feedback control of melanin to that of cortisol.

MELANIN AS A HORMONE

In reviewing the melanocytes of mammals, Billingham and Silvers (1960) came to the conclusion: 'If melanocytes do have functions other than pigmentary activity, probably none is indispensable.'

Since that review it has been suggested that melanin as free radical acceptor may influence intracellular metabolism by functioning as a repository for free radicals, which may be harmful to cellular function (Mason et al., 1960). Such a protective role apparently pertains to the function of melanin in the skin (Fitzpatrick, 1965). In the cutaneous inflammatory response the application of chlorpromazine, an electron donor, produced vacuolisation of leucocytes in the Caucasian response, but in the Bantu, however, phagocytosed melanin protected against this morphological change (Wassermann, 1968).

In view of the recent work which indicates melanin as a biochemically active substance, which may influence intracellular metabolism, and which circulates through the body, the function of melanin seems as far removed from pigmentation as is the case with other physiological pigments, e.g. haemoglobin (which also contributes to the skin colour).

In fishes and amphibians an active circulation occurs with visceral melanin deposits. In reptiles, however, a transitional stage in chromatic coordination is attained: 'whether it marks a stage in the 'advance' to speedy nervous control, or in retreat from it, is of course guess-work' (Waring, 1963).

With the hardy, thick integument which developed in the orders from reptiles to man, better protection is afforded to viscera against free radical formation by ultraviolet radiation and the circulation of melanin becomes of lesser importance (Wassermann, 1967).

The function of melanin, then, appears to have degenerated from that of a hormone in fishes and amphibians to that of a humoural substance produced and secreted locally in the 'epidermal melanin unit'. This may also be the case in the central nervous system of man, where free radical formation may significantly disrupt cellular function. Apparently the circulation of melanin is present wherever a hyperactive state of melanogenesis exists (e.g. ethnic pigmentation) or is induced (e.g. phenothiazine melanosis).

The concept of melanin as a hormone allows a definitive experimental approach to some clinical problems referred to later, and its function can be elucidated in terms of a known biochemical property. Recourse to vague hypotheses on pigmentary functions of melanin, e.g. survival value in tropical conditions, camouflaging and mate-selection, popular when no other function than pigmentation could be ascribed to melanin, now seems redundant.

Evidence presented by Rost et al. (1969) confirmed that melanocytes have the cytochemical and ultrastructural properties of those endocrine polypeptide cells grouped together by Pearse (1968, 1969) as the APUD series (Amine and amine Precursor Uptake and Decarboxylation). Rost et al. (1969) make the proviso that in the case of the melanocyte their main synthetic effort is the production of melanin and an associated polypeptide or protein.

In view of the evidence considered above, melanin may actually be considered a hormone, in which case the melanocyte conforms with the other endocrine cells in this series.

Ethnic pigmentation may be the secondary result of successful adaptation to tropical *disease*, and may also, through increased melanogenesis and the humoral function of melanin, allow man to endure better some diseases or make him increasedly susceptible to others. In the next section this concept will be discussed further.

REFERENCES

ABE, K., BUTCHER, R. W., NICHOLSON, W. E., BAIRD, C. E., LIDDLE, R. A. and LIDDLE, G. W. (1969): Adenosine 3′,5′-monophosphate (cyclic AMP) as the mediator of the actions of melanocyte stimulating hormone (MSH) and norepinephrine on the frog skin. *Endocrinology, 84,* 362.

ADADEVOH, B. K. (1967): The Nigerian and his endocrine system. *Lagos Notes Rec., 1,* 48.

ADADEVOH, B. K. (1968): Adrenocortical activity of the African. *J. trop. Med. Hyg., 71,* 259.

ADADEVOH, B. K. (1970): Endocrine patterns in the African: Clinico-biochemical assessment (Review). *Trop. geogr. Med., 22,* 125.

ADIJA, P. R., NEMURA, I. and WINNICK, T. (1965): Biosynthesis of ACTH and protein in slices of bovine anterior pituitary tissue. *Biochemistry, 4,* 246.

ALLBROOK, D. (1956): Size of adrenal cortex in East African males. *Lancet, 2,* 606.

ALLEN, B. M. (1916): The results of extirpation of the anterior lobe of the hypophysis and of the thyroid of *Rana pipiens larvae. Science, 44,* 755.

ARENS, L. and BROCK, J. F. (1954): Some aspects of the serum protein pattern of Africans. *S. Afr. J. clin. Sci., 5,* 20.

AWAD, N. A. (1958): Urinary 17-ketosteroid excretion, blood eosinophil level and adrenocortical function in adult male Egyptians. *J. trop. Med. Hyg., 61,* 204.

BARNICOT, N. A. and WOLFFSON, S. (1952): Daily urinary 17-ketosteroid output of African Negroes. *Lancet, 1,* 893.

BEARWOOD, C., GILBERT, C. and GILLMAN, J. (1962): Endocrine control of the plasma albumin/globulin ratio. *Nature (Lond.), 195,* 710.

BERSOHN, I. and OELOFSE, P. J. (1957): A comparison of urinary oestrogen levels in normal male South African Bantu and European subjects. *S. Afr. med. J., 31,* 1172.

BILLINGHAM, R. E. and SILVERS, W. K. (1960): The melanocytes of mammals. *Quart. Rev. Biol., 35,* 1.

BISCHITZ, P. G. and SNELL, R. S. (1959): The effect of testosterone on the melanocytes and melanin in the skin of the intact and orchidectomized male guinea-pig. *J. invest. Derm., 33,* 299.

BOULLE, P. (1968): A comparison of the oestrogen excretion during normal pregnancy in the racial groups of Durban. *S. Afr. med. J., 42,* 13.

BREATHNACH, A. S., BOR, S. and WYLLIE, L. A. M. (1966): Electron microscopy of peripheral nerve terminals and marginal melanocytes in vitiligo. *J. invest. Derm., 47,* 125.

BRÖNTE-STEWART, B., ANTONIS, A., ROSE-INNES, C. and MOODIE, A. D. (1961): An interracial study on the serum protein pattern of adult men in Southern Africa. *Amer. J. clin. Nutr., 9,* 596.

BURGERS, A. C. J. (1966): Biological aspects of pigment cell research. In: *Structure and Control of the Melanocyte,* p. 6. Editors: G. Della Porta and O. Mühlbock. Springer-Verlag, Berlin.

CARRUTHERS, R. (1966): Chloasma and oral contraceptives. *Med. J. Aust., 2,* 17.

CARRUTHERS, R. (1967): Chloasma and the 'Pill'. *Brit. med. J., 3,* 307.

CEHOVIC, G. (1962): Action des hormones mélanophorétiques sur la fonction thyroïdienne chez le Cobaye. *C.R. Acad. Sci. (Paris), 254,* 1872.

CHARMOT, G., GUIDICELLI, P., REYNAUD, R. and REGAUD, J. L. (1960): La dysprotéinémie commune de l'Africain. Essai d'interprétation. *Bull. Soc. Path. exot., 53,* 582.

CHERUBINO, M., BONACCORSI, P. and GALIOTO, G. B. (1966): Sulla melanocinesi delle cellule pigmentate dell'orecchio interno di *Rana esculenta* e di *Cavia cobaya.* Ricerche ormonali e ultrastrutturali. *Boll. Mal. Orecch., 84,* 353.

CLIFFORD, P. and BULDROOK, R. D. (1966): Endocrine studies in African males with nasopharyngeal cancer. *Lancet, 1,* 1228.

COOKE, J. N. C., JAMES, V. H. T., LANDON, J. and WYNN, V. (1964): Adrenocortical function in chronic malnutrition. *Brit. med. J.*, *1*, 662.

DAHLBERG, B. (1963): Urinary MSH determination as an index of pituitary function. *Ann. N.Y. Acad. Sci.*, *100*, 631.

DANCASTER, C. P. (1970): Thyrotoxicosis in the Bantu, with special reference to myopathy. *S. Afr. med. J.*, *44*, 695.

FITZPATRICK, T. B. (1965): Mammalian melanin biosynthesis. *Trans. St Johns Hosp. derm. Soc. (Lond.)*, *51*, 1.

FLAKS, J. (1948): The influence of testosterone propionate on pigmentation of the mammary nipples in female mice. *J. Endocr.*, *5*, 259.

FRIEDMAN, H. C. (1954): 17-Ketosteroid excretion in Indian males. *Lancet*, *2*, 262.

GELFAND, M. (1957): *The Sick African*, 3rd ed., p. 695. Juta and Co., Cape Town.

GOLDMAN, J. M. and HADLEY, M. E. (1969): In vitro demonstration of adrenergic receptors controlling melanophore responses of the lizard, *Anolis carolinensis*. *J. Pharmacol. exp. Ther.*, *166*, 1.

GOLDMAN, J. M. and HADLEY, M.E. (1970): Evidence for separate receptors for melanophore stimulating hormone and catecholamine regulation of cyclic AMP in the control of melanophore responses. *Brit. J. Pharmacol.*, *39*, 160.

GREEN, J. D. and HARRIS, G. W. (1947): The neurovascular link between the neurohypophysis and adenohypophysis. *J. Endocr.*, *5*, 136.

GREGG, W. I. (1966): Chloasma and the Pill. *New Engl. J. Med.*, *274*, 1432.

GUPTA, I. and BHIDE, N. K. (1967): Nature of adrenergic receptors on the skin melanophores of *Rana tigriana*. *J. Pharm. Pharmacol.*, *19*, 768.

HADLEY, M. E. and GOLDMAN, J. M. (1970): Adrenergic receptors and geographic variation in *Rana pipiens* chromatophore responses. *Amer. J. Physiol.*, *219*, 72.

HADLEY, M. E. and QUEVEDO JR., W. C. (1966): Vertebrate epidermal melanin unit. *Nature (Lond.)*, *209*, 1334.

HALL, P. F. (1969*a*): The influences of hormones on melanogenesis. *Aust. J. Derm.*, *10*, 125.

HALL, P. F. (1969*b*): Hormonal control of melanin synthesis in birds. *Gen. comp. Endocr.*, *Suppl. 2*, 451.

HARRIS, G. W. (1955): *Neural Control of the Pituitary Gland*. Arnold, London.

HENROTTE, J. G., KRISHNAMARTHI, G. and RANGANATHAN, G. (1960): Potassium tolerance tests in South Indian people. *Nature (Lond.)*, *187*, 328.

HIGGIN, D. and WOLFFSON, D. (1958): A comparison of 17-ketosteroid fractionation in West Africans and Europeans. *J. trop. Med. Hyg.*, *61*, 62.

JEGHERS, H. (1944): Pigmentation of the skin. *New Engl. J. Med.*, *231*, 122.

KALFF, M. W. (1970): A population study on serum immunoglobulin levels. *Clin. chim. Acta*, *28*, 277.

KAWAMURA, T., NISHIYAMA, S., IKEDA, S. and TAJIMA, K. (1964): The human *Haarscheibe*, its structure and function. *J. invest. Derm.*, *42*, 87.

KRIVOY, W. A. and GUILLEMIN, R. (1961): On a possible role of β-MSH in the central nervous system of mammalia: an effect of β-MSH in the spinal cord of the cat. *Endocrinology*, *69*, 170.

LADELL, W. S. S. (1964): Terrestrial animals in humid heat: Man. In: *Handbook of Physiology*, Sect. *4: Adaptation to the Environment*, Chapter 39, p. 641. Editors: D. B. Dill, E. F. Adolph and C. G. Wilber. American Physiological Society, Washington, D.C.

LANDE, S. and LERNER, A. B. (1967): The biochemistry of melanotropic agents. *Pharmacol. Rev.*, *19*, 1.

LERNER, A. B. (1959): Vitiligo. *J. invest. Derm.*, *32*, 285.

LERNER, A. B. (1960): Hormonal control of pigmentation. *Ann. Rev. Med.*, *11*, 187.

LERNER, A. B. (1971): On the etiology of vitiligo and grey hair. *Amer. J. Med., 51*, 141.

LERNER, A. B. and McGUIRE, J. S. (1964): Melanocyte stimulating hormone and adrenocorticotrophic hormone. Their relationship to pigmentation. *New Engl. J. Med., 270*, 539.

LERNER, A. B., SCHIZUME, K. and BUNDING, I. (1954): The mechanism of endocrine control of melanin pigmentation. *J. clin. Endocr., 14*, 1463.

LERNER, A. B., SNELL, R. S., CHANCO-TURNER, M. L. and McGUIRE, J. S. (1966): Vitiligo and sympathectomy. *Arch. Derm., 94*, 269.

LESCHI, J. (1947): Courbe de tolérance à l'ingestion du potassium chez des sujets de race noire. *C.R. Soc. Biol. (Paris), 225*, 1023.

LESCHI, J. (1948): Résultats obtenus chez des sujets de race noire soumis à l'ingestion de sel de potassium après injection de désoxycorticostérone. *C.R. Soc. Biol. (Paris), 227*, 1050.

LIPSCHUTZ, A. (1930): Über den Art der Pigmentbildung. *Virchows Arch. path. Anat., 276*, 676.

LUGG, J. W. H. and BOWNESS, J. M. (1954): Renal excretion of 17-ketosteroids by members of some ethnic groups living in Malaya. *Nature (Lond.), 174*, 1147.

MASON, H. S., INGRAM, D. J. E. and ALLEN, B. (1960): The free radical property of melanins. *Arch. Biochem., 86*, 225.

McFARLANE, H., TALERMAN, A. and STEINBERG, A. G. (1970): Immunoglobulins in Jamaicans and Nigerians with immunogenetic typing of myeloma and lymphoma in Jamaicans. *J. clin. Path., 23*, 124.

McGUINNESS, B. W. (1963): Melanocyte-stimulating hormone: A clinical and laboratory study. *Ann. N.Y. Acad. Sci., 100*, 640.

McGUIRE, J. S. and LERNER, A. B. (1963): Effects of tricosapeptide 'ACTH' and alpha-melanocyte-stimulating hormone on the skin color of man. *Ann. N.Y. Acad. Sci., 100*, 622.

McGUIRE, J. S. and MÖLLER, H. (1966): Differential responsiveness of dermal and epidermal melanocytes of *Rana pipiens* to hormones. *Endocrinology, 78*, 367.

MEIRING, P. DE V. (1967): Association between hypothyroidism and myasthenia gravis and a concept of generalized systemic auto-immunopathy. *S. Afr. med. J., 40*, 303.

MILNER, L. V. and CALITZ, F. (1971): Serum immunoglobulin levels in white, Asiatic and Bantu blood donors. *S. Afr. med. J., 45*, 683.

MISHIMA, Y. (1967): Electron microscopy of human cutaneous nerve pigmentation. *Brit. J. Derm., 79*, 611.

MODLIN, M., ISAACSON, L. C. and JACKSON, W. P. U. (1963): Normal Bantu urine. *S. Afr. med. J., 37*, 121.

NOTIDES, A. and GORSKI, J. (1966): Estrogen-induced synthesis of a specific uterine protein. *Proc. nat. Acad. Sci. (Wash.), 56*, 230.

NOVALES, R. R. (1963): Responses of cultured melanophores to the synthetic hormones α-MSH, melatonin and epinephrine. *Ann. N.Y. Acad. Sci., 100*, 1035.

NOVALES, R. R. and DAVIS, W. J. (1967): Melanin-dispersing effect of adenosine 3′,5′ monophosphate on amphibian melanophores. *Endocrinology, 81*, 283.

NOVIKOFF, A. B. (1967): Lysosomes in nerve cells. In: *The Neuron*, p. 319. Editor: Holger Hyden. Elsevier Publ. Co., Amsterdam.

OJIKUTU, R. O. (1965): Die Rolle von Hautpigment und Schweissdrüsen in der Klima-Anpassung des Menschen. *Homo, 16*, 77.

PARKINSON, L., GHYOOT, E., VAN VLIERBERGHE, R. and BÒNE, G. (1960): Adrenocortical responses of Bantu and Europeans to surgical stress. *Trans. roy. Soc. trop. Med. Hyg., 54*, 366.

PEARSE, A. G. E. (1968): Common cytochemical properties of cells producing polypeptide hormones (the APUD series) and their relevance to thyroid and ultimobronchial C cells and calcitonin. *Proc. roy. Soc. B*, *170*, 71.

PEARSE, A. G. E. (1969): The cytochemistry and ultrastructure of polypeptide hormone-producing cells of the APUD series and the embryologic, physiologic and pathologic implications of the concept. *J. Histochem. Cytochem.*, *17*, 303.

PHILLIPS, J. and BURCH, G. E. (1960): A review of cardiovascular diseases in the white and Negro races. *Medicine (Baltimore)*, *39*, 241.

POLITZER, W. M., BARRY, M. E. and KING, A. (1954): The effect of heat stress on mine workers with regard to loss of water and electrolytes. *S. Afr. J. med. Sci.*, *19*, 155.

POLITZER, W. M. and MUNOZ, J. A. (1962): Serum protein-bound iodine levels in Basuto school children. *S. Afr. med. J.*, *27*, 11.

POLITZER, W. M. and TUCKER, B. (1958): Urinary 17-ketosteroid and 17-ketogenic steroid excretion in South African Bantu. *Lancet*, 2, 778.

POLITZER, W. M. and WAYBURNE, S. (1957): Serum electrolytes and proteins in kwashiorkor. *Brit. J. Nutr.*, *11*, 105.

QUAMINA, D. B. E. (1967): Chloasma and the contraceptive pill. *Brit. med. J.*, 2, 638.

RILEY, P. A. (1970): Mechanism of pigment-cell toxicity produced by hydroxyanisole. *J. Path.*, *101*, 163.

RIMOIN, D. L., MERIMEE, T. J., RABINOWITZ, D., CAVALLIS-SPORZA, L. L. and McKUSICK, V. A. (1969): Peripheral subresponsiveness to human growth hormone in African Pygmies. *New Engl. J. Med.*, *281*, 1383.

ROBERT, P. (1941): Über die Vitiligo (zugleich ein Beitrag zur Frage der Pigmentbildung). *Dermatologica (Basel)*, *84*, 257.

ROBERTS, J. I. (1948): A comparison of haematological results in Europeans and Africans suffering from active malaria. *J. trop. Med. Hyg.*, *51*, 228.

ROBISON, G. A., BUTCHER, R. W. and SUTHERLAND, E. W. (1967): Adenyl cyclase as an adrenergic receptor. *Ann. N.Y. Acad. Sci.*, *139*, 703.

ROSEN, E. W., GEEFHUYSEN, J. and IPP, T. (1971): Immunoglobulin levels in protein calorie malnutrition. *S. Afr. med. J.*, *45*, 980.

ROST, F. W. D., POLAK, J. M. and PEARSE, A. G. E. (1969): Melanocyte relationship to cells of endocrine polypeptide (APUD) series. *Virchows Arch. B.*, *Cell Path.*, *4*, 93.

RUDMAN, D. (1963): Adipokinetic action of polypeptides on amine hormones upon the adipose tissue of various animal species. *J. Lipid Res. 4*, 119.

SCHALLY, A. V., BOWERS, C. Y., KUROSHIMA, A., ISHIDA, Y., REDDING, T. W. and KASTIN, A. J. (1965): Hormonal activities of beef and pig hypothalamus. In: *Proceedings, 23d International Congress of Physiological Sciences, Tokyo, 1965*, pp. 275–283. Editor: D. Noble. ICS 87, Excerpta Medica, Amsterdam.

SCHALLY, A. V., LIPSCOMB, S. and GUILLEMIN, R. (1962): Isolation and aminoacid sequence of a a_2-CRF from hog pituitary glands. *Endocrinology*, *71*, 164.

SCOTT, G. T. (1965): Physiology and pharmacology of color change in the sand flounder *Scopthalamus aquosus*. *Limnol. Oceanogr.*, *10, Suppl.*, R230.

SERRI, F. and CERIMELE, D. (1967): Connections between nerve fibers and dendritic cells in the skin of the fetus. In: *Advances in Biology of Skin, Vol. VIII: The Pigmentary System*, p. 31. Editors: W. Montagna and F. Hu. Pergamon Press, New York, N.Y.

SMITH, P. E. (1916): Experimental ablation of the hypophysis in the frog embryo. *Science*, *44*, 280.

SNELL, R. S. (1962): Effect of the melanocyte stimulating hormone of the pituitary on melanocytes and melanin in the skin of guinea-pigs. *J. Endocr.*, *25*, 249.

SNELL, R. S. (1964): Effect of the a-MSH of the pituitary on mammalian epidermal melanocytes. *J. invest. Derm.*, *42*, 337.

SNELL, R. S. (1967): Hormonal control of pigmentation in man. In: *Advances in Biology of Skin, Vol. VIII: The Pigmentary System*, p. 447. Editors: W. Montagna and F. Hu. Pergamon Press, New York, N.Y.

SNELL, R. S. and BISCHITZ, P. G. (1960): Effect of large doses of estrogen and progesterone on melanin pigmentation. *J. invest. Derm., 35*, 73.

SNELL, R. S. and TURNER, R. (1966): Skin pigmentation in relation to the menstrual cycle. *J. invest. Derm., 47*, 147.

STIRLING, G. A. and KEATING, V. J. (1958): Size of the adrenals in Jamaicans. *Brit. med. J., 2*, 1016.

SUCKLING, A. J. (1968): Serum gammaglobulin level as a racial characteristic. *J. med. Technol., 25*, 217.

SUTHERLAND, E. W., OYE, I. and BUTCHER, R. W. (1965): The action of epinephrine and the role of the adenyl cyclase system in hormone action. *Recent Progr. Hormone Res., 21*, 623.

SUTHERLAND, E. W. and ROBISON, G. A. (1966): The role of cyclic 3'5'-AMP in responses to catecholamines and other hormones. *Pharmacol. Rev., 18*, 145.

SUTHERLAND, E. W., ROBISON, G. A. and BUTCHER, R. W. (1968): Some aspects of the biological role of adenosine 3',5'-monophosphate (cyclic AMP). *Circulation, 37*, 279.

SWINYARD, C. A. (1940): Volume and cortico-medullary ratio of adult human suprarenal gland. *Anat. Rec., 76*, 69.

TALEISNIK, S. and ORIAS, R. (1965): An MSH releasing factor in hypothalamic extracts. *Amer. J. Physiol., 208*, 293.

TROWELL, H. C. (1960): *Non-infective Diseases in Africa*. Arnold, London.

VOITKEVICH, A. A. (1966): Interrelation of the nervous and endocrine factors in regulation of melanocytes. In: *Structure and Control of the Melanocyte*, p. 44. Editors: G. Della Porta and O. Mühlbock. Springer-Verlag, Berlin.

WARING, H. (1963): *Color Change Mechanisms of Cold-Blooded Vertebrates*. Academic Press, New York, N.Y.

WASSERMANN, H. P. (1965): Human pigmentation and environmental adaptation. *Arch. environment. Hlth, 11*, 691.

WASSERMANN, H. P. (1966): Leucocytes and melanin pigmentation. II. The leucocyte count in Africa. Review of the literature and an interracial study. *S. Afr. med. J., Suppl.*, 3.

WASSERMANN, H. P. (1967): Extension of the concept 'Vertebrate epidermal melanin unit' to embrace visceral pigmentation and leucocytic melanin transport. *Nature (Lond.), 213*, 282.

WASSERMANN, H. P. (1968): Phenothiazines and leucocytic melanin transport. *Agressologie, 9*, 241.

WASSERMANN, H. P. (1969): Melanin pigmentation and the environment. In: *Essays on Tropical Dermatology*, pp. 7-16. Editors: R. D. G. P. Simons and J. Marshall. Excerpta Medica, Amsterdam.

WASSERMANN, H. P. and HEYL, T. (1968): Quantitative data on skin pigmentation in South African races. *S. Afr. med. J., 42*, 98.

YAM, L. T., FINKEL, H. E., WEINTRAUB, L. R. and CROSBY, W. H. (1968): Circulating iron-containing macrophages in haemosiderosis. *New Engl. J. Med., 279*, 512.

ZIMMERMAN, A. A. and BECKER JR., S. W. (1959): Precursors of epidermal melanocytes in the Negro foetus. In: *Pigment Cell Biology*, p. 159. Editor: M. Gordon. Academic Press, New York, N.Y.

ZOUTENDYK, A. (1970): Auto-antibodies in South African whites, Coloured and Bantu. *S. Afr. med. J., 44*, 469.

Clinical aspects of ethnic pigmentation

*The most exciting era in the biology
of melanin has only just begun.*

T. B. Fitzpatrick (1965):
Mammalian melanin biosynthesis.
Trans. St. John's Hosp. derm. Soc. (Lond.), 51, 1.

Chapter XV

Ethnicity and disease:
General considerations on type-responsiveness

*As a point of departure in the study of
racial relationships in disease, it is
important not to be misled by the color of
the skin. The important consideration
is that skin color has caused separation
and selection resulting in the perpetuation and propagation of differing genetic
and environmental factors. These factors
then form the background upon which
racial differences in the occurrence and
manifestations of disease become possible.*

Phillips and Burch (1960).

1. The quotation above emphasizes the existence of a 'colour problem' as defined in Chapter I (ethnic pigmentation as a marker of particular populations) as well as a 'problem of colour': ethnic pigmentation markedly influences mate selection and group separation, and so aids the 'perpetuation and propagation of differing genetic and environmental factors.'
2. The very fact that skin colour differs in races implies that the physiological homeostat of melanogenesis and the functional activity of the epidermal melanin unit differs between ethnic groups. Furthermore, melanin itself is not an inactive end product of metabolism but a stable free radical which may influence cellular metabolism. Both genetic and endocrine factors are involved in this difference.
3. Finally, if, as I proposed, ethnic pigmentation was the secondary result of successful adaptation to tropical disease (or the lack of pigmentation the result of an environment without such a stressor), one would expect ethnic groups to respond differently to certain diseases. Thus, ethnic pigmentation identifies a type responsiveness, dependent on the activity of the reticuloendothelial system

(RES) as determined by endocrine adaptations. There is some evidence that similar responsiveness varies within an ethnic group according to the degree of pigmentation.

At the outset it should be stated that the author is fully aware of 3 facts: (1) Many ethnic differences in disease incidence and manifestation, in the past held to be peculiar to particular ethnic groups, can now be firmly related to particular sets of environmental and socioeconomic conditions. (2) Several countries and isolated communities (especially in Africa, but elsewhere in the world too) have only recently been explored medically (Marshall, 1969). With improved public health techniques and medication, and some decrease in the more serious infections and epidemic diseases, attention could only recently be diverted to the neglected areas of medicine. (3) Recent objective studies in sociological medicine have clarified the importance of cultural ethnic factors in disease prevalence and incidence (Susser and Watson, 1971; Brown, 1964) and this, too, requires consideration.

I use the word 'ethnicity' in the context in which Brown (1964, footnote p. 26) used it: 'Ethnicity refers to the cultural values and ways of behaviour that the members of a group have learned and transmit to their children, and which serve to tie them together . . . the term 'nationality background' has often been used as a rough equivalent for ethnic background. In those countries composed of many ethnic strains, such as the United States, reference to present nationality has limited practical usefulness,' but I also include in this definition the physiological differences which have evolved by natural selection.

ENVIRONMENT IN RELATION TO ETHNICITY AND DISEASE

The constancy of the *milieu intérieur* is maintained by homeostatic mechanisms, as discussed in previous Chapters. It is quite obvious that in different races the 'pigmentary homeostat' must have been set differently to achieve a steady state of hypo-, eu- and hypermelanism in whites, browns and blacks respectively.

While the *milieu intérieur* shows homeostatic stability, the *milieu extérieur* demands adaptation by the organism in order to survive successfully.

Environmental influences held pride of place in the explanation of ethnic pigmentation: '. . . the notion that the Negro's pigment adapts him for life in the tropics, has become so generally accepted into anthropological and medical lore, that a mere photobiologist needs some temerity to question it' (Johnson, 1965).

To question this notion some terminological explanations must be made.

Adaptation

In a sense, ethnic pigmentation may be regarded as an adaptation to the environmental stressor, ultraviolet radiation, and it would then constitute a morphological characteristic by which the individual was fitted for his environment.

Physiological adaptation is a term used by Prosser (1964) to indicate any property of an organism which favours survival in a specific (stressful) environment. Melanin as a sunscreen affords little survival value because lethal consequences develop late in life. As far as a thermal heat load is concerned another stressor is gained from the protection provided by melanin (Blum, 1961).

The term *'response'* refers to a direct reaction to an environmental stimulus, whether the response is adaptive or not, or whether it is morphological or strictly physiological (Prosser, 1964). All normal humans, whatever their ethnic colour, show a *response* to solar radiation (i.e. immediate pigment darkening and an increase in melanogenesis).

Selection

The selection concept in its Darwinian context denotes the 'survival of the fittest'. With the dubious *survival* value of melanin pigmentation (Blum, 1961) the hypothesis that the protective role of melanin may be a secondary result becomes more plausible. Quevedo (1969) thought that vertebrate pigmentation patterns may have developed early as a mechanism for protective colouration, and for attracting and distinguishing between sexes of the same species, and for further distinction between species.

1. If one assumes that the epidermal melanin unit was an *adaptation* to solar radiation, the *selective* factor must be sought elsewhere.

2. If ethnic pigmentation was merely the secondary result of an adaptation to disease stressors, which for survival required altered RES activity, as effected by endocrine changes, such pigmentation serves as identification of a physiological *milieu* which explains many of the clinical observations on ethnic differences in disease incidence and manifestation.

3. Such differences are usually attributed to environmental factors. These include the physical environment, but also the cultural environment. It is uncertain to what extent physical environment induced cultural evolution along particular lines, but incidentally, ethnic pigmentation also frequently identifies particular cultural values, behaviour, and socioeconomic circumstances which may, indirectly, have an influence on clinical manifestations. To differentiate cause and effect may, however, be difficult (Fig. 27).

DISEASE AS A SELECTIVE FACTOR

Palaeopathology

As an emerging branch of human biology, palaeopathology provides some interesting, although still meagre, data on the real processes and selective factors in human evolution.

Apparently man started off by inheriting several infections from his non-human primate forebears, and these were modified by climate, culture and natural selection. The geographical distribution of venereal syphilis and related

non-venereal diseases can now be explained as epidemiological phases and syndromes of treponematosis present in various forms on every continent.

   Tuberculosis has plagued man since Neolithic times. As man's culture established closer contact with his herds of livestock, a 'bridge' was established by
which an early mutant tubercle bacillus could cross and survive. This would
explain the discovery of tuberculosis of the spine in late Stone Age skeletons
(Goldstein, 1969).

   Settlement patterns may have been influenced by disease. 'Had the (American)
Indians not been decimated by Old World diseases, their population numbers
would eventually have increased to the point where New World diseases would
have become a public health problem' (Hoyme, 1969). He points out that
palaeopathology 'permits some speculation on the medical future of the Indians
had the Europeans and Africans not arrived with a cargo of pathogens' (Hoyme,
1969).

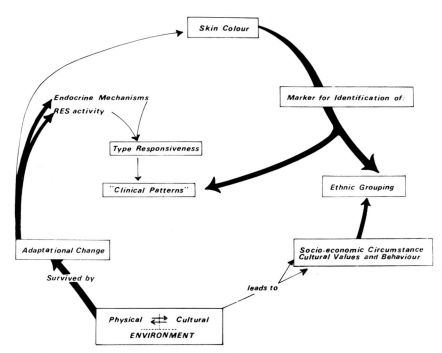

Fig. 27. Diagram of the relationship of skin colour to the physical and cultural
         environment. *Heavy arrows:* readily appreciated associations. *Light arrows:*
         lesser known associations.

   Migration between settlements can rapidly change the fertility/survival situation at a given site. Angel (1969) discussed the effects of falciparum malaria
on fertility in prehistoric Greece, and also the effects of diet (inferred from remains of plants, animal bones and shells), farming methods and invasions on
population growth. Porotic hyperostosis in skeletal remains allows a fairly accurate diagnosis of sicklaemia and thalassaemia, and palaeopathological findings

support the convincing present-day clinical assumption that the high incidence of sicklaemia and G-6-PD deficient erythrocytes enhanced protection against malaria as a lethal agent in tropical Africa.

Robb (1960) remarked on the distribution of blood group O in American Indians. Blood group A seems to be associated with susceptibility to smallpox and in preColumbian America smallpox may have selected a group O population. Apparently the small size of early groups of Indians in America and their distance apart accounts for the osteological evidence supported by reports from early travellers suggesting that, unlike in Africa, contagious diseases were a lesser problem than arthritis, nutritional and metabolic disturbances (Hoyme, 1969).

It is evident, therefore, that from prehistoric times the disease-stressor factor differed in various geographical areas. This would result in differing challenges to the RES, and variation in melanin pigmentation probably reflects variation in the adaptive response required of the RES.

Geographical pathology

The present-day counterpart of palaeopathology is geographical pathology, a study which aims at revealing the various degrees of successful adaptation reached in various communities.

Geographical pathology was defined as 'the comparative study of the incidence of disease and the distribution of physiological traits in people belonging to different communities throughout the world and the correlation of these data with features of the social and geographical environments, i.e. comparative studies between different ethnic, national and social groups' (Doll, 1959, p. 13).

For convenience, the 'social' and 'geographical' environments will be discussed separately. The former may determine mate selection for a particular pigmentation dominance and the latter may constitute a challenge to the RES which requires, in the case of tropical environments, a reduction in target organ sensitivity to, inter alia, ACTH which is accompanied by both increased RES reactivity and darker skin colour. They are more fully discussed below, with reference to their clinical significance.

GEOGRAPHICAL ENVIRONMENT

Ladell (1964), in his review on the physiological adaptation of man to humid heat, states that a temperate-climate man who readapts to tropical conditions is handicapped by a highly reactive endocrine system. He overadapts to heat and becomes hyperacclimatized. In the tropical anhidrotic asthenia syndrome (Allen and O'Brien, 1944; Ladell et al., 1944) there is 'no response to adrenocortical and to antidiuretic hormones, which suggests the failure is one of target organ response rather than of the endocrine glands themselves' (Ladell, 1964). The syndrome has not been described among indigenous tropical people, and this supports Ladell's hypothesis of 'tropical man's relative independence of en-docrine regulation.' By this he means that indigenous tropical man's endocrine system is not in a 'state of endocrine exhaustion' but rather that he does not need the 'permissive action' of adrenocortical hormones in an environment where water intake is high but salt intake low. Evidence of lesser adrenocortical function, as well as other endocrine differences in ethnic groups, has been discussed in Chapter XIV.

Reticuloendothelial system

The reticuloendothelial system as 'man's principal organ of defence' (Doan, 1957) exerts its defensive role by (1) phagocytosis and (2) the production of anti-bodies and cellular immunity. The immunological system consists of (1) a secre-tory part which produces antibodies or immunoglobulins in lymphocytes and plasma cells derived from lymphoid tissue in the tonsils, pharynx and intestinal tract and (2) a cellular mechanism operating through small lymphocytes derived from, and influenced by, the thymus.

The RES differs in its activity between ethnic groups: (*a*) Roberts (1948) re-ported an increased phagocytic ability for malarial pigments in Bantu, and some of our observations tend to support this finding of an increased phagocytic ability in Bantu leucocytes (Wassermann, 1964). The normal African frequently has enlarged supratrochlear lymph nodes, probably due to lymphoid hyperactivity (Scott, 1949; Chanarin 1949). (*b*) Dark races show a pattern of increased γ-globu-lins and decreased albumin levels in their serum proteins. This is determined genetically, and is not due to malaria.

As far as the specific immunoglobulin levels are concerned healthy Bantu male adults have about 40% more IgG, 30% more IgA and 32% more IgM than comparable whites, and in the case of healthy Asiatic males the IgG, IgA and IgM are respectively about 20%, 23% and 7% more than in white males (Milner and Calitz, 1971). This was confirmed in Jamaicans and Nigerians (McFarlane et al., 1970). It was found that IgG in African Negroes and Bantu reaches adult levels at 4–5 years of age, while IgM reaches adult levels at the age of 1 (McFarlane et al., 1970; Ho et al., 1971). This ethnic difference is well recognized and in addition to race also depends on age, sex and environmental factors. It is perhaps best summarized by Kalff (1970): 'Control groups used in the study of the immunoglobulin levels must be matched not only for age, sex and race, but also for several environmental factors, both changing and persistent. For any given individual living under particular environmental conditions, it is possible only to say whether his immunoglobulin levels fall within the average range of the region in which he lives. It does not yet seem justified to speak of 'normal' human immunoglobulin levels.' Whites living in comparable conditions in Africa did not show a significant difference from whites in Europe and the U.S.A. The protein pattern of a Bantu did not change on prolonged residence in the U.S.A. (10 years) (Ho et al., 1971). In fact, Suckling (1968) found that differences similar to those reported between whites and blacks existed between light- and dark-skinned whites.

Recently a comprehensive study was made of the low serum cholesterol levels in a particular Bantu tribe (the Masai of Kenya) (Ho et al., 1971). It is, however, common in other Bantu tribes, as well as in the Khoisan people, e.g. Kalahari Bushmen (Miller et al., 1968) and African Pygmies (Mann et al., 1962). The Masai are nomads with a high dietary cholesterol intake, comparable to that of whites, but they have little atherosclerosis and a persistently low cholesterol level. From their studies, Ho et al. (1971) conclude that this is due to a basically different genetic trait. They also have a low incidence of gallstones, which according to Ho et al. (1971), can be explained by the higher phospholipid/cholesterol ratio in their bile as compared to the converse situation in whites in New Zealand and the U.S.A. The reticuloendothelial system as well as cortisol influence cholesterol metabolism (Berliner and Dougherty, 1960). This 'unique biological characteristic of the Masai' may have had survival value in the primitive environment by developing high seromucous antibodies to protect them from invading micro-organisms (Ho et al., 1971). It not only agrees with the hypothesis I formulated elsewhere, but provides additional observational support.

SOME CLINICAL IMPLICATIONS OF ETHNIC TYPE-RESPONSIVENESS

Auto-immunity

The incidence of vitiligo varies from 0.14% in Russia to 3.0% in India. Many authors state that it is more common in dark-skinned races, but El Mofty (1968) thinks this may appear to be so more than it really is, because of the greater contrast between the normal and depigmented skin. The apparently higher incidence in females may, perhaps, be ascribed to their greater concern with cosmetic problems (El Mofty, 1968). Accurate statistics on the ethnic incidence of vitiligo are required, because of its association with organ-specific auto-immune disorders (Mackay, 1967; El Mofty, 1968; Cunliffe et al., 1968; Dawber, 1968; and Bor et al., 1969). This is even more important in view of the fact that Zoutendyk (1970) reports that auto-immune disease is rare in Bantu. There is not sufficient accurate information on the ethnic incidence of auto-immune disorders. Dancaster (1970) reporting on the rarity of thyrotoxicosis among Bantu in Natal, South Africa, suggests that this may be accounted for by their inability to form long-acting thyroid stimulator (LATS), an auto-antibody present in nearly all cases of Graves' disease.

The rarity of auto-immune thyroiditis in Bantu was also commented on by Oluwasanmi and Alli (1968) and Shee and Houston (1962). Zoutendyk's (1970) laboratory evidence is interesting and should be confirmed for other ethnic groups. He found thyroid auto-antibodies in 0.55% of Bantu, 9% of whites and 16.2% of Cape Coloureds (among 1618 consecutive blood specimens submitted for thyroid function tests). In 2850 consecutive direct Coombs' tests performed in his immunohaematology laboratory, in cases with suspected auto-immune conditions, a positive test was found in 1.5% of Bantu, 4.7% of whites and 5.2%

of Cape Coloureds. Similarly, circulating tissue antibodies against heart, kidneys and other organs, investigated in 540 patients, showed an incidence of 6% positive results in whites against 1.9% in Bantu. The Rose-Waaler test was the only laboratory procedure which did show a comparable incidence of positive results in Bantu, Cape Coloureds and whites (7.1, 8.2 and 8.4% respectively). Zoutendyk also provided evidence that Bantu respond normally to bacterial and viral antigens as seen in antitoxic and antibody levels in batches of pooled plasma from thousands of Bantu donors. In fact, the diphtheria-antitoxin level was found to be very much higher than one would expect in plasma pools from white donors (Zoutendyk, 1970).

RES pigmentation and cancer

The local protective effect of melanin in the skin, leading to protection from solar-induced skin cancer in Bantu, is considered in Chapter XVII.

Cellular immune mechanisms are of major importance in host resistance to cancer (Law, 1969). About a quarter of patients with carcinomas and sarcomas had a delayed skin reaction in response to intradermal inoculation of autologous tumour-cell extracts (Hughes and Lytton, 1964; Stewart, 1969).

This area of intensive current research activity could benefit from interracial studies. The following remark by Bonne (1937) still holds true today: 'There is a general feeling that cancer does not behave in the same way in the different races of mankind . . . It is obvious, however, that there would be a better chance of discovering racial influences on cancer, whether due to genetic factors or to habits of living, if we were in a position to compare its incidence in large and essentially diverse divisions of mankind rather than restricting ourselves to research within the limitations of a single one of these divisions, the white race.' The known difference in RES activity in whites and Bantu, and its relation to host resistance to cancer considerably narrows the field suggested by Bonne (1937).

Recent experience with immunosuppression has indicated the defensive role of immunosurveillance in protection against malignancy. The incidence of cancer is 100 times greater in immunosuppressed patients (Fahey, 1971) and a higher incidence of keratoacanthoma and skin cancer has also recently been reported (Walder et al., 1971). It is possible, too, that the increased RES activity of blacks combined with the protective role of melanin, protects against skin cancer.

Alternative possible hormone-RES relations in ethnic groups

There is evidence at present that patients with auto-immune disease have a genetically determined predisposition to form organ-specific antibodies. Thus there are 2 possible ways of interpreting the altered RES activity in different ethnic groups:

1. As I originally suggested, decreased adrenocortical activity could be the result of genetically determined enzyme deficiency, or subresponsiveness of the adrenal

glands. Cortisol is a powerful depressant of RES activity and depresses serum γ-globulin levels. (Nicol et al., 1956; Snell and Nicol, 1956).

Apart from the enhancement of pigmentation by such altered pituitary-adrenocortical axis function, reported differences in androgen and oestrogen levels may also exert some influence, either on the melanocytes directly or on the epidermal melanin unit (EMU) (see Chapter XIV).

Finally, target organ insensitivity to pituitary hormones (as demonstrated for pituitary growth hormone in Central African Pygmies) may allow the same effect, i.e. increased RES activity, and increased pigmentation due to high levels of trophic hormones.

2. On the other hand, cortisol is carried in the plasma by a specific serum protein, transcortin. It has a high affinity but a low capacity for cortisol and related drugs. Serum albumin has a low affinity but a high capacity for cortico-steroids (Lewis et al., 1971). The physiological function of cortisol is exerted by the free (unbound) fraction of hormone. Total cortisol levels may thus be within normal levels, but the free, physiologically active fraction may be low in the presence of a high protein-bound fraction. A similar situation probably exists for other hormones. The serum protein spectrum, which differs so markedly between ethnic groups, may thus influence hormone activity in different ethnic groups.

The complexity of endocrine differences in ethnic groups still requires further investigation.

THE SOCIAL ENVIRONMENT

'In every society systems of law, customs, moral imperatives and institutions mould the personalities and aspirations of successive generations; it is in this sense that man is said to be the victim of his social relationships' (Susser and Watson, 1971).

Mate selection according to skin colour stereotypes

Several studies relating the various aspects of body image to personality traits and the preferences for particular body types or attributes, such as height, weight, bust, waist, hips and other dimensions, have been made.

Lawson (1971) studied hair colour as an important aspect of body image. He points out that American culture has built up a number of images which relate to hair colour. (The dumb blonde; fast, dangerous blondes; 'gentlemen prefer blondes'; tall, dark, handsome male; the notion that 'opposites attract'.) He studied 240 students of psychology by a semantic differential procedure. All men considered dark males significantly superior to blond males on 9 traits, to red-headed males on 20, and blonde males to red-headed males on 10. Similar findings were recorded for the women. Both sexes seem to show a preference in order for dark, blonde and red-headed males respectively, which is the genetic order of dominance in the American population.

Each sex-hair group clearly seemed to prefer his own hair-colour group 'in a sort of trichocentrism.' The investigation failed to confirm the general belief that men prefer blondes. He points out that one could raise 'the further question about the degree to which verbal stereotypes compare with actual behaviour in dating, courtship and mate selection. At this time one could only speculate that there would be a consistency in stereotype and mate selection.'

Reflectance studies by Hulse (1967) on Japanese found a lighter skin colour in the higher social classes than in the middle and lower classes. Apparently social selection shows a preference for a light skin colour in that community.

The association of lighter skin colour with higher social class also occurs in South African Bantu, Cape Coloureds and Indians (in South Africa). In the United States a change in preference for mate selection has apparently occurred. The status advantage of light-skinned Negro women continues to hold. In the case of Negro men, marriages since 1960 indicate that the blackest men fare better in status acquisition than men with a lighter skin. The reverse holds true for men married before 1960 (Udry et al., 1971).

This colour-consciousness may, in actual fact, have clinical significance. Recently, Barr et al. (1972) gained the impression that most of the adult patients with a nephrotic syndrome seen in their hospital (Nairobi, Kenya), were young sophisticated English-speaking African women. (Their study found that 72% of the nephrotic females were able to speak English against 16% of the general medical in-patients.) In contrast to 11% of female medical in-patients using skin-lightening cream, 70% of the nephrotics were using or had used such cream. The creams contained aminomercuric chloride (5-10%), a compound known to cause the nephrotic syndrome under other circumstances (e.g. in the treatment of psoriasis). Mercury excretion in the urine was raised (mean: 150 μg/l) in those still using the cream on admission, lower (mean: 29 μg/l) in those who stopped before admission, and very low (mean: 6 μg/l) in those who had never used skin-lightening cream or only a preparation which did not contain mercury. This carefully studied group of patients can thus be said to have suffered an organic lesion of the kidneys as a side-effect of an alteration technology applied to the colour of their skin. Previous suggestions of the possible role of malaria in the aetiology of the nephrotic syndrome (Rees et al., 1972) could not be supported by that study.

Constitution and culture

Constitution may influence the process of learning and thus the acquisition of culture (Susser and Watson, 1971). In the first 72 hours of life black East African babies have greater motor activity than white babies (Geber and Dean, 1957). The skeleton of the former is apparently more mature than that of the latter (McKeown, 1960), and advanced motor activity depends on maturity of bone, muscle and brain (Tanner, 1957). Extrinsic factors may also be significant because African mothers handle their new-born more freely than white mothers handle theirs, and may thus stimulate motor activity (Williams, 1957). These 2 variables (physiological differences vs. cultural differences) are usually the only 2 considered. A study finding that motor activity in black babies was related to emotional strains of the mother during pregnancy was reported (Abramson et al., 1961).

Starting from pigmentation differences within an American Negro group, Horton and Crump (1958) suggested another possible explanation. They found that darker-skinned Negroes occur in greater proportion in the lower social class group: 35.7 and 42.8% respectively of the darker children came from families in socioeconomic Groups I and II (lower groups) whereas in the light group there was none in Group I, but all were equally divided (33.3%) in each of Groups II, III and IV. The medium group is more or less intermediate, with 7.9% in Groups I and IV, the bulk (44.7 and 39.8% respectively) being in the middle (Groups II and III). According to Myers and Yochelson (1948), in American culture, there are greater opportunities for the light-skinned individual to enhance his status. Horton and Crump (1958) conclude that light colour is generally associated with high socioeconomic status, and high socioeconomic status is, in turn, associated with such factors as heavier average birth weights and longer gestation periods and, thus, maturity. They also found that unmarried mothers had an incidence of 8.8% in the light group as against 32.5% in the dark group.

These 2 groups of studies contradict each other in a subtle way: The former group *observed* maturity difference in blacks and whites, and finds plausible explanations in physiological and cultural factors. The latter group found differences in socioeconomic status and opportunities for the lighter-skinned in contrast to the darker-skinned American Negro. From this, advanced maturity at birth is predicted for light-skinned American Negroes.

As, in this case, the *observations* differ from the *prediction*, only the former should be seriously considered.

ATTITUDES TOWARDS HEALTH IN ETHNIC GROUPS

A factor not always considered in the evaluation of interracial studies is the *attitude* of particular ethnic groups towards health. Longmore (1958) and Gelfand (1957) discussed the prominence of the subconscious fear which the Bantu have for the wrath of the spirits of their ancestors (even Bantu who may profess the Christian religion) should they consult white doctors. The Bantu rarely inquires into the nature of his complaint, rarely questioning the treatment given him; a situation very dissimilar to that of the white patient.

Marshall et al. (1970) examined the attitudes towards health in children of different races and of different socioeconomic status in the U.S.A., and found that whites have a more positive attitude towards health personnel and institutions, while on the average black children are much less concerned about sickness than whites. They could not, from their study, determine whether this difference was based on a 'culture of poverty' or was ethnically determined.

Such attitudes influence statistics. Only those seeking medical advice at institutions engaged in epidemiological research are likely to figure in the statistics. The more pronounced and grave the disease manifestations, the more likely that prejudice against institutions, fear of ancestral spirits and the witch-doctor would be overcome.

Insurance statistics on mortality and morbidity often serve as general guidelines to prognoses, and are applied to all ethnic groups. Blackburn and Parlin (1966), however, remark that in the U.S.A. 'insured lives are principally white men in middle income classes.'

Intelligence in ethnic groups

The ability to learn, drives, and behavioural traits have an important genetic component. Studies on identical twins in man have shown that ability to learn and reason has a genetic basis. As Ingle (1964) points out, race and colour are not valid criteria for judging the worth of an individual, but he very convincingly pleads for an investigation of racial differences in intelligence and ability rather than the assumption that such differences do not exist. Such ethnic differences as reported from intelligence tests may be doubted from the point of view that the tests are either not sensitive or not really applicable to interracial studies. On the other hand, the existence of differences may be accepted, but the genetic basis discounted, in a hypothesis which starts from cultural deprivation, poor prenatal and medical care resulting in undernutrition in infants, often of premature birth, who begin life with an intellectual handicap (Pasamanick, 1969). The influence of nutrition on intelligence is, however, controversial. The criteria for evaluating and interpreting intelligence are uncertain, and, further, a large number of factors other than nutrition have a bearing on the level of intelligence. Walker et al. (1970), reviewing the data relating to nutritional status and intelligence, conclude that 'on the basis of present evidence it cannot be maintained that huge proportions of the world's population are irreversibily damaged mentally because of episodes of poor nutrition in early life.'

CLINICAL ASPECTS OF ETHNIC PIGMENTATION

Ethnic pigmentation identifies a particular type responsiveness to the environment: the evidence available at present indicates that dark races have a hyperactive RES, due to endocrine adjustments. This modified activity of the RES allows effective resistance to exogenous insults, and apparently protects against the formation of autogenous antibodies with a low incidence of auto-immune disease in some races.

The social significance of skin colour is probably also related to at least one 'iatrogenic' disease following the use of skin-lightening creams.

The classification of ethnic factors involved in the clinical practice of medicine is made on the assumption that *melanin* may have an influence in the following ways:

1. It serves as an easily visible marker of particular ethnic groups and, through the 'problem of colour', is implicated in some sociological aspects of medical care (Chapter XVI).
2. By its sheer abundance in the eye and skin it may influence local physiological and drug responses of clinical importance (Chapter XVII).
3. Its distribution and function is genetically determined. Ethnic pigmentation is considered in relation to genetically determined diseases in which pigmentation anomalies are important (Chapter XVIII).
4. Melanin, as a stable free radical, influences intracellular oxidation-reduction reactions, and may, thus, be implicated in certain diseases in which a marked difference in ethnic incidence exists. This is particulary the case in the psychosis-dyskinesia-hyperpigmentation group of illnesses (Chapter XIX).

REFERENCES

ABRAMSON, J. H., SINGH, R. A. and MAMBO, V. (1961): Antenatal stress and the baby's development. *Arch. Dis. Childh.*, *36*, 42.
ADOLPH, E. F. (1956): General and specific characteristics of physiological adaptations. *Amer. J. Physiol.*, *184*, 18.
ALLEN, S. P. and O'BRIEN, J. P. (1944): Tropical anhidrotic asthenia. *Med. J. Aust.*, *2*, 335.
ANGEL, J. L. (1969): Paleodemography and evolution. *Amer. J. phys. Anthrop.*, *31*, 343.
BARR, R. D., REES, P. H., CORDY, P. E., KUNGU, A., WOODGER, B. A. and CAMERON, H. M. (1972): Nephrotic syndrome in adult Africans in Nairobi. *Brit. med. J.*, *2*. 131.
BERLINER, D. L. and DOUGHERTY, T. F. (1960): The reticulo-endothelial system and metabolism of cortisol and cholesterol. In: *Reticulo Endothelial Structure and Function*, p. 403. Editor: J. H. Heller. The Ronald Press Co., New York, N.Y.
BLACKBURN, H. and PARLIN, R. W. (1966): Antecedents of disease: Insurance mortality experience. *Ann. N.Y. Acad. Sci.*, *134*, 965.
BLUM, H. F. (1961): Does the melanin pigment of human skin have adaptive value? *Quart. Rev. Biol.*, *36*, 50.
BONNE, C. (1937): Cancer and human races. *Amer. J. Cancer*, *30*, 435.
BOR, S., FEIWEL, M. and CHANARIN, I. (1969): Vitiligo and its aetiological relationship to organ-specific auto-immune disease. *Brit. J. Derm.*, *81*, 83.
BROWN, E. L. (1964): *Newer Dimensions of Patient Care, Part III: Patients and People*. Russel Sage Foundation, New York, N.Y.
CHANARIN, I. (1949): Epitrochlear adenopathy in the Bantu. *S. Afr. med. J.*, *23*, 960.
CUNLIFFE, W. J., HALL, R., NEWELL, D. J. and STEVENSON, C. J. (1968): Vitiligo, thyroid disease and autoimmunity. *Brit. J. Derm.*, *80*, 135.
DANCASTER, C. P. (1970): Thyrotoxicosis in the Bantu, with special reference to myopathy. *S. Afr. med. J.*, *44*, 695.
DAWBER, R. P. R. (1968): Vitiligo in mature-onset diabetes mellitus. *Brit. J. Derm.*, *80*, 257.
DOAN, C. E. (1957): The reticulo-endothelial cells in health and disease. In: *Physiopathology of the Reticulo-endothelial System*, p. 290. Editors: B. N. Halpern, B. Benacerraf and J. F. Delafresnay. Blackwell Scientific Publications, Oxford.

DOLL, R. (1957): *Methods of Geographical Pathology*, p. 11 (report of the study group convened by the Council for International Organizations of Medical Sciences). Blackwell Scientific Publications, Oxford.

EL MOFTY, A. M. (1968): *Vitiligo and Psoralens*. Pergamon Press, Oxford.

FAHEY, J. L. (1971): Cancer in the immunosuppressed patient. *Ann. intern. Med., 75*, 310.

FITZPATRICK, T. B. (1965): Mammalian melanin biosynthesis. *Trans. St John's Hosp. derm. Soc. (Lond.), 51*, 1.

GEBER, M. and DEAN, R. F. A. (1957): The state of development of newborn African children. *Lancet, 1*, 1216.

GELFAND, M. (1967): *The African Witch (with Particular Reference to Witchcraft Beliefs and Practice among the Shona of Rhodesia)*. E. and S. Livingstone, Ltd., Edinburgh.

GOLDSTEIN, M. S. (1969): Human paleopathology and some diseases in living primitive societies: A review of the recent literature. *Amer. J. phys. Anthrop., 31*, 285.

HO, K. J., BISS, K., MIKKELSON, B., LEWIS, L. A. and TAYLOR, C. B. (1971): The Masai of East Africa: Some unique biological characteristics. *Arch. Path., 91*, 387.

HORTON, C. P. and CRUMP, E. P. (1958): Growth and development. III. Skin color in Negro infants and parents: Its relationship to birth weight, reflex maturity, socio-economic status, length of gestation and parity. *J. Pediat., 52*, 547.

HOYME, L. E. (1969): On the origins of New World paleopathology. *Amer. J. phys. Anthrop., 31*, 295.

HUGHES, L. E. and LYTTON, B. (1964): Antigenic properties of human tumours: Delayed cutaneous hypersensitivity reactions. *Brit. med. J., 1*, 209.

HULSE, F. S. (1967): Selection for skin colour among the Japanese. *Amer. J. phys. Anthrop., 27*, 143.

INGLE, D. J. (1964): Racial differences and the future. *Science, 146*, 375.

JOHNSON, B. E. (1965): Symposium report and discussion on light and melanin pigmentation of the skin. In: *Recent Progress in Photobiology*, p. 375. Editor: E. J. Bowen. Blackwell Scientific Publications, Oxford.

KALFF, M. W. (1970): A population study on serum immunoglobulin levels. *Clin. chim. Acta, 28*, 277.

LADELL, W. S. S. (1964): Terrestrial animals in human heat: Man. In: *Handbook of Physiology, Section IV: Adaptation to the Environment*, p. 625. Editors: D. B. Dill, E. F. Adolph and C. G. Wilber. American Physiological Society, Washington, D.C.

LADELL, W. S. S., WATERLOW, J. C. and HUDSON, M. F. (1944): Desert climate. Physiological and clinical observations. *Lancet, 2*, 491, 527.

LAW, L. W. (1969): Studies of the significance of tumor antigens in induction and repression of neoplastic diseases: Presidential address. *Cancer Res., 29*, 1.

LAWSON, E. D. (1971): Hair color, personality and the observer. *Psychol. Rep., 28*, 311.

LEWIS, G. P., JICH, H., SLONE, D. and SHAPIRO, S. (1971): The role of genetic factors and serum protein binding in determining drug response as revealed by comprehensive drug surveillance. *Ann. N.Y. Acad. Sci., 179*, 729.

LONGMORE, L. (1958): Medicine, magic and witchcraft among urban Africans on the Witwatersrand. *Cent. Afr. J. Med., 4*, 242.

MACKAY, I. R. (1967): Autoimmune aspects of three skin diseases: Pemphigus, cutaneous lupus erythematosus and vitiligo. *Aust. J. Derm., 9*, 113.

MANN, G. V., ROELS, O. A. and PRICE, D. L. (1962): Cardiovascular disease in African Pygmies: A study of the health status, serum lipids and diet of Pygmies in the Congo. *J. chron. Dis., 15*, 341.

MARSHALL, J. (1969): Epidemiology of skin diseases. In: *Essays on Tropical Dermatology*, p. 17. Editors: R. D. G. Ph. Simons and J. Marshall. Excerpta Medica, Amsterdam.

MARSHALL, C. L., HASSANEIN, K. M., HASSANEIN, R. S. and PAUL, C. L. (1970): Attitudes toward health among children of different races and socio-economic status. *Pediatrics, 46,* 422.

McFARLANE, H., TALERMAN, A. and STEINBERG, A. G. (1970): Immunoglobulins in Jamaicans and Nigerians with immunogenetic typing of myeloma and lymphoma in Jamaicans. *J. clin. Path., 23,* 124.

McGILL, P. E. (1971): Thyrotoxicosis in the African clinical and immunological observations. *Brit. med. J., 2,* 679.

McKEOWN, T. (1960): Influences affecting pre-natal growth in man. In: *Human Growth,* p. 93. Editor: J. M. Tanner. Pergamon Press, Oxford.

MILLER, K., RUBENSTEIN, A. and ASTRAND, P. O. (1968): Lipid values in Kalahari Bushmen. *Arch. intern. Med., 121,* 414.

MILNER, L. V. and CALITZ, F. (1971): Serum immunoglobulin levels in white, Asiatic and Bantu blood donors. *S. Afr. med. J., 45,* 683.

MYERS, H. J. and YOCHELSON, L. (1948): Color denial in the Negro. *Psychiatry, 11,* 39.

NICOL, T., SNELL, R. S. and BILBEY, D. E. J. (1956): Effect of cortisone on the defense mechanisms of the body. *Brit. med. J., 2,* 800.

OLUWASANMI, J. O. and ALLI, F. (1968): Goitres in Western Nigeria. *Trop. geogr. Med., 20,* 357.

PASAMANICK, B. (1969): A tract for the times: Some sociobiologic aspects of science, race and racism. *Amer. J. Orthopsychiat., 39,* 7.

PHILLIPS, J. H. and BURCH, G. E. (1960): A review of cardiovascular diseases in the white and Negro races. *Medicine (Baltimore), 39,* 241.

PROSSER, C. L. (1964): Perspectives of adaptation: theoretical aspects. In: *Handbook of Physiology, Section IV: Adaptation to the Environment,* p. 11. Editors: D. B. Dill, E. F. Adolph and C. G. Wilber. American Physiological Society, Washington, D. C.

QUEVEDO, W. C. (1969): 'Pigmentary Patterning' (panel discussion on the functions of melanin by M. S. Blois, T. B. Fitzpatrick, F. Daniels Jr. and W. C. Quevedo). In: *The Biologic Effects of Ultra Violet Radiation,* p. 325. Editor: F. Urbach. Pergamon Press, Oxford.

REES, P. H., BARR, R. D., CORDY, P. E. and VOLLER, A. (1972): Possible role of malaria in the aetiology of the nephrotic syndrome. *Brit. med. J., 2,* 130.

ROBB, D. (1960): Differential incidence of surgical and other disease. *N.Z. med. J., 59,* 271.

ROBERTS, J. I. (1948): A comparison of haematological results in Europeans and Africans suffering from active malaria. *J. trop. Med. Hyg., 51,* 228.

SCOTT, J. G. (1949): Epitrochlear adenopathy. *S. Afr. med. J., 23,* 1054.

SHEE, J. C. and HOUSTON, W. (1962): Clinical features of auto-immune thyroiditis. *E. Afr. med. J., 39,* 100.

SNELL, R. S. and NICOL, T. (1956): Effect of cortisone on the serum gamma globulin. *Nature (Lond.), 177,* 578.

STEWART, T. H. M. (1969): The presence of delayed hypersensitivity reactions in patients toward cellular extracts of their malignant tumours. I. The role of tissue antigen, non-specific reactions of nuclear material, and bacterial antigen as a cause of this phenomenon. *Cancer (Philad.), 23,* 1368.

SUCKLING, A. J. (1968): Serum gamma-globulin level as a racial characteristic. *J. med. Lab. Technol., 25,* 217.

SUSSER, M. W. and WATSON, W. (1971): *Sociology in Medicine, 2nd ed.* Oxford University Press, London.

TANNER, J. M. (1957): The state of development of new-born African children. *Lancet, 2,* 189.

UDRY, J. R., BAUMAN, K. E. and CHASE, C. (1971): Skin color, status and mate selection. *Amer. J. Sociol.*, *76*, 722.

WALDER, B. K., ROBERTSON, M. R. and JEREMY, D. (1971): Skin cancer and immunosuppression. *Lancet*, *2*, 1282.

WALKER, A. R. P., RICHARDSON, B. D. and WALKER, B. F. (1970): Nutrition and intelligence (editorial). *S. Afr. med. J.*, *44*, 717.

WASSERMANN, H. P. (1964): Studies on melanin-labelled cells in the human skin window. *S. Afr. J. Lab. clin. Med.*, *10*, 76.

WASSERMANN, H. P. (1965): Human pigmentation and environmental adaptation. *Arch. environm. Hlth*, *11*, 691.

WASSERMANN, H. P. (1969): Melanin pigmentation and the environment. In: *Essays on Tropical Dermatology*, pp. 7–16. Editors: R. D. G. Ph. Simons and J. Marshall. Excerpta Medica, Amsterdam.

WILLIAMS, C. D. (1957): The state of development of new-born African children. *Lancet*, *2*, 93.

ZOUTENDYK, A. (1970): Auto-antibodies in South African whites, Coloured and Bantu. *S. Afr. med. J. 44*, 469.

Chapter XVI

The 'problem of colour' in total medical care and social medicine

Skin colour, as a visible marker of ethnic groups, is intricately interwoven with social medicine and some urgent problems in the application of medical care; unfortunately, it is also interwoven with political philosophy.

GENERAL CONSIDERATIONS

The ethnic background of the patient in relation to the total medical care which he receives in the United States was discussed by Brown (1964, pp. 56–86). Patients differing considerably in physical appearance from the American norm (Negroes, American Indians, Japanese Americans, Chinese Americans) were fortunate in that the staff usually either made a mental note of the fact or entered it under the heading 'race' on the admission sheet. Patients who 'looked like Americans' were not questioned about their ethnic background and the staff was not alerted to the fact that patients of North German, Irish, Italian or English ancestry 'might react differently to the physical environment, treatment regime or even to their own bodily discomfort.' The psychosocial needs of those ethnic groups, not visibly different from the average American, consequently often passed unheeded. Several case reports were discussed, and the various reasons for attitudes were fully analysed (Brown, 1964, p. 27).

At present, treatment of racial groups within a particular country may be a philosophy of assimilation (the 'melting-pot' philosophy of the United States) or a philosophy of cultural pluralism (e.g. Switzerland). In a more abbreviated form the philosophies may be summarized as that of 'integration' and 'segregation'. Basically, it is sometimes believed that if different ethnic groups are integrated they will share equally in all the opportunities and advantages of the dominant group. Likewise, segregation is believed to withhold some opportunities and advantages from certain groups (Shaw, 1971). The important points which are frequently overlooked in this highly emotional controversy are: (1) Ethnic groups usually differ in social, cultural and religious backgrounds. Integration, while *offering* a uniformity in responsibility and community benefits also *requires* some degree of cultural, social and religious uniformity for harmony in daily living. If this involves minor concessions, integration becomes desirable, but if major concessions are required it is impossible to enforce them even under penalty of law. (2) The only basic human rights are those which ensure respect for the dignity of the individual. One must be fully aware of the uniqueness inherent in human variation, and this includes variation in cultural factors as well.

Philosophy of assimilation

Such a philosophy might be successful if each member of the community were gifted with a sensitive appreciation of the social and cultural factors important to other groups within the community. Such intensive and sensitive insight and understanding is unfortunately a superhuman requirement. Though it is an ideal to be pursued, at a more pragmatic level, it is at present unattainable.

An American nurse living in Israel described some of the difficulties encountered in adapting to Middle East Culture under the title 'Cultural Shock' (Weiss, 1971). She states: 'Cultural shock is a compound of all the minutiae of daily living, plus the discovery that certain words or gestures may convey completely different meanings in a different cultural setting.' Awareness of this problem of understanding a culture and social circumstances in which one was not born, bred and reared is evident especially in articles appearing in nursing journals (Donovan, 1970; White, 1970), because nurses naturally have closer individual contact with the patient than the doctor, whose contact is mainly professional and consists of (several) brief daily visits.

Britain has been described as a multiracial society (Parry, 1970), and the word immigrant was recognized as a 'highly emotive' word, which 'to some serves as a term of abuse. It is used by all of us as a euphemism for a person whose skin is coloured' (Carne, 1970). Stating that they have only made a beginning in the direction of establishing how different cultural problems affected the medical needs of immigrants and the delivery of medical care, Carne (1970) found that their task was made 'infinitely easier' by what they had learned. Discussing their emotional stress, Hashmi (1970) states that 'to ignore the culture from which the patient comes and its understanding would make it virtually impossible to understand the psychopathology of the related suffering.'

Schwab (1971) found that symptoms of depression are class-related and he developed social class profiles which he describes sufficiently clearly to accord with any practitioner's own experience. Lessening of social distance between patient and doctor/nurse increases emphatic understanding but lessens objectivity. Conversely, when social distance becomes great, objectivity is increased, but emphatic understanding is decreased. 'Our research showed that young doctors and nurses substantially underdiagnosed older medical patients' emotional illnesses. Furthermore, our white doctors and nurses consistently underdiagnosed black patients' emotional illnesses' (Schwab, 1971). He also states that 'communication is the essence of psychotherapy' and thereby also identifies unwittingly a major difference in medical care in the U.S.A. (where the American Negro speaks English) and in Africa (where the African Negro or Bantu, especially from rural areas, speaks only his own language, which is usually unintelligible to the white doctor or nurse).

Perhaps more mundane than emotional distress, the food which one enjoys is enjoyable because it is traditional to one's cultural milieu. Gordon and Kilgore (1971) discussed their experience with ethnic meal planning and found that this required, in addition to a sound knowledge of dietary science, consideration of food habits as influenced by 'area of rearing, ethnic background, religion and home traditions.' They state: 'Though belatedly, we are beginning to realize that food habits are a part of the total culture of a people, inextricably bound in with other aspects of daily living.' They present 6 ethnic menus for patients admitted to their New York long-term hospital.

It is not difficult to assemble various examples of ethnic disregard or a peculiar type of 'colour-blindness' in integrated hospital medical practice ranging from the examples quoted above to the problem of the best colour for skin sutures. These are traditionally black, and the colour is important only when they are being removed. Then it is desirable that they should be seen against the background of the patient's skin, so as to be grasped, cut and cleanly removed. Black sutures are difficult to distinguish in a dark hair-bearing area, in coloured patients and in wounds with encrusted blood. Tinckler (1972) found that red was the most suitable colour for skin sutures in Caucasians and Afro-Asians.

Philosophy of cultural pluralism

As in the Cantonal hospitals of Switzerland where particular ethnic (cultural) groups are served by hospitals staffed with people belonging to that culture, South Africa traditionally follows this philosophy.

The ideal is to accommodate patients belonging to a certain ethnic group in wards staffed by doctors and nurses belonging to the same group. Because of a chronic shortage of trained Cape Coloured and Bantu personnel, white staff at present, and for the immediate future, still have to bridge this deficiency. When several Bantu patients share a ward with Cape Coloured patients, they usually request to have their beds grouped together to make conversation easier. Personal discussion with many patients leaves no doubt in one's mind that hospital patients in South Africa prefer this 'apartheid' and would prefer completely separate wards, especially if the ward is staffed by nurses belonging to their own ethnic group.

Both philosophies may work well in particular situations. Cape Coloureds, American Negroes and whites would probably have little difficulty in becoming accustomed to integrated wards whether in South Africa or in the U.S.A., should they be willing to make some minor concessions. The Bantu and African Negro would find it extremely difficult because of the communication problem, and the religious, cultural and social differences which exist at present.

Probably, the ideal solution lies somewhere between these 2 opposed philosophies. While in the United States some blacks are demanding segregation as a solution, in South Africa some whites favour integration; in both instances this is envisaged with some further qualifications.

SOCIAL DISTANCES AMONG ETHNIC GROUPS IN AFRICA

'After all, man is subject to cultural determinism as well as a genetic disposition; and just as his cerebral activity depends on the integrity of his neurophysiologic

Fig. 28. The tropical belt across Africa, showing the endemic areas for
  (a) Bilharzia
  (b) Yellow fever
  (c) Relapsing fever and sleeping sickness
  (d) Plague and filariasis.
  (Modified from *Africa: Maps and Statistics*. Africa Institute of South Africa, Pretoria. By permission.)

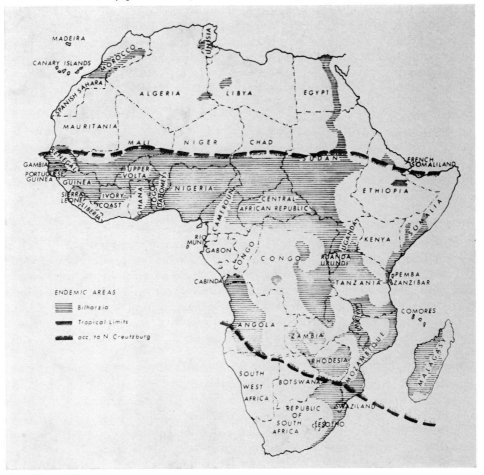

Fig. 28a. Bilharzia.

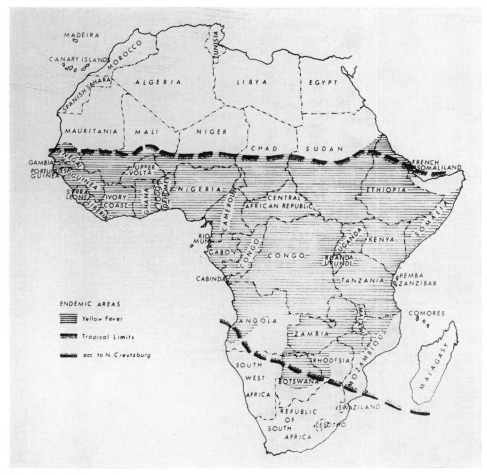

Fig. 28b. Yellow fever.

mechanisms, his self-esteem is a function of his social existence' (Schwab, 1971). To the inhabitant of Africa, the tendency of foreigners to suppose a homogeneity similar to that of Western Europe or North America is somewhat naïve. Africa is the second largest land mass of the earth and covers a fifth of the world's land surface but is inhabited by only about 1/12th of its people. Three distinct regions can be discerned:

(*a*) *North Africa* bordering on the Mediterranean with a predominantly non-negroid population;

(*b*) *Sub-Saharan or tropical Africa* with a mainly negroid population, and

(*c*) *Sub-Zambesian or Southern Africa,* with a predominantly Bantu-speaking black population, but also with the largest number of whites of European descent.

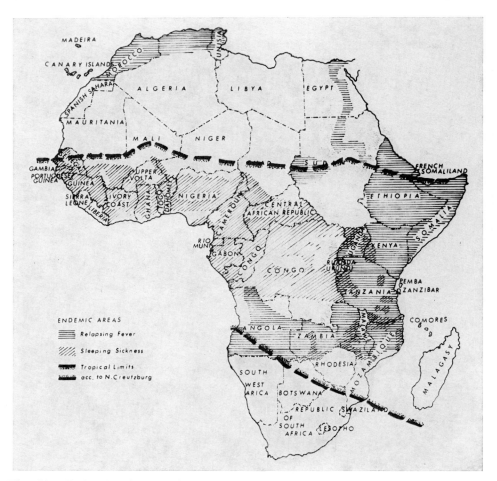

Fig. 28c. Relapsing fever and sleeping sickness.

Indians from India are widespread, mainly along the Eastern coastline; the Khoisan people (Hottentots and Bushmen) are virtually nearly extinct, and now mostly confined to South Africa. The Cape Coloured are mostly confined to the Western part of the Cape Province of South Africa.

The 3 regions are completely different in their geography, climate, economic and social structure as well as in their traditions and historical development (Fig. 28).

There are 3 main religions in Africa (Fig. 29):

1. **Tribal religions**

Magic is incorporated into tribal religion, although this differs between various nations. Many tribal religions believe in *animism and the ancestral cult (or*

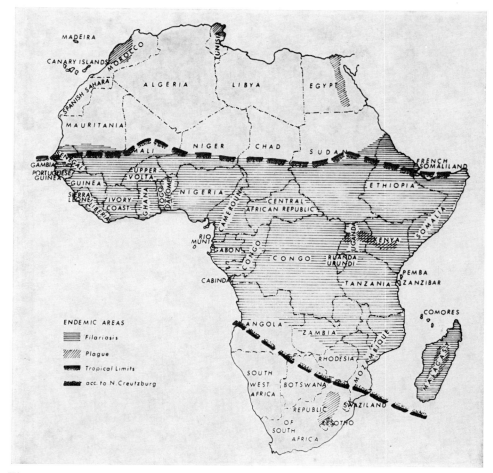

Fig. 28d. Plague and filariasis.

manism): In the former the 'soul' is an invisible yet material power which must be kept alive by natural or magical means after death when it has left the body; in the latter the family is regarded as a community of the living and the dead.

2. Islam

Founded by Mohammed in 622 A.D., Islam is the most widespread religion, not through missionary activity, but by cross-cultural assimilation. The animist finds magic in Islamic amulets and charms, the transitional group adheres to manism, and finally the fully Islamic (Moslem) religion adheres more firmly to the faith as proclaimed by Mohammed.

Popular among African Negroes and Bantus, who are by tradition polygamous, is the fact that Islam allows a man 4 wives. Most of the approximately 80

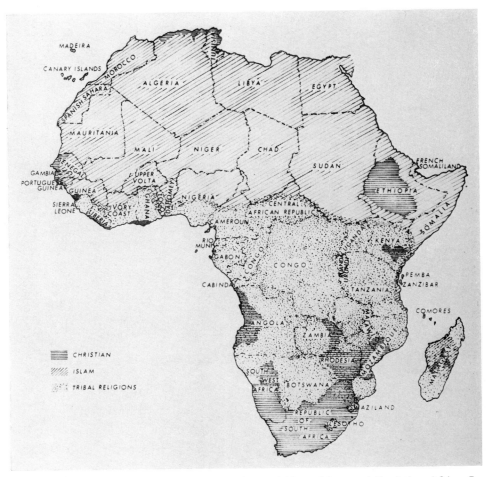

Fig. 29. Religions of Africa. (Modified from *Africa: Maps and Statistics*. Africa Institute of South Africa, Pretoria. By permission.)

million followers of Islam live in Egypt, Portuguese Guinea, Algeria and Sudan.

3. **Christianity**

Most of the 53 million Christians inhabit the Southern part of the continent, except for Ethiopia where the rapid spread of Islam in the 7th and 8th centuries was resisted. The majority are Roman Catholic (± 30 million) and Protestant (± 20 million). Christianity spread through missionary activity and was the major force in decreasing the belief in witchcraft, sorcery and magic and in establishing the principles of scientific medicine in the various regions of Africa.

In a confined area, e.g. Mali, the following social classes intermingle: The upper social class consists of merchants, rich but illiterate and religiously bigoted, and civil servants who are literate, well educated, religiously tolerant with a tendency to atheism. The lower strata consist of uneducated and semi-educated wage-earners, apprentices, small tradesmen and seasonal workers. Most are Moslem in name but hold traditional ideas about illness and its treatment (Imperato, 1970).

What follows is a generalisation which, with minor differences, applies to the larger part of the black community in Africa (Imperato, 1970; Gelfand, 1957, 1964).

The tribal Negro or Bantu does not enquire 'how', but rather 'why' he became ill. He may turn to the sorcerer, jinn, diviner, marabout, or witch-doctor to try and seek an answer.

The African (Bantu and Negro) is a fatalist; he seeks relief of symptoms, and if supernatural causes are not remedied by the witch-doctor, the herbalist may succeed with his old and well-tried remedies. The various types of 'medical practitioners' (witch-doctors, herbalists, sorcerers and scientific men) survive because the traditional beliefs (animism, magic, Islam, Christianity) determine the needs of the community with respect to its health care. Psychological care and organic cure are very much the same to a patient who is not interested in 'how' he became ill, but 'why'. If the sorcerer can allay his fears and symptoms his value to the patient equals that of the psychiatrist to the white patient of Western civilization. To a large extent, because of language and cultural barriers, the psychological needs of the patient are fulfilled by the witch-doctor and the organic health needs by scientific medicine. Although the situation is certainly changing, for many years to come this kaleidoscopic pattern will still dominate in large parts of the continent, because the type of health care is determined by the traditional beliefs of the community and the type of care they want (Figs. 30*a* and 30*b*).

It is interesting to compare this situation to that in Europe and the Far East, as done by Voorhoeve (1966). From the 15th century onward witchcraft in Europe receded with the revival of interest in ancient Greek civilization, but modern scientific medicine in the proper sense emerged only with the great scientific discoveries of the 19th century. Western medicine established a foothold in Indonesia (1851) and in Thailand (1889), and social class selection was immediately evident: the well-educated elite of the indigenous population received modern scientific medical views favourably, while the vast majority resisted the progressive approach and consolidated behind native witch-doctors and traditional medicine. Several decades elapsed before modern education and critical thinking achieved an effective break-through.

In the larger, Northern parts of Africa Western scientific medicine met with resistance until the end of the second World War. More, but nevertheless limited, success was achieved in Southern Africa from the turn of the century. Voorhoeve (1966) quotes Jelliffe's view that, in order to change effectively the hold of traditional medicine (in all tropical countries of the world), traditional customs should be divided into beneficial, neutral and harmful, and treated accordingly by medical practitioners.

Prolonged breast-feeding and feeding on demand are *beneficial practices* which lessen the incidence of kwashiorkor, and should be encouraged. *Neutral*

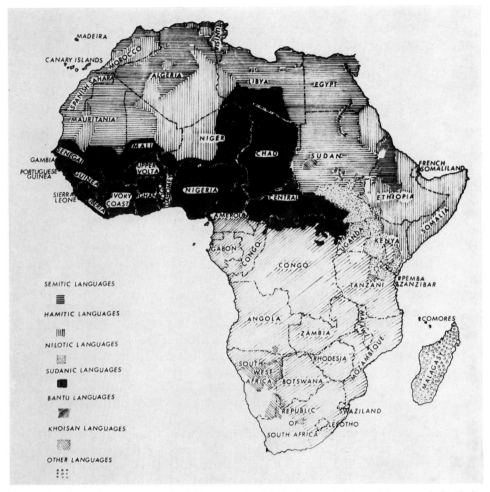

SEMITIC LANGUAGES

HAMITIC LANGUAGES

NILOTIC LANGUAGES

SUDANIC LANGUAGES

BANTU LANGUAGES

KHOISAN LANGUAGES

OTHER LANGUAGES

Fig. 30a. The languages of Africa. (Modified from *Africa: Maps and Statistics.* Africa Institute of South Africa, Pretoria. By permission.)

practices include the application of oil to the anterior fontanelle of the baby to 'keep cold out of the head'. To resist this tradition is to provoke the herbalist. Encouraging the tradition tactfully (but without overenthusiasm) enlists the herbalist's cooperation. *Harmful practices,* e.g. cow's urine and tobacco for convulsions in children, or ritual murder for 'medicine' from human organs, should of course be combated. This is most effectively achieved not only by fighting the custom, but by promoting health education at the same time.

This very brief survey does not do justice to the role of witch, witchcraft and superstition in traditional African medicine or its confrontation with scientific medicine, nor is the complexity of tribal ritual and custom in relation to medicine fully considered in all its ramifications. The reader is referred to the 2 monographs by Gelfand (1964, 1967) for an excellent and comprehensive discussion.

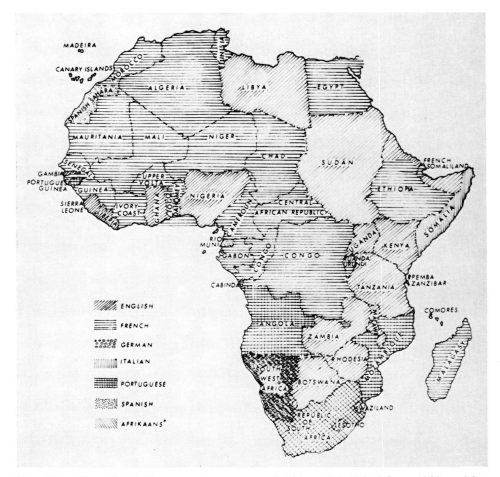

Fig. 30b. The official European languages of Africa. (Modified from *Africa: Maps and Statistics*. Africa Institute of South Africa, Pretoria. By permission.)

ECONOMICS, POLITICS AND HEALTH IN THE ETHNIC GROUPS OF AFRICA

'. . . the racial problem as we normally understand it is just a myth, a myth created to cover quite a different problem, that of the human instinct of competition. In this competition the skin is no more than a 'club-colour' or schooltie, which distinguishes the economically powerful from the economically weak' (Simons, 1961, p. 107).

Especially in Southern Africa 2 large economic societies exist: a white industrial and a black, predominantly peasant, society. The sociological background of differences in disease pattern in these societies is the same as exists everywhere where industrial and peasant societies are found. In comparison to men, female overall mortality is higher in peasant societies than in industrial societies. Fertility is held in high regard by people on a subsistence agriculture and barrenness is a ground for divorce. Anxiety about sterility accounts for many of the conversion hysterias in Zulu women (Loudon, 1959). Children are a form of social insurance, being able to provide for the parents when their ability for manual labour declines. The effect of large families in a country where rapid industrial development co-exists with a peasant society may be disastrous. Attempts at birth control by the 'pill' are regarded with suspicion of genocide amongst the uneducated, although its advantages are readily appreciated by the more educated in the community, regardless, of course, to which ethnic group they belong (see Susser and Watson, Chapter I, 1971).

The interest in traditional medicine originated from anthropological investigators, but the urgent and practical problems of malnutrition, paediatric disease and obstetric complications compelled medical investigators in many parts of Africa to take an active interest in traditional medicine, the economics and ergonomics of nutrition and the political scene.

Population growth

The population of developing countries increases at a rate of more than 3% per year, whereas the average international rate of growth is 1.7%. East Africa has the highest rate of population growth, predicted to double the population within the next 20 years. It is the literate, white-collar urban person who first limits his family size; who succumbs to the 'brain-drain' towards better pastures, while the poor and illiterate people living in slums have no interest in climbing the socioeconomic ladder and do not bother to limit or space their children (Brown, 1970).

In Africa, the 2 groups referred to above have differently coloured skins (this applies to the median of the groups; there are of course also poor whites and rich blacks. In South Africa, there are several black millionaires).

With population growth declining first, then, in the literate, economically strong section, which bears the burden of supporting technology and education not only of his own group but also of the large, poor and low-productive, but rapidly expanding group, the competition referred to by Simons in the quotation above (p. 215) becomes fierce. Many of the political problems of Africa stem from the fact that the modern 'white man's burden' in Africa is the economic support of a black majority which, often lacking in education and technological ability, yet exhibits a rapid population growth, because of its dependence on hands in a peasant economy, and has, of course, to be supported by the white group. This is the exact reverse of the American scene where the economically powerful are also numerically the majority group. This is, of course, a fruitful area for political agitators, who demand political control for an economically poor section. Recent political history in Africa demonstrates how the withdrawal of economically powerful white 'props' can lead to political instability when the economically weak start a scramble for power. In evolution there are no shortcuts, and the longest way round may even be the shortest way home as far as socioeconomic and cultural evolution are concerned.

A recent survey in Kenya indicated that although 90% of the educated Bantus around Kampala were interested in family planning, 90% of the respondents to the interview did not know of any methods of birth-control (Brown, 1970).

Childlessness by colour

The modern problem was partially enlarged further by advances in medical control of venereal disease. Veevers (1971) found that in the past childlessness has been more common among non-whites than among whites. To a large extent childlessness in non-whites was due to the relatively high incidence of venereal disease. Since 1950 this cause has declined rapidly while in many whites voluntary limitation of family size is not uncommon. In voluntary childlessness, population growth and health considerations are frequently mentioned. In modern highly advanced technological societies, career commitments, style of life, economic ambitions and, especially in cities, housing problems may be equally important (Gustavus and Henley, 1971; Rhodes, 1971). Bettering the socioeconomic and educational facilities is perhaps still the best method of population control.

Malnutrition

The inseparable counterpart of population growth is, of course, the feeding of the growing population. The problem of malnutrition in Africa is complex and includes agricultural technology, geographical factors (i.e. area suitable for cultivation, climatic factors), effective food storage and distribution, palatable cooking, effective sanitation (a problem especially in tropical climates) and the control of pests, micro-organisms and 'other disasters between the crop on the land and the food on the table' (Sofoluwe, 1970). Whiteman (1966) found great variation in beliefs and practices relating to food in a New Guinean community, but they were totally unaware of any relation of diet to good health.

Equally important are tribal taboos on articles of diet; the traditional diet (e.g. maize and cassava as the important providers of calories) may contain a low-quality protein lacking in tryptophane and leucine. In many Bantu tribes the custom of cooking and brewing beer in iron pots probably contributes largely to universal haemosiderosis in the Bantu. The iron in haemosiderotic livers oxidizes ascorbic acid, and in people on a marginal intake of vitamin C leads to osteoporosis and other manifestations of scurvy (Lynch et al., 1967; Schulz and Swanepoel, 1962; Smit and Swanepoel, 1962; Seftel et al., 1966).

Perception of social class

Urban Africans, studied in Johannesburg (Hurst, 1970), dichotomize their society, and clearly recognize educated and uneducated, westernized and tribal, Christian and heathen components. Classes have developed in urban African society which stress educational needs (middle class) and economic needs (working class), but class consciousness is 'as yet restricted to the very few who have assimilated western thought to such an extent that they are able to perceive such patterns' (Hurst, 1970).

What has been said of Africa, holds true for many parts of the world. 'This everpresent urge in one human being to try to rise above another is an essential stimulus for the development of mankind. Whenever necessary this instinct can lead to – or be associated with – group formation, be it only to consolidate a position in the struggle for life . . . and dominance' (Simons, 1961).

Ethnic pigmentation is not a factor which leads to bad human relations, but it marks:

1. GROUPS OF DIFFERENT CULTURAL, SOCIAL AND RELIGIOUS BACKGROUNDS

In some situations medical needs can best be provided by each group for its own members (segregation), and in others the differences are less marked and it becomes practical to provide medical care by integration of the groups. This is mainly a problem of providing effective organization, but the difficulties encountered are visibly underlined by the colour of the skin of the groups concerned.

2. GROUPS OF DIFFERENT ECONOMIC BACKGROUNDS AND POLITICAL POWER

If this situation is interpreted as the result of discrimination, *because* of the hereditary marking, friction develops. In many instances, but not always, the real causes may, for political expediency and in the struggle for power, be minimized.

As indicated, medical care may contribute to decreasing the distance between that group with a favourable population-growth/economic-support ratio and the one with an unfavourable ratio, and in this way, it might lessen friction between ethnic groups. The formation of social classes in black society defines certain common aspirations. Increasing class consciousness leads to awareness of the social position achieved and creates the need to consolidate this position. Unlike the situation in a homogeneously coloured community, in a multiracial society the normal team competition for social, economic and political dominance cannot be camouflaged.

REFERENCES

Brown, E. L. (1964): *Newer Dimensions of Patient Care, Part III: Patients as People.* Russel Sage Foundation, New York, N.Y.

Brown, R. E. (1970): Attitudes toward family planning among peri-urban Africans in Uganda. *Trop. Med. Hyg., 22*, 87.

Carne, S. (1970): The immigrant patient in general practice. *Proc. roy. Soc. Med., 63,* 629.

Donovan, H. (1970): Can we work with the Black Panthers. *Nursing Outlook, 18,* 34 (May).

Gelfand, M. (1957): *The Sick African: A Clinical Study,* 3rd ed., Chapter I. Juta and Company, Capetown.

Gelfand, M. (1964): *Medicine and Custom in Africa.* E. and S. Livingstone, Ltd., Edinburgh.

Gelfand, M. (1967): *The African Witch* (with particular reference to witchcraft beliefs and practice among the Shona of Rhodesia). E. and S. Livingstone, Ltd., Edinburgh.

Gordon, J. A. and Kilgore, V. (1971): Planning ethnic menus. *Hospitals, 45/21,* 87.

Gustavus, S. O. and Henley, J. R. (1971): Correlates of voluntary childlessness in a select population. *Soc. Biol., 18,* 277.

Hashmi, F. (1970): Immigrants and emotional stress. *Proc. roy. Soc. Med., 63,* 631.

Hurst, L. A. (1970): An investigation into the psychopathology of the Bantu-speaking people of the Witwatersrand. *Leech (Johannesburg), 40,* 52.

Imperato, P. J. (1970): Indigenous medical beliefs and practices in Bamako, a Moslem African city. *Trop. geogr. Med., 22,* 211.

Loudon, J. B. (1959): Psychogenic disorder and social conflict among the Zulu. In: *Culture and Mental Health,* p. 351. Editor: M. K. Opler. The MacMillan Press Ltd., New York, N.Y.

Lynch, S. R., Seftel, H. C., Torrance, J. D., Charlton, R. W. and Bothwell, T. H. (1967): Accelerated oxidative catabolism of ascorbic acid in siderotic Bantu. *Amer. J. clin. Nutr., 20,* 641.

Parry, W. H. (1970): Health and welfare of immigrants. *Proc. roy. Soc. Med., 63,* 633.

Rhodes, L. (1971): Socio-economic correlates of fertility in the metropolis: Relationship of individual and areal unit characteristics. *Soc. Biol., 18,* 296.

Schulz, E. J. and Swanepoel, H. (1962): Scorbutic pseudoscleroderma. An aspect of Bantu siderosis. *S. Afr. med. J., 36,* 367.

Schwab, J. J. (1971): Depressive illness: A sociomedical syndrome. *Psychosomatics, 12,* 385.

Seftel, H. C., Malkin, C., Schmaman, A., Abrahams, C., Lynch, S. R., Charlton, R. W. and Bothwed, T. H. (1966): Osteoporosis, scurvy and siderosis in Johannesburg Bantu. *Brit. med. J., 1,* 642.

Shaw, C. T. (1971): A detailed examination of treatment procedures of whites and blacks in hospitals. *Sociol. Sci. Med., 5,* 251.

Simons, R. D. G. Ph. (1958): Die Soziologische Bedeutung des Pigments. *Hautarzt, 9,* 452.

Simons, R. D. G. Ph. (1961): *The Colour of the Skin in Human Relations.* Elsevier Publ. Co., Amsterdam.

Smit, Z. M. and Swanepoel, H. (1962): Vitamin C metabolism in a case of scorbutic pseudoscleroderma with iron storage disease. *S. Afr. J. Lab. clin. Med., 8,* 72.

Sofoluwe, G. O. (1970): Promotive medicine. A boost to the economy of developing countries. *Trop. geogr. Med., 22,* 250.

Susser, M. W. and Watson, W. (1971): *Sociology in Medicine,* 2nd ed. Oxford University Press, London.

Tinckler, L. F. (1972): What is the best colour for skin sutures (Letter to the Editor). *Lancet, 1,* 353.

Veevers, J. E. (1971): Differential childlessness by color: A further examination. *Soc. Biol., 18,* 285.

VOORHOEVE, H. W. A. (1966): Traditional native and western medicine side by side in tropical countries. A review. *Trop. geogr. Med.*, *18*, 71.

WEISS, M. O. (1971): Cultural shock. *Nursing Outlook*, *19*, 40 (Jan.).

WHITE, E. M. (1970): Race relations: A call for action. *Nursing Outlook*, *18*, 31 (March).

WHITEMAN, J. (1966): Attitudes towards food in New Guinea. *Trop. geogr. Med.*, *18*, 159.

Chapter XVII

Ethnic differences in clinical manifestations
due to the sheer abundance of melanin

The differences in the amount of melanin formed in dark and white races may have clinical importance due to (1) mechanical effects, (2) biochemical effects and (3) the accumulation of drugs on melanin.

As an example of the first the eye will be considered, as an example of the second, skin pigmentation in relation to solar radiation will be discussed, and brief reference will be made to drug binding by melanin.

MELANIN AND THE EYE

As discussed earlier (p. 103), dark ethnic groups generally have heavily pigmented irides.

It is fairly common knowledge among practitioners who see many dark-skinned patients that a heavily pigmented iris dilates far less readily than one of a blue or intermediate colour, and also to a lesser extent. While 1 drop of 2% homatropine sufficiently dilates a pale iris in 10 to 20 minutes, several drops at intervals over a period up to 45 minutes may be required to dilate Negro or Bantu pupils, and even then such prolonged atropinization only gives about 75% of what would be considered maximal dilatation in the eyes of white patients (Somerset, 1962). The iris containing more pigment is somewhat thicker and so does not form folds easily when the pupil is dilated (Somerset, 1962). Another factor could be that stronger tropical sunlight may lead to relative hypertrophy of the sphincter in contrast to the dilator pupillae. Against this suggestion must be weighed the lesser degree of light scattering and reflection from the dark facial skin around the eye.

More recently, Emiru (1971) again studied this ethnic difference in response to mydriatics. It is evident that this peculiarity of response is indeed related to iris pigmentation because the Bantu albino reacts quite differently to the normally pigmented Bantu. Hailed in a recent editorial (1971) as a 'pioneer study',

Emiru's work is fully discussed and some possibilities for further investigation are considered.

Somerset (1962) also remarks on the poor response of the Negro eye to various types of operation for glaucoma of both the chronic-simple and closed-angle type: 'The very great abundance of pigment appears to hamper drainage and block normal and artificial exit channels.' Emiru (1971) attributes the rarity of acute closed-angle glaucoma in Bantus to this factor.

Pigment liberation into the anterior chamber of the eye may follow on the use of topical mydriatics, probably owing to rupture of degenerate cells of the pigment epithelium of the iris during contraction of the dilator pupillae (Aggarwal and Beveridge, 1971).

Into the same category as the masking of an erythema, exanthema or jaundice in the heavily pigmented skin, falls the difficulty of detecting corneal foreign bodies in the dark irides of dark races compared to the ease with which they can be detected in grey-blue irides. The lack of contrast between iris and pupil makes it more difficult to observe synechiae in dark-eyed people.

Most physicians discover the poor response to mydriatics in dark-skinned races, referred to above, when they are unable to perform ophthalmoscopy because of the heavy absorbance of light by the highly pigmented choroids. This requires dilation of the pupil for proper fundoscopy and, especially in a busy outpatient department, forcibly reminds one of the sluggish response of the dark iris to mydriatics.

MELANIN AND THE SKIN

The biological importance of adaptation to solar radiation is evident from Daniels' (1964) summary: '. . . the adaptations of man to solar radiation are of interest because they bridge levels of organization and function from the action of a single photon upon an electron in a molecule through all levels of organization of molecule, organelle, cell, organ, individual, to some of the most complicated social problems of our time.'

The stressor

The sun emits electromagnetic radiation which is a continuum of wavelengths from X-rays at the shorter to radio waves at the longer end. Ultraviolet radiation penetrated freely to the earth's surface before there was oxygen in the atmosphere and was a source of energy for synthesis of those organic compounds from which living systems arose (Sagan, 1961). Since chlorophylls appeared, life became possible by virtue of the screening effect on the shorter wavelengths of oxygen produced by photosynthesis. Oxygen is converted to ozone in the upper atmosphere by radiation of less than 240 nm. Absorption in the ozone layer, molecular scattering, and scattering and absorption by dust and water vapour in the atmosphere allow only those wavelengths longer than 297 nm to reach the earth. The upper limit of absorption of general protoplasm is between 310 and 320 nm, and this overlap of protoplasmic absorption and the shorter (ultraviolet) radiation which reaches the earth produce the photochemical effects on tissue clinically visible as sunburn. As the sun passes overhead, the amount of ultraviolet radiation varies with the amount of atmosphere which the rays have to penetrate. The air mass through which the rays have to pass is defined as the secant of the zenith angle multiplied by a factor which accounts for the curvature of the earth (Daniels, 1964). The greatest direct transmission occurs at an air mass of 1.0 with the sun directly overhead. This occurs only in the tropics, and at the equator this light passing through air mass 1.0 occurs at noon on 2 days of the year. Thus, latitude and season also partly determine the amount of ultraviolet radiation which reaches the surface of the earth in a particular area. Practically no sunburn radiation reaches the earth's surface when the zenith angle is greater than 70° (sun less than 20° above the horizon).

Furthermore, the total body dose of ultraviolet radiation also depends on the amount reflected from the surface of the earth. A fresh snowfield reflects about 85%, dry sand 17% and grass about 2.5% of sunburn radiation (Daniels, 1964).

In mid-summer at noon at latitude 40°N it takes at least 15 to 20 minutes of exposure to solar radiation to induce perceptible erythema in untanned white skin. The energy of this radiation is approximately equal to 67.5×10^3 μwatt/cm^2 (Pathak, 1967).

ULTRAVIOLET ACTION SPECTRUM

The UV radiation is often divided into short, medium and long UV sections denoted as UV-C (200–280 nm), UV-B (280–315 nm) and UV-A (315–400 nm).

An action spectrum is a collection of reciprocal values over a range of different wavelengths; usually these are reciprocal values of threshold doses for some effect. In the skin the effect is most commonly the threshold for erythema (minimal erythema dose (MED)) (Magnus, 1969).

Redness and pigmentation are the most important immediate responses to UV radiation. Progressing from UV-C to UV-A Breit and Kligman (1969) found that the erythema becomes more intense and more lasting. With increasing wavelength penetration becomes deeper, and with higher wavelengths histological evidence of greater depth of cellular damage can be demonstrated. The pattern of pigmentation response was, however, highly individualistic. Efficient tanners experienced much greater decrease in reflectance and the effects were long-lasting. It appeared that melanogenic potency increased proportionally with wavelength.

The absorption of shortwave UV is *almost* complete in the stratum corneum, while UV-A and visible light penetrate to the cutis and are absorbed primarily by the blood-vessels. The stratum corneum, apart from its light-scattering effects, contains absorbant molecules such as melanin granules, histidine, urocanic acid, small peptides, cholesterol and phospholipids, all of which absorb UV radiation especially in the shorter wavelengths. The stratum corneum of pigmented skin absorbs more radiation than the stratum corneum of white skin. Conversely, white stratum corneum transmits more radiation than pigmented epidermis, and is thus more susceptible to actinic damage. Between 5 and 15% of impinging wavelengths shorter than 320 nm (especially 240–260 nm and 300 nm) are transmitted through white epidermis. The erythemogenic wavelengths damage the venules and arterioles during the period of light absorption (Pathak, 1965).

Stress

To effect a photochemical change, radiation must be absorbed. Light which is not transmitted through a substance and not reflected or scattered at the surface, is absorbed by the substance. The effect of this absorption depends on the total energy rather than on the dose rate and duration of the exposure. Only a fraction of absorbed light is actually responsible for inducing a specific reaction; this depends on the number of molecules affected by the number of quanta absorbed (quantum yield).

PRIMARY REACTION

The absorption of light by a molecule raises the molecule to a state of higher electronic excitation, such as the 'triplet' or 'free radical' state. Such an exited molecule can lose the excess energy by a radiative process (fluorescence) or by a non-radiative process. It may enter into a chemical reaction with other molecules or the energy may be utilized to break down the structure of the original molecule. In the skin, molecules with ring structures and double bonds are readily activated by light. These include proteins, nucleic acids, porphyrins, carotenoids, and some sterols, e.g. vitamin D.

Epidermal protein is apparently unaffected by high dosages of UV radiation (Ogura et al., 1963). Changes in dermal protein, particularly collagen, may occur as a result of a direct photochemical reaction (Consden and Kirrane, 1967; Bottoms and Shuster, 1963).

It is extremely difficult to differentiate between the primary reaction and secondary changes as result of cell damage. Damage may involve deoxyribonucleic acid (DNA), amino acids (especially those containing a ring structure in their molecule), and bond disruption may occur (e.g. disulphide and sulphydryl groups) (Kusuhara and Knox, 1962). Other vulnerable molecules are cystine, glutathione and especially tryptophan substances and histidine.

Urocanic acid or 4-imidazoleacrylic acid is a deaminated product of histidine. It is an important constituent of human epidermis and is a significant absorbant of ultraviolet radiation (Tabachnick, 1957; Baden and Pathak, 1965; Everett et al., 1961). At erythemogenic energy levels in the short UV range urocanic acid isomerizes from a *trans* to a *cis* form. Baden and Pathak (1967) provided experimental evidence that urocanic acid might act as a photoprotective agent.

EFFECT OF LIGHT ON THE EPIDERMAL CELLS

The effect of light is evident from the activity of pigment cells, damage to keratinocytes and vitamin D synthesis.

EFFECT ON PIGMENT CELLS

The well-known result is, of course, a darkening of the skin. Both white and black skins are capable of darkening without any increase in the number of melanocytes. Szabo (1967) found a marked difference in response of melanocytes to light between various races and also between different regions of the skin of the same individual. A single exposure to UV radiation may cause an increase in melanocytes, but this is mainly in areas of the skin which are habitually covered. After multiple exposures there is an increase of melanocytes which is much greater in habitually covered areas than in habitually exposed areas. They tend to revert to their original number after cessation of repeated exposure. Mitchell's data (1963) support Szabo's contention (1967) that acute and chronic repeated exposure may show a different response, the melanocyte population reverting to its normal region-specific frequency upon chronic exposure.

Increased melanogenesis may, theoretically, be due to several of these factors. Pathak et al. (1965) could find morphological evidence of enhanced tyrosinase activity only.

CHANGES IN CELLS AND CELL ORGANELLES OTHER THAN MELANOCYTES

Cytological, histological and histochemical skin changes are fully described in general dermatological textbooks and some important studies are those of Daniels et al., 1961; Nix et al., 1965a, b; Fukuyama et al., 1967; Baden and Pearlman, 1964; Epstein et al., 1969. At present the lysosome merits most attention. Lysosomes, with their acid hydrolases, are disrupted by UV radiation in vitro (Weissmann and Dingle, 1961) and they are more susceptible to UV radiation damage than are the mitochondria or the plasma membrane (Desai et al., 1964). A relation between UV radiation on lysosomes, peroxidation and free radical formation has been proposed (Tappel et al., 1963). Johnson and Daniels (1969) showed that changes in acid phosphatase activity in epidermis of skin exposed to UV radiation are consistent with the rupture of lysosomes.

VITAMIN D SYNTHESIS

The discovery of the antirachitic properties of UV-irradiated sterol fractions of foods is well known. UV irradiation of ergosterol yielded crystalline vitamin D (Angus et al., 1931), initially named calciferol and now vitamin D_2. Irradiated 7-dehydrocholesterol yields vitamin D_3 and this may be produced by UV irradiation of the skin, as 7-dehydrocholesterol normally occurs in the skin, especially in the Malpighian cells (Reinertson and Wheatly, 1959). As 19 cm^2 of skin contains sufficient precursors to provide the daily requirement of this vitamin (Wheatly and Reinertson, 1958), the limiting factor is apparently the amount of sunshine required for biosynthetic conversion to the active vitamin. The dubious survival value of ethnic pigmentation as protection against environments which may lead either to rickets or to vitamin D toxicity was considered on p. 59. Recently, Hodgkin et al. (1973) confirmed that in Britain a low intake of vitamin D and inadequate solar radiation in Asians frequently leads to rickets and osteomalacia.

Protection against solar radiation

The deleterious effects of solar radiation are in the short term those of sunburn, and in the long term solar damage which may lead to skin cancer.

Man is, in general, fairly well protected against solar radiations by the physical scattering of light in the atmosphere aerosol, the changing position of the sun's incident rays relative to the earth's surface, the seasonal changes and the varying reflective potentialities of its surface (snow, soil and grass). This protection is further extended by man's upright posture, presenting a limited area for irradiation. Cultural development added the protection of clothes roughly suitable to the environment.

The skin protects against solar radiation in several ways: The epidermis is a multi-layered turbid medium which enhances scattering of rays and absorbs the shorter UV radiation effectively to allow minimal penetration to the dermal papillae. It contains protective substances, e.g. urocanic acid, and the unique polymer melanin.

VITAMIN A AND SUN PROTECTION

Cluver (1964) suggested that oral vitamin A before exposure to the sun, protects against sunburn. Cluver and Politzer (1965) demonstrated a fall in serum vitamin A within 1 hour of sun exposure and suggested this was due to uptake of vitamin A by the skin. This could not be confirmed by Anderson (1969). The work of Findlay and Van der Merwe (1965) showed that the total plasma vitamin A was 100 times the amount in the skin, and a fall in plasma levels to 50% would mean that the skin absorbed 50 times its normal content. Anderson's (1969) experiments failed to demonstrate any protective function of vitamin A against sunburn.

PROTECTION BY MELANIN

The protective potential of melanin is great: first as an optical filter with general absorption in the UV and visible spectrum, secondly as a repository for free radicals generated by the action of ultraviolet radiation and thirdly, by the arrangement in nuclear caps, specific protection is afforded to a vulnerable organelle and macromolecule (DNA), where it serves as free radical repositories in close proximity to the nucleus.

IMMEDIATE PIGMENT DARKENING

Immediate pigment darkening (IPD) or the Meirowsky phenomenon occurs in all races (Kooij and Scott, 1954) but is more noticeable in fair-skinned individuals. The action spectrum in this case is the wavelengths longer than those of the spectrum for sunburn. Pathak et al. (1962a, b) found that the assumed spectrum between 300 to about 440 nm was incorrect and that it actually extends from 300 to 700 nm. Longwave UV radiation evoked IPD more effectively than shortwave UV radiation. During IPD the melanocyte count does not change. A redistribution of melanin granules in the Malpighian cells, and changes in optical density take place during IPD but no evidence of a transfer of granules from melanocytes to Malpighian cells could be found (Pathak, 1967).

No convincing evidence for the suggestion that IPD is due to the oxidation of a colourless, reduced pigment already present in the epidermal cells (Miescher and Minder, 1939) was found until recently. The hypothesis was that the darkening was due to a reversible process in which monomer units were transformed from the reduced to the oxidized state. Pathak (1967) presented evidence from electron spin-resonance (esr) studies supporting this suggestion. Stripped of technical detail, the evidence is that human skin exhibits a stable esr signal before radiation only if it is pigmented, and the amplitude of the intrinsic-melanin free radical signal is related to the degree of melanization. Both natural and synthetic melanins prepared by oxidation of dopa have a stable esr signal because a free radical is trapped in the melanin polymer (Blois et al., 1964). UV and visible radiation (wavelength 320–700 nm) enhanced this intrinsic melanin signal in pigmented skin only, and not in white skin. The free radicals generated in the polymer were stable for 24 hours at 77° K but decayed rapidly at room temperature. The stable intrinsic melanin signal present in pigmented skin was not destroyed by warming. These results suggest that IPD is an oxidation reaction which involves the generation of unstable, semiquinone-like free radicals in melanin. The absorption of light (320–700 nm) causes the detachment of protons and the formation of semiquinone-like radicals.

The action spectrum of free radical generation in white skin was found to be limited to wavelengths below 320 nm and this action spectrum thus overlaps with that for sunburn (250-320 nm). Esr signals in white skin indicate that at least 2 different free radicals are generated by irradiation with UV light: one in the epidermal proteins, particularly by short UV radiation; and the other in melanin, induced by a broader action spectrum which includes both short and long wave UV radiation and visible radiation (Pathak, 1967).

MELANOGENESIS (DELAYED PIGMENTATION)

Both the short UV radiation spectrum and the broader action spectrum (including long UV radiation and visible light) can initiate the formation of new melanin. Following IPD (which may be accompanied by slight hyperaemia and mild erythema) fading or disappearance of IPD follows within 1 to 3 hours after irradiation. Pigmentation reappears at the exposed site after an interval of between 48 and 72 hours. The melanin was new melanin in both white and pigmented skin as shown by tyrosinase activity in biopsies. Pathak et al. (1962a, b) demonstrated that tyrosinase activity was present, in all biopsied areas, only after an interval of 72 hours had elapsed since the irradiation. Dendritic arborization of melanocytes was prominent.

While the relative melanogenic efficacy of light differs according to wavelength, those less than 320 nm being the most effective initiators of both erythema and melanogenesis, it should be remembered that over 50% of the radiation reaching the earth's surface is within the range 320 to 700 nm and less than 20% in the shorter range. Furthermore these longer wavelengths penetrate to the dermal papillae.

The melanogenesis which follows on the vasodilatation includes the whole activity of the epidermal melanin unit, i.e. the synthesis of all stages of melanosomes and their transfer to keratinocytes. The biological role suggested by Mason et al. (1960) for melanin has thus been proved by subsequent research results: 'Melanin may act in some organisms as a biological electron-exchange polymer able by means of its capacity for oxidation and reduction and its stable free radical state, to protect a melanin-containing tissue or associated tissues against reducing or oxidizing, which might otherwise set free radicals capable of disrupting metabolism.'

FRECKLING (EPHELIDES)

These occur only on exposed skin and reference to their ethnic incidence has already been made (p. 90). Histologically, freckles are collections of large, functionally-active type-specific melanocytes which respond more rapidly to UV light than do those of people without the trait. These cells apparently transmit 'inherently different capacities for melanogenesis to their descendants in the epidermis' (Breathnach, 1965). The melanocytes, although more active, are significantly fewer than in adjacent skin and the melanosomes produced by the melanocytes in the 2 areas differ from one another in size, shape, internal structure and degrees of melanization.

CARCINOGENESIS IN SOLAR DAMAGED SKIN

There is little doubt that sunlight is an aetiological factor in human skin cancer. Exposed areas are most vulnerable, and fair-skinned whites are most susceptible. In browns (Cape Coloureds and American Negroes) there is a much lower incidence than in whites, and in blacks it is virtually unknown. It is also more prevalent in outdoor workers, and this partly accounts for the much higher incidence in white males as compared to white females. Mitchell (1970) performed a light- and electron-microscopic study of premalignant and malignant lesions arising in solar damaged skin. An excellent description of the morphological evolution to fully developed malignancy and an extensive discussion of possible correlations with experimental carcinogenesis are given in this paper.

Even in the apparently clear-cut difference in the incidence of skin cancer between ethnic groups as seen in regions close to the equator with more sunshine hours, other factors, the relative importance of which it is difficult to assess at present, come into play (Belisario, 1969). Assuming the greater susceptibility to skin cancer in a white individual in the tropics, whether he develops the manifest disease or not will depend on whether he works in an office or on the land, whether he spends his free time sunbathing in the early morning or late afternoon, his clothing and of course his basic complexion. Walker (1959) postulated that the low incidence of rodent ulcers in dark races might be related to poor nutrition in addition to the effects of pigmentation, but being a *poor* white with malnutrition does not, apparently, reduce vulnerability. Differences in reticuloendothelial system (RES) activity may also be involved in the relative immunity of darker races (see p. 196).

SOLAR CIRCULATING FACTOR AND MELANOMAS

While prolonged exposure to the sun is known to be an aetiological factor in the development of carcinoma of the skin in people with poor tanning ability, the melanocyte in the skin is at least similarly exposed to sunlight, and although it is not embryologically a part of the skin, harmful effects of radiation may exert some influence. An association between melanoma and sunlight was suspected for a long time. The incidence of malignant melanoma varies with latitude and Caucasian mortality rate increases towards the Equator (Lancaster, 1956). Patients with malignant melanoma usually have greater exposure to sunlight than the general population (Gellin et al., 1969).

Lee and Merrill (1970) analysed epidemiological data on sunlight and melanoma and suggested that lentigo maligna, melanoma and superficial spreading melanoma on exposed sites are likely to be a direct traumatic effect of sunlight. According to them, nodular melanoma of non-exposed sites was more likely to be the effect of materials released by sunlight-irradiated skin which circulate and cause malignant change in melanocytes remote from the damaged area. This hypothetical material was provisionally called a 'solar circulating factor' and thought to have fairly specific properties.

From observations which they tabulated (Lee and Merrill, 1970), they inferred that this factor (alone or in combination) stimulates malignant change in pigment cells. It is produced by skin in response to sunlight, and circulates in the plasma. A latent period of several decades is not necessary and it has a strong bias towards production of nodular melanoma. Melanocyte chalone is a possible candidate for this action, but in an editorial comment a long list of potential contenders for this role is considered (*Lancet*, 1971).

Lee and Merrill's (1970) suggestion of melanocyte chalone as a 'reasonable candidate' is supported by Bullough and Laurence (1968), who postulate that locally reduced levels of chalone in melanoma or rapid loss via the blood-stream may account for the paradox of the concurrence of a high mitotic rate and mitosis-inhibiting chalone in melanoma extracts. Mohr et al. (1968) reported a high incidence of temporary tumour regressions with pigskin chalone extracts in animals.

A virus may be concerned, which might be activated by sunlight as in the case of lesions of herpes simplex mouse leukaemia (Kaplan, 1967).

The argument of ocular melanoma in Negroes should be considered with some caution; the conjunctiva is frequently pigmented in Negroes (p. 105) and thus would not necessarily constitute a valid model. Other clarifying remarks by Levene (1971) should be taken into account in evaluating these studies.

MELANIN (CUTANEOUS AND EXTRACUTANEOUS) AND DRUGS

Lindquist (1973) reviewed the literature and added his own elegant studies on the significance of melanin affinity of drugs. He concluded that melanin affinity is an important factor in the development of drug-induced lesions in skin, hair, reticuloendothelial system, eye, inner ear, and brain stem. He advised pre-clinical testing of new drugs for melanin affinity. He emphasized that toxicity of drugs with melanin affinity should be carefully investigated in pigmented experimental animals. The significance of this advice with regard to the various ethnic groups of the world is obviously of immediate and prime importance.

REFERENCES

AGGARWAL, J. L. and BEVERIDGE, B. (1971): Liberation of iris pigment in the anterior chamber. *Brit. J. Ophthal.*, *55*, 544.

ANDERSON, F. E. (1969): Studies in the relationship between serum vitamin A and sun exposure. *Aust. J. Derm.*, *10*, 26.

ANGUS, T. C., ASHEW, F. A., BOURELILLON, R. B., BRUCE, H. M., CALLOW, R. K., FISHMANN, C., PHILPOT, J. ST. L. and WEBSTER, T. A. (1931): Crystalline anti-rachitic substance. *Proc. roy. Soc. B*, *108*, 340.

BADEN, H. P. and PATHAK, M. A. (1965): Urocanic acid in keratinizing tissue. *Biochim. biophys. Acta (Amst.)*, *104*, 200.

BADEN, H. P. and PATHAK, M. A. (1967): The metabolism and function of urocanic acid in skin. *J. invest. Derm.*, *48*, 11.

BADEN, H. P. and PEARLMAN, C. (1964): The effect of ultraviolet light on protein and nucleic acid synthesis in the epidermis. *J. invest. Derm.*, *43*, 71.

BELISARIO, J. C. (1969): Epidemiology of the commoner skin cancers, solar kera-toses and keratoacanthomas. The importance of skin pigment and sunshine. In: *Essays on Tropical Dermatology*, p. 91. Editors: R. D. G. Ph. Simons and J. Marshall. Excerpta Medica, Amsterdam.

BLOIS, M. S., ZAHLON, A. B. and MALING, J. E. (1964): Electron spin resonance studies on melanin. *Biophys. J.*, *4*, 471.

BOTTOMS, E. and SHUSTER, S. (1963): Effect of ultraviolet light on skin collagen. *Nature (Lond.)*, *199*, 192.

BREATHNACH, A. S. (1965): Electron microscopy of melanocytes in freckling and in certain hypopigmentary conditions. In: *Recent Progress in Photobiology*. Editor: E. J. Bowen. Blackwell Scientific Publications, Oxford.

BREIT, R. and KLIGMAN, A. M. (1969): Measurement of erythemal and pigmentary responses to ultraviolet radiation of different spectral qualities. In: *The Biologic Effects of Ultraviolet Radiation (with emphasis on the skin)*, p. 267. Editor: F. Urbach. Pergamon Press, Oxford.

BULLOUGH, W. S. and LAURENCE, E. B. (1968): Melanocyte chalone and mitotic control in melanomata. *Nature (Lond.)*, *220*, 137.

CLUVER, E. H. (1964): Sun trauma prevention. *S. Afr. med. J.*, *38*, 801.

CLUVER, E. H. and POLITZER, W. M. (1965): Sunburn and vitamin A deficiency. *S. Afr. J. Sci.*, *61*, 306.

CONSDEN, R. and KIRRANE, J. A. (1967): Action of ultraviolet light on soluble collagens. *Nature (Lond.)*, *215*, 165.

DANIELS JR., F. (1964): Man and radiant energy: Solar radiation. In: *Handbook of Physiology, Sect. IV: Adaptation to the Environment*, p. 969. Editors: D. B. Dill, E. F. Adolph and C. G. Wilber. American Physiological Society, Washington, D.C.

DANIELS JR., F., BROPHY, D. and LOBITZ JR., W. C. (1961): Histochemical responses of human skin following ultraviolet irradiation. *J. invest. Derm.*, *37*, 351.

DAVIS, N. C. (1971): Sunlight and melanomas. *Lancet*, *1*, 803.

DESAI, I. D., SAWANT, P. L. and TAPPEL, A. L. (1964): Peroxidative and radiation damage to isolated lysosomes. *Biochim. biophys. Acta (Amst.)*, *86*, 277.

EDITORIAL (1971): Pupillary mobility and skin colour. *Brit. med. J.*, *2*, 252.

EDITORIAL (1971): Sunlight and melanoma. *Lancet*, *1*, 172.

EMIRU, V. P. (1971): Response to mydriatics in the African. *Brit. J. Ophthal.*, *55*, 538.

EPSTEIN, J. H., FUKUYAMA, K. and DOBSON, R. L. (1969): Ultraviolet light carcinogenesis. In: *Biologic Effects of Ultraviolet Radiation (with emphasis on the skin)*, p. 551. Editor: F. Urbach. Pergamon Press, Oxford.

EVERETT, M. A., ANGLIN JR., J. H. and BEVER, A. T. (1961): Ultraviolet induced biochemical alterations in the skin. I. Urocanic acid. *Arch. Derm.*, *84*, 717.

FINDLAY, G. H. and VAN DER MERWE, R. W. (1965): Epidermal vitamin A and sunburn in man. *Brit. J. Derm.*, *77*, 622.

FUKUYAMA, K., EPSTEIN, W. L. and EPSTEIN, J. H. (1967): Effect of ultraviolet light on RNA and protein synthesis in differentiated epidermal cells. *Nature (Lond.)*, *216*, 1031.

GELLIN, G. A., KOPF, A. W. and GARFINKEL, L. (1969): Malignant melanoma. A controlled study of possibly associated factors. *Arch. Derm.*, *99*, 43.

HODGKIN, P., KAY, G. H., HINE, P. M., LUMB, G. A. and STANSBURY, S. W. (1973): Vitamin D deficiency in Asians at home and in Britain. *Lancet*, *2*, 167.

JOHNSON, B. E. and DANIELS JR., F. (1969): Lysosomes and the reactions of skin to ultraviolet radiation. *J. invest. Derm.*, *53*, 85.

KAPLAN, H. S. (1967): On the natural history of the murine leukaemias: Presidential address. *Cancer Res.*, *27*, 1325.

KOOIJ, R. and SCOTT, F. P. (1954): Primêre of direkte pigmentasie van die huid as gevolg van sonlig in Suid Afrika. *S. Afr. med. J.*, *28*, 433.

KUSUHARA, M. and KNOX, J. M. (1962): Changes in sulfhydryl and disulphide groups in animal skin following a single exposure to ultraviolet light. *J. invest. Derm.*, *39*, 287.

LANCASTER, H. O. (1956): Some geographical aspects of the mortality from melanoma in Europeans. *Med. J. Aust.*, *1*, 1082.

LEE, J. A. H. and MERRILL, J. M. (1970): Sunlight and the aetiology of malignant melanoma: A synthesis. *Med. J. Aust.*, *2*, 846.

LEVENE, A. (1971): Sunlight and melanomas (Letter to the Editor). *Lancet*, *1*, 855.

LINDQUIST, N. G. (1973): Accumulation of drugs on melanin. *Acta radiol. (Stockh.)*, *Suppl. 325.*

MAGNUS, I. A. (1969): Biologic action spectra, introduction and general review. In: *The Biologic Effects of Ultraviolet Radiation (with emphasis on the skin)*, p. 175. Editor: F. Urbach. Pergamon Press, Oxford.

MASON, H. S., INGRAM, D. J. E. and ALLEN, B. (1960): The free radical property of melanins. *Arch. Biochem.*, *86*, 225.

MIESCHER, G. and MINDER, H. (1939): Untersuchungen über die durch langwelliges Ultraviolett hervorgerufene Pigmentdunkelung. *Strahlentherapie*, *66*, 6.

MITCHELL, R. E. (1963): The effect of prolonged solar radiation on melanocytes of the human epidermis. *J. invest. Derm.*, *41*, 199.

MITCHELL, R. E. (1967): Chronic solar dermatosis: A light and electron microscopic study of the dermis. *J. invest. Derm.*, *48*, 203.

MITCHELL, R. E. (1970): Aspects of carcinogenesis in solar damaged skin. *Aust. J. Derm.*, *11*, 14.

MOHR, U., ALTHOFF, J., KINZEL, V., SUSS, R. and VOLM, M. (1968): Melanoma regression induced by 'chalone': A new tumor inhibiting principle acting in vivo. *Nature (Lond.)*, *220*, 138.

Nix Jr., T. E., Nordquist, R. E., Scott, J. R. and Everett, M. A. (1965a): An ultrastructural study of nucleolar enlargement following ultraviolet irradiation of human epidermis. *J. invest. Derm.*, *45*, 114.

Nix Jr., T. E., Nordquist, R. E., Scott, J. R. and Everett, M. A. (1965b): Ultra-structural changes induced by ultraviolet light in human epidermis: Basal and spinal layers. *J. invest. Derm.*, *45*, 52.

Ogura, R., Knox, J. M. and Kusuhara, M. (1963): A polygraphic study on the effects of ultraviolet light on scales epidermis, dermis and serum. *J. invest. Derm.*, *40*, 37.

Pathak, M. A. (1965): Action spectra and biophysical changes in skin. In: *Recent Progress in Photobiology*, p. 381. Editor: E. J. Bowen. Blackwell Scientific Publications, Oxford.

Pathak, M. A. (1967): Photobiology of melanogenesis: Biophysical aspects. In: *Advances in Biology of Skin, Vol. VIII: The Pigmentary System*, p. 397. Editors: W. Montagna and F. Hu. Pergamon Press, Oxford.

Pathak, M. A., Riley, F. C. and Fitzpatrick, T. B. (1962a): Melanogenesis in human skin following exposure to longwave ultraviolet and visible light. *J. invest. Derm.*, *39*, 435.

Pathak, M. A., Riley, F. C., Fitzpatrick, T. B. and Curwen, W. L. (1962b): Melanin formation in human skin induced by longwave ultraviolet and visible light. *Nature (Lond.)*, *193*, 148.

Pathak, M. A., Sinesi, S. J. and Szabo, G. (1965): The effect of a single dose of ultraviolet radiation on epidermal melanocytes. *J. invest. Derm.*, *45*, 520.

Reinertson, R. P. and Wheatley, V. R. (1959): Studies on the chemical composition of human epidermal lipids. *J. invest. Derm.*, *32*, 49.

Sagan, C. (1961): On the origin and planetary distribution of life. *Radiat. Res.*, *15*, 174.

Somerset, E. J. (1962): *Ophthalmology in the Tropics*, p. 3. Ballière, Tyndall and Cox, London.

Szabo, G. (1967): Photobiology of melanogenesis: Cytological aspects with special reference to differences in racial coloration. In: *Advances in Biology of Skin, Vol. VIII: The Pigmentary System*, p. 379. Editors: W. Montagna and F. Hu. Pergamon Press, Oxford.

Tabachnick, J. (1957): Urocanic acid, the major acid soluble, ultraviolet-absorbing compound in guinea pig epidermis. *Arch. Biochem.*, *70*, 295.

Tappel, A. L., Sawant, P. L. and Shibko, S. (1963): Lysosomes: distribution in animals, hydrolytic capacity and other properties. In: *Lysosomes*, p. 78. Editors: A. V. S. de Reuck and M. Cameron. J. and A. Churchill Ltd., London.

Walker, J. (1959): Basal-cell carcinoma: Speculations on possible factors influencing its low incidence among the non-European races in South Africa. *S. Afr. med. J.*, *33*, 394.

Weissmann, G. and Dingle, J. T. (1961): Release of lysosomal protease by UV irradiation and inhibition by hydrocortisone. *Exp. Cell Res.*, *25*, 207.

Wheatley, V. R. and Reinertson, R. P. (1958): The presence of vitamin D precursors in human epidermis. *J. invest. Derm.*, *31*, 51.

Chapter XVIII

Ethnic pigmentation: Aspects of some congenital and genetic anomalies of pigmentation

Of the various physiological processes which control human pigmentation, least is known of genetic control. What we know definitely is that ethnic pigmentation is genetically determined. This involves the genetic code, transmitted by chromosomes to all the cells which ultimately result from the union of sperm and ovum. It is natural to concentrate on the enzymatic control of melanin formation in melanocytes (i.e. the transcription and translation of the code), but in the case of pigmentation the transmission of the code is equally important, for the melano*blast* originates in the neural crest together with other primitive ganglion cells, and, after it has differentiated into a melanocyte, migrates to various definitive sites, of which skin, eye, hairbulbs and meninges are the best known and studied.

No clinician can fail to be intrigued by the pigmentary patterns which occur in some well-known syndromes (even though they are rare and only occasionally encountered) and also by the markedly consistent occurrence of some pigment anomalies (e.g. freckling and naevi) in certain syndromes (e.g. Down's syndrome and lentiginosa-profusa syndrome with its cardiac anomalies). The question arising in each individual case is: how is *ethnic pigmentation* associated with these anomalies? There is an ethnic difference in the incidence of pigmented naevi, a prominent feature of Down's syndrome. Frequency of anomalies of the neural tube differs in various ethnic groups, as does Waardenburg's syndrome, a defect perhaps related to anomalous development in the neural crest (Deol, 1970).

Because little is known of either the genetics of ethnic pigmentation in man or the biological significance of melanin, I arranged some reported observations on genetic and congenital conditions associated with pigment anomalies and what I could ascertain about the ethnic incidence of such anomalies. This is certainly an area where data on ethnic incidence are very incomplete.

A genetically determined predisposition to a particular malformation or disease may depend on (1) a chromosome abnormality, (2) a mutant gene of large effect, or (3) a deviation from the normal, dependent on numerous genes, individually of small effect on the particular character.

I have followed the above arrangement to classify the congenital and hereditary pigment anomalies associated with other defects which are of more general
medical interest.

CHROMOSOME ABNORMALITIES AND PIGMENTARY EFFECTS

Monosomy

In the Turner syndrome or ovarian agenesis syndrome an X-chromosome is
lacking. The pigmentary anomaly, an extraordinarily high number of pigmented
naevi, is much less conspicuous than the other features of the syndrome but was
mentioned by Turner (1938). Ethnic differences in the incidence of pigmented
naevi are, thus, of little clinical importance. Recently, Cheah and Lim (1971)
reported ocular melanosis (melanosis bulbi) in a Chinese boy with a male Turner
syndrome. Apparently, this was not reported before. Other pigmentary associations of the syndrome include vitiligo and café-au-lait spot (Polani, 1961).

Trisomy 21

Down's syndrome or mongolism has the sacral or mongolian spots as pigmentary
anomaly.
1. The high incidence of mongolian spots in dark ethnic groups may decrease
the clinical importance of this feature in the early suspicion of Down's syndrome.
2. As in most trisomies, the frequency is influenced by maternal age. The likeli-
hood of a mother of 25 having an affected baby is 1/2000 against 1/100 if she
is over 40 years. Especially in tribal Bantu where polygamy is still a usual
custom, most children are born to fairly young mothers. This may in part account
for Gelfand's (1957, p. 535) observation that Down's syndrome is extremely
rare in the Bantu.

Chromosome breaks

Two autosomal recessive conditions show multiple chromosome breaks and
endoreduplication. Most constantly associated with *Fanconi's panmyelopathy*
is the finding of pigmentary anomalies (80% of cases), with skeletal, renal and
hepatic anomalies and, of course, aplastic anaemia. In *Bloom's syndrome*
telangiectasia and a sun-sensitive skin occurs in association with dwarfism. In
the case of Fanconi's anaemia which we studied (Wassermann et al., 1969) the
pigmentary anomalies first drew our attention to the existence of the syndrome.
The patient was one of the earliest cases treated by androgens and steroids
(McDonald and Goldschmidt, 1952) and she was at the time of our study asymptomatic for several years. A relapse was brought on by an upper respiratory-tract
infection. The interest lies in the frequent association of pigmentary defects with

panmyelopathy and an increased liability to leukaemia. The genetic defect determines a biochemical abnormality which either renders the chromosomes liable to break or which impairs their normal repair.

Chromosome mapping

Ocular albinism, inherited as an X-linked recessive characteristic, allowed the localization of the gene for ocular albinism at a measurable distance from the gene for colour-blindness and G-6-PD deficiency in the red blood cells. Colour-blindness (Squires, 1942) and G-6-PD deficiency has a high incidence in Bantu, but I could find no statistics on the incidence of ocular albinism in Bantu.

PIGMENTATION AND MUTANT GENES OF LARGE EFFECT

Central nervous system

Accepting the view that the melanocyte is a masked primitive neuron which migrates from the neural crest to its definitive position in the skin, it would be expected that with defective development of, or defective migration from, this area, pigmentary anomalies may be associated with anomalies related to neural tube malformations in any race (Fig. 31).

Neural tube malformations have a multifactorial origin. They are dependent on a genetic component as well as an environmental component. To clarify the various interrelated factors, the effect of migration and mixed marriages on neural tube malformations were explored (Carter, 1970). Migration will not alter gene frequencies in the migrating populations except by selection over a century or more. Climatic factors would change immediately, while dietary habits would change more slowly. Studies by Leck (1969) confirmed the low incidence of anencephalus and spina bifida among West Indian immigrants. This was similar to the low incidence observed in West and Central African Negroes, whether in their African area of origin, in the United States, or in Birmingham (England) via the West Indies. The lower socioeconomic classes normally have a high incidence of neural tube malformation. The immigrants retained their low incidence even when they were among the lower socioeconomic groups of the country to which they migrated, stressing the importance of genetic factors in this regard.

The frequency of neural tube malformations (in ascending order) among babies born at Birmingham (England) as related to their mother's birthplaces were found to be: West Indies, England, India and Pakistan, and Ireland. The world's highest frequency in Ireland is well established, and probably a high incidence is also present among the Sikhs in the Punjab (Carter, 1970).

The few children born to Irish wives of West Indian men have had the high Irish incidence of neural tube malformations. There are still too few data to show whether West Indian mothers married to Irishmen would retain their low incidence (Carter, 1970).

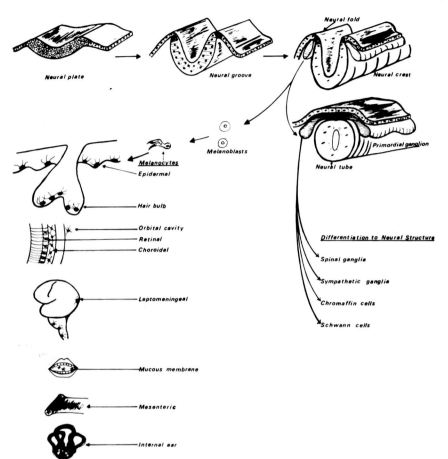

Fig. 31. Common origin of melanocytes and primordial neural ganglia from the neural crest. A mutant gene of large effect may influence both pigmentation and neural structures.

DEAFNESS

The apparent rarity of the Waardenburg syndrome in dark races (discussed on p. 85 may perhaps be related to ethnic differences in neural tube malformation.

Abnormalities of pigmentation and of the inner ear occur together in hereditary syndromes in several species of mammals including man (Deol, 1970), but his statement that the pigmentary abnormalities are always of the white spotting kind is questionable, as congenital deafness and multiple lentigines have been reported (Capute et al., 1969). In all cases the abnormalities of the inner ear appear to be confined to the cochlea and the saccule. There is severe degeneration of the organ of Corti, stria vascularis, spiral ganglion and the macula of the saccule.

Although the association of congenital deafness and hypopigmentation was known since the early 19th century, and reported in various mammals, Deol

(1970) also searched for, and found, the association in mice. Since Waardenburg's syndrome was described in 1951, he conducted a systematic investigation. The inner ear is normally heavily pigmented in a precise pattern. He ruled out the possibility that the pigment performs an essential function in the inner ear on the evidence that albino mice which have melanocytes but no pigment do not show the inner ear abnormality. The possibility that the melanocyte (apart from its pigment formation) may have an essential function is thought unlikely (Deol, 1970). The synthesis of experimental and clinical data by Deol (1970) is convincing: genes causing this syndrome primarily affect the neural crest, wholly or partially before its differentiation into the melanoblasts and the ganglionic primordia. The acoustic ganglion originates (at least partly) in the neural crest. The pigmentary defect, then, may be due to anomalous melanoblasts, and the inner ear defect the direct and indirect consequence of the anomaly of the acoustic ganglion (Deol, 1970). This theory is very similar to the one proposed by Fisch in 1959 (Soussi, 1965).

Congenital deafness and pigmentary changes have been reported in man as shown in Table VII.

Table VII

Congenital deafness and pigmentary changes in man

Syndrome	Author
1. Waardenburg's syndrome	Waardenburg (1951)
2. Sex-linked albinism with congenital deafness	Ziprkowski et al. (1962)
3. Dominant albinism and congenital deafness	Tietz (1963)
4. Recessive piebaldness and neural deafness	Woolf et al. (1965)
5. Conductive deafness, osseous defects, mitral insufficiency, short stature and heavy freckling	Forney et al. (1966)
6. Congenital neural deafness and multiple lentigines	Capute et al. (1969)

It would appear that Deol's hypothesis might explain 1 and 4 in Table VII and perhaps 6 too. There is some evidence that an ethnic difference in prevalence exists in Waardenburg's syndrome (p. 85). It is apparently rare in those races known to have a low incidence of other neural tube malformations. Trowell (1960) lists congenital deafness as a condition not yet reported in Bantu. It would be of interest to know whether or not Waardenburg's syndrome has a high incidence in the Irish (who have the highest incidence of neural tube malformation).

Ethnic eye colour and the Waardenburg syndrome

As stated elsewhere (p. 105), dark irides are practically universal among Bantu and Negroes. Waardenburg thought that all cases of blue eyes in Negroes of pure descent were *formes frustes* of the Waardenburg syndrome. Soussi (1965) thoroughly studied the genetics of blue-eyed Bantu and concluded that 'normal' blue eyes can exist as a simple genetical variation in Negroid individuals. This is presumably owing to a mutation at a different locus from the gene for the Waardenburg syndrome.

More data on the ethnic incidence of Waardenburg's syndrome are needed. Quite recently, Dr. Elizabeth Rose (personal communication, 1972) drew my attention to the apparently high incidence of Waardenburg's syndrome in Transkei Bantu. This requires confirmation, and especially in other parts of South Africa, as the area in which the high incidence occurred is an area with a remarkably high incidence of oesophageal carcinoma. It may be a genetically selected group of Bantu, not necessarily representative of this ethnic group in general.

Recently, Amini-Elihou (1970) described a case of Waardenburg's syndrome in a Swiss family where the 6 children, including dizygotic twins, and the mother were affected to varying degrees. There was palmo-plantar hyperkeratosis in 4 children, and severe mental retardation in both twins. Other collaterals of the family included several cases of oligophrenia, and 1 case of congenital deafness, 1 with cardiac malformation and a person with piebaldism. She gives a very complete review of the syndrome, and concludes that it is inherited as an autosomal dominant with variable penetrance and expression.

The defect probably occurs between the 8th and 10th week of pregnancy, when the face, first branchial arch and neural crest develop (Amini-Elihou, 1970).

NEUROFIBROMATOSIS AND ALBRIGHT'S SYNDROME

Café-au-lait hypermelanotic macules occur in neurofibromatoses and in Albright's syndrome. They are usually few in number and often unilateral over the bone lesions, while in neurofibromatosis they tend to be generalized and irregular. Axillary freckle-like pigmentation is characteristic of neurofibromatosis, and usually occurs in greater numbers than in Albright's syndrome. Although the borders are more often smooth in contrast to the 'coast of Maine' appearance in Albright's syndrome, Benedict et al. (1968) did not consider that clinical features of an isolated café-au-lait spot in neurofibromatosis could be distinguished from those of the pigmented macules in Albright's syndrome. Microscopically, however, in split-skin preparations giant pigment granules in the keratinocytes and/or melanocytes were present in neurofibromatosis but not in Albright's syndrome. In a case of Albright's syndrome in a Bantu woman, and several cases of neurofibromatosis in Cape Coloureds, the author confirmed this microscopic finding (unpublished observations).

In black children 2 café-au-lait spots occurred in 5% against 2% of white children. The diagnostic significance of multiple café-au-lait spots should therefore be considered in relation to the ethnic group of the patient (see p. 91).

RARE SYNDROMES WITH NO KNOWN ETHNIC PREDILECTION

Incontinentia pigmenti

Approximately 60% of patients with this hereditary, often congenital, condition demonstrate ectodermal defects, e.g. dental, ocular and central nervous system anomalies as well as changes in the hair and nails (Pfeiffer, 1959). There is a marked predilection for females.

Moynahan's syndrome

Moynahan (1962) described a syndrome which he believed to be a disorder of the neural crest. The patients had dwarfism, multiple symmetrical lentigines, genital hypoplasia and congenital mitral stenosis with psychic infantilism and mental deficiency.

Giant pigmented naevus with involvement of the meninges and malignant melanoma

This is a complex clinical entity with cutaneous pigmented naevi, frequently in a dermatomal distribution, neurofibromatosis and neural tube defects (e.g. spina bifida), and malignant melanoma which may develop early in life or even be present at birth. Death is usually due to communicating hydrocephalus (Reed et al., 1967).

Hypopigmentation

Apart from its association with congenital deafness, tuberous sclerosis with its clinical triad of adenoma sebaceum, epilepsy and mental retardation, is accompanied by congenital white (hypomelanotic) macules in 85% of patients; their high incidence is of diagnostic significance. It is a rare disease with apparently no ethnic predilection. The hypopigmented macules would, of course, be more easily visible in a dark skin than in those patients with a light complexion.

Mental deficiency

Apart from the specific syndromes, it is noteworthy that in several congenital conditions with pigmentary anomalies, mental deficiency occurs, as shown in Table VIII.

Table VIII

Congenital pigmentary anomalies associated with mental deficiency

Anomaly	Reference
Pulmonary stenosis, café-au-lait spots	Watson (1967)
Symmetrical moles and genital hypoplasia	Moynahan (1962)
Unilateral lentigines	Cappon (1948)
Profuse lentiginosis, progressive cardiomyopathy, mental retardation (and other anomalies)	Moynahan and Polani (1968)

The association of central nervous system anomalies with pigmentation anomalies appears to be rather common, probably due to the common origin of neural crest, primitive integument and central nervous system; a vulnerable region where a mutant gene of large effect may cause such a combinaton of anomalies. It is especially the rarity of neural tube defects and the Waardenburg syndrome in dark races which must be stressed and further investigated as to its ethnic incidence.

NUMEROUS GENES OF INDIVIDUALLY
SMALL EFFECT ON THE PARTICULAR CHARACTER

The rather arbitrary decision to group the following systems under this heading is because of the difficulty, in terms of our present concept of pigmentation, in finding a reasonable basis to relate the various findings to a single factor, although in both cases a single gene effect has been proposed.

The syndromes are merely enumerated as they are rare and a particular ethnic distribution is not yet evident.

Cardiovascular system

Differences in the ethnic incidence of various cardiac diseases were reviewed by Phillips and Burch (1960), and more recently in respect to South African races by the late Velva Schrire (1971).

Of the associated hereditary pigmentary and cardiac anomalies the most interesting is the lentiginosis profusa syndrome, variously designated as cardio-cutaneous syndrome, multiple lentigines syndrome and 'leopard syndrome' (Pickering et al., 1971; Lynch, 1970) where *leopard* may be used as a muemonic for features of the syndrome (Gorlin et al., 1969): *l*entigines, *e*lectrocardiographic changes, *o*cular hypertelorism, *p*ulmonary stenosis, *a*bnormalities of genitalia (hypoplasia), *r*etardation of growth and *d*eafness. Most cases reported were in whites, but Smith et al. (1970) described a Negro family with the syndrome. Somerville and Bonham-Carter (1972) described and reviewed the cardiological findings. *Interestingly, Selmanowitz et al. (1971) proposed a theory that mutation in the stem cell pool in the neural crest of embryonic life may account for the prominent features of the syndrome.*

Gastrointestinal tract

The Peutz-Jeghers syndrome of mucocutaneous lentigines and intestinal polyposis needs no further description. Sommerhaug and Mason (1970) found ureteral polyposis associated with the syndrome in a white man. André et al. (1966) found oesophageal polyposis. From Dormandy's review (1957), which discusses polyps in the bladder, renal pelvis, bronchus and nasal passages, it seems likely that a generalized tendency toward polyp formation exists in the Peutz-Jeghers syndrome. Histologically, the polyps are hamartomas. The dominant gene seems to determine both the pigmentation pattern and the polyp formation. Apparently no particular differences occur in its ethnic incidence.

The skin pigmentation appears before the age of 10, and gradually fades in the 2nd and 3rd decades and may be lost by the age of 40. In the mouth it remains permanently.

Recently, Kieselstein et al. (1969) reported a family where the Peutz-Jeghers syndrome was associated with polycystic kidney disease (a condition often associated with cysts of liver, pancreas, lungs or spleen and other genitourinary and cardiac defects, as well as with aneurysms of the cerebral vessels). In 3 males of the family an abnormally long Y-chromosome was found, a chromosome change which may occur in mongolism, hypogonadism and other anomalies.

Polyposis of the gastrointestinal tract is important clinically for the premalignant nature of familial polyposis of the colon. There are, however, several associated features of familial polyposis of the colon: (*a*) osteomata of mandible, skull or long bones, (*b*) multiple epidermoid cysts, lipomas and fibromas (Gardner's syndrome), (*c*) desmoid tumours, (*d*) abnormal proliferation of fibrous tissue, e.g. keloids and peritoneal adhesions, (*e*) polyposis of the small intestine and (*f*) gastric polyposis.

The pigmentation of colonic polyposis is said to occur on the torso and limbs, but not on the face, buccal mucosa or lips, as in the case of Peutz-Jeghers syndrome. Recently, however, I saw a white woman with Peutz-Jeghers type of pigmentation, no small intestinal or colonic polyps, but a family history of colonic polyposis. She is being followed up.

Familial polyposis and the rareness of adenomata of the colon were considered as 'striking' by McQuaide and Stewart (1972) who described the first extensive study among a Bantu family. They refer to 2 cases reported in Bantu and to a comment that familial polyposis 'has been seen' in Uganda. This intriguing association with other anomalies, with pigmentation and with a differential ethnic incidence requires further study.

REFERENCES

AMINI-ELIHOU, S. (1970): Une famille suisse atteinte du syndrome de Klein-Waardenburg associé à une hyperkératose palmo-plantaire et à une oligophrénie grave. *J. Génét. Hum.*, *18*, 307.

ANDRÉ, R., DUHAMEL, G. and BRUAIRE, M. (1966): Syndrome de Peutz-Jeghers avec polypose oesophagienne. *Bull. Soc. méd. Hôp. Paris*, *117*, 505.

BENEDICT, PH., SZABO, G., FITZPATRICK, T. B. and SINESI, S. J. (1968): Melanotic macules in Albright's syndrome and in neurofibromatosis. *J. Amer. med. Ass.*, *205*, 618.

CAPPON, D. (1948): Case of unilateral lentigines with mental deficiency. *Brit. J. Derm.*, *60*, 371.

CAPUTE, A. J., RIMOIN, D. L., KONIGSMARK, B. W., ESTERLY, N. B. and RICHARDSON, F. (1969): Congenital deafness and multiple lentigines. *Arch. Derm.*, *100*, 207.

CARTER, C. (1970): Ethnic origin and neural tube malformations. *Develop. Med. Child Neurol.*, *12*, 372.

CHEAH, J. S. and LIM, K. H. (1971): Melanosis bulbi in a Chinese boy with Turner's syndrome. *Aust. N.Z. J. Med.*, *1*, 83.

DEOL, M. S. (1970): The relationship between abnormalities of pigmentation and of the inner ear. *Proc. roy. Soc. A, 175*, 201.

DORMANDY, T. L. (1957): Gastrointestinal polyposis with mucocutaneous pigmentation. *New Engl. J. Med.*, *256*, 1093.

FORNEY, W. R., ROBINSON, S. J. and PASCOE, D. J. (1966): Congenital heart disease, deafness and skeletal malformations: A new syndrome? *J. Pediat.*, *68*, 14.

GELFAND, M. (1957): *The Sick African*, 3rd ed. Juta and Co., Cape Town.

GORLIN, R. J., ANDERSON, R. C. and BLAW, M. (1969): Multiple lentigines syndrome. *Amer. J. Dis. Childh.*, *117*, 652.

KIESELSTEIN, M., HERMAN, M. D., WAHRMAN, J., VOSS, R., GITELSON, S., FEUCHT-WANGER, M. and KADAR, S. (1969): Mucocutaneous pigmentation and intestinal polyposis (Peutz-Jeghers syndrome) in a family of Iraqi Jews with polycystic kidney disease. *Israel J. med. Sci.*, *5*, 81.

LECK, I. (1969): Ethnic differences in the incidence of malformations following migration. *Brit. J. prev. soc. Med.*, *23*, 166.

LYNCH, P. J. (1970): Leopard syndrome. *Arch. Derm.*, *101*, 119.

McDONALD, R. and GOLDSCHMIDT, B. (1952): Pancytopenia with congenital defects (Fanconi's anaemia). *Arch. Dis. Childh.*, *35*, 367.

McQUAIDE, J. R. and STEWART, A. W. (1972): Familial polyposis of the colon in the Bantu. *S. Afr. med. J.*, *46*, 1241.

MOYNAHAN, E. J. (1962): Multiple symmetrical moles, with psychic and somatic infantilism and genital hypoplasia. *Proc. roy. Soc. Med.*, *55*, 959.

MOYNAHAN, E. J. and POLANI, P. (1968): Progressive profuse lentiginosis, progressive cardiomyopathy, short stature with delayed puberty, mental retardation or psychic infantilism, and other developmental anomalies: a new familial syndrome. In: *Acta, XIII Congressus Internationalis Dermatologiae, 1967, München, Vol. II*, p. 1543. Editors: W. Jadassohn and C. G. Schirren. Springer-Verlag, Berlin.

PFEIFFER, R. A. (1959): Das Syndrom der Incontinentia pigmenti (Bloch-Siemens). *Münch. med. Wschr.*, *101*, 2312.

PHILLIPS, J. H. and BURCH, G. E. (1960): A review of cardiovascular diseases in the white and Negro races. *Medicine (Baltimore)*, *39*, 241.

PICKERING, D., LASKI, B., MACMILLAN, D. C. and ROSE, V. (1971): 'Little Leopard' syndrome. *Arch. Dis. Childh.*, *46*, 85.

POLANI, P. E. (1961): Turner's syndrome and allied conditions. *Brit. med. Bull.*, *17*, 200.

REED, W. B., STONE, V. M., BODER, E. and ZIPRKOWSKI, L. (1967): Pigmentary disorders in association with congenital deafness. *Arch. Derm.*, *95*, 176.

SCHRIRE, V. (1971): Heart disease in Southern Africa with special reference to ischaemic heart disease. *S. Afr. med. J.*, *45*, 634.

SELMANOWITZ, V. J., ORENTREICH, N. and FELSENSTEIN, J. M. (1971): Lentiginosa profusa syndrome (multiple lentigines syndrome). *Arch. Derm.*, *104*, 393.

SMITH, R. F., PUHCICCHIO, L. U. and HOLMES, A. V. (1970): Generalized lentigo: Electrocardiographic abnormalities, conduction disorders and arrhythmias in three cases. *Amer. J. Cardiol.*, *25*, 501.

SOMERVILLE, J. and BONHAM-CARTER, R. E. (1972): The heart in lentiginosis. *Brit. Heart J.*, *34*, 58.

SOMMERHAUG, R. G. and MASON, T. (1970): Peutz-Jeghers syndrome and ureteral polyposis. *J. Amer. med. Ass.*, *211*, 120.

Soussi, J. (1965): The incidence of blue eyes in South African Negroes with special reference to the Waardenburg syndrome. *S. Afr. J. med. Sci.*, *61*, 243.

Squires, B. T. (1942): Colour vision and colour discrimination amongst Bechuana. *Proc. roy. Soc. S. Afr.*, *29*, 29.

Tietz, W. (1963): A syndrome of deaf mutism associated with albinism showing dominant autosomal inheritance. *Amer. J. hum. Genet.*, *15*, 259.

Trowell, H. C. (1960): *Non-infective Disease in Africa.* Arnold, London.

Turner, H. H. (1938): A syndrome of infantilism, congenital webbed neck and cubitus valgus. *Endocrinology*, *23*, 566.

Waardenburg, P. J. (1951): A new syndrome combining developmental anomalies of the eyelids, eyebrows, and nose root with pigmentary defects of the iris and head hair with congenital deafness. *Amer. J. hum. Genet.*, *3*, 195.

Wassermann, H. P., Fry, R. and Cohn, J. H. (1969): Fanconi's anaemia: Cytogenetic studies in a family. *S. Afr. med. J.*, *42*, 1162.

Watson, G. H. (1967): Pulmonary stenosis, café-au-lait spots and dull intelligence. *Arch. Dis. Childh.*, *42*, 303.

Woolf, C. M., Dolowitz, D. A. and Aldous, H. E. (1965): Congenital deafness associated with piebaldness. *Arch. Otolaryng.*, *82*, 244.

Ziprkowski, L., Krakowski, A., Adam, A., Costeff, H. and Sade, J. (1962): Partial albinism and deafmutism. *Arch. Derm.*, *86*, 530.

Chapter XIX

Melanin and the biochemistry of neuropsychiatric phenomena in ethnic groups

THE PIGMENTATION-DYSKINESIA-PSYCHOSIS TRIAD

A relationship of pigmentation to schizophrenia and extrapyramidal disease has been considered for several decades. Only during the past decade, however, was melanin recognized as a stable free radical, and interest in the triad was renewed when it became obvious that compounds with electron-transfer properties (phenothiazines, copper and manganese) bear a relationship to dyskinetic symptoms in man. As a side-effect, pigmentation may follow on large dosage, long-term phenothiazine therapy. Phenothiazines may also give rise to dyskinesia. L-Dopa, a precursor of melanin, has emerged as the drug of choice in the treatment of parkinsonism, but may be complicated by psychiatric manifestations (Van Wieringen, 1972). During our early studies on the circulation of melanin, I had the impression that parkinsonism was rare in Bantu and schizophrenia perhaps more frequent. It was at that stage that the first reports on phenothiazine melanosis were made, and Cotzias et al. (1964) and Cotzias (1966) first reported on manganese, melanins and the extrapyramidal system. Proctor (1971) emphasized the dyskinesias associated with alcaptonuria (striatal-nigral ochronosis), L-dopa therapy and the Lesch-Nyhan syndrome. In all cases there are chronic elevations in the levels of substances with strong electron-donor properties, schizophrenia-like psychosis and hyperpigmentation (except in homocystinuria which has hypopigmentation). Other conditions related to this clinical triad are manganese poisoning, phenothiazine therapy, hepatolenticular degeneration (Wilson's disease), haemochromatosis and chronic iodism (Proctor, 1971).

As schizophrenia and parkinsonism are the 2 most common conditions among these diseases, the one responding to an electron donor and the other to a melanin precursor, with therapeutic side-effects in either case resembling the symptoms of the other condition, these 2 conditions will be considered in relation to ethnic pigmentation.

PROBLEMS IN ASSESSING
ETHNIC INCIDENCE OF SCHIZOPHRENIA

Schizophrenia and social class

Schizophrenia is heavily concentrated in the lowest social classes. This well-established finding may be interpreted in 2 ways: either social disadvantages increase the incidence of schizophrenia, or the nature of the disease determines the class position of the schizophrenic (Dunham et al., 1966; Van den Haag, 1966; Rinehart, 1966).

Schizophrenia and ethnicity

Piedmont's (1966) study on ethnic factors was based on the assumption that there are several levels of causality or influence involved in schizophrenia, and that the patient's interpersonal functioning is affected regardless of the level of the primary aetiological agent. Rationally, the cause of schizophrenia could be sought in the individual's interpersonal relations, and the development of schizophrenia is analogous to the development of normal personalities.

His study concerns normal Polish and German populations and 30 schizophrenics from each ethnic group, tested in 9 parameters of personality, evaluated by chi-square tests. When classified by social and economic status rather than ethnicity, differences were not statistically significant but it was so for ethnic classification. Thus, he concluded that ethnicity, and not social or economic status, accounted for the observed differences in the distribution of the patients (Piedmont, 1966).

Diagnosis of schizophrenia

In view of the shortage of psychiatrists in many cultures and countries, Lin's (1953) remark that 'accurate comparative data on mental disorders in different cultures are woefully inadequate' is pertinent to the problem. The remark by Cooper (1934) was quoted as relevant to the situation in 1953: 'The information needed can be obtained only by personal field study, by anthropologists who have had psychiatric training, or preferably by psychiatrists who have had anthropological training. Our chief desiderata are: exact statistics of incidence, detailed descriptions of types of mental disease, and thorough studies of individual cases to determine aetiology and mechanisms.' These considerations certainly apply to comparison of statistics of one geographical area to another.

When evaluating differences in ethnic incidence as reported in the literature, differing diagnostic criteria in different cultural settings (e.g. the U.S.A. versus England and Wales) further complicate the assessment (Kramer, 1963). Katz et al. (1969*b*) found that the ethnic background of the psychiatrist was very likely to influence the type of symptomatology or emotional state that he would perceive in a certain kind of patient.

Ethnic manifestations in symptomatology

The symptomatic manifestations of schizophrenic syndromes vary in different ethnic groups (Schooler and Candill, 1964). The study by Katz et al. (1969*a*) is a model for the methodological care they brought to bear on this problem. Ethnic groups in Hawaii were studied and the results statistically evaluated. Whites were significantly higher in 'hostile belligerence, anxious intropunitiveness and excitement' while Japanese rated significantly higher in 'retardation, apathy and disorientation'.

The American Negro and the Black African

Very important in this field is the confusion of 'American Negro' with 'Black African'. The Cape Coloured, with whom the American Negro should be compared, shows a far less defined difference in incidence from that of whites than is the case with Bantu and Negroes in Africa.

REPORTED ETHNIC INCIDENCES COMPARED

For reasons stated above, it is best to separate the American studies on American Negroes and whites from studies on the ethnic incidence in Africa. Differences in diagnostic criteria in different cultural settings are thus minimized. The psychiatrist reporting on the incidence should be responsible for diagnosis of patients from both ethnic groups.

U.S.A.

Schizophrenia occurred more commonly among American Negroes than among whites in the State of North Carolina as judged by admission rates (Vitols, 1961). The literature before 1961, as reviewed by him, agreed with his findings of a higher incidence of schizophrenia in American Negroes compared to whites (Wagner, 1938; Malzberg, 1935, 1953, 1959; Ripley and Wolf, 1947; Faris and Dunham, 1939; Carothers, 1948; Frumkin, 1954). Faris and Dunham (1939) suggested that people, regardless of race, tend to show a higher incidence of schizophrenia when living in an area populated predominantly by another race. If this was true, the incidence of schizophrenia in South African whites should be the reverse of that in the U.S.A., as the 1 : 3 ratio of blacks to whites is 3 : 1 in South Africa. (Such, however, was not the case on statistical investigation – see below.)

The criticism levelled at these studies is mainly theoretical rediscussion of the reported results rather than the presentation of new data. Thus Fischer (1969) objects to the survey designs which compared the 'admission to treatment' incidence rather than a 'true prevalence' incidence. He was also concerned that the 'myth of more mental illness among Negroes than whites' may be joined to similar myths such as the 'myth of inferior Negro intelligence' and that this may be used by 'racists as rationale for segregatory practices.' Both Fischer (1969) and Pasamanick (1963) correctly emphasize the importance of sociological factors in the aetiology of schizophrenia. The criticism should be taken into account in subsequent studies, but it does not convince me that the available data can be completely disregarded. It would, at most, suggest that the data are not conclusive as far as the American Negroes, compared to the American whites, are concerned. (This would agree with the situation in Cape Coloureds as compared to white South Africans.)

Africa

Although Laubscher (1937) first suggested an ethnic difference, and Moffson (1954) found that the percentage of first admissions to the Weskoppies Hospital, Pretoria, over a 3-year period varied between 43 and 50.5% in Bantu as compared to between 19.5 and 23% for whites, it is only recently that several studies on the black races in Africa were reported. Toker (1966) discussed the whole spectrum of mental illness as observed in white and Bantu populations in the Republic of South Africa. Like Moffson (1954), he found that schizophrenia was the most common mental disorder amongst the Bantu in state mental hospitals, but only the second most common in the white hospital population. The 4 major types (simple, hebephrenic, catatonic and paranoid) occurred in both racial sections. Poverty might be an important sociological factor in this difference. Walton (1962) found schizophrenia a very common condition in Bantu, but concluded that schizophrenia in the case of Bantu often takes a more benign course than in the case of whites. These experiences are in agreement with the observations of Forster (1962) that schizophrenia is the most frequent psychosis in Ghana, and that of Collomb (1959) that this is also the case in French West Africa. Toker (1966), Walton (1962) and Forster (1962) found depression extremely rare in Bantu but common in whites, although this was not found so elsewhere in Africa.

In Bantu acute schizophrenia, which recovers within 4 to 7 days, was often found to be the result of marihuana (dagga) smoking. In contrast to whites, this drug was smoked by many Bantu at the time of these studies and it was used by several African tribes in religious rites. The use of marihuana is, of course, at present increasing among the youth of all ethnic groups in a permissive society.

As compared to whites, evidence for a higher incidence of schizophrenia in black races (Bantu, Negro) is stronger than the evidence for a higher incidence in brown races (American Negro, Cape Coloured). In all situations, however, socioeconomic factors may be important but at present it is not possible to assess the relative importance of the one or the other in the reported differences in the ethnic incidence of schizophrenia.

Assuming that ethnic incidence *suggests* that melanin plays a role in the aetiology of schizophrenia, the following must be considered: (*a*) how melanin might be involved in this difference and (*b*) whether there is any support from non-ethnic pigmentation for the involvement of melanin biology in schizophrenia.

Melanin may be involved in 2 ways: (1) as '*a problem of colour*' which would emphasize the sociological problem of ethnic and colour stereotypes or (2) as a *biochemical product* produced by metabolic processes, and having biochemical reactivity.

Melanin causing a 'problem of colour'

This was considered by Vitols (1961): 'For the Negro, especially the female, the shade of her skin is of great concern. She has much higher marriage value and chance for advancement if she is light-coloured, while the male has more difficulty if he is lighter-coloured than his mate. It is believed that skin colour among Negroes is related to prestige. Darker-skinned persons are seen as having lower status' (Vitols, 1961). Other factors such as the impact of one lighter skinned child in a family and the question of doubtful parentage could be important. To this may be added external factors of segregation as well as integration.

Melanin as a biochemical substance

This may be connected to either the biosynthesis of melanin or to melanin *per se*. In the latter case effectiveness of drug therapy might differ between ethnic groups. Haupt (1963) compared the response of different ethnic groups with schizophrenia to various forms of somatic therapy. No significant difference was found in response to electroconvulsive therapy but it was less effective than either chlorpromazine alone or in combination with other drugs. It was statistically significant that the response rate of Cape Coloured and whites was better than that of Bantu and Indians. I suggested (Wassermann, 1968) that this might be related to the affinity of chlorpromazine for melanin or to the increased excretion of unconjugated drug metabolites reported in the American Negro and in patients with phenothiazine melanosis (Forrest et al., 1963; Bolt and Forrest, 1968).

On the other hand, melanin may be formed as the result of metabolic processes operative in schizophrenia, and this possibility is considered below:

NON-ETHNIC PIGMENTATION AND SCHIZOPHRENIA

Involvement of melanin is suggested in the studies reporting pigmentation as an important concomitant symptom in schizophrenia. Analysis of the literature suggests that: (1) increased pigmentation occurs in schizophrenia and that (2) some metabolic diseases, accompanied by increased pigmentation, may be associated with psychotic manifestations.

In 1952, before the active interest in hallucinogens, Osmond and Smythies reported on the similarity of ingested mescaline experience to the psychological changes reported in schizophrenia. Mescaline is structurally similar to adrenalin, and Osmond and Smythies (1952) suggested that a derivative from adrenalin might be present and causally related to schizophrenia. Originally they considered adrenochrome as the responsible product, but later favoured adrenolutin as the responsible agent. Both these substances induce psychological manifestations in animals and in man, involving in the latter changes in perception,

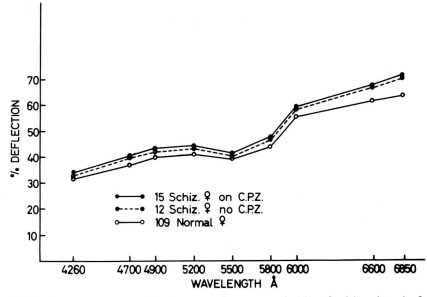

Fig. 32. Reflectance spectrophotometry of unexposed skin of schizophrenic females (15 on chlorpromazine, 12 not on chlorpromazine), as compared to 109 normal white females.

thinking and mood. The adrenochrome theory of schizophrenia was reviewed by Hoffer (1964). Relevant to further discussion is his remark that adrenochrome 'is readily polymerized to darkly coloured pigments, and this could account for the increased pigmentation of some patients.' The formation of rheomelanin, a soluble melanin with esr signals identical to melanin, from adrenolutin, adrenochrome and many other primary amines, was demonstrated by Hegedus and Altschule (1967, 1968, 1970).

On the basis that adrenochrome and adrenalin are derived from tyrosine, Lea (1955) assumed that the hypothesis of Osmond and Smythies (1952) indicates an abnormal tyrosine metabolism. He correlated abnormal pigmentation, a negative association with allergy, defective ascorbic acid metabolism and abnormal products in the urine of schizophrenics with an abnormal tyrosine metabolism. Lea (1955) quoted Hoskins to the effect that disturbances of the adrenosympathetic system, 'which is involved in pathological pigmentation', were one of the most constant features of schizophrenia. His reference to Loehner's (1938) description of melanosis in schizophrenia is unfortunate as this was almost certainly a case of Addison's disease with psychosis and the favourable response to adrenal extracts would be expected. Lea's deduction that a preponderance of the dark type of individual should be found in schizophrenics was investigated by studying 1008 cases of schizophrenia in comparison with 5127 cases of injury in American soldiers. The results were, however, not convincing.

Greiner and Nicholson's (1965) finding that schizophrenia was associated with abnormal, increased melanogenesis was investigated by reflectance spectrophotometry by Robins (1972a). In 76 patients with schizophrenia untreated by phenothiazines and matched with 76 non-schizophrenic psychiatric controls, and 80 normals, he found that schizophrenics had *less* melanin than the controls, but did not differ from the normal series. These observations agree with our findings in a much smaller series of schizophrenics and normal whites (Wassermann and Heyl, unpublished) (Fig. 32).

POSSIBLE BIOCHEMICAL ASSOCIATIONS

Van der Kamp (1963) further developed the adrenergic hypothesis. A genetic factor in schizophrenia was assumed, but the location of this genetically-determined enzymatic defect was uncertain. He pointed out that there are only 5 molecular changes in the conversion of phenylalanine to adrenalin, but that this could be achieved in 120 different ways, with 30 possible intermediates. Dopa, as one of the intermediates, may increase melanin if there is an enzymatic block and shunt between dopa and dopamine in schizophrenia. Evidence for this was found in the circulation of melanin in schizophrenics: 'At our hospital we were able to demonstrate abnormal pigments in the lymphocytes of our chronic schizophrenics.'

McIsaac (1961) approached the biochemical aetiology of schizophrenia from the finding of serotonin (5-hydroxytryptamine) in the brain (Twarog and Page, 1953), the observation that this substance is related to reserpine tranquilization (Brodie and Shore, 1957), and Woolley and Shaw's (1954) suggestion that serotonin depletion may be involved in the aetiology of schizophrenia, a possibility also mooted by Gaddum (1954).

The structural similarity between various hallucinogens (lysergic acid diethylamide, psilocybin and bufotenin) and serotonin has been pointed out by McIsaac (1961). As far as melanin is concerned, adrenalin, nor-adrenalin and serotonin lead to a clumping of melanin granules in the melanocytes of amphibian skin, and such clumping is reversible by ergotamine. Clumping by melatonin, a methylated N-acetyl-serotonin, does not show reversibility by ergotamine. The clumping of granules by serotonin, however, is reversible by the L-methylated-lysergic acid, butanolamide. This substitution also leads to loss of the hallucinogenic properties of the parent substance (Berde and Cerletti, 1956). *McIsaac (1961) thus suggested a defect in transmethylating enzymes in schizophrenia.*

In the human skin window the effect of 5-HT could be studied if a monoamine oxidase inhibitor was administered concurrently with the response. Melanophagocytosis was stimulated and a tendency to vacuolization of the macrophages was noted. Local application of D-methyllysergic acid butanolamide (UML-491, Sandoz) inhibited this reaction, and increased numbers of basophils were noted (Wassermann, 1961) These findings agree with the general observation that agents which clump melanin in melanocytes of lower vertebrates decrease pigmentation in mammals. Lerner and Case (1959) suggested that pigment granule movement in amphibian melanocytes may be the result of drug effects on the cell membrane. The cell-membrane effect of hallucinogens apparently influences melanocyte responses. Apart from its mental manifestations, these drugs could be involved at the lysosomal level of influence on melanin biology (see p. 163).

Phenothiazines as therapeutic drugs with marked benefit in schizophrenia once again suggested a relationship of melanin to schizophrenia.

Since discovery of phenothiazine melanosis in schizophrenic patients, intensive study was done in this area. It could be shown that the highest phenothiazine content of all organs in a patient treated with phenothiazines occurred in the hair, a finding compatible with the formation of a chlorpromazine-melanin adduct. Other studies reported that the eye melanin concentrated phenothiazines in laboratory animals up to 30 times above the expected rate as calculated per weight of tissue (Forrest et al., 1963). Forrest et al. (1966) were able to show that the adduct is a chlorpromazine-melanin charge-transfer complex. Blois (1965) found that intraperitoneally administered chlorpromazine localized in vivo in tissues containing melanin. The major portion of the drug is apparently reversibly bound to the melanin.

While phenothiazine therapy in schizophrenics brought melanin pigmentation forcibly to attention again as a rare side-effect, its increased occurrence in schizophrenia was suspected before phenothiazine therapy. Greiner and Nicholson (1965) thought, from autopsy material obtained prior to the phenothiazine era, that increased deposits of melanin could be found in cases with schizophrenia. They suggested that diffuse melanin deposition normally accompanies schizophrenia, but that this is intensified by chlorpromazine. White and Bantu schizophrenics on phenothiazines were compared with matched controls and normal subjects by reflectance spectrophotometry. The drug-treated schizophrenics did not differ from the drug-treated controls, although they were more pigmented than normals (Robins, 1972*b*). The conclusion of Robins (1972*b*) that melanosis is a non-specific drug effect is not necessarily in conflict with that of Forrest et al. (1966) that those patients who developed a melanosis excreted various unconjugated metabolites derived from 7-hydroxychlorpromazine, in contrast to those patients who did not develop a melanosis. The study by Forrest et al. (1966) does, however, suggest a genetic predisposition to melanosis. As I pointed out earlier, from our study, the findings of Robins (1972*a, b*) of no increase in *skin* pigmentation in schizophrenics does not exclude increased *internal* deposition of melanin (Wassermann, 1968).

SCHIZOPHRENIC SYNDROMES IN METABOLIC DISTURBANCES ASSOCIATED WITH HYPERPIGMENTATION

Pellagra

In pellagra the triad of dementia, diarrhoea and dermatitis, which is associated with melanin deposition in the epidermis, presents a further clinical model for the aetiology of schizophrenia. The beneficial effect of nicotinamide in pellagra can be explained on the basis of correcting a vitamin deficiency. The dementia, however, may respond in a similar way to the improvement reported in schizophrenia treated with nicotinamide: the removal of methyl groups by excretion of the methylated metabolites of nicotinic acid and nicotinamide.

Pellagra results not only from a deficiency of nicotinic acid, but also from a tryptophan deficiency. This amino acid is the precursor of nicotinic acid, and of 5-HT (serotonin).

Therapy of tuberculosis with isoniazid in the higher dosage initially used, caused pellagra-like skin lesions and also quite frequently gave rise to a psychosis resembling schizophrenia.

Vitamin B_{12} deficiency and hyperpigmentation

Hyperpigmentation, especially over the knuckles of the fingers and in the palmar creases, has been reported as a sign of vitamin B_{12} deficiency. Vitamin B_{12} deficiency has also been reported in schizophrenia, but some contradictory findings were reported. In a recent study on this subject 2 cases of vitamin B_{12} deficiency were found among 150 cases of schizophrenia and both responded to vitamin B_{12} therapy (Henderson et al., 1966).

The most consistent evidence for the metabolic reactions of vitamin B_{12} concerns its connection with the neogenesis of methyl-groups or as a co-factor in transmethylation reactions, as in the biosynthesis of methionine.

RETICULOENDOTHELIAL ACTIVITY IN SCHIZOPHRENIA

A long-standing hypothesis relates schizophrenia to modified activity of the reticuloendothelial system. Kallman (1938) advanced the theory of a hereditary reticulum cell inadequacy in schizophrenia, while Hoffer et al. (1954) suggested a noxious metabolite as a stimulant of the reticuloendothelial system. Beattie (1966) reports refractory anaemia in 210 schizophrenics, associated with benign or malignant reticulum cell hyperplasias in 10. This is a far higher incidence (10/210) than in other mental diseases (7/1216). She suggests a possible parallel to mongolism where the chromosomal anomaly is associated with a very high incidence of leukaemia.

A high incidence of abnormal lymphocytes and increased lymphocyte counts were described in schizophrenia (Itten, 1914; Meyer, 1956) as well as a corresponding abnormal bone-marrow (Hirata-Hibi and Fessel, 1964). Many of these cells suggest the type of change seen in viral infections and in immunological stimulation (Fessel and Hirata-Hibi, 1963). Thus, ethnic differences in RES reactivity may also be implicated in differences in the incidence of schizophrenia.

AUTO-IMMUNE THEORY

Burch (1964) postulated an auto-immune origin for schizophrenia, and Heath and Krupp (1967) described a globulin, presumably an antibody, with immuno-fluorescent techniques, in certain brain cell nuclei. Two editorial comments (*Brit. med. J.*, 1967; *Lancet*, 1967) discussed these findings. These results could not be confirmed, and the incidence of serum antibody in schizophrenics was not higher than in controls (Whittingham et al., 1968).

To summarise: The ethnic incidence of schizophrenia supports other evidence that melanin may be involved in the aetiology of schizophrenia. Possible relationships vary from a function as free radical sink for melanin, to defective transmethylation enzymes which would divert the metabolism of various primary amines, all known to be able to give rise to melanins. While Greiner and Nicholson's (1965) suggestion of increased melanogenesis in schizophrenia *not* treated by phenothiazine could not be confirmed by reflectance studies of the skin (Robins, 1972*a, b*), this does not exclude increased internal melanin deposits. Indeed, Greiner (1968) remarked that increased liver pigmentation may be marked in the absence of skin-eye pigmentation, but that *with* skin-eye melanosis, internal melanosis was always marked.

To locate the metabolic defect more closely, evidence from the role of melanin in, and the ethnic incidence of, parkinsonism should be considered.

PARKINSONISM

The commonest form of parkinsonism is the idiopathic form (paralysis agitans). A postencephalitic form followed an epidemic of encephalitis lethargica after the 1914–1918 World War, but new cases have apparently not been noted over the last 4 decades. It may also follow on cerebral arteriosclerosis, or following manganese and carbon monoxide poisoning or as a side-effect of phenothiazine, reserpine or haloperidol therapy.

A prominent neuropathological finding in parkinsonism is a quantitative decrease in melanin granules in the cells of the substantia nigra. Biochemical interest in parkinsonism centred around the catecholamine biosynthetic pathway for many years, both the intermediates (dopa, dopamine) and the respective enzymes involved in the synthesis (tyrosine hydroxylase, L-dopa decarboxylase, dopamine β-hydroxylase) received intensive study (reviewed by Sandler, 1972).

Carlsson (1959) first suggested that dopamine is involved in the control of motor functions. Barbeau et al. (1962) and Birkmayer and Hornykiewicz (1962) reported initial trials of L-dopa in parkinsonism. The early paper by Cotzias et al. (1964) bore the provocative title of 'melanogenesis and extrapyramidal disease' and they thought at that stage that neurological malfunction might follow on the deposition of a metal ion in the melanin of the basal ganglia. Their later studies, however (Cotzias et al., 1967), fully confirmed the significant therapeutic effect of L-dopa in parkinsonism. Subsequent research has shown fairly convincingly that L-dopa exerts its effect by virtue of its role as a precursor of dopamine, the transmitter substance at the dopaminergic synapses in the central nervous system. This is, as will be discussed later, an oversimplification of the effect of L-dopa in parkinsonism.

I know of no interracial studies which attempted to define, in quantitative terms, the amounts of neuromelanin present in different races. Pigmentation of the leptomeninges was found to correlate with skin pigmentation (Lewis, 1969), and in guinea-pigs melanocytes of the inner ear responded to hormonal influences just like skin melanocytes (Cherubino et al., 1966). Differences in melanin content of the substantia nigra and locus caeruleus in different ethnic groups may thus be expected, but have yet to be confirmed. Rolston (1972) suggested a correlation between iris pigmentation and that of the substantia nigra. Even quantitatively similar melanin may differ qualitatively, as in the case of skin and eye melanin which shows ultrastructural differences in melanosomes (Lerche and Wulle, 1967). The presence of neuromelanin in a column of cells extending throughout the human adult brain stem was only recently reported (Bazelon et al., 1967) and Fenichel and Bazelon (1968) in their study of 44 brain stems of children found that melanin was not consistently present at birth, but begins to accumulate during the first 5 years increasing steadily throughout childhood, so that at adolescense the dorsal motor nucleus, locus caeruleus and substantia nigra were well pigmented. They considered their results as favouring the hypothesis that 'neuromelanin deposition results from an active neurochemical process, and not as a by-product of aging.' It is probable that ethnic differences in neuromelanin exist, but they have not yet been demonstrated.

ETHNIC INCIDENCE OF EXTRAPYRAMIDAL DISEASE

When considering the circulation of melanin and its possible relation to melanin pigmentation of the basal ganglia, I became interested in the ethnic incidence of parkinsonism (Wassermann, 1965).

I realized that I had not yet seen a case of parkinsonism in a Bantu; the neurologist on our staff (Dr. A. van Wieringen) was able to recall a single case observed personally. Since starting the evaluation of L-dopa therapy at the Karl Bremer Hospital, 40 white patients and 3 Cape Coloured patients were found to be suffering from parkinsonism (Van Wieringen and Wright, 1972). Among 7420 white, 5496 Cape Coloured and 617 Bantu admissions to the Department of Internal Medicine the incidence per 1000 admissions was 2.15 and 1.2 for whites and Cape Coloureds respectively. No case of parkinsonism was observed in the 617 Bantu admissions. (The low number of Bantu admissions is due to the relative size of white, Cape Coloured and Bantu populations in this area.)

The incidence of neurological disease in various geographical areas is difficult to assess and ethnic incidence is thus poorly represented in statistics. The reasons for this state of affairs were suggested by Cosnett (1964): (1) The degree of rapport necessary between doctor and patient for proper neurological examination and diagnosis, which is often impossible to achieve when dealing with patients of different civilization and language. (This, of course, applies to psychiatric patients as well.) (2) The time-consuming nature of neurological examinations limits finesse in diagnosis in the face of a huge work-load. (3) In those areas where specialized facilities are at a premium and great distances are involved, the chronicity of many neurological diseases hinders follow-up. Many patients attend hospital once only. Where adequate facilities for neurological diagnosis and treatment exist, these are often 'monopolized by the acutely and curably ill, while investigations of an academic nature must necessarily take second place.' He refers to the few general surveys made in Africa by Cook (1901), Muwazi and Trowell (1944), Hutton (1956) and Reef et al. (1958). All those reviews make reference to the scarcity of extrapyramidal disease among Bantu. Reef et al. (1958) found 7 cases of parkinsonism among 1384 Bantu *neurological* cases at the Baragwanath Hospital. Cosnett (1964) reported on 1302 Zulu patients consecutively hospitalized with neurological diseases at the Edendale Hospital. Under the heading of 'unusually rare conditions' are included demyelinating disorders of all types, cerebral tumours, cerebellar disease, migraine and trigeminal neuralgia, muscular disorders and striatal disorders. Amongst striatal disorders, idiopathic parkinsonism was 'relatively rare', only 3 cases being observed. The remainder were either postencephalitic or arteriosclerotic parkinsonism. All of these together accounted for 1% of the neurological diseases observed.

Australia

Jenkins (1966) in his study on the epidemiology of parkinsonism in Victoria found not one case in all the aboriginal settlements surveyed. Due to the small numbers in the population, this is not statistically significant but nevertheless he remarks on the impression that blacks are protected from this disease. He quotes I. Cooper's personal communication as to the apparent rarity of the disease in American Negroes.

U.S.A.

Goldberg and Kurland (1962) found that the age-adjusted mortality for whites in the U.S.A. was 3 times the rate for American Negroes. Williams (1966) found that the average annual death rate per 100,000 population at all ages was 1.8, 1.9, and 1.6 for all whites, male and female whites respectively. The corresponding figures for American Negroes were 0.4, 0.5 and 0.3 respectively. This trend existed through all age groups over 55 years of age. Over 65 years of age the mortality rates for parkinsonism are 15.0 for whites against 4.1 for American Negroes or a white/black ratio of 3.66.

Available statistics, as in the case of the ethnic incidence of schizophrenia, leave much to be desired but the available evidence strongly suggests a reversal of the position as regards schizophrenia: Parkinsonism, not uncommon among whites, is rare among blacks.

BIOCHEMICAL MECHANISMS

It is not clear how the decreased pigmentation of the substantia nigra in parkinsonism is related to dopamine or L-dopa therapy, a synaptic transmitter and precursor of melanin respectively. Neuromelanin may indicate active catecholamine metabolism; there is some evidence that melanin is deposited in those neurons which are most active in catecholamine synthesis (Bazelon et al., 1967; Hillarp et al., 1966). Marsden's (1965) suggestion that dopa, as an evolutionary remnant which is no longer needed to provide dopamine, is channeled to dopaquinone and melanin, was thought to be incorrect (Hornykiewicz, 1966). Cotzias et al. (1964), after suggesting that some of the features of parkinsonism may be due to the melanin deficit, made an unsuccessful trial of melanocyte-stimulating hormone in parkinsonism (Cotzias et al., 1967). Birkmayer (1970) found that the substantia nigra of patients with parkinsonism who failed to respond to L-dopa therapy contained no melanin. This, perhaps, indicates the severity of the anatomical defect (Sandler, 1972).

The mode of action of L-dopa in parkinsonism is also not clear. One of the anomalous situations in the hypothesis that L-dopa raises the dopamine content of dopaminergic nerve endings is the slow time course of the therapeutic response (Calne et al., 1969; Cotzias et al., 1969), while dopamine generation is rapid (Pletscher et al., 1967). Minor pathways of dopa metabolism thus still require active study (Sourkes, 1971a, b; Sandler, 1972).

Chlorpromazine, which has a beneficial effect on schizophrenia may, as a side-effect, produce extrapyramidal symptoms. It was suggested (Sourkes, 1971) that chlorpromazine blocks the dopamine sensitive receptor at the dopaminergic synapse. Reserpine interferes with the storage of dopamine in the vesicles at the dopaminergic nerve ending, while α-methyltyrosine blocks the formation of L-dopa by inhibiting tyrosine hydroxylase. The 3 different sites of action all result in a nigrostriatal lesion.

Stein and Wise (1971) recently suggested that schizophrenia is caused by an aberrant metabolite, 6-hydroxydopamine. This is an auto-oxidation product of dopamine which induces specific degeneration of peripheral sympathetic nerve endings with marked and long-lasting depletion of noradrenalin. Chlorpromazine prevents the depletion of brain noradrenalin by 6-hydroxydopamine. They thus related the genetic defect in schizophrenia to a deficiency of dopamine β-hydroxylase activity. Such a defect would lead to the release of dopamine instead of noradrenalin at noradrenergic nerve endings. This dopamine would then be auto-oxidized to 6-hydroxydopamine.

In parkinsonism the somewhat reduced levels of hypothalamic noradrenalin and brain 5-hydroxytryptamine return to normal after monoamine oxidase (MAO) inhibition, but not in the case of striatal dopamine (Bernheimer and Hornykiewicz, 1963). Sandler (1970) suggested that 6-hydroxydopamine might be generated endogenously in patients with parkinsonism, and cause neuronal degeneration in areas with a high dopamine concentration.

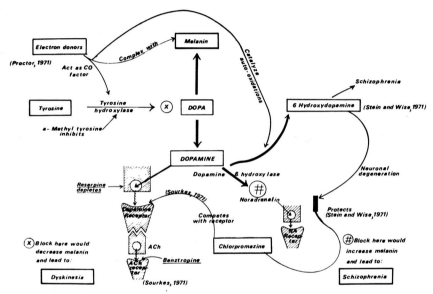

Fig. 33. The dyskinesia-schizophrenia-pigmentation triad. Diagrammatic summary of concepts of Proctor (1971), Stein and Wise (1971) and Sourkes (1971a).

It is disputed whether or not L-dopa is responsible for the intellectual improvement in patients with parkinsonism treated with this drug. Depression may become marked (Van Wieringen, 1972) and can be treated with imipramine without recurrence of parkinsonism (Jenkins and Groh, 1970a, b). In eldery arteriosclerotic subjects delirium or a state resembling acute toxic delirium may result. Some dopa metabolites are potentially hallucinogenic, and may involve o-methylation at the 4-position (Smythies et al., 1967; Shulgin et al., 1969).

With dopamine at a junctional position in the synthesis of both melanin and noradrenalin these findings can be tentatively summarized as follows:

In parkinsonism, an aberrant metabolic pathway leads to decreased dopamine in dopaminergic nerve endings. This may also result from inhibition of tyrosine hydroxylase by α-methyltyrosine, which would reduce both the dopa and dopamine content of the striatum. In such a case, whether neuromelanin is derived from dopa or from dopamine, reduced neuromelanin synthesis would result. There are sufficient anomalies in this simplified version of L-dopa action as being that of increasing dopamine content, to postulate that other metabolites may be concerned; of these it was suggested that 6-hydroxydopamine might be involved in neuronal degeneration in areas of high dopamine concentration (Sandler, 1970). Stein and Wise (1971), in relating 6-hydroxydopamine to the cause of schizophrenia, place melanin pigmentation firmly in a sketchy pathway which should nevertheless be rewarding to further research.

In Figure 33 I have summarized my interpretation of the relationship of the work of Sourkes (1971), Proctor (1971) and Stein and Wise (1971) to the dopa-melanin-dopamine-noradrenalin metabolic pathway and its tentative relation to skin pigmentation.

There remains, however, a further problem regarding schizophrenia. Parkinsonism may result from decreased dopamine formation, depletion of dopamine in nerve endings, receptor competition by chlorpromazine or increased acetylcholine sensitivity but, as visualized in Figure 33, only decreased dopa and dopamine formation would be expected to be associated with decreased melanin synthesis. Similarly, in schizophrenia, in the absence of decreased dopamine β-hydroxylase activity, increased electron donor levels may stimulate sufficient auto-oxidation of dopamine to 6-hydroxydopamine without affecting melanin synthesis. Such alternate mechanisms may explain the 'schizophrenic spectrum of disorders' referred to by Wender (1972).

ETHNIC VULNERABILITY

Because ethnic differences in incidence of these particular clinical disorders may easily be interpreted as suggesting a particular *tendency* toward these disorders in particular ethnic groups, it should be stated that what appears to be tentatively located in this metabolic pathway are 2 areas of *vulnerability*. Under a particular set of circumstances, whites may find their tyrosine-dopa conversion to be sufficiently limited to make them vulnerable to dyskinetic manifestations, just as blacks may have a vulnerable site at dopamine-noradrenalin conversion.

A further factor which may be briefly alluded to at this stage is the modified RES activity which has been briefly discussed above in relation to schizophrenia. Several somatic manifestations occur in schizophrenia; Osmond and Smythies (1952) tabulated these as excessive adrenocortical activity, vascular changes, disturbances in carbohydrate metabolism, defective detoxicating mechanisms in the liver, and skin pigmentation. These may, according to the discussion so far, be secondary manifestations. Altered RES function may be related to increased adrenocortical activity, the vascular and carbohydrate disturbances to disturbed adrenergic neuron function. The lesser adrenocortical activity and increased RES function of dark races may indicate vulnerability due to a particular type responsiveness to the environment.

REFERENCES

Asuni, T. and Pillutla, V. S. (1967): Schizophrenia-like psychoses in Nigerian epileptics. *Brit. J. Psychiat.*, *113*, 1375.

Barbeau, A., Sourkes, T. L. and Murphy, G. F. (1962): Les catécholamines dans la maladie de Parkinson. In: *Monoamines et Système nerveux central. Symposium Bel-Air 1961*, p. 247. Editor: J. de Ajuriaguerra. Masson et Cie., Paris.

Bazelon, M., Fenichel, G. M. and Randall, J. (1967): Studies on neuromelanin. I. A melanin system in the human adult brainstem. *Neurology (Minneap.)*, *17*, 512.

Beattie, M. K. (1966): Anaemia and reticulum cell hyperplasia in schizophrenia. *Brit. J. Psychiat.*, *112*, 1285.

Berde, B. and Cerletti, A. (1956): Über den Melanophoreneffekt von D-Lysergsäure-diethylamid und verwandten Verbindungen. *Helv. physiol. Acta*, *14*, 325.

Bernheimer, H. and Hornykiewicz, O. (1963): Monoaminooxydase-Hemmer und Dopamin-Noradrenalin- und 5 Hydroxytryptamin-Stoffwechsel im Gehirn Parkinson-Kranker Menschen. *Naunyn-Schmiedeberg's Arch. exp. Path. Pharmak.*, *245*, 52.

Birkmayer, W. (1970): Failures in L-dopa therapy. In: *L-Dopa and Parkinsonism*, p. 12. Editors: A. Barbeau and F. H. McDowell. F. A. Davis Co., Philadelphia, Pa.

Birkmayer, W. and Hornykiewicz, O. (1962): Der L-Dioxyphenylalanin (L-DOPA) Effekt beim Parkinson Syndrom des Menschen: Zur Pathogenese und Behandlung des Parkinson Akinesie. *Arch. Psychiat. Nervenkr.*, *203*, 560.

Blois, M. S. (1965): On chlorpromazine binding in vivo. *J. invest. Derm.*, *45*, 475.

Bolt, A. G. and Forrest, I. S. (1968): Metabolic studies of chlorpromazine induced hyperpigmentation of the skin in psychiatric patients. *Agressologie*, *9*, 201.

Brodie, B. B. and Shore, P. A. (1957): A concept for a role of serotonin and nor-epinephrine as chemical mediators in the brain. *Ann. N.Y. Acad. Sci.*, *66*, 631.

Burch, P. R. J. (1964): Schizophrenia: Some new aetiological considerations. *Brit. J. Psychiat.*, *110*, 818.

Calne, D. B., Stern, G. M., Laurence, D. R., Sharhey, J. and Armitage, P. (1969): L-Dopa in postencephalitic parkinsonism. *Lancet*, *1*, 744.

Carlsson (1959): The occurrence, distribution and physiological role of catecholamines in the nervous system. *Pharmacol. Rev.*, *11*, 490.

Carothers, J. C. (1948): A study of mental derangement in Africans and attempt to explain its peculiarities more especially in relation to the African attitude to life. *Psychiatry*, *11*, 47.

Cherubino, M., Bonaceorsi, P. and Galioto, G. B. (1966): Sulla melanocinesi delle cellule pigmentate dell'orecchio interno di *Rana esculenta* e di *Cavia cobaya*. Ricerche ormonali e ultrastrutturali. *Boll. Mal. Orecch.*, *84*, 353.

Collomb, H. (1959): Problems of African psychiatry (South of the Sahara). *Review and Newsletter, transcult. Res. ment. Hlth Probl.*, *6*, 34.

Cook, A. R. (1901): Notes of diseases met with in Uganda Central Africa. *J. trop. Med. Hyg.*, *4*, 175.

Cooper, J. M. (1934): Mental disease situation in certain cultures. A new field for research. *J. abnorm. soc. Psychol.*, *29*, 10. Cited by Lin (1953).

Cosnett, J. E. (1964): Neurological disorders in the Zulu. *Neurology (Minneap.)*, *14*, 443.

Cotzias, G. C. (1966): Manganese, melanins and the extrapyramidal system. *J. Neurosurg.*, *24/2, Suppl.*, 170.

Cotzias, G. C. and Papavasiliou, P. S. (1969): Therapeutic studies of parkinsonian patients: longterm effects of D-L and L-dopa. In: *Progress in Neurogenetics, Vol. I*, pp. 357–365. Editors: A. Barbeau and J. R. Brunette. ICS 175, Excerpta Medica, Amsterdam.

COTZIAS, G. C., PAPAVASILIOU, P. S., VAN WOERT, M. H. and SAKAMOTO, A. (1964): Melanogenesis and extrapyramidal diseases. *Fed. Proc., 23*, 713.

COTZIAS, G. C., VAN WOERT, M. H. and SCHIFFER, L. M. (1967): Aromatic amino-acids and modification of parkinsonism.*New Engl. J. Med., 276*, 374.

DUNHAM, H. W., PHILLIPS, P. and SRINIRASAN (1966): A research note on diagnosed mental illness and social class. *Amer. Sociol. Rev. 31*, 223.

EDITORIAL (1967): Antibodies in schizophrenics. *Brit. med. J., 3*, 569.

EDITORIAL (1967): Antibody, antimind? *Lancet, 1*, 828.

FARIS, R. E. L. and DUNHAM, H. W. (1939): *Mental Disorders in Urban Areas: An Ecological Study of Schizophrenia and Other Psychoses.* University of Chicago Press, Chicago, Ill.

FENICHEL, G. M. and BAZELON, M. (1968): Studies on neuromelanin. II. Melanin in the brainstems of infants and children. *Neurology (Minneap.), 18*, 817.

FESSEL, W. J. and HIRATA-HIBI, M. (1963): Abnormal leucocytes in schizophrenia. *Arch. gen. Psychiat., 9*, 601.

FIELD, M. J. (1968): Chronic psychosis in rural Ghana. *Brit. J. Psychiat., 114*, 31.

FISCHER, J. (1969): Negroes and whites and rates of mental illness: Reconsideration of a myth. *Psychiatry, 32*, 428.

FORREST, F. M., FORREST, I. S. and ROIZIN, L. (1963): Clinical, biochemical and post mortem studies on a patient treated with chlorpromazine. *Agressologie, 4*, 259.

FORREST, I. S., BOLT, A. G. and ABER, R. C. (1968): Metabolic pathways for the detoxication of chlorpromazine in various mammalian species. *Agressologie, 9*, 259.

FORREST, I. S., FORREST, F. M., BOLT, A. G. and SERRA, M. T. (1966): An attempt to correlate urinary chlorpromazine excretion with clinical response to drug therapy. In: *Proceedings, 5th International Congress, C.I.N.P., Washington, D.C.*, p. 1186. Editors: H. Brill, J. O. Cole, P. Deniker, T. Hippius, P. D. Bradley. ICS 129, Excerpta Medica, Amsterdam.

FORSTER, E. B. (1962): The theory and practice of psychiatry in Ghana. *Amer. J. Psychother., 16*, 7.

FRUMKIN, R. (1954): Social factors in schizophrenia. *Sociol. Res., 38*, 383.

GADDUM, J. H. (1954): *Ciba Foundation Symposium on Hypertension.* Little, Brown and Co., Boston, Mass.

GOLDBERG, I. D. and KURLAND, L. T. (1962): Mortality in 33 countries from diseases of the nervous system. *Wld Neurol., 3*, 444.

GREINER, A. C. (1968): Phenothiazines and diffuse melanosis. *Agressologie, 9*, 219.

GREINER, A. C. and NICHOLSON, G. A. (1965): Schizophrenia-melanosis: Cause or side-effect? *Lancet, 2*, 1165.

HARRIS, A. (1942): Skin pigmentation with dementia. *Lancet, 2*, 125.

HAUPT, F. J. G. (1963): *Somatic Therapy of Schizophrenia in South African Mental Hospitals, Vol. II.* Thesis, University of Pretoria.

HEATH, R. G. and KRUPP, I. M. (1967): Schizophrenia as an immunologic disorder. I. Demonstration of antibrain globulins by fluorescent antibody techniques. *Arch. gen. Psychiat., 16*, 1.

HEGEDUS, Z. L. and ALTSCHULE, M. D. (1967): Studies on aminochromes. I. Behaviour of adrenochrome added to human plasma. *Arch. int. Physiol. Biochim., 75*, 690.

HEGEDUS, Z. L. and ALTSCHULE, M. D. (1968): Studies on aminochromes. III. Transformation of epinephrine, adrenochrome and adrenolutin into plasma-soluble melanins during incubation in human blood plasma. *Arch. Biochem., 126*, 388.

HEGEDUS, Z. L. and ALTSCHULE, M. D. (1970): Studies on rheomelanins. I. The formation of rheomelanins in human blood plasma from catecholamines, from L-dopa and from some of their derivatives. *Arch. int. Physiol. Biochim., 78*, 443.

HENDERSON, J. G., STRACHAN, R. W., BECK, J. S., DAWSON, A. and DANIEL, M. (1966): The antigastric antibody test as a screening procedure for Vit. B_{12} deficiency in psychiatric practice. *Lancet*, 2, 809.

HILLARP, N., FUXE, K. and DAHLSTROM, A. (1966): Demonstration and mapping of central neurons containing dopamine, noradrenaline, and 5-hydroxytryptamine and their reactions to psychopharmaca. *Pharmacol. Rev.*, 18, 727.

HIRATA-HIBI, M. and FESSEL, W. J. (1964): The bone-marrow in schizophrenia. *Arch. gen. Psychiat.*, 10, 414.

HOFFER, A. (1964): The adrenochrome theory of schizophrenia: A review. *Dis. nerv. Syst.*, 25, 173.

HOFFER, A., OSMOND, H. and SMYTHIES, J. (1954): Schizophrenia: A new approach. II. Result of a year's research. *J. ment. Sci.*, 100, 29.

HOPE, J. and ADAMS, R. D. (1966): Schizophrenia, paranoia, puerperal and endocrine psychoses. In: *Principles of Internal Medicine*, Chapter 216, p. 1284. Editors: T. R. Harrison, R. D. Adams, I. L. Bennett, W. H. Resnik, G. W. Thorn and M. M. Wintrobe. McGraw-Hill Book Co. Inc., New York, N.Y.

HORNYKIEWICZ, O. (1966): Dopamine (3-hydroxytyramine) and brain function. *Pharmacol. Rev.*, 18, 925.

HURST, L. A. (1970): An investigation into the psychopathology of the Bantu-speaking people of the Witwatersrand. *Leech (Johannesburg)*, 40, 52.

HUTTON, P. W. (1956): Neurological disease in Uganda. *E. Afr. med. J.*, 33, 209.

ITTEN, W. (1914): Zur Kenntnis hämatologischer Befunde bei einigen Psychosen. *Z. ges. Neurol. Psychiat.*, 24, 341.

JENKINS, A. C. (1966): Epidemiology of Parkinsonism in Victoria. *Med. J. Aust.*, 2, 496.

JENKINS, R. B. and GROH, R. H. (1970a): Mental symptoms in parkinsonian patients treated with L-dopa. *Lancet*, 2, 177.

JENKINS, R. B. and GROH, R. H. (1970b): Psychic effects from levodopa. *J. Amer. med. Ass.*, 212, 2265.

KALLMAN, F. J. (1938): *Genetics of Schizophrenics*. New York, N.Y.

KATZ, M. M., COLE, J. O. and LOWERY, H. A. (1969b): Studies of the diagnostic process: the influence of symptom perception, past experience and ethnic background on diagnostic decisions. *Amer. J. Psychiat.*, 125, 109.

KATZ, M. M., SANBORN, K. O. and GUDEMAN, H. (1969a): Characterizing differences in psychopathology among ethnic groups in Hawaii. *Social Psychiat.*, 47, 139.

KETY, S. S. (1970): Genetic-environmental interactions in schizophrenia. *Trans. Stud. Coll. Phycns Philad.*, 38, 124.

KIMMICH, R. A. (1960): Ethnic aspects of schizophrenia in Hawaii. *Psychiatry*, 23, 97.

KRAMER, M. (1963): Some problems for international research suggested by observations on differences in first admission rates to the mental hospitals of England and Wales and of the United States. In: *Proceedings, Third World Congress of Psychiatry, Vol. I*, p. 153. University of Toronto Press, Toronto.

LAUBSCHER, B. J. F. (1937): *Sex, Custom and Psychopathology*. Routledge and Kegan Paul, London.

LEA, A. J. (1955): Adrenochrome as the cause of schizophrenia: An investigation of some deductions from this hypothesis. *J. ment. Sci.*, 101, 538.

LERCHE, W. and WULLE, K. G. (1967): Über die Genese der Melaningranula in der embryonalen menschlichen Retina. *Z. Zellforsch.*, 76, 452.

LERNER, A. B. and CASE, J. D. (1959): Pigment cell regulatory factors. *J. invest. Derm.*, 32, 211.

LEWIS, M. G. (1969): Melanoma and pigmentation of the leptomeninges in Ugandan Africans. *J. clin. Path.*, *22*, 183.

LIN, TSUNG-YI (1953): A study of the incidence of mental disorder in Chinese and other cultures. *Psychiatry*, *16*, 313.

LOEHNER, C. A. (1938): The therapeutic effect of adrenal cortex extract on the psychotic patient. *Endocrinology*, *23*, 507.

MALZBERG, B. (1935): Mental disease among Negroes in New York State. *Hum. Biol.*, *7*, 471.

MALZBERG, B. (1953): Mental disease among Negroes in New York State. *Ment. Hyg. (N.Y.)*, *37*, 450.

MALZBERG, B. (1959): Mental disease among Negroes. *Ment. Hyg. (N.Y.)*, *43*, 422.

MARSDEN, C. D. (1965): Brain pigment and catecholamines. *Lancet*, *2*, 1244.

McISAAC, W. M. (1961): A biochemical concept of mental disease. *Postgrad. Med.*, *30*, 111.

MEYER, F. (1956): Die Bedeutung des R.E.S. für die Pathogenese und Therapie der Geisteskrankheiten. *Psychiat. Neurol. med. Psychol. (Lpz.)*, *8*, 365.

MOFFSON, A. (1954): Admissions to Weskoppies Hospital. *S. Afr. med. J.*, *28*, 662.

MUWAZI, E. M. K. and TROWELL, H. C. (1944): Neurological disease among African natives of Uganda, a review of 269 cases. *E. Afr. med. J.*, *21*, 2.

OSMOND, H. and SMYTHIES, J. (1952): Schizophrenia: A new approach. *J. ment. Sci.*, *98*, 309.

PASAMANICK, B. (1963): Some misconceptions concerning differences in the racial prevalence of mental disease. *Amer. J. Orthopsychiat.*, *33*, 72.

PIEDMONT, E. B. (1966): Ethnicity and schizophrenia: A pilot study. *Ment. Hyg. (N.Y.)*, *50*, 374.

PLETSCHER, A., BARTHOLINI, G. and TISSOT, R. (1967): Metabolic fate of L-(^{14}C)-dopa in cerebrospinal fluid and blood plasma of humans. *Brain Res.*, *4*, 106.

PROCTOR, P. (1971): Psychosis, dyskinesia and hyperpigmentation. *Lancet*, *1*, 1069.

REEF, H., LIPSCHITZ, R. and BLOCK, J. (1958): Neurological disorders at Baragwanath hospital: a survey. *Med. Proc.*, *4*, 292.

RINEHART, J. W. (1966): On diagnosed mental illness and social class. *Amer. Sociol. Rev.*, *31*, 545.

RIPLEY, H. S. and WOLF, S. (1947): Mental illness among Negro troops overseas. *Amer. J. Psychiat.*, *103*, 499.

ROBINS, A. H. (1972a): Skin melanin concentrations in schizophrenia. I. Patients untreated by phenothiazines. *Brit. J. Psychiat.*, *121*, 613.

ROBINS, A. H. (1972b): Skin melanin concentrations in schizophrenia. II. Patients treated by phenothiazines. *Brit. J. Psychiat.*, *121*, 615.

ROLSTON, R. (1972): Personal communication.

SANDLER, M. (1970): The role of minor pathways of dopa metabolism. In: L-*Dopa and Parkinsonism*, p. 72. Editors: A. Barbeau and F. H. McDowell. F. A. Davis Co., Philadelphia, Pa.

SANDLER, M. (1972): Catecholamine synthesis and metabolism in man: Clinical implications (with special reference to Parkinsonism). In: *Handbook of Experimental Pharmacology: Catecholamines* pp. 845-899. Editors: H. Blaschko and E. Muscholl. Springer-Verlag, Berlin.

SCHOOLER, C. and CANDILL, W. (1964): Symptomatology in Japanese and American schizophrenics. *Ethnology*, *3*, 172.

SHULGIN, A. T., SARGENT, T. and NARANJO, C. (1969): Structure-activity relationships of one-ring psychotomimetics. *Nature (Lond.)*, *221*, 537.

SMARTT, C. G. F. (1960): Problems and prospects of psychiatry in Tanganyika. *E. Afr. med. J.*, *37*, 480.

SMYTHIES, J. R., JOHNSTON, V. S., BRADLEY, R. J., BENINGTON, F., MORIN, R. D. and CLARK, L. C. (1967): Some new behaviour-disrupting amphetamines and their significance. *Nature (Lond.)*, *216*, 128.

SOURKES, T. L. (1971*a*): Actions of levodopa and dopamine in the central nervous system. *J. Amer. med. Ass.*, *218*, 1909.

SOURKES, T. L. (1971*b*): Possible new metabolites mediating actions of L-dopa. *Nature (Lond.)*, *229*, 413.

STAINBROOK, E. (1952): Some characteristics of the psychopathology of schizophrenic behaviour in Bahaian society. *Amer. J. Psychiat.*, *109*, 330.

STEIN, L. and WISE, C. D. (1971): Possible etiology of schizophrenia: Progressive damage to the noradrenergic reward system by 6-hydroxydopamine. *Science*, *171*, 1032.

TOKER, E. (1966): Mental illness in the white and Bantu populations of the Republic of South Africa. *Amer. J. Psychiat.*, *123*, 55.

TWAROG, B. M. and PAGE, I. H. (1953): Serotonin content of some mammalian tissues and urine and method for its determination. *Amer. J. Physiol.*, *175*, 157.

VAN DEN HAAG, E. (1966): On diagnosed mental illness and social class. *Amer. Sociol. Rev.*, *31*, 544.

VAN DER KAMP, H. (1963): Prognostic determinants in schizophrenia. *J. Neuropsychiat.*, *5*, 118.

VAN WIERINGEN, A. (1972): Observations on patients with Parkinson's disease treated with L-dopa therapy. II. Side-effects and analysis of therapeutic failures. *S. Afr. med. J.*, *46*, 1308.

VAN WIERINGEN, A. and WRIGHT, J. (1972): Observations on patients with Parkinson's disease treated with L-dopa. I. Trial and evaluation of L-dopa therapy. *S. Afr. med. J.*, *46*, 1262.

VITOLS, M. M. (1961): The significance of the higher incidence of schizophrenia in the Negro race in North Carolina. *N.C. med. J.*, *22*, 147.

WAGNER, P. S. (1938): A comparative study of Negro and white admissions to the Psychiatry Pavilion of the Cincinnati General Hospital. *Amer. J. Psychiat.*, *95*, 167.

WALTON, H. (1962): Psychiatric practice in a multiracial society: Modifications required in clinical approach. *Comprehens. Psychiat.*, *3*, 255.

WASSERMANN, H. P. (1961): *Die Effekt van 5 H-T. op die Ontwikkeling van die Limfosiet soos waargeneem in die Inflammatoriese Respons.* Thesis, University of Stellenbosch.

WASSERMANN, H. P. (1965): The circulation of melanin. Its clinical and physiological significance. Review of the literature on leucocytic melanin transport. *S. Afr. med. J.*, *39*, 711.

WASSERMANN, H. P. (1968): Phenothiazines and leucocytic melanin transport. *Agressologie*, *9*, 241.

WASSERMANN, H. P. (1970): Melanokinetics and the biological significance of melanin. *Brit. J. Derm.*, *82*, 530.

WENDER, P. H. (1972): Adopted children and their families in the evaluation of nature-nurture interactions in the schizophrenic disorders. *Ann. Rev. Med.*, *23*, 355.

WHITTINGHAM, S., MACKAY, I. R., JONES, I. H. and DAVIES, B. (1968): Absence of brain antibodies in patients with schizophrenia. *Brit. med. J.*, *1*, 347.

WILLIAMS, G. R. (1966): Morbidity and mortality with parkinsonism. *J. Neurosurg.*, *24*, 2 Suppl., 138.

WOOLLEY, D. W. and SHAW, E. (1954): A biochemical and pharmacological suggestion about certain mental disorders. *Science*, *119*, 587.

Chapter XX

An holistic concept of ethnic pigmentation

The aim of this monograph was to present ethnic pigmentation in the perspective gained from the possible significance of the circulation of melanin in man. As mononuclear cells are mainly responsible for this transport, the differences in leucocyte counts in ethnic groups had to be investigated as no satisfactorily controlled studies were available at the time. The most plausible explanation for the Bantu leucocyte count appeared to be decreased adrenocortical function. This allowed extrapolation of a cause-and-effect nature to the increased serum γ-globulin levels found in these groups, and then eventually to the hypothesis as I formulated it: An adaption of the reticuloendothelial system (RES) to a disease-stressed environment through decreased adrenocortical activity and, incidentally, increased pigmentation. This hypothesis explains several clinical observations.

It may explain the evolution of man from a homogeneously coloured species to one of heterogeneously coloured races: Man's defencelessness against his environment, his early migration, and his limited technological ability would allow selection, in geographically isolated areas, of the RES responsiveness most suitable to his local environment, and this would be marked by a particular skin colour. Before technology enabled easier and more effective travel, migrations on foot would most likely lead to isolation of groups by geographical barriers. In time, adaptation to the environment would, as outlined, lead to differently pigmented people in various localities.

There can be speculation on the extent to which the art of writing (discovered in Egypt ca. 3,300 B.C. and in Mesopotamia ca. 4,000 B.C.) accelerated the scientific and technological acumen of ancient Greece and Rome, allowing both easier travel and rediscovery of those isolated communities which now had become differentially marked in skin colour. In rediscovering his fellowmen, now in various colours, it is perhaps the art of writing and the dissemination of written histories which allowed a great acceleration of science and culture on the European continent; this allowed the white man to rediscover the black, brown and yellow men. Rediscovery of his fellowmen also accentuated the difference in degrees of sophistication and civilization attained. The 'geographical colour bar' has now been completely removed by technology. The 'cultural colour bar' still exists. Sociological 'experiments' are still in progress, and no significant advances have, to my mind, been made yet.

Early interest in ethnic pigmentation had a few important results: (1) It became absorbed in the developing concepts on evolution. Darwin's concept of 'the survival of the fittest' allowed misapplication of scientific theory in allocating superior and inferior ranks of 'fitness' to various races. The consequences may still be seen in fairly recent political history. (2) The interest in the phenomenon of ethnic pigmentation became diverted to a specialized *dermatological* field of interest. This was largely stimulated by the pigment responses to radiation, the problem of malignant melanoma, and the availability of cutaneous pigmentation for study by sophisticated technology. Inevitably, the biology of pigment elsewhere in the body became of secondary importance. Ethnic differences in various physiological parameters as well as differences in the incidence, and also manifestations, of disease, found ready explanations in an environment vastly different from the sophisticated culture of Western Europe and that established by its emigrants all over the earth. Skin colour also tagged cultural differences, and rendered cultural conflicts highly visible.

At the beginning of the 1960's, a *function* for melanin could not yet be postulated. Nevertheless Blum (1961) was able to point out that its survival value is extremely limited. On discovery of its paramagnetic properties, its protective function could, however, be rationally explained, and the activation of the transport system by phenothiazines and the consequent internal deposition of melanin confirmed its affinity for electron donors, and its possible function wherever it occurs intracellularly. This allows the consideration of melanin as a hormone: a substance produced by particular cells, transported by the blood and exerting a regulating effect at a distance from where it was produced. (A 'scattered' endocrine organ was perhaps more of a conceptual innovation at that stage than it is today in view of Pearce's (1969) concept of the APUD cell series: 'A diverse group of endocrine cells situated in, or outside, known endocrine glands.' These cells, 6 of which produce named polypeptide hormones and 12 others of which produce ether biogenic amines or unknown compounds, are named APUD because of their 3 most reliable cytochemical characteristics: *a*mine and amine *p*recursor *u*ptake and *d*ecarboxylation.)

In considering the origin of melanin, the melanocyte is certainly the most important producer of this pigment from tyrosine through dopa. The cell derives from the neural crest and is a modified neuron, as is the adrenal medulla which is derived from the sympathetic portion of the autonomic nervous system. In the latter, dopa is decarboxylated to dopamine and eventually oxidized to noradrenalin, and methylated to adrenalin. The clinical implications of these relationships have been considered in this section.

The greater task of defining the function of melanin in biology in general is beyond the scope of this monograph. A leucocytic transport of melanin can be demonstrated in sponges, coelenterates and flatworms in the absence of a vascular system, the circulation of melanin thus being phylogenetically older than the circulation of blood. In vertebrates, melanocytes could be demonstrated in a 150 million year old *ichthyosaurus* (references cited by Wassermann, 1965). A circulation of, and intricate association with, leucocytes is evident also in insects. Oenocytoids (an insect leucocyte) contain tyrosinase, they may form pigment and melanise implants and they may be involved in the biosynthesis of dopamine, which permeates the epidermis (Mills and Whitehead (1969) in a personal communication to Jones (1970)).

Thus, melanin is no recent biological development, but its association with reticuloendothelial function can be traced to the simplest animals. It exerts a protective function through its paramagnetic properties even in plants (Szent-Györgyi, 1968).

While this monograph has sketched the various lines of thought which I have pursued over the past decade, and which I investigated in the few areas for which I had facilities, much remains to be done. I am convinced that a sharp distinction should be drawn between the *visibility* of melanin, the *function* of melanin and the *result* of melanin deposition wherever it occurs. Study of the ethnicity of disease in relation to differences in RES function among races may be rewarding. Elucidation of the differences in endocrine function is an urgent requirement in this regard. Perhaps no other pigment so forcibly underlines the truth of Sumner's (1937) statement: '*From whatever direction we approach the study of life, we cannot escape the phenomena of colour.*'

REFERENCES

BLUM, H. F. (1961): Does the melanin pigment of human skin have adaptive value? *Quart. Rev. Biol.*, *36*, 50.

JONES, J. C. (1970): Hemocytopoiesis in insects. In: *Regulation of Hematopoiesis, Vol. I*, pp. 7–66. Editor: A. S. Gordon. Appleton-Century-Crofts, New York, N.Y.

PEARCE, A. G. E. (1969): The calcitonin secreting C cells and their relationship to the APUD cell series (Abstract). *J. Endocr.*, *45*, 13.

SUMNER, F. B. (1937): Color and pigmentation. Why they should interest us as biologists. *Sci. Mthly (N.Y.)*, *44*, 350.

SZENT-GYÖRGYI, A. (1968): Bio-electronics. *Science*, *161*, 988.

WASSERMANN, H. P. (1965): The circulation of melanin – its clinical and physiological significance. *S. Afr. med. J.*, *39*, 711.

Index